The Complete
HOME ELECTRICIAN

The Complete
HOME ELECTRICIAN:
Techniques,
Projects and Materials
Edited by Mike Lawrence

ORBIS · LONDON

Printed in Yugoslavia
ISBN: 0-85613-986-6

Acknowledgements
Photographers: Jon Bouchier, Simon Butcher,
Paul Forrester, Jem Grischotti, Keith Morris, Karen Norquay,
Ian O'Leary, Roger Tuff.

Artists: Roger Courthold Associates, Bernard Fallon,
Nick Farmer, Val Hill, Trevor Lawrence, Linden Artists,
David Pope, Peter Robinson, Mike Saunders, Ian Stephen,
Ralph Stobart, Ed Stuart, Universal Studios, Craig Warwick,
Brian Watson, David Weeks.

CONTENTS

Introduction – Understanding electrics 6

1 Tools and accessories 11
Plugs and fuses 12
Cable and flex 14
Electrical wiring accessories 16
Tools for electrical jobs 19

2 Basic techniques 22
Ceiling lights and switches 23
Adding a power point 27
Running circuit cables 31

3 Lighting 36
Lighting design 1: the basics 37
Light bulbs and tubes 40
Lighting design 2: the planning 43
Fluorescent lighting 46
Decorative lights 50
Installing wall lights 54
Installing recessed lighting 58
Installing track lighting 62
Two-way switching 66

4 Power circuits 71
Adding new radial circuits 72
Installing an RCCB 76
Fitting an electric shower 79
Wiring for cookers 84
Installing shaver sockets 88
Replacing an immersion heater 92
Fitting a waste disposal unit 96
Fitting an extractor fan 100
Fitting a ceiling fan 104
Installing wall heaters and towel rails 108

5 Electrics outdoors 111
Running cable underground 112
Providing power in the garage 116
Installing outdoor lights 121
Installing garden lighting 126
Fitting a pond pump and fountain 130

6 Updating and rewiring 134
Planning to update your electrics 135
Improving light and power in the kitchen 139
Rewiring a house 1: inspection 144
Rewiring a house 2: starting work 149
Rewiring a house 3: finishing off 153
Using gridswitches 158

7 Miscellaneous projects 160
Fitting door bells 161
Fitting an entryphone 165
Installing a burglar alarm 167
Installing convenience controls 171

Appendix – Maintenance and repairs 175
Tracing electrical faults 176
Extending flex safely 180
Servicing electrical appliances 1 182
Servicing electrical appliances 2 186

Index 190

Understanding ELECTRICS

In theory, you could do electrical jobs knowing nothing about electricity, given accurate step-by-step instructions. But you can't deal with any part of an electrical installation in isolation — everything is linked. And unless you understand how each part of the system works you have no way of knowing if you are making a mistake. With electricity, ignorance is dangerous.

We're all familiar with lights and power sockets, but how does the electricity reach them so we can use it? In fact, electricity enters your home along one thick cable (the service cable), passes through a large 'service fuse' and into a meter which records the amount you use. Everything up to and including that meter belongs to the electricity board, and is their responsibility. Everything beyond is the householder's property, which is perhaps why installations vary so much.

In a modern installation — one wired in the last 30 years — there are two wires carrying electric current that lead from the meter to what is called the consumer unit. These wires are known as the meter tails — one is termed live, the other neutral.

On the inlet side of the consumer unit there's a switch with which you can turn off the power altogether, but the unit's principal job is to divide up the power and send it round your home through a network of cables.

These cables are organized into circuits. There are circuits for lights, power sockets and so on, each with its own fuse in the consumer unit. The cables themselves run under the floor, above the ceiling and may even be visible on wall surfaces, although more often they are buried within them.

In older installations, instead of a consumer unit there may be individual fuse boxes protecting separate circuits. And each of these fuse boxes will have an isolating switch to cut off power to the circuit it controls. These fuse boxes are connected direct to the meter by

> **WARNING:** *Electricity is dangerous. Before touching any part of the fixed wiring in your home, turn off the power at the main switch so you can be sure no current is flowing anywhere in the system.*

live and neutral meter tails. Alternatively the fuse boxes may be supplied from a distribution board which in turn is connected to the meter.

Sometimes, even with a consumer unit you may find separate fuse boxes. This is normally the result of the system having been extended.

What are circuits?

If you take a battery, and connect a wire to the positive (+) terminal, and another to the negative (−), then bring the free ends of the wires together, electricity will flow from positive to negative along them. That's a circuit. You can build a torch bulb and holder into it to prove it works. Break the circuit by cutting one wire, and the light goes out (the flow of current has stopped), and it will stay out until the cut ends are rejoined. That's a simple switch.

Of course, the circuits in your home are a good deal more complex than that, and their design varies according to whether they supply lights, power sockets or whatever. Even the electricity is different. Instead of flowing in one direction, it goes back and forth 50 times a second — hence its name *alternating current*, or AC for short.

But the principle is the same., Think of 'live' as positive, 'neutral' as negative, and you will see that for any appliance such as an electric fire to work it must have wires connecting it to the live and neutral terminals in the consumer unit. Those wires may be contained in a single cable, but the link must always be there, with switches *en route* to make or break it, and for safety reasons, switches are on the live wire.

What are fuses?

The main service cable has its fuse; the various circuits have theirs in the consumer

unit or fuse box and if you remove the back of a flat-pin plug you'll find a fuse in there.

Think of an electric light bulb. It gives out light because electricity passing through the filament (the fine wire just visible inside the bulb) makes it very hot. If you pass enough electricity through any wire, it will also heat up. If that wire happens to be a circuit cable, an appliance flex, or the service cable to the meter, then the consequences would. be serious. So, to protect them, a weak link called a fuse is built into the circuit.

Most fuses are just thin pieces of wire. They can be fitted to rewirable fuse carriers, in which case you can replace them, or they may be in ceramic cartridges, in which case you throw them away and fit another. In any event, the fuse's thickness is described in terms of how much electricity — expressed in amps — is theoretically needed to melt it.

The word 'theoretically' is important because, in fact, fuses aren't particularly accurate or reliable. For this reason, a more sensitive device called a miniature circuit breaker (MCB) may be used instead. It's just a switch that turns off automatically when danger threatens. Once the fault responsible for the overload is put right, you switch on again.

Why cables?

It would be far too complicated to wire a house like a battery and bulb circuit using individual wires. Instead, the copper wires carrying the electricity are encased in PVC insulation to stop them touching and making their circuit in the wrong place — what's called a short circuit — and then bound together in PVC sheathing to form a cable. In this way, the live, neutral and earth wires can be run as one, even though each one is still connected up separately.

Different kinds of cable are used for different jobs. For full details of the most common types, see pages 14 and 15.

Earthing

The purpose of the earth wire within the cable is to make up the earth continuity conductor (ECC). This is an essential safety feature of any electrical installation. Its role is to act as a 'safety valve' in the event of a fault, causing a fuse to blow or an MCB to trip to isolate a faulty circuit or faulty appliance from the mains supply. In doing so it could prevent the risk of fire or someone being electrocuted.

Earth wires are connected to the metal parts of switches, socket outlets, fittings and appliances (and even plumbing) in a really up-to-date system. Electricity will flow along the line of least resistance, so that if by some mishap any of these parts became live (by coming into contact with a live conductor) the earth wire would offer a line of 'less' resistance. In effect the faulty current would travel along the earth wire rather than through a person touching the live metal part. And the extra current passing through one circuit would

be sufficient to blow the fuse or activate the MCB.

Unfortunately this doesn't always happen – so, for added safety, a special device called a residual current circuit breaker (RCCB) can be fitted to detect the slightest leakage of current to earth. It shuts off the power within milliseconds – quickly enough to save a life – at the first sign of a fault.

RCCBs can be added to an existing system, or included within the consumer unit in a new installation. They usually protect all the circuits in the house and also act as a mains on/off switch.

Ring circuits

For getting electricity to the power points, the most common system of wiring is what's called a 'ring' circuit. Wired in 2.5mm² two-core and earth cable, most homes have one such circuit for each floor of the house.

The two-cores and the earth wire are connected to their terminals in the consumer unit (or fuse box) and then pass through each power socket in turn before returning to their respective terminals in the consumer unit (fuse box). The circuit is protected by a 30A

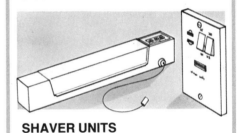
YOUR ELECTRICITY SUPPLY

Neutral · Live · Meter · Circuit cables · Consumer unit · 1 · Meter tails · To earthing point · Electricity Board's sealed fuse

Circuit cable · Circuit cable · 2 · Fuse box · Fuse box · To earth · To earth · To other fuse boxes · Distribution board

3 · 'White' meter · Time clock · Consumer unit for off-peak circuits · Consumer unit · To earth

Where your electricity supply enters the house, the cable passes first of all to the electricity board's main fuse, and then to the electricity meter. From there two meter tails to the electrical distribution equipment. It will be one of three types.
1 a modern house will have a one-piece consumer unit.
2 in an older home you may find a number of separate switched fuse boxes, each controlling one circuit.
3 if you use off-peak electricity, this will be metered separately, and there will be a time clock for the off-peak circuits.

Trevor Lawrence

fuse. The advantage of this system is it allows the cable to cope with more sockets than if it made a one-way trip (see Radial circuits –right). In fact, you are allowed as many sockets as you like on the ring, so long as the floor area served by the circuit doesn't exceed 100 sq metres (1,080 sq ft). What's more, you can increase the number of sockets by adding 'branch lines' off the ring. These are called 'spurs' and break into the ring via a junction box, a spur connection unit, or an existing socket. You are allowed as many spurs as

there are sockets on the ring, and each spur can supply one single, double or triple socket, or one fixed appliance via a fused connection unit. Until a recent change in the IEE Wiring Regulations, a spur could feed two single sockets, and you may find such spurs on your existing circuits.

Of course, with all those sockets, there is a risk of overloading the circuit, but in the average family home it's unlikely that you'll have enough sockets in use at any one time. The circuit may carry up to 30 amps of current

which is equivalent to having appliances and portable lamps using 7,200 watts of power all switched on together. It's doubtful that you would want all this on at the same time, but it's wise not to go above this level of power use. If the circuit does overload, the fuse will blow. or the MCB will switch off.

Radial circuits

Unlike ring circuits, radial circuits consist of a single cable that leaves the fuse box and runs to one or more sockets. In older homes in the UK, before ring circuits were introduced, all power circuits were wired as radials. Since homes had (and needed) only a few sockets, individual circuits were usually run to each one from the fuse box. The sockets themselves were rated at 2A, 5A or 15A, and had round holes to accept round-pin plugs. Such circuits will probably have been wired in rubber- or lead-sheathed cables, which deteriorate with age (see pages 14 and 15), and are not able to satisfy the far greater electrical demands of a modern household. It's wise to have such circuits examined by a qualified electrician, and best of all to have them replaced.

Radial circuits are, however, also used in modern wiring systems where a ring circuit could be inappropriate for some reason. There are two types, with different current-carrying capacity.

A 20A radial circuit uses 2.5mm² cable and

A ring circuit originates from a 30A fuseway in the consumer unit. Protection may be by an MCB rather than a rewirable or cartridge fuse.

Spurs are sometimes added when the ring circuit is installed to save on the wiring runs. They are usually connected at a three-terminal junction box.

Socket outlets on a ring circuit take the fused 13A flat-pin plug. They can have one, two or three outlets on the faceplate; the best have switches.

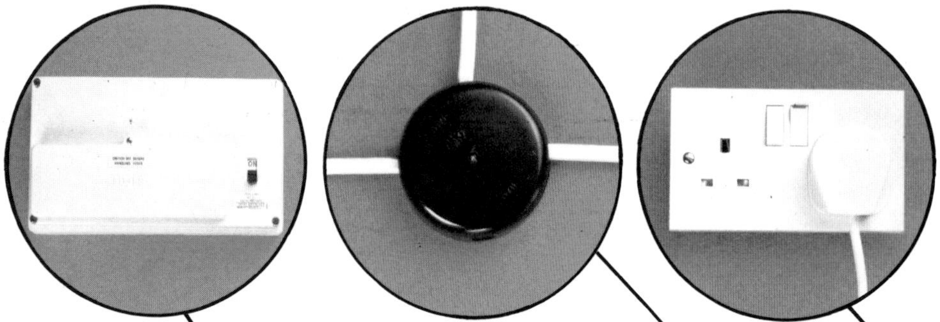

Jem Grischotti

THE RING CIRCUIT

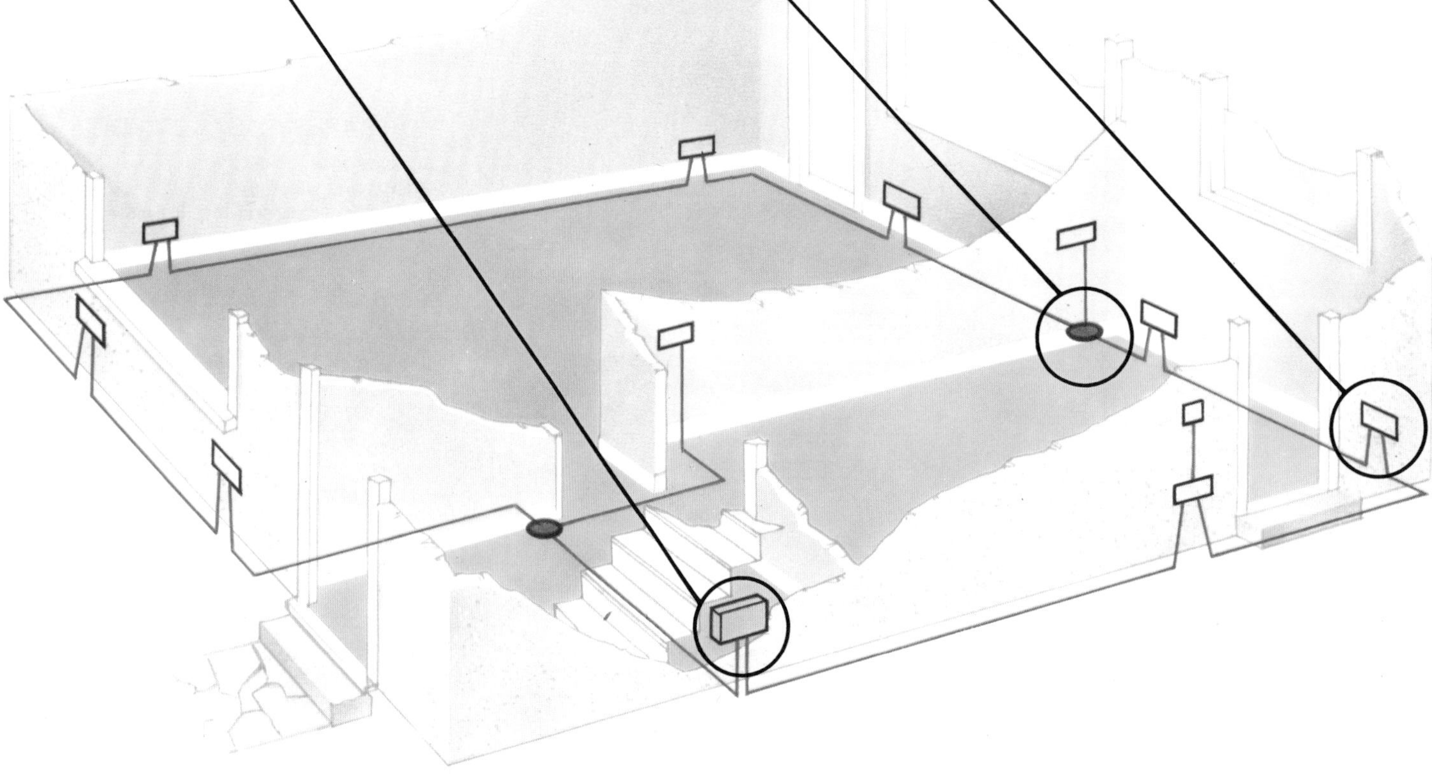

Trevor Lawrence

is protected by a 20A fuse (rewirable or cartridge) or an MCB in the consumer unit (or fuse box). It can supply an unlimited number of 13A socket outlets and fixed appliances using 3kW of power or less, providing they are within a floor area not exceeding 20 sq metres (about 215 sq ft).

The other type of circuit is the 30A radial which is wired in 4mm² cable and can feed a floor area of up to 50 sq m (540 sq ft). It can be protected by a 30A cartridge fuse or MCB, but not by a rewirable fuse.

These restrictions on floor area mean that several radial circuits would have to be installed to cover the same area as a ring circuit. This is one of the reasons why the 'ring' is now the most common method of wiring in the UK, but radial circuits can supplement an overworked ring circuit.

Special purpose circuits

In addition to rings and radials, your home may have special circuits which supply only one outlet or appliance. Cookers, immersion heaters, instantaneous showers and the like are wired in this way and each has its own individual fuse. In effect, these circuits are just radials that have had both the cable and fuse sizes 'beefed up' to cope with the often heavy demands of the appliances they supply — for example, a large family-size cooker might need a 45A fuse, and 6mm² or even 10mm² cable.

Because electric night storage heaters all come on together they could overload a ring circuit; consequently each one is supplied by

The various radial power circuits originate from fuseways in a consumer unit or from individual fuse boxes. They are protected by fuses or MCBs.

Modern radial circuits have sockets that take 13A flat-pin plugs. Older radials with lead or rubber-sheathed cable take round pin plugs.

Even if you have ring circuit wiring, radial circuits are used for special purposes, such as supplying a cooker. It may also contain a 13A socket outlet.

A fused connection unit sometimes supplies a fixed appliance on a radial circuit. This could be a wall mounted heater or an immersion heater.

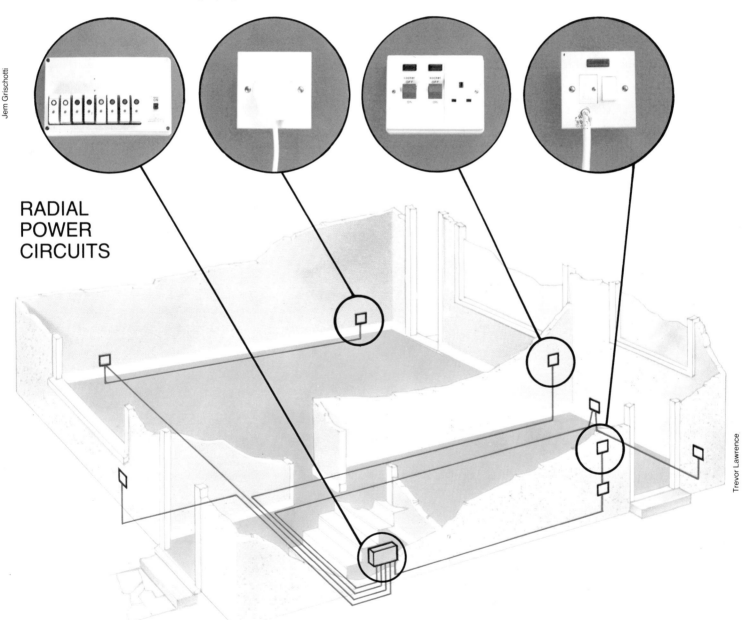

RADIAL
POWER
CIRCUITS

Jem Grischotti

Trevor Lawrence

LIGHTING CIRCUITS

LOOP-IN LIGHTING

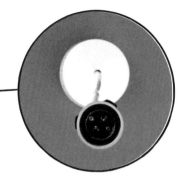

The cable on a loop-in lighting circuit links each ceiling rose in turn. The switch cable also connects into the rose as does the flexible cord for the lampholder.

JUNCTION BOX SYSTEM

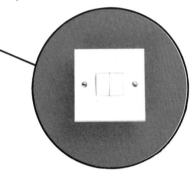

A two-gang switch enables two lighting points to be controlled individually from the same point. Switches can be surface-mounted or flush.

Trevor Lawrence

Jem Grischotti

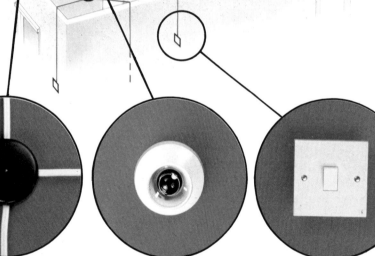

With junction box wiring the main cable runs between four-terminal junction boxes. The other cables go to the lighting point and the switch.

Batten holders are used to fit a light close to the ceiling. In bathrooms, they must have a 'skirt' to prevent contact with metal on the fitting or bulb.

The simplest switch is a one-gang type mounted on a faceplate. They can be either surface mounted or recessed to be flush with the wall.

a separate radial circuit protected by a 20A fuse. The fuses are housed in a separate consumer unit which is linked to a sealed time clock and uses off-peak electricity.

Lighting circuits

Two systems of wiring lighting circuits are in common use, and it is not unusual for an installation to contain a little bit of each. One is called the loop-in system; the other the junction (or joint) box system.

With the loop-in system, a cable (normally 1.0mm² but sometimes 1.5mm²) leaves a 5A fuse in the consumer unit (or fuse box) and is connected to the first in a series of special loop-in ceiling roses. From this rose, one cable goes onto the next in the series, and another takes the power down to the switch controlling the light and back up through the light itself.

The junction box system uses the same idea but, instead of going from rose to rose, the cable from the consumer unit (or fuse box) passes through a series of junction boxes. From each box, one cable goes to the ceiling rose or light, and another to the switch that controls it. This system is particularly useful, for example, when fitting wall lights as there is little space at the back of a wall light fitting for looping-in.

Lighting circuits are rated at 5 amps, which means they can take a load of up to 1,200 watts. In effect, they could supply 12 lamp-holders containing bulbs of 100W each or smaller. But as you may want to fit bulbs with higher wattages, it is usual for a lighting circuit to supply up to eight outlet points, so separate circuits are required for each floor.

Strictly speaking it's better to arrange the circuits so that there is more than one on each floor — this means that you won't be in total darkness if a fuse in the consumer unit blows.

CHAPTER 1

TOOLS & ACCESSORIES

Before you can contemplate carrying out any electrical work in
your home, you must make sure you are familiar with all the
components that go to make up the system.

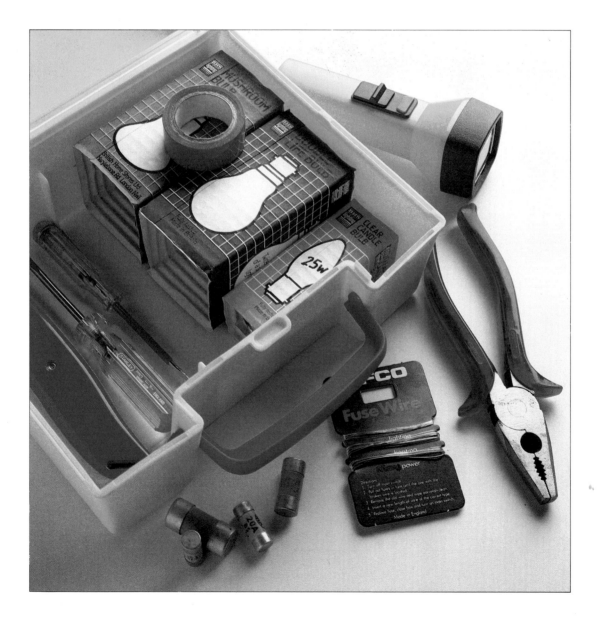

PLUGS & FUSES

Fuses and plugs are the two parts of a home's electrical system that most closely concern the householder and it's important to know what they do and how to use them.

FUSES

A fuse is a safety device inserted into an electrical circuit to protect the mains wiring or any appliance from damage by overloading. This can be caused by anything from too many appliances overloading a particular circuit to a short circuit within an appliance, its plug or in some other part of the system. Basically the fuse is a thin wire that melts ('blows') and breaks the circuit if too much current flows through it. Circuit fuses are located in the house's main fuse box or consumer unit. Fuses are also fitted in modern plugs.

Circuit fuses

Circuit fuses protect the fixed wiring and apparatus, and if they 'blow' no equipment will operate on the circuit affected.

Every circuit fuse has a current rating in amps (A) appropriate to the rating of the circuit, and is colour-coded: white is for a 5A fuse (for lighting circuits), blue for a 15A, yellow for a 20A, red for a 30A (ring circuit) and green for a 45A (cooker circuit).

There are two types of circuit fuse – rewirable and cartridge. A rewirable fuse is the least sensitive method of protection, but it can be mended easily by connecting fuse wire of the correct rating between the terminals of the fuse carrier.

In a cartridge fuse, the fuse wire is enclosed in a clip-in ceramic cartridge filled with quartz powder (sand) and if it blows you simply replace the whole cartridge. Unlike the rewirable fuse where it's possible to fit the wrongly rated fuse wire, it's impossible to fit a larger amperage cartridge as the size of fuse holder usually depends on the rating of the circuit to which it is fitted. The only exception to this is with 15A and 20A fuses which are the same size, but as the cartridges are colour-coded, a mistake is avoidable.

BE PREPARED

● Make a list of which circuit does what (eg, no 1: downstairs lighting) and keep it by the main fuse box or consumer unit

● Keep a fuse wire card containing adequate lengths of each rating, a small screwdriver and a torch near the fuse box or consumer unit ready for emergencies

● If the consumer unit contains cartridge fuses, always keep at least two spare fuses of each current rating in a plastic bag and hang it nearby.

Miniature circuit breaker (MCB)

MCBs can be fitted instead of circuit fuses in modern consumer units. An MCB is a switching device that is activated by the surge of current caused by overloading or a short circuit. It has the advantage that it can be reset at the push of a button or the flick of a switch – unless the fault that caused it to switch off in the first place is still present.

MCBs are more sensitive and faster reacting than circuit fuses. Some kinds have the same colour-coding as conventional circuit fuses; others are labelled with the circuit rating.

Residual Current Circuit Breaker (RCCB)

An RCCB may sometimes be fitted in conjunction with the house's earthing system, and usually protects all circuits in the house. It cuts off the power supply if it detects an electric current flowing to earth – this is what happens when someone receives an electric shock, or insulation fails on a mains cable. An RCCB is activated by far less current than is necessary to blow a fuse or trip an MCB, and operates within a fraction of a second.

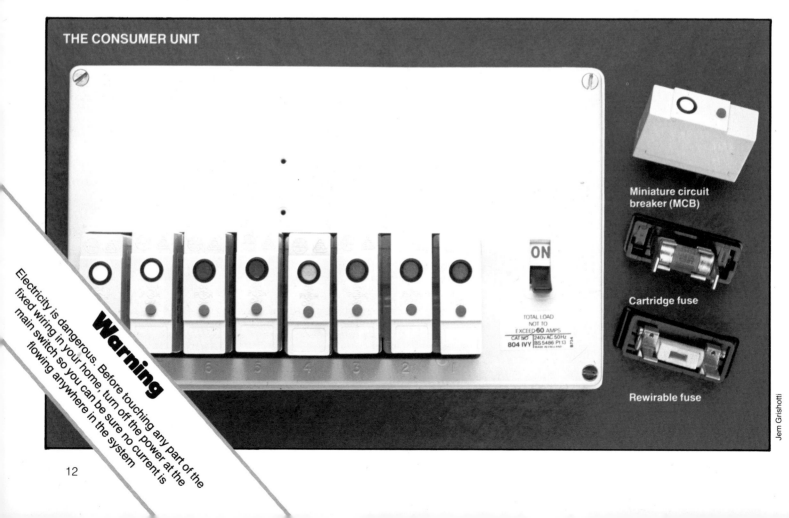

THE CONSUMER UNIT

Miniature circuit breaker (MCB)

Cartridge fuse

Rewirable fuse

Warning Electricity is dangerous. Before touching any part of the fixed wiring in your home, turn off the power at the main switch so you can be sure no current is flowing anywhere in the system

Craig Warwick

Jem Grishotti

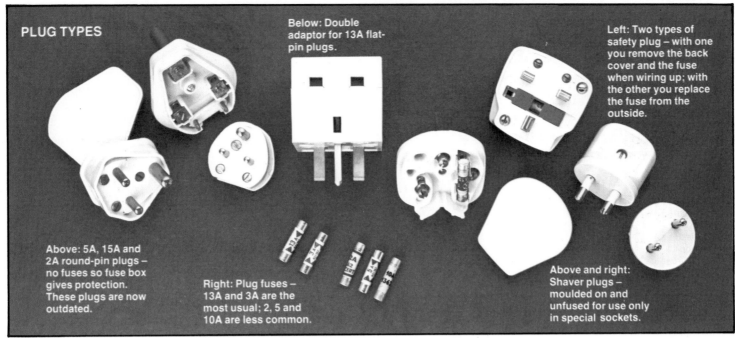

Below: Double adaptor for 13A flat-pin plugs.

Left: Two types of safety plug – with one you remove the back cover and the fuse when wiring up; with the other you replace the fuse from the outside.

Above: 5A, 15A and 2A round-pin plugs – no fuses so fuse box gives protection. These plugs are now outdated.

Right: Plug fuses – 13A and 3A are the most usual; 2, 5 and 10A are less common.

Above and right: Shaver plugs – moulded on and unfused for use only in special sockets.

Jem Grischotti

Circuit fuses and faults

If a circuit fuse blows immediately after it has been mended, the cause could be a fault in an appliance, in the circuit wiring or in a socket outlet. A fixed appliance such as a shower unit or immersion heater (which has no plug or intermediate fuse) could also be to blame. Such faults should be investigated by a qualified electrician.

Continuous blowing of a lighting circuit fuse is probably caused by a short circuit in the flex or lampholder of a pendant light.

Plug fuses

Modern 13A flat-pin plugs contain fuses that protect the individual appliance and its flex in case a fault occurs. When they blow they only isolate the appliance concerned, so other appliances plugged into the main circuit will still function.

Plug fuses are of the cartridge type which fit neatly into a carrier in the plug, but are a different size to circuit cartridge fuses. The two standard ones have current ratings of 3A and 13A and are colour-coded red and brown respectively. Fit a 3A fuse for appliances rated at less than 700 watts, a 13A fuse otherwise (and always for colour TV sets). Plug fuses can also be fitted into connection units used to supply fixed appliances such as a night storage heater or a freezer.

When a plug fuse blows

If an appliance doesn't work, the most likely cause is a blown plug fuse. Replace it with a new one of the correct rating for the appliance (see above), then put the plug back in the socket and switch on. If nothing happens, check that the socket is live by plugging in an appliance that you know is working. Should this not work, check the circuit fuse.

PLUGS

The function of a plug is to connect a portable appliance (eg a lamp or power tool) to the fixed wiring via a socket outlet anywhere around the house.

The modern standard plug is a 13A fused three-pin plug, which has flat pins. There is also a moulded-on unfused two-pin plug used exclusively for electric shavers in conjunction with a special socket outlet. In older installations, instead of 13A plugs, round-pin plugs with current ratings of 2A, 5A and 15A are used. These are not fused.

A recent development is a 13A fused plug that is moulded onto the PVC sheathing of the flex and can't be dismantled. However, it's possible to change the fuse by lifting up a flap between the pins of the plug. It's also possible to change the fuse in some conventional plugs without removing the plug top. If you ever need to replace a moulded-on plug you have to cut off the flex as close to the plug as possible and replace it with a conventional 13A plug.

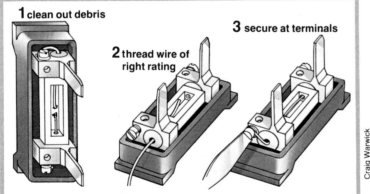

1 clean out debris

2 thread wire of right rating

3 secure at terminals

Craig Warwick

Replacing circuit fuses

Turn off the main on/off switch on the fuse box or consumer unit before tackling the repair. With a rewirable fuse, you may have to remove each in turn to locate the one that's blown. Always use fuse wire of the correct rating for the circuit when you make the repair – don't be tempted to use a higher rated one even if the fuse continues to blow. Don't make the wire taut between the terminals as this will reduce the current rating, resulting in over-heating and premature failure of the fuse wire. NEVER fit any other metallic object into a fuse carrier.

If a cartridge fuse blows, and you've no list of the circuits (or it is not obvious which circuit has been affected), turn off the main switch and remove each cartridge in turn. Test it by holding it across the open end of a switched-on metal torch, with one end of the fuse on the casing and the other on the end of the battery. A sound fuse will light the torch. Alternatively, use a continuity tester (available from electrical stores). Replace the blown fuse with a new one of the correct rating.

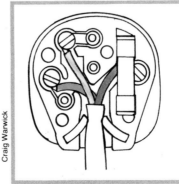

Craig Warwick

Plugs and earthing

Most electrical appliances are fitted with three-core flex (see pages 14-15). When plugged in, the earth wire (green/yellow) is linked to the house's earthing and ensures that the appliance is properly earthed. Two-core flex is for double-insulated appliances. Left: A correctly-wired 13A plug.
REMEMBER
BL (Bottom Left) = BLue
BR (Bottom Right) = BRown.

CABLE & FLEX

Two types of wiring are used in the domestic electrical circuits. Fixed cables are normally concealed, and carry electrical current to switches, ceiling lights, and socket outlets. Flexible cords (flexes) connect portable appliances and light fittings to the fixed wiring.

Fixed wiring

This consists mostly of PVC-sheathed cable containing three copper conductors (cores). The core insulated in red PVC is the 'live' and the one in black the 'neutral' though in lighting circuits in the cable to the switch both the black and red are live. (The black core is required to have a piece of red sleeving on it to indicate this, although this is often omitted by incompetent electricians. Cables having two red conductors are made for contract work, but rarely stocked and sold retail). The third core is the earth and this is uninsulated, but when exposed after the sheathing is removed ready for wiring up it must be sleeved in green/yellow striped PVC before being connected to the earth terminal. In some wiring circuits PVC-sheathed cables having one core only are used, for example, where a live core is looped out of a switch or a neutral core is looped out of a light, to supply an additional light or lights. Three-core and earth cable is used for two-way switching. The conductors are insulated in red, blue and yellow; the colour coding is for purposes of identification only.

Cables

PVC-sheathed and insulated, two-core and earth

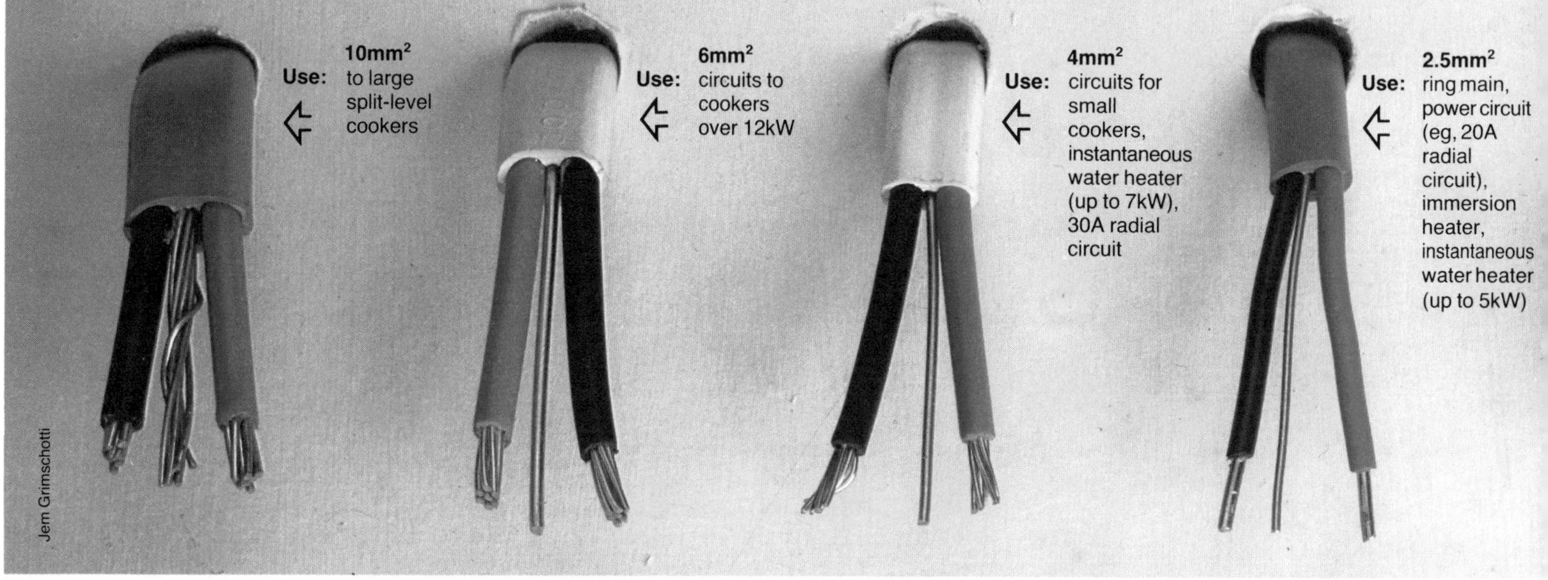

Jem Grimschotti

Use: 10mm² to large split-level cookers

Use: 6mm² circuits to cookers over 12kW

Use: 4mm² circuits for small cookers, instantaneous water heater (up to 7kW), 30A radial circuit

Use: 2.5mm² ring main, power circuit (eg, 20A radial circuit), immersion heater, instantaneous water heater (up to 5kW)

Flexible cords

Flexible cords are made in various sizes and current ratings and the types you'll most often come across are: *parallel twin unsheathed, circular PVC-sheathed, circular braided, unkinkable* and *heat-resisting.* Each conductor is made up of a number of strands of copper and it is this which gives the cord its flexibility.

The insulation used round the conductors now conforms to an international colour coding standard – brown denotes the live wire, blue the neutral, and green/yellow the earth, when it is part of the flex. Transparent or white insulation is used for a flex that carries a low current and where it doesn't matter which wire is connected to the live and neutral terminals of an appliance. It is used mainly for table lamps that need no earth.

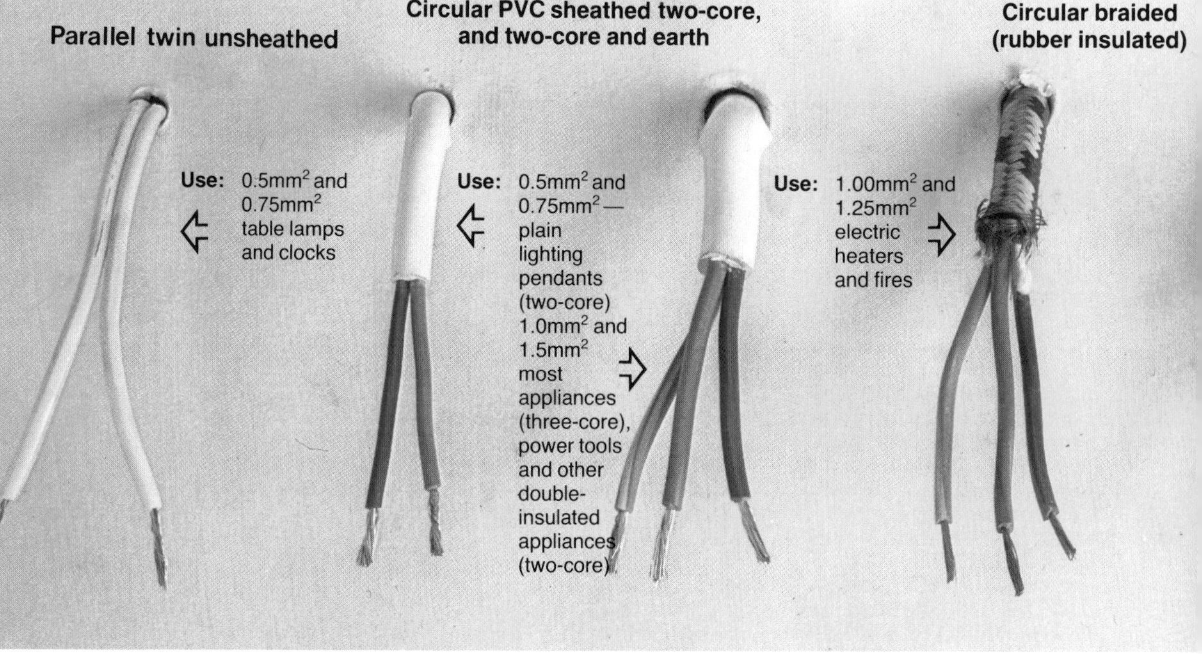

Parallel twin unsheathed

Use: 0.5mm² and 0.75mm² table lamps and clocks

Circular PVC sheathed two-core, and two-core and earth

Use: 0.5mm² and 0.75mm² — plain lighting pendants (two-core) 1.0mm² and 1.5mm² most appliances (three-core), power tools and other double-insulated appliances (two-core)

Circular braided (rubber insulated)

Use: 1.00mm² and 1.25mm² electric heaters and fires

14

Cables for fixed wiring

Most domestic wiring is now supplied in metric sizes which refer to the cross-sectional area of one of the conductors, whether it is composed of one or several strands of wire. Most common sizes of cable are 1.0mm² and 1.5mm² used for lighting, and 2.5mm² used for power circuits.

Cable with grey sheathing is intended to be concealed in walls or under floors; white sheathing is meant for surface mounting.

PVC-sheathed and insulated, three-core and earth

1.5mm²
Use: lighting circuit, immersion heater (1.0mm² also used for lighting)

1.0mm²
Use: two-way switching for lighting circuit (1.5mm² also available)

Unkinkable

Use: 1.25mm² and 1.5mm² electric irons, percolators and kettles

Heat-resisting

Use: 0.5mm² and 0.75mm² lighting pendants with 100W-200W bulbs 1.25mm² and 1.5mm² immersion heater

---

Safety with electricity

● never work on a circuit with current on. Turn off at mains and isolate circuit by removing relevant fuse. Keep this with you until you restore supply
● never touch plugs and sockets with wet hands
● remove plugs from socket when working on appliance
● always use the correct fuse wire when mending a fuse

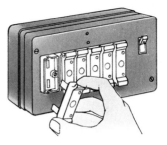

The importance of earthing

Earthing is an essential safety feature of all wiring systems. To complete a circuit, electricity either flows down the neutral conductor of the supply cable or it flows to earth. That is why you get a shock if you touch a live wire. The idea of earthing is to connect all metal fittings and appliances in the house with a good conductor – the 'earth wire' in cables and flexes. If a fault occurs that makes this metal live, the presence of the earth wire prevents the voltage from rising much above earth voltage. At the same time, the fault greatly increases the current being drawn to the metal via the supply conductor, and this current surge is detected by the circuit fuse, which

'blows' and cuts off the current flow (see pages 12-13).

The earth conductor links socket outlets and appliances (via their plugs) and is connected to a main earthing terminal at the house fuse box or consumer unit. This is usually connected to the outer metal sheath of the underground supply cable.

All metal pipework in the house is also earthed by being connected to the earth terminal – this is called 'cross bonding'.

Old wiring

Some old installations may still be using lead-sheathed or tough rubber-sheathed (TRS) wiring, with the conducting wires insulated in vulcanized rubber, or vulcanized rubber insulated, taped and braided

wire. These insulating materials deteriorate with age (about 25-30 years) so the wiring can become dangerous. Therefore it really does need to be replaced with modern PVC-sheathed and insulated cable.

The right connection

The plug is the vital link between any electrical appliance and the mains and must be connected up correctly if it is to do its job properly. With flex in the new colour codes, connect the BRown core to the Bottom Right terminal, the BLue core to the Bottom Left one and the green-and-yellow core (if present) to the top terminal. With cores in old colour codes, Red goes to the bottom Right terminal, BLack to Bottom Left and green to top.

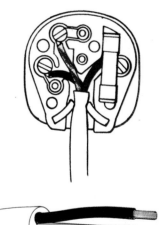

Old colour codes

Before the introduction of new international colour codes, flex used red insulation to denote the live conductor, black for the neutral and green for the earth.

Warning: Electricity is dangerous

Before touching any part of the fixed wiring in your home, turn off the power at the main switch so you can be sure no current is flowing anywhere in the system.

ELECTRICAL WIRING ACCESSORIES

Without electrical wiring accessories you could never make use of the power carried round your home by the various circuit cables. These accessories include such things as power sockets, light switches and much more besides. Here are some of the most useful.

It's a good idea to have a thorough knowlege of the available accessories when you plan a wiring job. That way you'll know what to use, and both when and where to use it. If you're fairly new to the world of home electrics then the chances are that you'll have to follow to the letter any guide that you're using. But instructions, however good, cannot cover every eventuality and a wide knowledge of what accessories are available will help you to prepare for the job and also save you extra work. Once you know what the various types of accessories do, and the special features that they have, you'll be able to distinguish easily between those that will do a particular job and those that won't. Then you'll be able to work out exactly what you require before you go to the retailers and that way not risk making a fool of yourself. Before you go laying out a lot of money, it's important to understand a few technical terms that will help you to avoid making expensive mistakes.

Terms to know
Most accessories are rated at a certain number of amps, which indicates the amount of current the fitting can carry or control in complete safety. Under normal

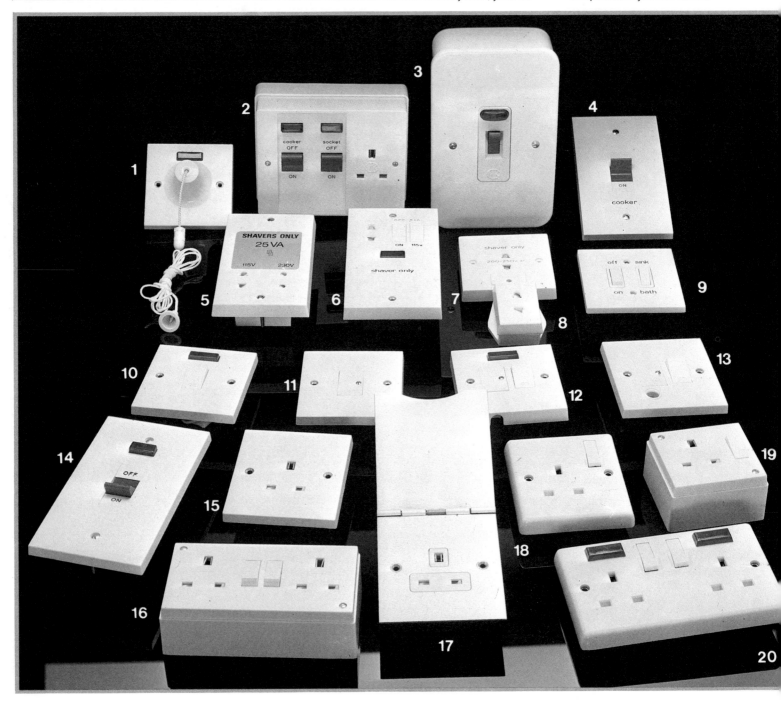

circumstances, a rating of 13A means that the accessory is for use on a ring circuit or its spurs, and any other rating means the fitting is designed to form part of a purpose-made radial circuit.

In the latter case, the current rating you need depends on what the circuit feeds and should therefore match the current rating of the fuse in the consumer unit controlling that circuit. But there are exceptions. A shaver socket, for example, may overload above 2A, yet is quite safe if connected to a 5A lighting circuit. And fused connection units won't be rated at all as you decide their rating when the fuse is put into the carrier.

Next, there are a number of terms that classify switches. You'll find some described as SP (single-pole) and others as DP (double-pole). When a switch is described as SP it means that when it is turned off, it breaks only the live side of the circuit. A DP switch, on the other hand, breaks both the live and neutral sides, and so ensures total disconnection.

SP switches are used mainly in lighting circuits (because they have a low current rating), while DP switches are used in most power circuits (because these have a higher current rating). It's all a question of safety; obviously

the DP switch is the safer and is therefore used in most high rating circuits.

The other important expression you must understand is what is meant by a switch or socket having a certain number of gangs. This is, in fact, straightforward. Where switches are concerned, the number of gangs tells you how many separate switches you have built into a single face plate. With power sockets, the number of gangs refers to the number of plugs the socket will take without the need for an adaptor plug. An adaptor plug is not to be recommended as you can risk the danger of fire.

Decorative aspects
The days of all electrical accessories being finished in the same material are now, thankfully, long gone. The variety of different styles, colours and materials that are available make it possible for light switches, sockets and other accessories to be incorporated in the overall interior design.

That's really all you need to know if you're buying accessories for an electrics job in your home. You may well come across other odd expressions and terms but you'll find most of them explained satisfactorily in Chapter 1, pages 6-10.

POWER CIRCUIT ACCESSORIES

1 Ceiling switches with a higher current rating than a lighting ceiling switch are ideal for use in the bathroom to control appliances such as instantaneous electric showers.

2 Cooker control units are rated at 45A and incorporate a 13A power socket and two switches to control both cooker and socket.

3, 10, 14 DP switches are used to control permanently connected appliances such as water heaters and are rated at 20, 45, or 60A. Some 20A models have a flex outlet and many are fitted with pilot lamps.

4 Cooker switches are merely DP switches which control the power to the cooker. They are safer than a cooker control unit as you can't risk the danger of fire by trailing a kettle flex across a boiling ring.

5, 6 Shaver supply units are suitable only for electric shavers. A built-in transformer allows them to be connected to the power circuit, and an isolator provides complete safety for use in a bathroom. All have on/off switches and some a voltage selection switch for different models of shavers.

7 Shaver socket outlets don't have built-in transformers to lower the voltage which means that they must be wired into the lighting circuit and are not safe to be used in bathrooms.

8 Shaver adaptors will fit into any 13A plug and are protected by a fuse and a safety shuttered outlet.

9 Dual switches are used for controlling dual element immersion heaters – those with one element heating only the top part of the tank and another heating the entire tank. The unit has two switches, one controlling power, the other directing that power to one element or the other.

11-13 Fused connection units connect permanently the flex of an appliance, such as a freezer, to the power circuit. There is less risk of accidental disconnection than with a plug and socket, and a fused unit can be used to 'down-grade' the current for a spur off the ring circuit and so make it safe to use for a light. They are available with switches, lights and flex outlet holes.

15-20 13A socket outlets are for use with 13A square-pin plugs. One- and two-gang versions with switches and neon lights are available. They can be surface or flush-mounted or set in the floor – in which case they are fitted with a protective cover. There are versions fitted with earth leakage circuit breakers for extra protection and round-pin sockets are also available.

CABLE OUTLETS

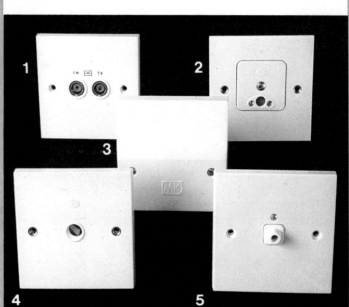

1 Aerial sockets can have either single or double outlets and allow you to use your outside aerial for both the television and the FM frequency of your radio.

2 Fused clock connectors are really specialised versions of the fused connection unit and were used to connect mains-operated clocks (now no longer made). They are also used in the installation of some extractor fans and can be flush or surface-mounted.

3 Cooker connection units are nothing more than purpose-built terminal blocks which allow you to connect the trailing cable of an electric cooker to a concealed, fixed cable run from the cooker control unit. They incorporate a clamp plate that protects the

cable and connections in case the cooker is moved.

4 Flex outlet plates are similar to blank plates but a hole in the face plate allows the flex of an appliance directly into the DP cable run. This set-up should really only be used on radial circuits designed for a specific job, such as providing power for a bathroom towel rail in conjunction with a fused connection unit. So, they are used in much the same way as a cooker connector – where it is impractical to pass the flex of the appliance directly into the DP switch or fused connection unit.

5 Telephone cord outlets have a moulded outlet designed to carry standard telephone cable. Double outlet models are available.

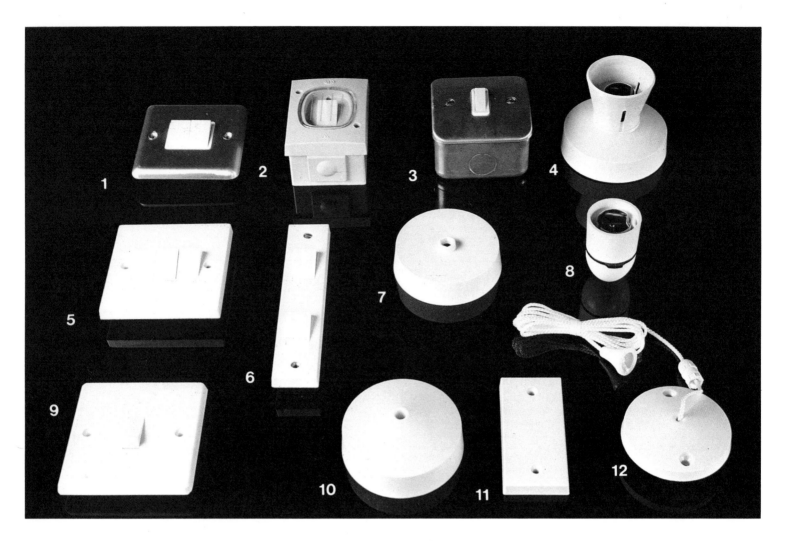

LIGHTING ACCESSORIES

1, 5, 9 Plate switches are rated at 5A, and are used in ordinary lighting circuits. They have up to six gangs and most can be connected for two-way switching.

2 Sealed switches are used where the switch is likely to be exposed to water or the elements.

3 Metal clad switches are surface-mounted and are used when the switch needs extra protection – such as in a garage or else where it is likely to get knocked.

4 Battenholders are for lights that are surface-mounted on a wall or ceiling. They can be used in a junction box lighting circuit, at the end of a fused spur from a power circuit, or wired into a loop-in lighting circuit.

6 Architrave switches, so-named because they can fit into the decorative surround of a doorway, are about 32mm (1¼in) wide.

7, 10 Ceiling roses connect the lighting circuit's cables to the pendant light flex. Most have their terminals arranged for the loop-in system, but two terminal versions for use in a junction circuit are also available. When used with a heavy pendant light, the rose should have a strain wire clamp which takes the weight off the conductor cores in the light flex.

8 Lampholders fit on a pendant light's flex and hold the bulb and lamp shade in position. They should be heat resistant and in bathrooms it's essential to use one with a deep protective shield for extra safety.

11 Blank plates allow you to seal off a mounting box when it is no longer in use so saving you the extra work of removing it.

12 Ceiling switches are rated at 5A for the lighting circuit and are the only sort of light switch permitted in a bathroom where stringent safety regulations apply.

MOUNTING BOXES

1 Accessories of all types can be fitted in surface-mounted boxes.

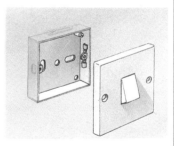

2 Light switches can be flush-mounted in plaster-depth boxes.

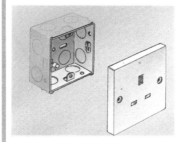

3 Power circuit accessories need deeper boxes than light switches – 35mm (1⅜in) is the commonest.

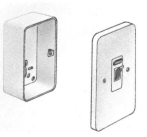

4 Extra-deep boxes are needed for flush-mounting some accessories. Fit with care in single-brick walls.

18

TOOLS FOR ELECTRICAL JOBS

Electrical work, like so many other jobs about the home, can be carried out more successfully and more quickly if you have the right tools to hand. Here is a selection of what you will need for installation work, and also to enable you to cope with emergencies.

To carry out electrical work properly without causing damage to cables and other household fittings, you'll need to have the right tools for the job. Most DIY enthusiasts will already have many of the tools needed for such heavy work as raising and replacing floorboards and chopping out chases in walls to bury cables. Very often the car tool kit will produce spanners for dismantling appliances when renewing flexible cords or heating elements.

Nevertheless, if you are contemplating carrying out your own electrical installation work, you should assemble a tool kit to cope with all the jobs you are likely to encounter. That way not only will you find the work much easier, but you'll also be able to ensure that the final result reaches a professional standard that will give you great satisfaction.

Screwdrivers
A minimum of three straight-tipped screwdrivers is required: a small, thin-bladed electrician's screwdriver for reaching shrouded grub screws in electrical fittings; and medium and large size normal screwdrivers. A selection of crosshead screwdrivers may also be helpful in dealing with Pozidriv and similar screws.

There are two other screwdriver types which you may find useful: a ratchet screwdriver with a chuck to accept a range of different driver bits, and an offset screwdriver. The latter is a simple steel bar, the ends of which are bent at right angles and terminate in a straight tip at one end and a crosshead tip at the other. It is ideal for reaching awkward screws, particularly when servicing electrical appliances.

Bradawls
A bradawl is needed for piercing holes in timber and plaster to mark the position of fixing screws for appliances and their mounting boxes or brackets.

Pliers
Pliers are among the essential tools for electrical work. They are used to grip and bend wire, and to hold small items such as nuts and washers in confined spaces.

Electrician's pliers are similar to engineer's pliers but have insulated handles suitable for working with voltages of 240 volts or above. However, remember you should never carry out any work on an installation unless the power has been turned off, so the presence of insulated handles is only an extra safeguard.

Complementing the standard electrician's pliers should be a pair of long-nosed pliers, which may also be obtained with insulated handles.

Cutters and strippers
Small side cutters are used for cutting the ends of fuse wires when rewiring circuit fuses, and for trimming cable and flex cores when making connections. The jaws are shaped to get close in to the work and still allow knuckle room to grip the handles.

A pair of wire strippers of the adjustable type to fit the various sizes of insulated conductor will permit the insulation to be removed efficiently without damaging the conductor itself. Also available is a cable stripper which will remove the outer sheathing of a cable without cutting into the insulation of the conductors inside. This is much safer than using a knife.

SPECIALIST TOOLS

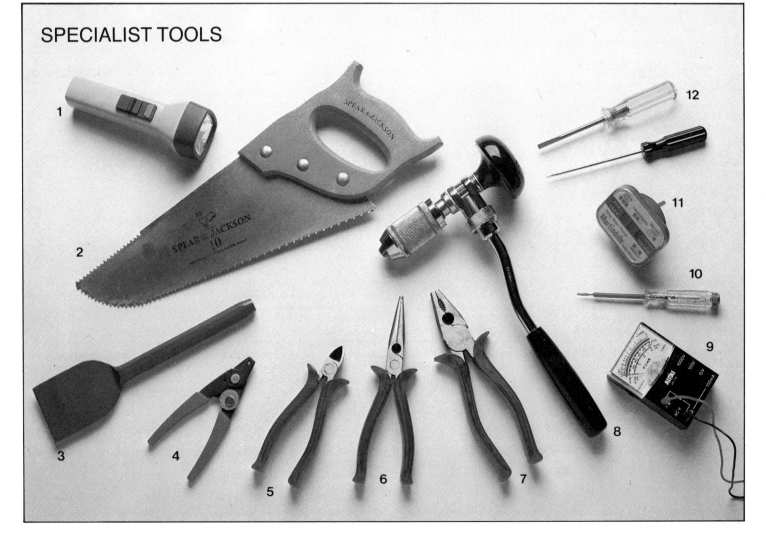

GENERAL-PURPOSE TOOLS

Handyman's knife
If you can't get hold of the type of cable stripper mentioned previously, a handyman's knife will do for trimming the insulation and cable sheathing, providing it is used carefully. Also, it it useful for trimming floor coverings when lifting and replacing floorboards.

Grips and wrenches
Where metal conduit, armoured and mineral-insulated cables are used, an adjustable spanner will be

SPECIALIST TOOLS
There are a number of specialist tools (below) which are essential for any electrical installation work. These will enable you to get perfect results with the minimum of effort.

KEY
1 *Torch*
2 *Flooring saw*
3 *Floorboard chisel*
4 *Adjustable wire strippers*
5 *Side cutters*
6 *Long-nosed pliers*
7 *Snub-nosed pliers*
8 *Joist brace*
9 *Continuity tester*
10 *Neon screwdriver*
11 *Ring-main tester*
12 *Screwdrivers*

needed. A companion tool is the locking wrench which also has adjustable jaws, but they can be locked on to the workpiece to apply great pressure, leaving the hands free.

Hammers
Ideally, your tool kit should include three types of hammer, and you may already have some of them. A claw hammer is used for general work, a pin hammer for fixing cable clips and a club hammer for driving cold chisels.

Chisels
A selection of cold chisels will make installing cable runs and mounting boxes easier. A short, sharp, small-diameter chisel should be used for chopping out cable chases and recesses in plaster. Deeper recesses in brickwork and masonry can be cut with a thicker 150 to 200mm (6 to 8in) long chisel. A longer (at least 300mm/12in) thin chisel is ideal for cutting holes through brick walls.
   The electrician's bolster chisel is useful for lifting floorboards; you drive it between the boards to split off the tongues and then lever them upwards. The wide blade spreads the load.
   Since a certain amount of wood cutting is involved in laying cables

beneath floors, a set of general-purpose wood chisels will also prove to be invaluable.

Saws
Various types of saw are needed in electrical work since metal, wood and plastic need to be cut.
   For cutting plastic trunking, floorboards and other timber, you'll need a tenon saw.
   Cutting down into floorboards and removing the tongues when lifting boarding can be done with a special floorboard saw. This has a curved blade, allowing the waste material to be cleared quickly from the groove the saw cuts, and so reducing the likelihood of damaging adjacent woodwork when cutting across a board. The tip of the back edge of the blade is set at an angle with cutting teeth to allow cuts to be made right up to a skirting board without the handle fouling the wall.
   A padsaw is useful for cutting timber in confined spaces and for making holes in ceilings to accept mounting boxes for light fittings.
   Metal fittings and large cables, including the armoured variety, may be cut with an adjustable hacksaw, which will take 200 to 300mm (8 to 12in) long blades. Finally, small sawing jobs and shortening fixing screws can be carried out with a junior hacksaw.

Your tool box (above) should contain many general-purpose tools that will help you with your electrical jobs, as well as being useful for other repairs. Screwdrivers, chisels, drill bits and saws are all vital. In addition, it's a good idea to keep a number of spare electrical accessories in case of an emergency.

Drills
A hand drill should be available for light drilling of plastic or thin metal, and can also be used for drilling small holes in brickwork and masonry.
   Alternatively, a power drill is a better bet providing, of course, that you already have a live circuit from which to operate it. Pick one with a large chuck capacity, and give serious consideration to buying a drill with an optional hammer action, which will be a great help when drilling into masonry.

Drill bits
A set of masonry drill bits is necessary for drilling brickwork. If you have a power drill with a hammer action make sure the drill bits are suitable for this; not all are.
   For drilling holes in metal and plastic boxes, a selection of high-speed twist drills is a must.

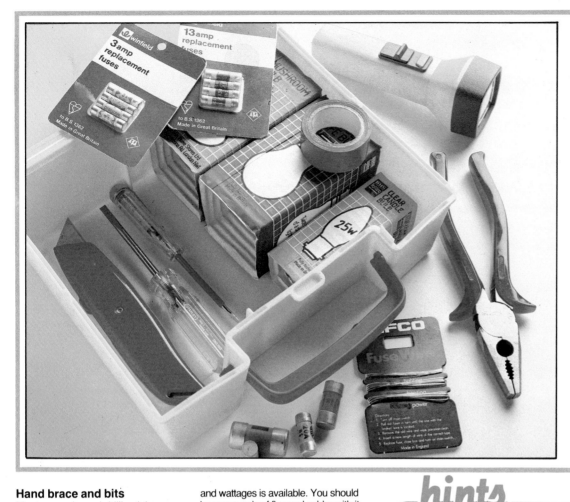

Even if you're never likely to carry out any electrical installation work in your home, you're sure to have to cope with running repairs to your system when things go wrong. So you can find the tools and materials you will need when the lights go out, buy a small box and assemble an emergency tool kit you can keep near to the fuse board so you can always find it when you need it. Include a torch, a pair of pliers, a handyman's knife, a couple of screwdrivers, some PVC insulating tape and fuse wire or replacement fuses of appropriate types. It's also worth adding two or three spare light bulbs. Label the box, and always replace any components of the kit if they are used.

Emergency procedures
Before dealing with any repair, make sure that the circuit is safe to work on. If a fuse has blown, you should turn off the mainswitch and identify which circuit it is. Remove the fuse carrier and renew the wire or cartridge, or reset the MCB. Never undertake any work with wet hands and always make sure that you have sufficient light by which to see.

Hand brace and bits
Most general wood-drilling jobs can also be accomplished with a conventional carpenter's ratchet brace and a set of auger bits. However, drilling through joists often presents problems due to their close spacing. A special compact joist brace is made for this purpose and has a ratchet lever immediately behind the chuck.

Measuring tape
A retractable steel tape is essential for the accurate positioning of switches and other accessories. A 3m (10ft) one will do for installation work, but a longer one will be useful when estimating cable runs.

Plumb bob
The position of vertical runs of cable can be determined accurately with the aid of a plumb bob and line. It can also be used to carry a draw wire down into a hollow partition where it can be hooked out at the switch position.

Spirit level
Switch and accessory boxes need to be level, and a small spirit level is ideal for setting them correctly.

Soldering iron
For servicing and repairing electrical appliances, you will need a soldering iron to unsolder and remake connections. A range of sizes and wattages is available. You should keep a supply of flux and solder with it. FACTFINDER 57.

Testers
Two testers that every home electrician should have are a neon tester (usually in the form of a small screwdriver) and a continuity tester.

The neon tester is used to determine if a terminal is live. Place the tip of the tester blade on the terminal and a finger on the metal cap at the end of the tester's handle. This completes a circuit, causing a neon bulb in the handle to light if there is power. A built-in resistor prevents electric shocks.

Battery-powered testers are relatively cheap to buy. The most popular type has metal probes, and such a device will test cartridge fuses and other conductors of low resistance, continuity being indicated by a positive meter reading. Some models double as mains testers.

High resistance items, such as light bulbs and heating elements, should be checked with a special high-resistance tester.

Another useful tester takes the form of a 3-pin plug and is used for checking the cable connections at a socket. It has neon indicators to show whether the socket is wired correctly, has faulty earth, live or neutral connections, or reversed live and neutral connections.

hints

● When lifting a floorboard, lever the end clear of the floor and lay a long cold chisel across the adjacent boards to support it in this raised position. Continue levering, moving the chisel as you go, until the board can be removed.

● A flooring saw with its specially shaped blade will allow you to cut through floorboards right up to skirting boards without the handle touching the wall. It may also be used for cutting through the tongues of T & G boarding.

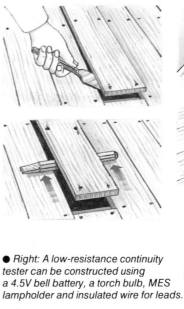

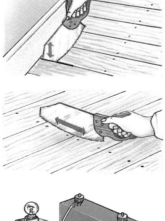

● Right: A low-resistance continuity tester can be constructed using a 4.5V bell battery, a torch bulb, MES lampholder and insulated wire for leads.

CHAPTER 2

BASIC TECHNIQUES

There are a few basic tasks that you will be carrying out over and over again as you improve and extend your home's electrics, so it pays to learn some of the tricks employed by professional electricians.

CEILING LIGHTS AND SWITCHES

Most ceiling lights are positioned centrally in a room to give general lighting. But by adding another light, or changing the position of an existing fitting, you can highlight particular areas and enhance the decoration.

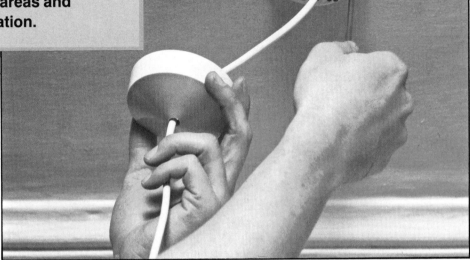

Keith Morris

Putting in a new pendant ceiling light and switch, or changing the position of an existing one, usually presents few problems – even if you have little or no experience of electrical work.

A pendant is the most common ceiling light and consists of a lampholder wired to a length of flexible cord which hangs from a ceiling rose. Another type can be plugged into the ceiling rose – in this case the flexible cord has to have a special fitting which slots into a batten holder.

Know your system

Installing a new ceiling light requires making a simple connection into a nearby lighting circuit either by inserting a junction box or at an existing loop-in rose and then running a cable to a switch. In order to connect into the circuit you'll first need to know how the lights in your house are wired and which lights belong to which circuit. Then you'll be able to work out whether you can actually add another light to the circuit that is nearest to the new light's position.

There are two principal methods of wiring a lighting circuit. In the loop-in method the cable runs from ceiling rose to ceiling rose, stopping at the last one on the circuit, and the switches are wired into the roses. With the junction box system the cable runs to a number of junction boxes each serving a switch and a light. You may well find that both methods have been used in the same circuit to simplify and reduce the cable runs.

It's possible to connect into a nearby rose provided it's a loop-in type. You can check this simply by turning off the power and unscrewing the rose cover. A loop-in rose will have more than one red insulated wire going into the central terminal bank of the three in-line terminal banks. However, it can be quite fiddly to fit another cable, given that the terminal banks are very small, so you might find it easier to insert a junction box in the main circuit. And if there isn't a loop-in rose you'll have to use this method anyway.

Earthing for lighting circuits

Modern lighting circuits are protected by an earth. But if you've got a fairly old system (it's

likely to be based on junction boxes), you might find that it doesn't have one. So when you're extending such a circuit, you're now required to protect the new wiring, light fitting and switch by installing an earth. Consequently, you have to use two-core and earth cable for the extension, which will most probably connect into the existing circuit at a junction box. You then have to run a 1.5mm^2 earth cable from this point to the main earthing point.

Circuit additions

Usually there's a lighting circuit for each floor of a house and in a single storey dwelling there are likely to be two or more. But it's easy to identify the individual circuits simply by switching on all the lights, turning off the power and taking out a 5A fuse from the consumer unit or switching off an MCB. When you restore the power you'll know that the lights that remain off all belong to the same circuit.

Generally speaking, a lighting circuit serves six to eight fixed lighting points. In fact it can serve up to 12 lampholders provided the total wattage of the bulbs on the circuit doesn't exceed 1,200 watts. This means that unless other lights have previously been added – wall lights for example – there shouldn't be a problem of connecting in another light.

Remember, when adding up the bulb wattages, a bulb of less than 100 watts counts as 100 watts and not its face value.

The place for lights

Apart from bathrooms, where special regulations apply, you can position lights and switches in any place you like inside the house. But bear in mind they are there to fulfil a function, so switches, for example, should be conveniently located – by a door is often the most satisfactory position. Usually they are set on the wall 1.4 metres (4ft 6in) above floor level. But they can be higher or lower to suit your needs.

You mustn't install pendant lights, especially plain pendants with exposed flexible cords, in a bathroom. This is for your safety. Flexes can become frayed, and if, say, you tried to change a bulb while standing in the bath and touched an exposed conductor you could electrocute yourself. Consequently, all light fittings here must be of the close-mounted type and preferably totally enclosed to keep out condensation. If instead you use an open batten lampholder it must be fitted with a protective shield or skirt which makes it impossible for anyone changing the bulb to touch the metal parts.

A wall-mounted switch must also be out of reach of a person using the bath or shower. In modern small bathrooms, however, this is often impossible. The alternative is to place the switch just outside the room by the door, or to fit a special ceiling switch operated by an insulating cord which doesn't have to be out of reach of the bath or the shower.

PREPARING THE CABLE RUN

1 Raise the floorboard above the proposed location of the new light and any others necessary for laying the power supply and switch cables.

2 Mark the position of the new rose, then bore a 12mm (½in) hole. Where the cable crosses a joist, drill a 16mm (⅝in) hole 50mm (2in) below the top.

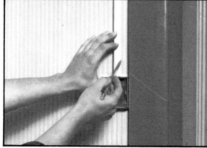

3 If the new rose can't be screwed to a joist, drill a 12mm (½in) hole in a wooden batten to coincide with the hole in the ceiling and fix the batten in position.

4 If flush-fitting the switch and chasing in the cable, use a mounting box and a length of conduit to mark their positions on the wall.

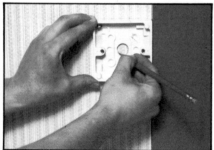

5 To prevent disturbing the decoration in one room, you can bring the switch cable down the other side of the wall and surface-mount the switch.

6 Use a small bolster chisel and club hammer to channel out a groove in the wall to take the switch cable and to chop out the recess for the switch.

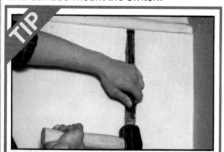

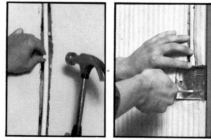

7 With cornices, make the channel in the wall first, then drive a long cold chisel gently up the back.

8 Fix the conduit in place with old nails, although you can also use clout nails. Drill and plug the fixing holes for the box and screw it into place.

Mounting box: MK

Keith Morris

Ready Reference

LIGHTING BASICS

● Extensions to lighting circuits are usually wired in 1.00mm² two-core and earth PVC-sheathed and insulated cable.
● You can extend from an existing rose only if it is of the loop-in variety with three banks of terminals; such roses can accommodate up to four cables. If you have older roses, extensions must be made via a junction box.

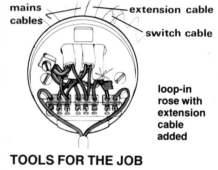

mains cables — extension cable — switch cable

loop-in rose with extension cable added

TOOLS FOR THE JOB

Electrician's pliers have cutting edges on the jaws and insulated handles.
Wire strippers can be adjusted to the diameter of the insulation to be stripped.
Handyman's knife – ideal for cutting back the sheathing of the cable.
Screwdrivers – a small one is best for the terminal fixing screws and a medium sized one for the fixing screws on the rose and switch.

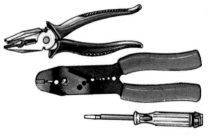

HOW TO STRIP CABLE

● Use handyman's knife to cut sheathing between neutral and earth cores.
● Use wire strippers to remove core insulation.

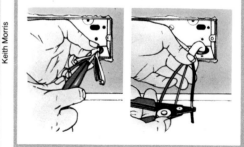

LAYING THE CABLE

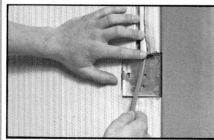

1 *Run the cable from where it joins the existing circuit to the new rose and lay in the switch cable. Allow 200mm (8in) for connections.*

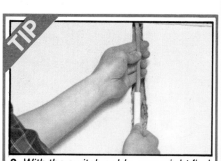

2 *With the switch cable, you might find it easier to pull down the required length and then slide on the conduit before fixing it in place.*

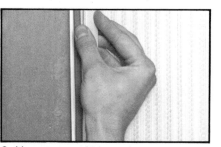

3 *It's not a good idea to leave cable exposed on a wall. When surface-mounting, the cable should be laid in PVC trunking with a clip-on cover.*

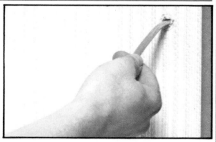

4 *If the cable is brought down on the other side of the wall to the switch, you'll need to drill a hole through so the cable enters the back of the box.*

FIXING THE SWITCH

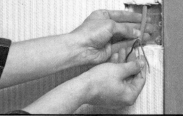

1 *After making good, strip back about 100mm (4in) of sheathing; take off 15mm (5/8in) of insulation and bend over the exposed wire; sleeve the earth wire.*

2 *Because the switch is wired into the 'live' of the circuit, the black wire is live and not neutral; mark it as such with red PVC tape.*

3 *Connect the earth wire to the earth terminal of the metal box and the two conductors to the terminals on the back of the faceplate.*

4 *Make sure a surface-mounted box is square before connecting the switch. With a flush fitting squareness can be adjusted when attaching the faceplate.*

Keith Morris

Switch: MK

Putting in switches

There is a great variety of switches available, but all perform the same function of breaking or completing an electrical circuit so you can turn the light off or on. Modern switches are of the rocker type; a one-gang switch has a single switch on the faceplate; a two-gang switch has two switches on the same faceplate, and so on. Dimmer switches are slightly different in that you can vary the power flowing to the bulb (so reducing or increasing its brightness) by rotating a control knob.

With a new light, you can either connect it into an existing switch position (fitting a two-gang switch in place of a one-gang one, for example) or a new switch. Depending on how you connect into the existing circuit, you'll have to run the switch cable above the ceiling from a rose or a junction box down the wall to where you are going to locate it. If you want to conceal the cable on the down drop you'll have to cut a shallow channel – which will damage the existing decoration – or you can surface-mount it in trunking.

Making the connection

Once you've decided where you want to put the light fitting and switch, you then have to decide where it's best to make the connection into the existing circuit.

Wiring runs may require some detective work to find out what each cable is doing – you don't want to connect into a switch cable by mistake. This may mean climbing into the roof space or raising a few floorboards. You'll need to do this anyway to run in the new cables to the required positions. As cable is expensive, it's best to plan your runs to use as little as possible. But when you measure along the proposed route, don't forget to allow about 200mm extra at the switch, rose and junction box for stripping back the conductors and joining in.

Changing the position of a ceiling light is even easier than adding a new one. If after you've turned off the power you undo the existing rose you'll see immediately the type of lighting circuit you are dealing with.

If there is only a black, a red and an earth wire going into it on the fixed wiring side then you have a junction box system. All you have to do is to disconnect the wires from the rose and reconnect them to the respective terminals of a new three-terminal junction box that you'll have to put in directly above the old fitting. You can then lead off another cable from this junction box to the re-positioned ceiling rose. The switch remains unaffected.

If the rose is a loop-in type, you have to carry out a similar modification, but this time the switch wires have to be incorporated in the new junction box, which must be a four-terminal type.

FITTING THE NEW ROSE AND LAMPHOLDER

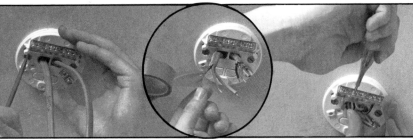

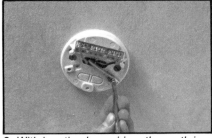

1 *Fix the new rose to the ceiling. Strip back 75mm (3in) of sheathing and 10mm (³/₈in) of insulation from the conductors, and sleeve the earth wires.*

2 *With loop-in wiring you'll need to wrap red PVC tape round the black wire (inset) then make the connections to the terminals as illustrated.*

3 *With junction box wiring, the earth is connected to the earth terminal, the black conductor goes to the neutral bank and the red to the SW terminal.*

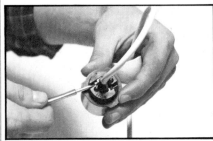

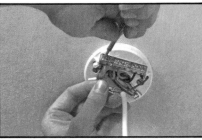

4 *Strip back the sheathing and insulation of one end of the flex and connect the blue and brown conductors to the two terminals of the lampholder.*

5 *Screw on the cap and then slip the rose cover over the flex. Cut the flex to length and prepare the free end for connecting to the rose.*

6 *At the rose, connect the blue conductor to the terminal on the neutral side and the brown to the SW side. Hook the wires over the cord grips.*

CONNECTING INTO THE CIRCUIT

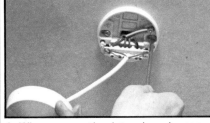

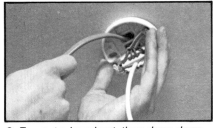

1 *When connecting into a loop-in rose, undo the fixing screws and pull the fitting a little way from the ceiling. But keep all the wires in place.*

2 *Tap out a knockout, then draw down through it about 200mm (8in) of the cable that leads to the new ceiling rose, or else feed the cable up from below.*

3 *Prepare the cable by stripping back about 75mm (3in) of sheathing and 10mm (³/₈in) of insulation from the conductors. Sleeve the earth wire.*

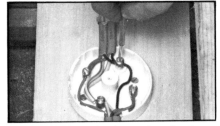

4 *Connect the earth to the earth terminal, the black to the neutral terminals and the red to the central in-line terminals.*

5 *When connecting in at a junction box, use a four-terminal type mounted on a batten. Connect the wires to the terminals as shown.*

6 *When taking out an old loop-in rose, disconnect the switch and feed cables and connect up the two feed cables as shown in a three-terminal junction box.*

ADDING A POWER POINT

Electrical equipment is now used more and more in the home, so an extra power socket is always useful. Here's how to fit one.

Keith Morris

There's nothing really difficult about installing a new power point. It's easier than putting in a new light as you don't have to worry about a switch cable.

Ever since the early 1950s. the power supply to the sockets has almost always been wired as a ring circuit (see Chapter 1, pages 6-10). And any house rewired since then will almost certainly have had this system installed. This means that once you've decided where you want the new outlet point – by a shelf in the living room for a hi-fi system, or over a worktop in the kitchen, for example – all you then have to do is to run a 'branch' or 'spur' to it from a convenient point on a nearby ring circuit.

The connection could be made at any socket on the ring (unless it already has a spur coming from it), or by using a three-terminal junction box inserted into the cable run. Each spur can have one single, double or triple socket fitted to it, or else a fused connection unit. Until a recent change in the Wiring Regulations, you were allowed two single sockets on a spur, but this is no longer permitted.

Checking your circuits
Although it's very likely that your house has ring circuits for the power supply, it's important to make sure. A ring circuit serves a number of 13A power outlets, and the sockets themselves take the familiar three-pin plugs with flat pins. But having this type of socket doesn't necessarily mean you've got a ring circuit – a new radial circuit may have been installed with these fittings, or an old radial circuit may simply have been modernised with new socket outlets. Chapter 1 explains the distinction.

First you've got to check whether you've got a modern consumer unit or separate fuse boxes for each of the circuits. Having a consumer unit is a fair indication that you've got ring circuit wiring, and if two cables are connected to each individual 30A fuseway in the unit this will confirm it. Normally each floor of the house will have a separate ring circuit, protected by a 30A fuse or MCB.

If you have separate fuse boxes, look for the ones with 30A fuses. If they have one supply cable going into them and two circuit cables coming out, this indicates a ring circuit.

It's easy to identify the sockets on any particular circuit simply by plugging in electrical appliances, such as table lamps, turning off the power and then removing a 30A fuse from the fuse box or consumer unit, or switching off a 30A MCB. When you restore the supply, the equipment that remains off will indicate which sockets are on the circuit.

Dealing with radial circuits
Where a house hasn't got ring circuits, then the power sockets will be supplied by some form of radial circuit. Because there are different types of radial circuit, each governed by separate regulations controlling the number and location of sockets on the circuit, the size of cable to be used and the size and type of circuit fuse protecting it, you should only add a spur to an existing radial circuit if you can trace its run back to the fuse box or consumer unit and identify its type, and if it has been wired up in modern PVC-sheathed cable throughout.

If you've still got unfused 15A, 5A and 2A round-pin plugs, then this is a sure sign of very old radial circuits, which were installed more than 30 years ago. Rather than extending the system you should seriously consider taking these circuits out and replacing them with ring circuits, as the wiring will almost certainly be nearing the end of its life. You'll then be able to position the new sockets exactly where you want them. If you're in any doubt about the

circuitry in your house you should contact your local electricity authority or a qualified electrician before carrying out any work.

Adding a spur to a ring
Once you've established you're dealing with a ring circuit and what sockets are on it, you'll need to find out if any spurs have already been added. You can't have more spurs than there are socket outlets on the ring itself. But unless the circuit has been heavily modified, it's unlikely that this situation will arise. You'll also need to know where any spurs are located – you don't want to overload an existing branch by mistake.

You can distinguish the sockets on the ring from those on a spur by a combination of inspecting the back of the sockets and tracing some cable runs (see *Ready Reference*, page 28). But remember to turn off the power first.

When you've got this information, you can work out whether it's feasible to add to the ring circuit. And you'll have a good idea where the cable runs.

Installing the socket
It's best to install the socket and lay in the cable before making the final join into the ring, since by doing this you reduce the amount of time that the power to the circuit is off.

You can either set the socket flush with the wall or mount it on the surface. The latter is the less messy method, but the fitting stands proud of the wall and so is more conspicuous.

FLUSH FITTING IN A BRICK WALL

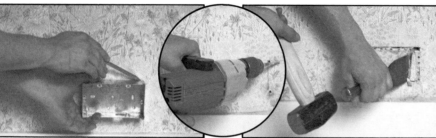

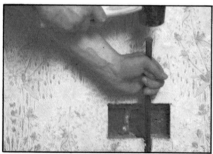

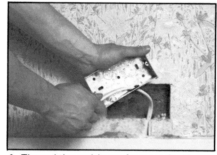

1 *Decide where you want to position the socket, then pencil round the mounting box as a guide for where to chop out the wall.*

2 *Drill slightly within the pencil lines to the depth of the mounting box, then work along the lines with a bolster chisel before chopping out the recess.*

3 *Channel a cable run down the back of the skirting using a long, thin cold chisel. Alternatively, use a long masonry bit and an electric drill.*

4 *Thread the cable up from under the floor, through some PVC conduiting behind the skirting and into the mounting box.*

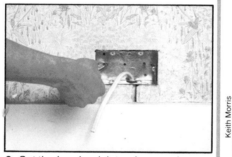

5 *Push the box into position, then use a bradawl to mark where the fixing holes are to go in the recess. Remove the box and drill and plug the holes.*

6 *Set the box back into place and screw it tightly into the recess. Check that it is level, and then make good if necessary with plaster or filler.*

Flush-fixing a socket on a plasterboard wall is a little more involved.

If you choose to surface-mount the socket, all you have to do is to fix a PVC or metal box directly to the wall after you've removed the knockout (and, if metal, use a grommet) where you want the cable to enter. The socket can then be screwed directly to this.

Laying in the cable

Because cable is expensive, it's best to plan the spur so that it uses as little cable as possible. When you channel cable into a wall you'll need to chase out a shallow run, fix the cable in position with clips, then plaster over it. But the best method of all is to run the cable in oval PVC conduiting. It won't give any more protection against an electric drill, but it'll prevent any possible reaction between the plaster making good and the cable sheathing. Always channel horizontally or vertically, and never diagonally, so it's easier to trace the wiring run when you've completed decorating. You can then avoid the cable when fixing something to the wall.

Normally the cable will drop down to below floor level to connect into the circuit. Rather than remove the skirting to get the cable down

Ready Reference

WARNING
The power supply to the sockets will probably be wired as a ring circuit. You can add a spur to this provided the number of spurs doesn't exceed the number of sockets on the ring.

CABLE SIZE
New spurs should be in 2.5mm^2 cable

CHECKING OUT A RING CIRCUIT
These instructions assume that your installation conforms to the Wiring Regulations. If it seems to have been modified in an unauthorised way, get a qualified electrician to check it.

TURN OFF THE POWER SUPPLY. Start by undoing a socket near where you want to install the new socket.

AT A SINGLE SOCKET
One cable entering
Socket is on the end of a spur. There could be another single socket on the branch.
Action: trace cable. If it goes to another single socket and this socket has only two cables going to it, then you have found an intermediate socket on the spur. It it goes to a double socket where there are three cables, then the single socket is the only socket on the spur. It's the same if the cable goes to a junction box.

Two cables entering
Socket is probably on the ring (see above). You can connect a spur into this.
Action: You'll need to trace the cable runs. If the cable is the only one going to another single socket, then the socket is on a spur. If the cable makes up one of two cables in another socket then it's on the ring.

Three cables entering
Socket is on the ring with a spur leading from it.
Action: to check which cable is which you'll need to trace the cable runs.

AT A DOUBLE SOCKET
One cable entering
Socket is on a spur. You can't connect a new socket from this.
Two cables entering
Socket is on the ring. You can connect a spur into this.
Three cables entering
Socket is on the ring with a spur leading from it. Checking to see which cable is which is the same as for a single socket with three cables. You can't connect a spur from this socket.

Keith Morris

FLUSH FITTING IN A PLASTERBOARD WALL

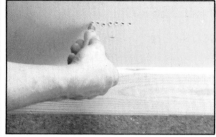

1 Knock along the cavity wall to locate a stud near where you want the socket. Pierce the wall with a bradawl to locate the centre of the upright.

2 Position the box centrally over the stud and pencil round it. Be as accurate as you can because eventually the box should fit neatly in the opening.

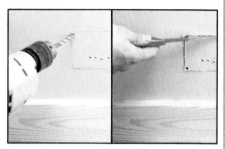

3 Drill the corners of the guidelines. Push a pad saw (or keyhole saw) into one of them and cut along the lines. The plasterboard will come out in one piece.

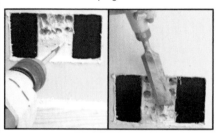

4 Once you've exposed the stud, you'll need to remove some of the wood so the box can be fully recessed. You can do this with a drill and chisel.

5 Use a long drill bit to drill down through the baseplate of the stud partition. Try and keep the drill as upright as possible.

6 Lay the cable from the point where it joins the main circuit and thread it up through the hole in the baseplate and into the box.

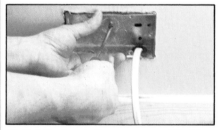

7 Set the box in the recess and fix it in place by screwing to the stud. The cable end can now be prepared and connected to the socket terminals.

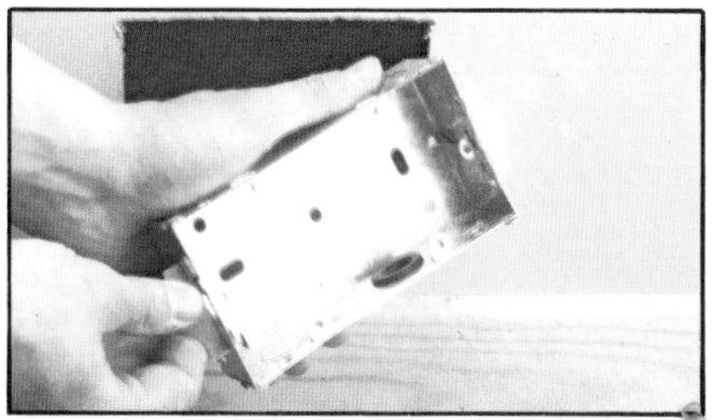

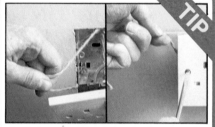

8 Where there is no stud to fix to, fit special lugs to the box sides. These press against the plasterboard's inner face when the faceplate is attached.

9 Before manoeuvring the box into the recess, thread some string through the front so you can hold it in position.

CONNECTING THE NEW SOCKET

1 Strip back the sheathing of the cable by running a sharp knife down the side of the uninsulated earth. Avoid damaging the other cores.

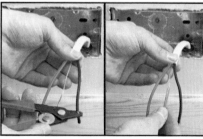

2 Set the wire strippers to the correct gauge and remove about 9mm (³/₈in) of insulation from the cores. Sleeve the earth core in green/yellow PVC.

3 Connect the three cores to the relevant terminals of the socket, making sure no exposed core is showing. Then screw the socket into position.

Jem Grischotti

Keith Morris

the back you can use a long steel cold chisel to chip out a groove. You'll then have to drill down through the end of the floorboard with a wood bit. Alternatively, you can use a long masonry bit with an electric drill to complete the task.

But if the floor is solid, the ring is usually in the ceiling void above, in which case the branch will drop down from the ceiling. And this will involve a considerable amount of channelling out if you want to install the new socket near floor level.

Stud partition walls also present a few problems. If the socket is near the floor, you should be able to get a long drill bit through the hole you cut for the socket to drill through the baseplate and floorboard. You can then thread the cable through. But if the socket is to be placed higher up the wall, noggings and sound insulation material may prevent the cable being drawn through the cavity. In this case you will probably have to surface-mount the cable.

In fact, surface-mounting is the easiest method of running the cable. All you do is fix special plastic conduit to the wall and lay the cable inside before clipping on the lid. But many people regard this as an ugly solution.

When laying cable under ground floor floorboards you should clip it to the sides of the joists about 50mm (2in) below the surface so that it doesn't droop on the ground. Cable in the ceiling void can rest on the surface.

When you have to cross joists, you'll need to drill 16mm (⅝in) holes about 50mm (2in) below the level of the floorboards. The cable is threaded through them and so is well clear of any floorboard fixing nails.

Connecting into the circuit

If you use a junction box, you'll need one with three terminals inside. You have to connect the live conductors (those with red insulation) of the circuit cable and the spur to one terminal, the neutral conductors (black insulation) to another, and the earth wires to the third. Sleeve the earth wires in green/yellow PVC first.

You might decide that it's easier to connect into the back of an existing socket rather than use a junction box, although this will probably mean some extra channelling on the wall. Space is limited at the back of a socket so it may be difficult to fit the conductors to the relevant terminals. However, this method is ideal if the new socket that you're fitting on one wall is back-to-back with an existing fitting. By carefully drilling through the wall a length of cable can be linked from the old socket into the new.

CONNECTING INTO THE CIRCUIT

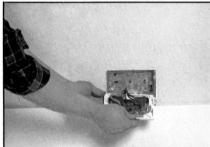

1 *Unscrew a nearby socket to check that it's on the ring – normally there'll be two red, two black and two earth wires. Sometimes the earths are in one sleeve.*

2 *Usually it's easier to push the new cable up into the mounting box from below the floor, although you might prefer to take it the other way.*

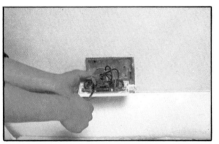

3 *Prepare the cores and sleeve the earth of the new cable, then connect them into the appropriate terminals on the back of the socket.*

4 *If installing a junction box use a three-terminal type. Connect the red conductors to one terminal, the blacks to another and the earths to a third.*

SOCKET MOUNTINGS

Metal boxes are recessed into the wall and provide a fixing for the socket itself. Knockouts are provided in the back, sides and ends to allow the cable to enter the box. Rubber grommets are fitted round the hole so the cable doesn't chafe against the metal edges.

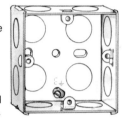

Elongated screw slots allow box to be levelled when fixed to wall.

Adjustable lugs enable final adjustments to level of faceplate on wall.

Boxes are usually 35mm deep, but with single-brick walls boxes 25mm deep should be used, along with accessories having deeper-than-usual faceplates.

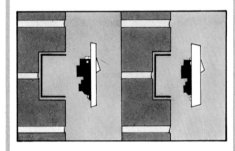

Lugs can be fitted to a metal box so that it can be fitted into stud partition walls.

Surface-mounted boxes (usually white plastic) are 35mm deep, and are simply screwed to the wall surface where required.

TIP: FIT SAFETY PLATES

Safety plates can be fitted to sockets to prevent young children playing with them.

PROBLEMS

● **Crumbly plaster** There's little that can be done other than cutting back to sound plaster. Position the box and socket as required then make good the surrounding area.
● **Poor bricks** Because of soft bricks you can quite easily chop out too big a recess for the box. Pack the recess with dabs of mortar or plaster.
● **Cavity walls** To prevent breaking through into the cavity only chop out a recess big enough to take a shallow box, about 25mm (1in) deep.

RUNNING CIRCUIT CABLES

The hardest part of the average electrical job is running the cables: it takes up a lot of time and a lot of effort. But there are certain techniques used by experts which can make it much easier.

B efore you get involved in the details of how to install the wiring, there's one simple question you must answer. Does it matter if the cable runs show? This is because there are only two approaches to the job of running cable. Either you fix the cable to the surface of the wall, or you conceal it. The first option is far quicker and easier but doesn't look particularly attractive; it's good enough for use in, say, an understairs cupboard. For a neater finish, using this method, you can smarten up the cable runs by boxing them in with some trunking. Many people, however, prefer to conceal the wiring completely by taking it under the floor, over the ceiling, or in walls.

TYPICAL CABLE RUNS

More and more electrical equipment is now being used in the home. And the chances are that sooner or later you will want to install a new power point, wall or ceiling light, or another switch. In which case you will have to get power to your new accessory. To do that will involve running cable from an existing circuit or installing a completely new one. Running cable to a new appliance can be the hardest part of any job and, as the illustration on the right shows, you will be involved in trailing cable across the roof space or ceiling void, channelling it down walls and threading it behind partitions as well as taking it under floorboards. But it's much easier than it seems. There are a number of tricks of the trade that will make any electrical job simpler and less time consuming. For example, once you can 'fish' cable, the daunting task of running it under a floor is simple.

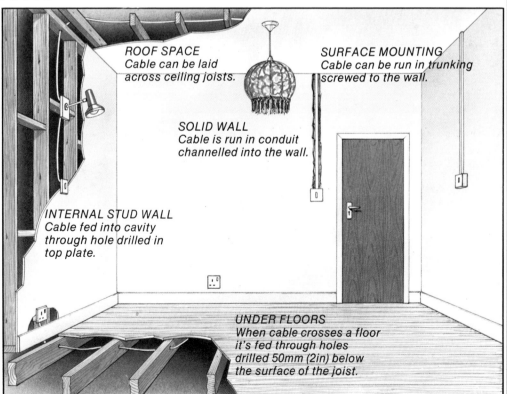

ROOF SPACE
Cable can be laid across ceiling joists.

SURFACE MOUNTING
Cable can be run in trunking screwed to the wall.

SOLID WALL
Cable is run in conduit channelled into the wall.

INTERNAL STUD WALL
Cable fed into cavity through hole drilled in top plate.

UNDER FLOORS
When cable crosses a floor it's fed through holes drilled 50mm (2in) below the surface of the joist.

SURFACE MOUNTING CABLE

1 *To run cable in trunking, cut the trunking to length and fix the channel half to the wall with screws and wall plugs at 450mm (18in) centres.*

2 *Run the cable and press it firmly into the channel as far as it will go, carefully smoothing it out to avoid kinks and twists.*

3 *Next, snap the trunking's capping piece over the channelling, tapping it firmly along its length with your hand to lock it into place.*

4 *If the cable is to be on show, merely secure it every 225mm (9in) with cable clips. Fit them over the cable and drive home the fixing pins.*

Planning the route

Having made your decision you must now work out a suitable route for the cable to follow.

If it is to be surface-mounted – with or without trunking – run the cable around window and door frames, just above skirting boards and picture rails, down the corners of the room, or along the angle between wall and ceiling. This not only helps conceal the cable's presence, but also protects it against accidental damage. This last point is most important, and is the reason why you must never run cable over a floor.

With concealed wiring, the position is more complicated. When running cable under a floor or above a ceiling, you must allow for the direction in which the joists run – normally at right angles to the floorboards – and use an indirect route, taking it parallel to the joists and/or at right angles to them.

When running cable within a wall, the cable should *always* run vertically or horizontally from whatever it supplies, *never* diagonally.

Surface-mounting techniques

If you are leaving the cable on show, all you need do is cut it to length, and fix it to the surface with a cable clip about every 225mm (9in), making sure it is free from kinks and twists. With modern cable clips, simply fit the groove in the plastic block over the cable and drive home the small pin provided.

Surface mounting cable within trunking involves a bit more work. Having obtained the right size of PVC trunking, build up the run a section at a time, cutting the trunking to length with a hacksaw. Once each piece is cut, separate it into its two parts – the

Ready Reference

RUNNING CABLE

You can mount cable:
● on the surface of a wall or ceiling
● concealed within the wall, above the ceiling or below the floor.

SURFACE-MOUNTED CABLE

This should be run above skirting boards, round window and door frames and in the corners of rooms to disguise the run and protect the cable. Never run cable across a floor.

Fix the cable in place every 225mm (9 in) with cable clips. Make sure the cable isn't kinked or twisted.

For a neater finish run the cable in PVC trunking, which you can cut to length using a hacksaw. Fix the channel part of the trunking to the wall first with screws and wall plugs at roughly 450mm (18in) centres. Then lay in the cable and clip the cover in position – tap it with your fist to ensure a tight fixing.

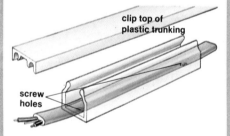

clip top of plastic trunking

screw holes

CONCEALED WIRING

To conceal a cable in a solid wall run it down a channel (chase) chopped in the surface and plaster over it. For added protection it's best to run the cable in PVC conduit and plaster this into the channel.

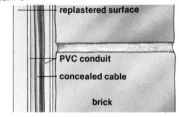

replastered surface

PVC conduit

concealed cable

brick

Concealed wiring should always be run vertically or horizontally from the fitting it supplies; never run it diagonally. This makes it easier to trace the runs in the future, when the wall has been decorated, and will prevent you drilling into the cable.

channelling and capping – and fix the channel to the wall with screws and wall plugs at roughly 450mm (18in) intervals (you may have to drill screw clearance holes in the channelling yourself).

Continue in this way until the run is complete. Turn corners by using proprietary fittings or by angling the ends of two pieces of trunking to form a neatly mitred joint, then run in the cable. Press this firmly into the channel and finish off by snapping the capping pieces firmly into place.

Concealing cables in walls

There are two ways to conceal cable in a wall. With a solid wall, chop a channel (called a 'chase') out of the plaster using a club hammer and bolster chisel, carefully continuing this behind any skirting boards, picture rails, and coverings. You could now run the cable in this chase and plaster over it. However, to give the cable some protection, it is better to fit a length of PVC conduit into the chase and run the cable through this before replastering.

To continue the run either above the ceiling or through the floor before you position the conduit, use a long drill bit so you can drill through the floor behind the skirting board. If a joist blocks the hole, angle the drill sufficiently to avoid it.

With a hollow internal partition wall, the job is rather easier, because you can run the cable within the cavity.

First drill a hole in the wall where the cable is to emerge, making sure you go right through into the cavity. Your next step is to gain access to the timber 'plate' at the very top of the wall, either by going up into the loft, or by lifting floorboards in the room above. Drill a 19mm (¾in) hole through the plate, at a point vertically above the first hole, or as near vertically above it as possible.

All that remains is to tie the cable you wish to run to a length of stout 'draw' wire – single-core earth cable is often used – and then to tie the free end of this wire to a length of string. To the free end of the string, tie a small weight, and drop the weight through the hole at the top of the wall. Then all you do is make a hook in a piece of stout wire, insert it in the cavity, catch hold of the string and pull it (and in turn the draw wire and cable) through the hole in the room below.

What are the snags? There are two. You may find that, at some point between the two holes, the cavity is blocked by a horizontal timber called a noggin. If this happens, try to reach the noggin from above with a long auger bit (you should be able to hire one) and drill through it. Failing that, chisel through the wall surface, cut a notch in the side of the noggin, pass the cable through the notch, and then make good.

The second snag is that you may not be

CHASING OUT SOLID WALLS

1 Mark out the cable run using a length of conduit, and chop a channel ('chase') in the wall to receive it, using a club hammer and a bolster chisel.

2 Continue the chase behind any coving, skirting board, or picture rail by chipping out the plaster there with a long, narrow cold chisel.

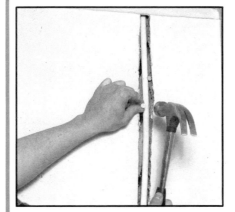

3 Cut a length of PVC conduit to fit, and lay it in the chase, securing it temporarily with clout nails driven into the wall's mortar joints.

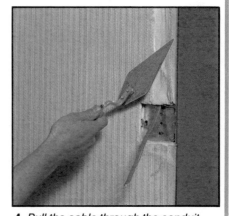

4 Pull the cable through the conduit, then make good the wall by filling in over the conduit with plaster or cellulose filler.

able to reach the top plate to drill it. In which case, either give up the idea of having concealed wiring, or try a variation on the second method used to run cable into the cavity from below the floor.

Here, it is sometimes possible to lift a couple of floorboards and drill up through the plate forming the bottom of the wall. Failing that you have to take a very long drill bit, drill through the wall into the cavity, then continue drilling through into the timber plate. You can now use the weighted string trick to feed the cable in through the hole in the wall, and out under the floor.

Running cable beneath a floor

The technique for running cable beneath a suspended timber floor depends on whether the floor is on an upper storey and so has a ceiling underneath, or is on a ground floor

with empty space below. If it's a ground floor, it may be possible to crawl underneath and secure the cable to the sides of the joists with cable clips, or to pass it through 19mm (¾in) diameter holes drilled in the joists at least 50mm (2in) below their top edge. This prevents anyone nailing into the floor and hitting the cable.

If you cannot crawl underneath, then the cable can be left loose in the void. But how do you run it without lifting the entire floor? The answer is you use another trick, called 'fishing'.

For this, you need a piece of stiff but reasonably flexible galvanised wire, say 14 standard wire gauge (swg), rather longer than the intended cable run, and a piece of thicker, more rigid wire, about 1m in length. Each piece should have one end bent to form a hook.

Lift a floorboard at each end of the

COPING WITH STUD WALLS

1 *Drill a hole in the wall where the cable is to emerge, then bore a second hole in the wooden plate forming the top of the wall.*

2 *Tie a weight to a length of string and lower this through the hole in the wall plate. Tie the free end of the string to a stout 'draw' wire.*

3 *If the weight gets blocked on its way to the hole in the wall, use a long auger bit to drill through the noggin obstructing it.*

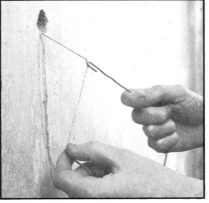

4 *Fish out the weighted string through the hole in the wall, using a piece of wire bent to form a hook. Now, pull through the draw wire.*

5 *Tie the draw wire to the cable you wish to run, then return to the hole in the wall's top plate, and use the string to pull up the draw wire.*

6 *Then use the draw wire to pull the length of cable through. Remember, do this smoothly and don't use force if there's an obstruction.*

Ready Reference

TRICKS OF THE TRADE

Hollow internal partition wall
Drill a hole in the top or bottom plate, then drill another in the wall where the cable is to emerge. Drop a weighted piece of string through one of the holes and hook it out through the other. Use this to pull through a stout draw wire which is attached to the cable.

● if the weighted piece of string gets obstructed by a noggin or its way to the hole in the wall, use a long auger bit to drill through the noggin.

● don't pull the cable through with the weighted string – the string tends to snap

● never run cable down the cavity of an external wall– treat these as solid walls.

Under floors
Use a technique known as fishing:
● lift the floorboards at either end of the run
● thread stiff wire beneath the floor through one hole and hook it out of the other with another piece of wire
● use the longer piece of wire to pull the cable through.

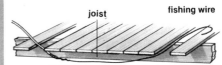

joist   fishing wire

cable with draw wire attached

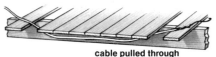

cable pulled through

● if there's a gap beneath a ground floor you can 'fish' the cable diagonally across the room under the joist

● if the gap under the joists is large enough you can crawl in the space clipping the cable to the joists

● where the cable crosses the joists at right angles, run it through holes drilled 50mm (2in) below their top edges.

Over ceilings
If you can get above the ceiling into a loft, you can clip the cables to the joists. Otherwise you'll have to 'fish' the cable across (see above).

If you can't get above the ceiling and fishing doesn't work you'll have to surface-mount the cable.

proposed cable run and feed the longer piece of wire, hook end first, into the void through one of the resulting gaps in the floor. Hook it out through the second gap using the shorter piece of wire, and use it to pull through the cable in the same way as the draw wire used to pull cable through a hollow wall.

This technique is also used where there is a ceiling below the floor, and where you wish to run cable parallel to the joists, but in this case, check for any ribs and struts between the joists which might stop the fish wire getting through. Do this with the aid of a small mirror and a torch. If there is an obstruction, lift the floorboard above it, and drill a hole through which the cable can pass.

If the cable is to run at right angles to the joists, lift the floorboard above the line of the cable run, and feed the cable through holes drilled in the joists, 50mm (2in) below their top edge.

And what about solid floors? Obviously there is no way to run cable beneath these. Instead run the cable around the walls of the room, surface-mounting it just above the skirting board.

Running cable above a ceiling

Running cable above a ceiling is essentially the same as running it below a suspended timber floor. In fact, if there is a floor above the ceiling, it is generally easier to tackle the job from there, rather than from the room below.

If running the cable above the ceiling means taking it into the loft, then you can tackle it in much the same way as if you were running it below a suspended ground floor. If you cannot gain access to the loft, fish the cable through. If you can get into the loft, run the cable by hand, clipping it to the sides of the joists where it runs parallel to them.

You can run the cable at right angles to the joists by passing it through holes as already described, but this is frowned on by many electricians. Instead, they prefer to run it parallel to the joists as far as the 'binder' – the large timber cross-member linking the joists. They then clip the cable to the binder to traverse the ceiling, before running it to the desired position, again working parallel to the joists.

Unfortunately, there are situations in which running cable above a ceiling is almost impossible. The main ones are where the ceiling is solid concrete, as in many modern flats; where the ceiling is below a flat roof; and where, although there is a floor above the ceiling, you can't get at it (again this applies mainly to flats).

In the last two instances, if you intend the cable to run parallel to the joists, you may be able to fish it through. If not, you will have to treat the ceiling as if it were solid, and that means surface mounting the cable.

FISHING CABLE ABOVE CEILINGS

1 Take a piece of stiff wire and. check that it is just longer than is needed to reach between the cable's entry and exit holes in the ceiling.

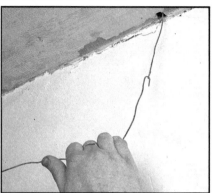

2 Feed the wire into one hole, fish it out of the other with a second piece of wire, then tie the cable to the first wire and pull it through.

RUNNING CABLE UNDER FLOORS

1 When running cable parallel to the joists, fish it through in the same way as if fishing through cable above a ceiling.

2 If the cable or fish wire will not pull through, check under the floor for obstructions, using a small mirror and a reasonably powerful torch.

3 For cable runs at right angles to the joists, drill holes in the joists 50mm (2in) below their tops, angling these if the drill is too long to fit in.

4 Carefully thread the cable through the holes, without stretching it so that it chafes against the side of the hole and damages the insulation.

CHAPTER 3

LIGHTING

Improving your home's lighting is one of the most dramatic moves
you can make – the range of fittings and the switching systems
available today virtually make it possible to decorate your home
just by using lighting effects.

LIGHTING DESIGN 1: the basics

There is more to lighting your home than meets the eye, and well-designed lighting schemes can enhance every room in the house. To start with, you need to grasp some of the basic principles.

In most homes the standard of room lighting leaves something to be desired. Interior design generally has made immense strides in recent years, yet even new homes are built with a lighting specification left over from the dark ages – literally. Builders still follow what is known quaintly as the Builder's Norm – one pendant light in the centre of each room, switched by the entrance door – a standard that hasn't changed since the days of gas lighting, although in small rooms the gas light would often be a wall bracket fitting. You may be lucky enough to find the occasional wall light – in the lounge or bedroom, for example – but even homes that have been extensively modernised are unlikely to have anything much more adventurous.

This is a pity, because there is now a very wide range of attractive and versatile light fittings available, and a glance around many public buildings will show you some of the effects they can produce if used with a little flair. Installing fittings like these in your home isn't difficult, and the difference that well-designed lighting can make to every room in the house has to be seen to be believed.

How much light do you get?

Electric lamps – tungsten-filament bulbs and tubes and fluorescent fittings – are rated in watts (W). This tells you how much electricity the lamp uses when lit; it doesn't directly indicate how much light the lamp gives off (although it's obvious that a 100W lamp will be brighter than a 40W one), nor does it tell you how much useful light is provided or in what direction. The amount and quality of light needed for different tasks or effects varies widely; lighting to illuminate the dining table, the kitchen worktops or the family silver will differ from lighting for reading, sewing or lulling a child to sleep.

The actual amount of light emitted from a lamp is measured in units called lumens. Some lamps burn more efficiently that others, emitting more lumens per watt. Generally speaking, coiled-coil pear-shaped clear and pearl bulbs (see pages 40-42) have the highest efficiency in lumens/watt; next come mushroom-shaped bulbs, double-life bulbs and finally single-coil bulbs. What's

more, the actual wattage of the bulb is also a factor; a 40W coiled-coil bulb has an output of 390 lumens (9.75 lumens/watt) while a 100W bulb of the same type emits 1260 lumens (12.6 lumens/watt).

Fluorescent tubes, as is widely known, are much more efficient light emitters than tungsten filament lamps. For example, a 40W warm white tube gives out 1950 lumens (48 lumens/watt) and an 80W tube of the same colour gives 3730 lumens (44 lumens) watt). On average, fluorescent tubes give about four times as much light as light bulbs of the same wattage.

How much light do you need?

When you're planning a lighting scheme these figures (see *Ready Reference* for a summary) will come in very useful. The other figure you need to know is how much light to provide in a given area. A rough and ready figure to work to for general lighting is 22 watts per sq m (2W/sq ft), and if seeing what you are doing was the only criterion for satisfactory illumination, it could be used without variation. However, several other factors have to be taken into account, including the type and position of the light fitting chosen, whether the lighting of a surface or object is direct or indirect, and the colour and reflectivity of the surface being lit. So as a general guideline it's a good idea to take the 22W/sq m figure as the minimum overall lighting required in each room, and to regard any additional local lighting as being supplementary to this. To

Ready Reference

LIGHT OUTPUT OF LAMPS

Fluorescent tubes are more efficient emitters of light (measured as lumens/watt) than coiled bulbs, which in turn are more efficient than single-coil ones. The outputs given below in lumens are for pearl bulbs and 'warm white' tubes.

Bulb wattage	Output	Lumens/W
15W single-coil	110	7.33
25W single-coil	200	8.00
40W coiled-coil	390	9.75
60W coiled-coil	665	11.08
75W coiled-coil	880	11.73
100W coiled-coil	1260	12.60
150W coiled-coil	2040	13.60

Tube wattage	Output	Lumens/W
15W (450mm/18in)	500	33.33
20W (600mm/2ft)	780	39.00
30W (900mm/3ft)	1450	48.33
40W (1.2m/4ft)	1950	48.75
65W (1.5m/5ft)	3120	48.00
85W (1.8m/6ft)	3730	43.88

LIGHTING LEVELS

Aim to provide at least the following light levels in each room in the house:
● living room, dining room, bathroom, landing, hall, stairs – 100 lumens/sq m
● kitchen, reading area – 200 lumens/sq m
● bedrooms, garage – 50 lumens/sq m.

WHERE THE LIGHT GOES

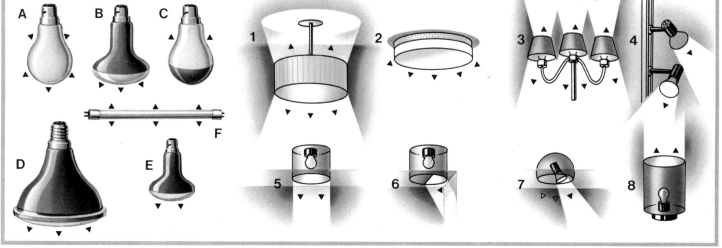

Below: How light is emitted from various lamp types – GLS (A), ISL (B), CS (C), PAR (D), small spot (E) and fluorescent (F).

Below: The direction of light emitted may be modified by the type of fitting chosen. Shown here are a pendant (1), close-

ceiling fitting (2), wall light (3), track spot-light (4), downlighter (5), wall washer (6), eyeball (7) and uplighter (8).

give a worked example, a living room measuring 6x4m (20x13ft) would need an overall lighting level of 6x4x22 = 528 watts.

The other point you need to take into account is that the amount of illumination you get – the amount of light falling on a surface – depends on how far it is from the light source. Double the distance and the level of illumination is halved.

Light bulbs and tubes

We tend to think of light bulbs and tubes as emitting light at random in all directions, and this is certainly true of the ordinary (GLS) bulb and the standard tungsten or fluorescent tube. But other types of lamp are available that emit light only in certain directions because the bulb or tube surface is coated with reflective or opaque material. For example, the internally-silvered (ISL) bulb has an internal reflector that covers the neck and sides of the bulb, resulting in a controlled beam that is ideal for projecting light onto walls and for spotlighting objects. The crown-silvered (CS) bulb has the reflector on the crown of the bulb, so that light is projected backwards into the fitting; when used with a parabolic reflector dish, the result is a parallel beam of light like that produced by a car head-lamp. The PAR (parabolic aluminised reflector) lamp combines the CS optics into a single sealed unit that can provide spot or flood lighting.

Types of light fitting

There are four principal types of light fitting with which these various lamps can be used, and the type of fitting chosen may further modify the beam of light that the lamp itself emits, so giving you additional flexibility in

the design of your lighting effects. The four types are: ceiling-mounted (pendant or close-fitting); wall-mounted; concealed (including 'downlighters' and 'wall-washers'), and free-standing (table, or standard lamps and 'uplighters').

Pendant fittings, the most familiar type, range from a plain lampholder carrying a decorative shade to multi-light fittings suspended from a ceiling plate by chains or a rod. Some give a general light output, others mainly direct downward and/or upward depending on the style of shade chosen. Rise-and-fall fittings are simply pendants with a spring-loaded flex extender concealed in the ceiling plate.

Close-ceiling fittings are mounted on the ceiling surface as an alternative to pendant fittings, and so by definition emit light in an overall downward direction only. They are usually fitted with a translucent glass or plastic cover, which may be coloured. Fluorescent fittings of various types also come into this category.

Wall-mounted fittings can range from simple brackets holding plain or decorative bulbs, with or without shades, to spot and flood fittings. Uplighters (see below under 'Free-standing fittings') can also be wall-mounted.

Concealed fittings include downlighters and wall-washers, both of which are usually recessed into the ceiling. Downlighters are cylindrical housings and usually contain an ISL bulb, so providing a fairly well-defined beam pointing to the floor. Wall-washers have either an adjustable aperture or an eye-ball-type fitting that directs light downwards *and* to one side, allowing a ceiling-mounted

fitting to 'wash' a nearby wall with light.

Free-standing fittings need little description – table and standard lamps come in a very wide range of models and offer general or local lighting according to type. The one comparatively unfamiliar member of this group is the uplighter, which bounces reflected light off ceilings and walls and is an excellent source of background or concealed light.

The effect of colour schemes

The colour scheme used in any room can have a profound effect on the level of lighting it requires. It goes without saying that dark wallcoverings and carpets will absorb a lot of light, so that a greater light wattage will have to be provided than if the room has white walls and pale furnishings.

The colour of walls and ceilings is particularly important when you plan to use a lot of indirect lighting, although this doesn't mean you have to have pale surfaces; you simply need more wattage. It's certainly true that you can achieve more dramatic lighting effects (at the expense of the general level of illumination) in rooms decorated in rich, deep colours.

Light and shadow

Before we begin to deal with the more detailed planning of lighting schemes, the last ground rule to remember – and one of the most important, too – concerns the problem of positioning lights to avoid glare and the creation of hard shadows. This is mainly solved by the correct choice of fitting for the job, and its careful positioning in the room. The illustrations opposite summarise some of the commonest problems and show how they can be overcome.

AVOIDING GLARE AND HARD SHADOWS

Living rooms *A central light is no good for reading as it casts shadows on the page.*

Position a reading lamp behind you, and provide indirect lighting near TV sets.

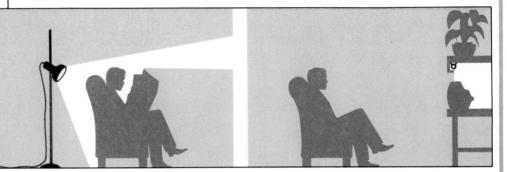

Dining rooms *Avoid fittings where the naked lamp is close to eye level and glares diners.*

Fit a rise-and-fall fitting, and provide two fittings above long tables.

Workrooms *A wrongly-positioned lamp means that you are working in your own shadow.*

Fit a concealed lamp above the work surface, adding an adjustable one for typing.

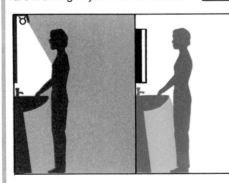

Bathrooms *Concealed lighting above mirrors leaves faces in shadow. Better illumination is provided by fittings at each side of the mirror.*

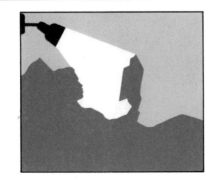

Bedrooms *Position reading lights on the wall above your head (and switch them at the bedside).*

Children's rooms *If night-time light is needed, provide it indirectly, or install a dimmer switch.*

LIGHT BULBS AND TUBES

You're always going to need artificial light, and so you should know what types of light bulbs and fluorescent tubes are available. Here's a brief summary.

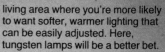

There are two basic types of electric lamps in common use in the home. (We know them as light bulbs or tubes, but the professionals call them all lamps.) These are the filament lamp, a direct descendant of Thomas Edison's early bulbs, and the fluorescent tube, which has only come into widespread use in the past 30 years.

The filament lamp works on much the same principle as those early lamps that were produced over a hundred years ago. Electricity is passed through a wire which is suspended inside a glass envelope. Resistance to its passage produces heat, and when a certain temperature is reached, the conductor – called the filament – emits light. Today these filaments are made of tungsten that has been formed into coiled spirals, and the glass envelopes hold an inert gas such as argon that helps stop the filament from burning out. Previously the filament was suspended in a vacuum.

The range of filament lamps on the market is tremendous. They are available in different sizes, shapes and colours, and also come in a tube form that provides a more intense light and which is easily concealed above worktops and such like.

A fluorescent tube, on the other hand, has no filament; instead it has an electrode at each end and the tube is filled with a small amount of mercury vapour that glows when the lamp is switched on. This, in itself, doesn't produce much light, but it does produce quite a lot of invisible ultra-voilet light which causes the chemicals lining the inside of the tube to glow (or fluoresce) very brightly.

What about watts?
The power of a lamp is expressed in terms of wattage; so a 150W lamp will produce considerably more light that a 40W one. However, not all light fittings will accept the most powerful lamps, and as most are marked with their upper wattage limit, you should check beforehand – otherwise you risk damaging the fitting.

When deciding upon the actual level of light and the type of lamps you want, there are certain guidelines to bear in mind that may make things easier for you. As a rule, with general lighting from filament lights, you should be aiming at around 10 to 15 watts of lighting for every square metre of floor area in the room – although it obviously won't all be in use at any one time. With fluorescent lighting, the requirements are somewhat less; about 3 watts per square metre for general lighting, and between 8 and 10 watts per square metre for well-lit areas.

Light fittings
It's no good just buying a lamp without examining the light fitting in which it will be used. It's important to check the type of cap your fitting will accept.

Filaments lamps usually have either a bayonet cap, which comprises two small prongs that lock the lamp into the lampholder, or an Edison screw cap that is threaded like a large torch bulb and is screwed into the lampholder. There is also the single-centre contact usually found on filament tubes only. Fluorescent tubes nowadays almost always have bi-pin endcaps – two pin contacts that slot into the terminals of the fluorescent light fitting itself. Very old fittings may, however, need a tube with bayonet end caps like those on filament lamps.

Which types to choose
The type of light you want is also an important factor when deciding on the type of lamp to choose. In certain rooms, such as the kitchen, for example, the brighter the light the better. And, of course, you'll want a light that casts few shadows. In that case the answer is to use fluorescent lighting. However, this bright and sometimes slightly harsh light would hardly be suitable for a

living area where you're more likely to want softer, warmer lighting that can be easily adjusted. Here, tungsten lamps will be a better bet.

Remember, the real secret to lighting a room successfully lies in giving it variety. In your living room, it's no good having just one high-wattage lamp in the centre of the ceiling, as you'll never be able to alter the mood and atmosphere successfully. You should really aim for a lamp that will provide satisfactory general light, and then supplement it with light over specific areas or for special decorative effects. So, in a kitchen although fluorescent lights will be adequate, you might well have filament reflector bulbs fitted into down-lighters above certain worktops.

Cost is another factor. As the majority of tubes require special fittings, fluorescent lighting can work out to be quite dear, whereas most filament lamps will fit into lampholders and can therefore be changed around quite frequently. A recent development is a two-contact fluorescent lamp that will fit into a standard fitting. But it is important to remember that most of the cost of lighting a room lies in the amount of electricity used; the actual lamp itself represents only about 10 per cent of the cost. So, using what is called a coiled coil filament bulb will cost more initially, but the light is brighter and actually costs less to run. Similarly, although fluorescent tubes cost more to buy than filament lamps, they do give between three and five times as much light for a given number of watts as a filament bulb and have a much longer life, usually lasting between 5000 and 7500 hours compared to the average of 1000 hours for an ordinary filament lamp.

REFLECTOR LAMPS

These lamps have a special silver coating to reflect the light in a particular way. There is a wide variety available and when looking for a replacement it's a good idea to take your old lamp to the shop with you.

1

GENERAL LIGHTING

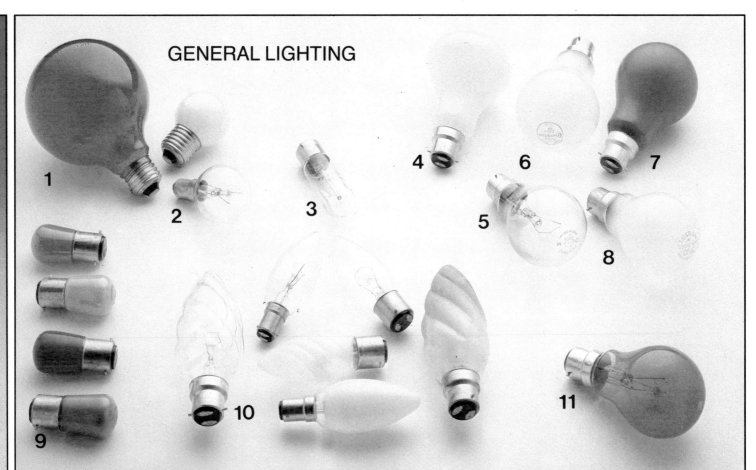

1 Decor round lamps are designed for use with open type, ornamental shades where the lamp could be conspicuous. They give less light than other General Lighting Service (GLS) lamps.
2 Round (ball) lamps are normally used in small decorative fittings.
3 Single cap tubes are specially suited for bedside lights.
4 Mushroom lamps should be used in shallow fittings or where the lamp itself will be partly visible. Their silica coating gives them a softer and more diffuse light than pearl lamps.

5 Clear glass lamps are used in reflector fittings and chandeliers. The filament is visible and shadows sharp and hard.
6 Pearl lamps give a diffused light. The inside of the glass envelope is roughened by special treatment but there is no subsequent loss of light.
7 Coloured lamps usually have bayonet caps and range from 15 to 100W. Colours are amber, blue, green, pink, yellow and red. Low wattage lamps are safe outside without extra protection but others require special fittings.

8 Long-life bulbs give slightly less light than an equivalent standard lamp, but will have more than double the lifespan.
9 Pigmy lamps are 15W and are normally used for outdoor festoons, where they fit into special waterproof holders; good for wall lights too.
10 Candle lamps are used extensively in wall lights and chandeliers.
11 Fireglow lamps give the warm glow behind simulated log and coal electric fires. They're sometimes fitted with three-pin bayonet caps, so check your holder before buying one.

1 Internally silvered lamps (ISL lamps) are silvered round the base and sides. This throws the light forward and gives a broad beam.

2 Crown silvered lamps have the top of the envelope silvered to control the amount of glare and produce a narrow beam suitable for spotlights.

3 ISL lamps with the stem silvered.

4 Parabolic aluminized reflector (PAR) lamps have armoured glass for outside use.

TUBES

1 SL lamps are a recent development and combine the efficiency and economy of the fluorescent tube with the convenience of an ordinary GLS lamp. They come with either Bayonet caps or Edison screws, and so can fit into any standard lampholders. As they are quite heavy you should check that your lampholder can take the extra weight.

2 Circular fluorescent tubes come in one of two diameters. There is the 300mm (12in) version which is 32W and the 400mm (16in) that can be either 40 or 60W. They are specially suited for use in bathrooms and come only in warm white.

3 Architectural tubes are often used to light paintings and pictures when a fluorescent tube would give too much light. They usually have special peg caps.

4 Double cap filament tubes are used in the same way as architectural tubes. They have single centre contacts.

5 Fluorescent tubes come in a number of different sizes and colours. The standard diameter is 38mm, while slimline tubes are only 26mm diameter. Miniature tubes, complete with miniature bi-pins, are perfect for installing above worksurfaces and are 15mm in diameter. Colours range from a bluish white to a warm pink white. If you want a fluorescent tube in a living area, it's best to aim for Deluxe warm white which will most closely match the yellow light given off by a filament lamp. Fluorescent tubes are particularly useful for lighting kitchens as they cast few shadows.

6 Tungsten Halogen lamps give an intense light from a small glass envelope. Special gas increases the efficacy of the filament and these lamps are being increasingly used in low voltage spotlamps in the home.

7 Linear filament tubes are used in the same way as other filament tubes and are specially useful for lighting a prominent painting or decorative feature.

TYPES OF CAP

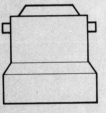

1 Bayonet caps (BC) are fitted to most filament lamps. Usually 22mm in diameter, smaller lamps often have a 15mm version.

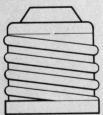

2 Edison screw (ES) caps range from the miniature size on Christmas tree lamps to the giant that is seen on lamps over 300W.

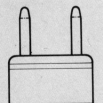

3 Bi-pin end caps are fitted to most fluorescent tubes. The pins act as contacts and the caps are sized according to the tube diameter.

4 Single-centre contacts are normally fitted to filament tubes, although some tubes have peg caps.

LIGHTING DESIGN: 2 the planning

Once you're familiar with the basic principles of lighting design, you can go on to some more detailed planning of your lighting and start to turn ideas into reality.

The lighting you choose for your home should meet two criteria: it should be functional, giving you light where you need it (and in the right quantity), and it should be decorative, enhancing the looks of the room concerned while conserving its character. The type of fitting chosen for each light source is of great importance (see pages 37-39) – certain fittings excel at particular jobs – but its positioning is ultimately responsible for helping to create exactly the effect you want.

Above all, the aim must be to provide a balanced mixture of light and shadow; uniformly bright lighting is stark and cheerless, while deep shadows are simply depressing. You can do this for the most part using fittings with tungsten light bulbs, or with fluorescent tubes concealed in some way and used for perimeter lighting. An unshielded fluorescent fitting, whether linear or circular, gives an overall flat lighting effect with no shadows, which robs a room of its character and makes it appear almost two-dimensional – satisfactory in a kitchen or garage, perhaps, but not for visual comfort in a living room.

Lamp positions

There are a few simple guidelines to bear in mind when planning the positions of light fittings. The first golden rule is to ensure that naked bulbs cannot be seen by anyone in the room, whether standing, sitting or even lying (after all, you'll see most of your bedroom lighting effects from the bed). You can avoid this by judicious choice of fittings and shades, and also by thinking about the height of the fitting; examples are using a rise-and-fall fitting over a dining table, and setting wall lights low rather than high above bedheads.

Secondly, aim for an acceptable level of lighting throughout the room, even when local lights are providing extra illumination at individual points. This avoids creating pools of hard, dark shadows.

Thirdly, use lighting to highlight special features in the room; these can range from the obvious – an attractive fireplace or a group of pictures – to the sort of feature often ignored, such as a run of beautiful curtains that could be lit from above by perimeter

LIGHT EFFECTS

You can create various effects by 'washing' walls with light. For perfect and graded washes, use wallwashers with reflector floods – all 150W for a perfect wash, in decreasing wattages for a graded one. For spill and scallop washes, use downlighters to graze the wall with light.

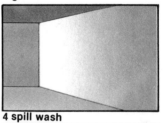
1 perfect wash

2 graded wash

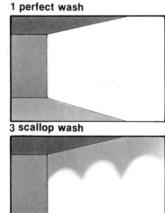
3 scallop wash

4 spill wash

lighting (behind pelmets) or wallwashers.

Lighting for special jobs

One activity needing good localised lighting is reading, and here a reflector lamp, table or standard lamp placed behind the chair gives the best illumination without glare. Where sewing is involved, even brighter illumination is needed, and a spotlight (wall-mounted or freestanding) is the best choice. For writing at a desk, a fluorescent or tungsten tube concealed behind a pelmet above the desk (or below its top shelf) will illuminate the whole desk surface and eliminate hand shadows; if a typewriter is being used, add an adjustable lamp to one side of the desk to illuminate the keyboard without creating glare. Lastly, amongst leisure pursuits,

television watching comes fairly high, and here the aim should be to reduce contrast glare from the tube by providing low-level lighting behind the set – a dimmed wall light in an alcove, or a table lamp or standard lamp behind and to one side of the set.

In the kitchen, the first priority is good task lighting over work areas, and the best solutions are a ceiling-mounted fluorescent tube or track-light fitting over the sink and hob areas, and lighting above worktops concealed behind battens fixed to the underside of wall cupboards.

In the bedroom, the specific needs are bedhead lighting (two directional lights in shared bedrooms allow one person to read, the other to sleep) and good lighting at dressing tables, where the light should shine

LIGHTING FOR DOWNSTAIRS ROOMS

The best way to plan and co-ordinate your home lighting scheme is with a simple floor plan on which the position of fixtures and fittings are marked. This example is intended to show the scope you have for planning alternative lighting effects. In the living room the range of fittings allows general and task lighting, while wallwashers, track lighting and perimeter fittings allow a choice of lighting effects to be achieved. In the kitchen a central spotlight group back up the general and task lighting provided by fluorescent fittings on the ceiling and over the worktops.

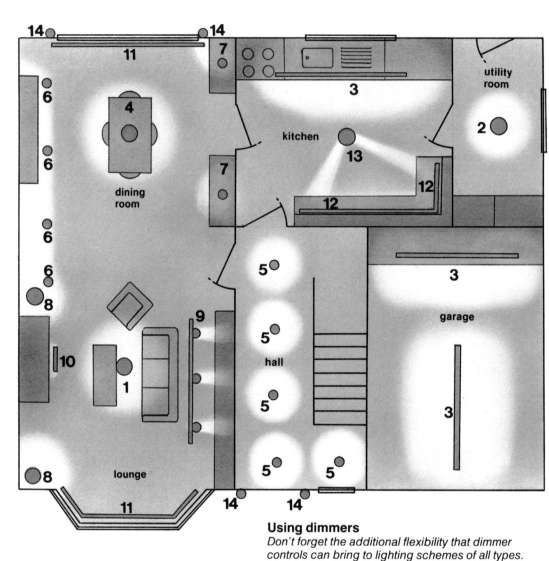

KEY
1 *Centre pendant fitting*
2 *Close-ceiling fitting*
3 *Fluorescent tube fitting*
4 *Rise-and-fall fitting*
5 *Recessed downlighters*
6 *Recessed wallwashers*
7 *Table lamps*
8 *Standard lamps*
9 *Track fitting with spotlights*
10 *Picture strip light*
11 *Perimeter lighting*
12 *Strip lighting over worktops*
13 *Ceiling-mounted spot group*
14 *Outside light*

Using dimmers
Don't forget the additional flexibility that dimmer controls can bring to lighting schemes of all types.

on the face, not the mirror. Table lamps or striplights at each side of the mirror offer the best lighting balance. The same point also applies to lighting next to mirrors in the bathroom, but make sure any lights chosen are switched from a point out of reach of bath, basin or shower.

One other specific form of task lighting is worth considering, and that is lighting in wardrobes and storage cupboards. Strip lighting positioned above the inner face of the door frame, or down each side if shelves would be in shadow, is the simplest answer, and control can be automatic if door switches are used. Remember that the circuit to such lights also requires an ordinary plateswitch, wired into the spur between the mains supply and the automatic switch/switches.

Room lighting
Apart from individual task lighting, every room needs more general illumination, and this can be provided in many different ways. Here are some of your options.

In the living room, the central pendant light (if fitted) should be an attractive feature unlit as well as lit. The same applies to wall lights, table and standard lamps too. Other forms of lighting tend to be more functional in their appearance – wallwashers and downlighters recessed into the ceiling, track lighting carrying spotlights above a display unit or a range of pictures, or perimeter fluorescent lighting hidden behind cornices or pelmets. Remember that an open-topped pelmet allows light to travel upwards and reflect off the ceiling. Where you are installing a run of

downlighters or wallwashers, it's a good idea to have them individually switched so you can vary the areas of the room that are illuminated.

In the dining room the use of rise-and-fall fittings over dining tables has already been covered. What is needed in addition is some fairly subdued background lighting – say, wall lights or wallwashers illuminating the sideboard/serving area, or perimeter lighting throwing light downwards over curtains.

The landing, hall and stairs is one area of the home where good, bright lighting is essential; safety must take preference over 'mood', so that all parts of the stairwell are clearly lit without glare. Light should fall on the treads, with the risers in shadow. Suspended fittings must not be so low as to

LIGHTING FOR UPSTAIRS ROOMS

As with the downstairs, a simple floor plan makes it much easier to decide on what sort of lighting to provide for the various rooms. There is obviously less need for flexibility in bedrooms and bathrooms, but still plenty of scope for practical or restful effects to be achieved.

The most important points shown here include good lighting on landing and stairs (with the stair treads illuminated and the risers in shadow), adjustable light fittings at bedheads and over desks and dressing tables, and additional lighting in the bathroom for shaving, making up and showering.

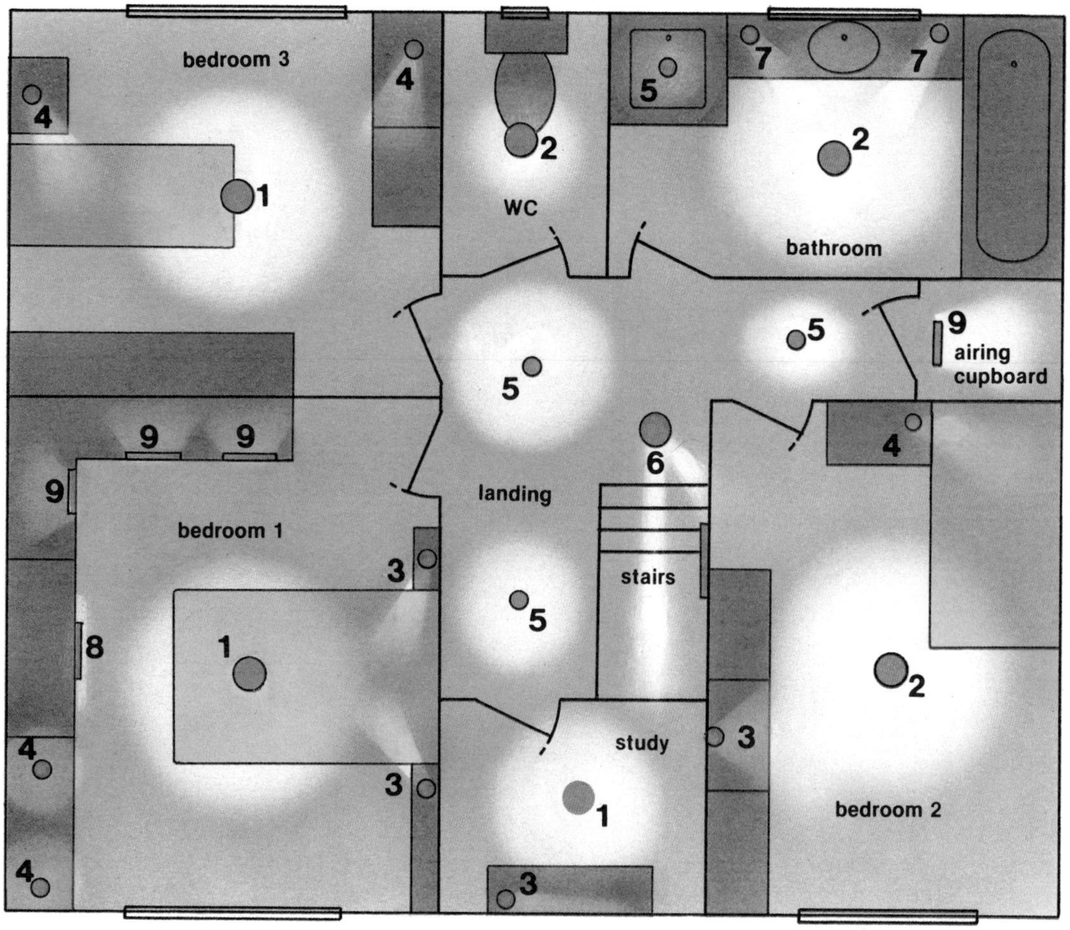

KEY
1 *Centre pendant fitting*
2 *Close-mounted ceiling fittings*
3 *Adjustable wall light*
4 *Adjustable table lamp*
5 *Recessed downlighters*
6 *Ceiling-mounted spot group*
7 *Wall-mounted strip light*
8 *Picture strip light*
9 *Strip lights for cupboard interiors (with door switches)*

For more information on choosing and installing lights and light fittings, see pages 37-42 and 46-70.

For more information on choosing and installing lights and light fittings, see pages 37-42 and 46-70.

impede passage on the staircase. Down-lighters can work extremely well if installed in the landing ceiling above an open flight; otherwise aim to light the flight from at least two positions so that it is evenly illuminated.

In kitchens you will need some sort of general lighting in addition to 'task' lighting over work surfaces. In a small kitchen this could be provided by the main ceiling-mounted fluorescent fitting, but you could experiment with either a close-ceiling fitting (easy to clean) or even track lighting carrying a number of spotlights directed towards the walls. If you eat in your kitchen too, add a rise-and-fall fitting over the table so you can turn off the fluorescent tube at meal-times and enjoy a softer light. Island bars are best illuminated with downlighters mounted

directly above the bar surface.

Bedroom background lighting can be as simple or as sophisticated as you wish – ornate pendants, simple centre fittings, perimeter lighting or wall lights. However, do include two-way switching of whatever arrangements you choose, so that you aren't having to leap in and out of bed to turn lights on and off.

Lastly, in bathrooms a close-ceiling light, or even a fitting recessed into the ceiling itself, is the best way to provide even lighting over the whole room.

Drawing up your plans
The simplest way to plan your home lighting is to use sketch plans on which you can mark the positions of major pieces of furniture and

the locations where task lighting will be required. The examples shown here illustrate the principle and help to give some idea of the scope and flexibility you have.

As you work out your requirements, don't hesitate to experiment with portable lamps and dummy fittings to see what effects you can achieve. For example, you can make up an extension cable carrying three or four lampholders with cardboard shades to try out the effect of a row of downlighters and wallwashers, or get a helper to hold spotlights in various positions in the room while you decide on the best angle and fitting height to choose. Light fittings and lamps are comparatively expensive, and a little time spent experimenting in this way will be worthwhile in the long run.

FLUORESCENT LIGHTING

Fluorescent lighting is glare-free and casts no hard, irritating shadows. It is therefore ideal for certain areas of the home, particularly the kitchen, bathroom, workroom and garage.

Many people have mixed feelings about fluorescent lights because of the nature or 'colour' of the light they emit. Admittedly they are not the best form of main lighting for living or dining areas as the light is harsh compared to ordinary tungsten filament light and doesn't give a relaxed atmosphere to the room. Nevertheless, they are ideal where good all-round lighting is required.

Fluorescent lighting can be fitted at any lighting point. However, an ordinary ceiling rose on a loop-in circuit will require some minor modification to the fixed wiring. This is not a difficult operation.

Types and uses

There are two basic types of fluorescent fitting – linear and circular – and both are made in a range of sizes. Circular tubes, in particular, are becoming more popular as they greatly improve the light output from a ceiling point and can be fitted flush to the ceiling and disguised with an attractive glass diffuser. The straight tubes likewise spread light evenly in a room, again often aided by a diffuser. In this case it's usually a corrugated or dimpled cover which is clipped over the fitting.

Fluorescent lights come in a variety of sizes; as a result they can be used for all sorts of purposes in kitchens, bathrooms, and in more specialised areas. For example, small tubes are ideal for concealed lighting in alcoves and can be hidden behind pelmets or baffles to highlight curtains drawn across a window. Sometimes they are used to feature cornices against the ceiling. There is also a type available which resembles a tungsten filament light bulb and can be used in an ordinary lampholder. And as the tubes last for 5,000 to 7,500 hours – about five year's average use – this more than compensates for the extra cost.

Installation and running costs

Fluorescent lights are more costly to install than a normal light, but because they are more efficient at turning electricity into light than a filament lamp they are cheaper to run. And they also have a longer life. In fact a 100W filament lamp will give light for ten hours for one unit of electricity (1 kilowatt/hour) while a 1500mm (5ft) tube will give four times as much light for the same cost over the same period.

The fluorescent fitting

There are two parts to a fluorescent fitting. The lamp itself is a long, thin glass tube, which is coated on the inside with a powder that fluoresces – gives off light – when the fitting is switched on. The tube contains argon gas, which is similar to neon, and a small amount of mercury, and at each end there is a tiny heater (electrode) which is coated in a special chemical. In some fittings there is more than one tube.

The other part of the fitting is the control gear. This is made up of several different components including a starter and 'choke' or 'ballast', and is responsible for starting up the light when it's switched on and controlling it when it's operating.

Most manufacturers sell an integral unit which incorporates both a tube and linear metal box designed to take the control gear. But they don't always have to be together. In fact, in some situations it's probably a good idea that they aren't. If you want to highlight some curtains, for example, you could conceal the tube behind a pelmet board or a baffle, holding it in place with spring clips about 150mm (6in) from the material. It should be connected to the control gear, which can be mounted on a solid surface nearby, using 0.5mm² (3 amp) or 0.75mm² (6 amp) flex. As the choke can

KNOW YOUR WIRING

If you are replacing a pendant fitting with a fluorescent light, you first need to check what type of wiring is at the ceiling rose. It doesn't matter whether you've got one of the neat, modern roses or an older style one mounted on a pattress or block as it will have to be removed before putting up the new fitting.

With loop-in wiring you might find two, three or four cables going into the rose. The black core of the switch cable going to the switch (SW) terminal should be wrapped with red PVC tape as it is live and not neutral, but in many cases you'll see this hasn't been done.

If you have junction box wiring there'll only be one cable going into the rose.

Don't be alarmed if there's no earth on

How the light works

In an ordinary tungsten bulb electricity flowing through the filament causes it to heat up to a white heat and so emit visible light. In a fluorescent tube there's no filament, but the electricity flowing between the two heater elements at each end causes the mercury vapour in the tube to emit ultraviolet (invisible) light. This is converted to visible light by the fluorescent powder on the inside of the tube.

In order to get an electric current to flow in the tube a high voltage is needed initially when the light is switched on. And it's the function of the choke and starter to provide this. At the same time the starter also has to heat up the elements. Once the light is operating, the starter switches itself off while the choke and power factor correction capacitor (PFCC) regulate the current flowing through the tube.

There are two types of starter. The thermal type has a tiny heating element which acts like a thermostat and turns off the current in the starter circuit when the elements are hot enough and current is flowing in the tube. The more common starter is the two-pin 'glow' type which doesn't have its own internal heating element.

Quick-start fittings

Some fittings have 'quick start' ballasts that don't need a starter, but a special tube is required with a metal strip running along its length, which is earthed at the lampholders at either end. When the light is switched on the current passes down the tube immediately – so there is no flick-flick effect or delay in the tube lighting. This type of fitting needs to be earthed. The manufacturers' catalogues usually contain details and circuit diagrams.

get rather warm, the control gear should have some ventilation.

Given the positions where most fluorescents are used, it's unlikely you'll want to be able to control their brilliance. If you do you'll need to use a special dimmer and modify the fitting.

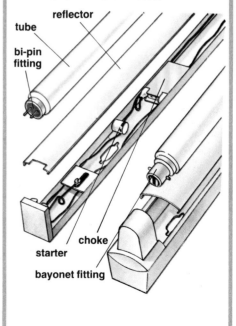
Loop-in wiring system

the lighting circuit, because two-core cable was once used for wiring. But when putting in the fluorescent light you'll have to make a separate connection to the main earthing

Rose on a junction box system

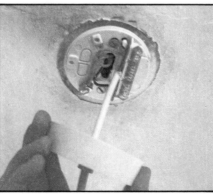

terminal. You'll have to run two-core and earth cable from the junction box to the fitting and then a single core 1.5mm^2 earth cable to the consumer unit.

MODIFYING LOOP-IN WIRING

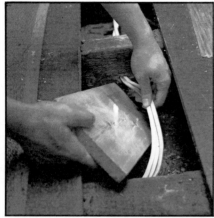

1 Before installing the four-terminal junction box, you have to fix a wooden batten between the joists near the lighting point.

2 Screw the junction box to the batten – it makes fixing the cores that much easier – and draw the cables into the ceiling void, then run them to the box.

3 Take earths to one terminal, red cores of the supply cables to another, black neutrals to a third and black switch core with red PVC to the fourth.

4 Lay a length of 1.0mm² two-core and earth cable from the lighting point to the junction box, strip back the sheathing and prepare the cores.

5 After you've sleeved the earth core and connected it to the earth terminal, take the red to the switch terminal and the black to the neutrals.

6 Follow the same procedure if you have to extend the lighting cable on an existing junction box system, and don't forget to screw on the cover.

Colour range

Fluorescent tubes are manufactured to give off different types of light. In all there are 13 different colours to choose from. These range from the very cold white 'northlight' to the warmer yellow colours. Most of the fittings sold in retail lighting shops are supplied with a tube marked 'warm white' – a colour that isn't really warm when compared with the yellow light given out by an ordinary filament lamp. The tubes giving a yellow light are listed as 'de luxe warm white'.

Some fittings such as the very useful circular fluorescents with their diffusers and some of the 25/26mm slimline tubes are available in 'warm white' or the colder 'natural'. The very neat 15/16mm miniature tubes are available in three or four colours, but not in 'de luxe warm white'. 'Warm white' tubes are ideal for the kitchen, but they're not really acceptable for living rooms except for lighting small areas displaying ornaments or paintings, for example. Here the colder colour of the fluorescent can be compensated by tungsten lighting elsewhere in the room. Colours such as 'daylight' and 'natural' are not really suitable for the home except for display cabinets.

Installing the fitting

You can install a fluorescent fitting almost anywhere instead of an existing tungsten filament lamp. If you want to connect the fitting to an existing lighting point, you'll first need to inspect the fitting or rose that's already there to see how the circuit is wired. If there is only one cable going into the rose or fitting on the fixed wiring side – ie, there's one black and one red insulated core and possibly an earth wire – then the circuit is wired on the junction box system. All you have to do when putting up the fluorescent light is to connect the cores to the relevant terminals in the fitting – black to the 'N' terminal, red to the 'L' terminal and the earth (which should be sleeved in green/yellow PVC) to the 'E' terminal.

However, if you've got loop-in wiring where there are two or more cables going into the fitting or rose, then some small modifications are necessary as there are no loop-in terminal facilities on a fluorescent fitting. All you have to do is to draw the cables back into the ceiling void or loft space and fit the cores to the relevant terminals of a four-terminal junction box. You then have to run a short piece of 1.0mm² two-core and earth flat PVC-sheathed cable from the junction box to the fluorescent light and connect it to the terminals.

If, as in many circuits, there is no earthing at the lighting point, it's necessary to run 1.5mm² green/yellow PVC-insulated cable from the fluorescent fitting back to the earthing terminal block in the consumer unit.

CONNECTING THE FITTING

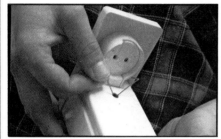

1 Remove the diffuser and tube from the fitting and take off the backplate cover by undoing the retaining screws and prising out the spring clips.

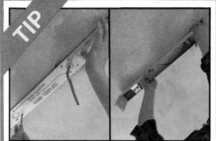

2 Use the template supplied with the fitting – or the backplate itself – to test that the fixing holes are sound; then screw the fitting into position.

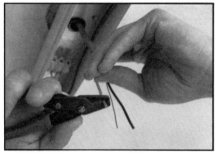

3 If you've had to lay in a new cable, strip back the sheathing and prepare the cores. Don't forget, there should be a rubber grommet round the cable entry.

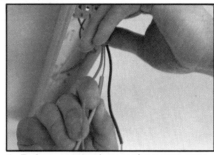

4 Before connecting up the cores, you need to slip a length of green/yellow PVC sleeving over the earth wire so there is no exposed wire in the fitting.

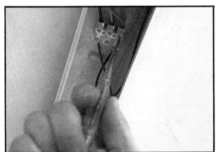

5 Push the cores well into their terminals and screw down the retaining screws. The back of the earth terminal is connected to the metal backplate.

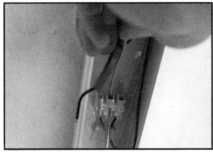

6 If you're using the existing lighting cable and it's only two-core, you'll have to run a separate earth core from the fitting to the main earthing point.

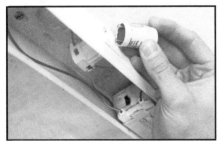

7 Push the starter into its socket, which you'll find on the outside of the backplate. You have to twist it clockwise to secure it in position.

8 Replace the cover of the backplate and refit the spring clips. The tube is inserted in the holders at each end, which spring outwards for easy fitting.

Ready Reference

FAULTS AND REMEDIES

Turn off the power at mains when carrying out repairs other than changing the tube itself.

FAULT Tube flickers and is reluctant to light, or tube glows at each end but fails to start.
Solution Faults could be due to malfunctioning starter; if so fit new one. Or it could be an ageing tube. Look for tell-tale signs of blackening at ends of tube; if present fit new tube of same size and type.
FAULT Tube glows at one end and flashes.
Solution Check tube connections. If pin holders damaged or bent, fit new holder.
FAULT Strong oily smell.
Solution Check the choke for signs of burning and replace it making sure you use the correct type to match the wattage of tube.

REPLACING A STARTER

A simple operation – locate the starter, push in and twist anti-clockwise to remove. Replace with a new one of the same type.

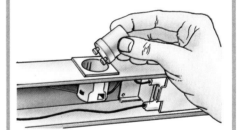

REPLACING A TUBE

With a bayonet-type fitting (1), push in and twist the tube against the spring-loaded lampholders. With a bi-pin tube (2), simply pull back one of the spring-loaded end brackets.

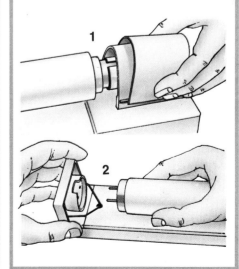

DECORATIVE LIGHTS

There is a tremendous range of decorative ceiling lights from which to choose. Normally they replace an existing rose and pendant fitting. They're not difficult to install but they may require some modification to the existing wiring.

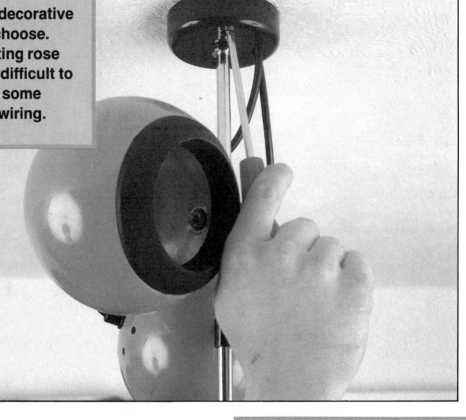

Lighting in a room has become more sophisticated. Whereas a central light was once the only form of lighting, giving uneven illumination and shadowy corners, you can now use spotlights, concealed lighting, wall-washers and downlighters, as well as table and standard lamps, to create more interesting lighting effects.

But the central light still has an important role to play. The tendency is for it to be more decorative and less functional; to be an attractive feature in a room even when turned off. You can, of course, always change lampshades to transform an ordinary pendant fitting, but there is now an ever-increasing number of decorative fittings which replace the pendant ceiling rose entirely. Whether they are ornate chandeliers, glass and brass lanterns or modern designs in multi-coloured acrylics, the choice is so large there is something to match the decoration in any room.

These fittings either hang down from the ceiling on a rod, chain or cord, or are close-mounted on the surface.

Close-mounted fittings are the answer to many lighting problems in smaller houses and flats, or in houses with low ceilings, because they give a good general spread of light and are unobtrusive.

As general room lights, ceiling-mounted spotlights can make a room look rather bare and cold. However, you can use other lights to supplement them. You can also use lighting track to enable more than one spotlight to be used from the same lighting point. Sometimes, particularly in smaller houses, bulky lighting track can look obtrusive. You can remedy this by recessing it into the ceiling, but you'll have to make sure that the track you buy is suitable.

Rise-and-fall pendants enable you to adjust the height of a light simply by pulling it down to the required level. They have particular uses other than over a dining table. Breakfast bars and through-room conversions from kitchen to dining room are becoming increasingly popular, and rise-and-fall pendants are ideal here because they can be pushed out of the way when the meal is finished.

Inspecting the fitting

Although the designs of decorative fittings vary enormously, there are only three ways in which they can be connected to the main lighting circuit. The method you adopt will depend on the type of fitting and the way the lighting circuit has been wired.

If you have a close-mounted fitting this will probably have a plastic or metal backing plate which you have to screw to the ceiling. You'll find three connectors attached to the plate and these take the cores of the circuit cable (red to live or 'L', black to neutral or 'N' and the earth to the earth terminal). If the lighting circuit isn't earthed (ie, if it's wired in two-core cable), and the fitting has a metal backing plate, then this needs to be earthed. You'll need to run a 1.5mm^2 green/yellow insulated earth wire from the terminal on the plate right back to the earthing terminal at the consumer unit or fuse box. If there's no earth terminal on the plate then you'll have to drill a small hole and insert a nut, bolt and washer set to which you can fix the earth wire. The glass or plastic cover of the fitting is screwed or clipped to the backing plate so that the bulb is totally enclosed.

If you've got a pendant-type fitting this will have either a two-core or three-core flex. Two-core flexes are used when a fitting is mainly made of plastic or a non-conductive material. If a fitting contains metal parts,

FITTING A BESA BOX

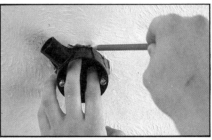

1 *Disconnect the rose and draw the cables back into the ceiling void. Then mark the position of a terminal BESA box on the ceiling surface.*

4 *Push the BESA box into the recess and screw it to the joist. Alternatively, fix a batten between the joists and screw the box in place to this.*

INSTALLING A JUNCTION BOX

1 Mount a four-terminal junction box on a batten fixed between two joists. Disconnect the cables from the loop-in rose and draw them back to this position.

3 Lay a length of 1.0mm² two-core and earth cable from the lighting point to the junction box and prepare the ends, remembering to sleeve the earth core.

2 Connect the live cores to one terminal, the neutrals to a second and the earths to a third. The black of the switch cable goes to a fourth.

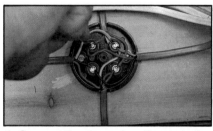

4 Connect the sleeved earth core to the earth terminal, the black core to the neutral terminal and the red core to the switch terminal (top left).

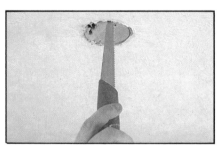

2 Cut out the circular section of ceiling using a pad saw or keyhole saw. Make sure the cables are well out of the way to prevent damaging them.

5 With loop-in wiring, draw the feed and switch cables into the BESA box. Wrap red PVC insulating tape round the black core of the switch cable.

TIP

3 If the lighting point is partly under a joist. use a wood bit in a power drill to cut away part of the joist to the depth of the BESA box.

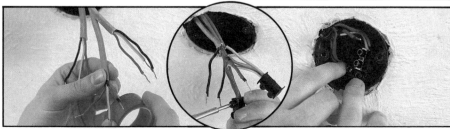

6 Connect the lives, neutrals and earths up to three separate connectors, and the taped switch core to a fourth (inset). Push all four up into the BESA box.

Ready Reference

TYPES OF DECORATIVE LIGHT

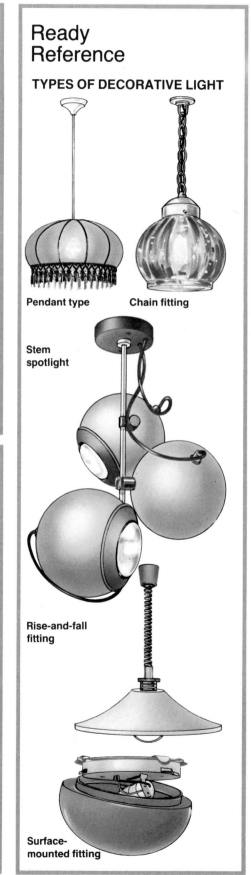

Pendant type   **Chain fitting**

Stem spotlight

Rise-and-fall fitting

Surface-mounted fitting

SURFACE-MOUNTED FITTING

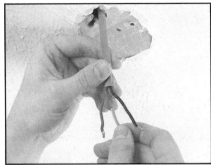

1 Unscrew the ceiling rose to inspect the wiring. If it's the loop-in type you'll need to remove it and install a junction box (see page 51).

2 Lay a cable from the junction box to the lighting point, prepare the cores and sleeve the earth in green/yellow PVC sleeving.

3 Screw the fixing bar of the fitting into position. You should be able to use the same fixing holes that were used for the original rose.

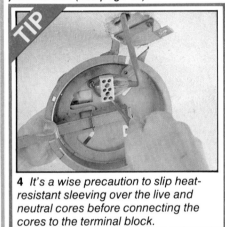

4 It's a wise precaution to slip heat-resistant sleeving over the live and neutral cores before connecting the cores to the terminal block.

5 The base plate can then be screwed to the fixing bracket. Pull out the lever and slide it round so that the fixing catches are fully recessed.

6 Insert a bulb into the lampholder and position the cover. Rotate the lever so the catches slip under the rim to secure it, then push the lever out of sight.

even a lampshade ring, then it must be earthed and so it should have a three-core flex. This is particularly necessary for pendants, which are suspended from a flat, metal ceiling-plate by a chain, and for the type where the flex runs down a hollow rod to the lights, as in some stem spotlights.

Making the connection
In all probability, your fitting will not connect directly to a ceiling rose and so you'll first have to remove the rose. But remember that before you carry out any electrical work you must turn off the power first. If you've got lighting track you can connect the flex from an existing ceiling rose into it, but this isn't a very neat method.

Once you've unscrewed the rose cover you'll be able to tell what type of wiring you've got – junction (joint) box or loop-in (see Ready Reference). However, it's not so obvious to see how the fitting connects to the wiring when the rose is removed. The fixing plates of, for example, pendants which you have to attach to the ceiling don't have a provision for connecting the flex of the fitting to the circuit wiring.

Close-mounted fittings
Probably the simplest combination is to have a close-mounted fitting with junction box wiring. You should be able to draw the mains cable through the fitting base plate, screw the plate to the ceiling and then connect the cable cores to the fitting terminal block. But if you've got loop-in wiring there's no facility for dealing with all the cores. The best thing to do is to draw all the cables back into the roof space or ceiling void and install a four-terminal junction box. You can then lead a single cable from this into the fitting.

Installing a pendant-type fitting
Despite the fact that there is a wide range of pendant-type fittings, they are connected up in basically the same way. Some are attached to the ceiling by a flat, metal plate which may have a decorative cover. With this type of fitting there is no provision for linking the flex to the lighting circuit, although some modern fittings have a base plate deep enough to take terminal connectors which allow the circuit wiring and the flex of the fitting to be joined together.

Where there is no space behind the base plate to fit connectors, you'll have to install a BESA box. This is now more commonly referred to as a terminal conduit box and it provides a protected recess in the ceiling for housing the connectors for joining the lighting circuit to the flex. Connectors have to be fitted regardless of whether you have loop-in or junction box wiring.

The boxes are made of metal or tough PVC and if you use the metal type you'll need to earth it. Sometimes, however, there is no earthing terminal, so you'll have to wrap the earths round one of the fixing screws – a fiddly job – or you can drill a hole and insert a nut, bolt and washer set to which you can attach the earth. PVC boxes don't need to be earthed.

To install the box, you'll need to cut out a small circle of ceiling so the box can be set flush to the surface. If your existing ceiling rose is screwed to a joist, you may need to drill out some of the joist to position the box. And if you can't do this you'll have to install a wooden batten between the joists and screw the box to this (see Ready Reference on facing page).

PENDANT-TYPE FITTINGS

1 With stem spotlights there may be room in the base plate for the terminal connectors, particularly if you have junction box wiring.

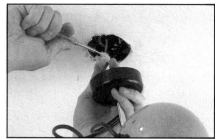

2 If you install a BESA box to deal with loop-in wiring, attach the blue flex to the connector housing the neutrals and the brown to the taped switch core.

3 With a chain fitting there's usually no room behind the base plate to connect the wiring to the flex so you'll have to install a BESA box.

4 The flex of the fitting is threaded through the chain which is suspended from a hook on the base plate to take the weight of the lampholder and shade.

RISE-AND-FALL FITTING

1 Install a BESA box in the ceiling and connect the cores of the circuit cables to the relevant connectors. Then screw the base plate and hook to the box.

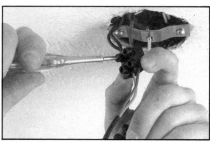

2 The flex will probably be attached to a terminal block. Connect the neutral cores to the blue flex connector and the switch core to the brown one.

3 The rise-and-fall unit can now be slipped over the hook and the up-and-down movement adjusted by tightening or loosening the control screw.

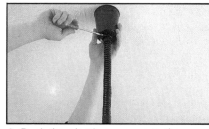

4 Push the plastic cover up to the ceiling to conceal the rise-and-fall unit and secure it in position with a grub-screw. Then fit the shade and bulb.

Ready Reference

BESA BOXES
Otherwise known as terminal conduit boxes. Install them where there is no room behind the base plate of the fitting to join the circuit cable to the flex. They are made of metal or tough PVC.

WAYS OF FIXING A BESA BOX
The box must be recessed into the ceiling and screwed to a joist or fixing batten.

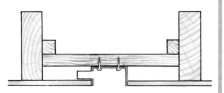

DEALING WITH THE WIRING
With loop-in wiring you will usually have to remove the loop-in rose and install a BESA box. Connect the mains and switch cables to the flex from the fitting using terminal connectors as shown (A). With junction-box wiring you may not need a BESA box unless the fitting is suspended from one; connect the single feed cable either directly to the terminals on the fitting, or use terminal connectors (B).

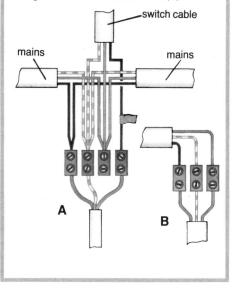

INSTALLING WALL LIGHTS

Ceiling lights are simple and effective, but if you want a lighting scheme that is a little more exciting, more decorative and more versatile, they are not enough. One solution is to fit wall lights. Here's how.

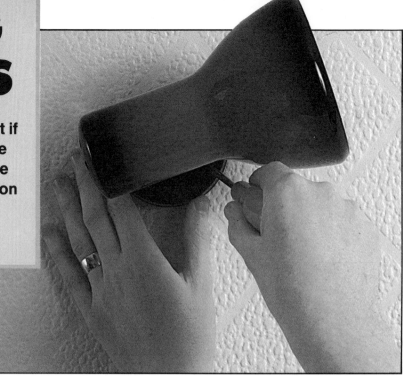

There are two keys to a really successful lighting scheme: variety and versatility. Variety, because having a uniform level of light throughout a room is just plain boring. And versatility because your lighting needs change from one part of the room to another. In a living room, for example, you may prefer the overall lighting level to be fairly low and restful, but you will still need pools of intense light for reading, or perhaps simply to show off decorative feature like pictures, plants or ornaments. That's where wall lights come in. They are very good at creating interesting pools of light.

Choosing a light

With so many wall lights to choose from where do you start? It really depends on what you want the light to do. Few provide a light you can put to practical use. Most are purely decorative.

The traditional wall light is a good example. It normally has a low wattage, candle-shaped lamp, mounted on a wooden base, and concealed behind a pretty parchment shade, so that it spreads a fan of soft light across the wall.

More recent versions take the imitation candelabra and gaslight theme still further, having ornate brass, copper, and aluminium stems, and, instead of shades, translucent bowls in plain, coloured, frosted, smoked, and sculpted glass or plastic. They tend to use more powerful bulbs, and can be made to light the top or bottom of the wall, but the net result is the same. They are for looking at, rather than seeing by.

This is also true of many modern wall light designs. There are, for example, cylindrical fittings open at top and bottom to spread a shaft of light in two directions, either vertically or horizontally.

Still attractive, but producing a more useful light, there are the fully enclosed fittings. 'Opals', for example, create a beautifully soft, even light, and look rather like round, square or rectangular blocks of milky glass or plastic. For those who prefer more ornate lights, sculpted glass versions (they look like cut crystal) are also available. Enclosed fittings are particularly handy

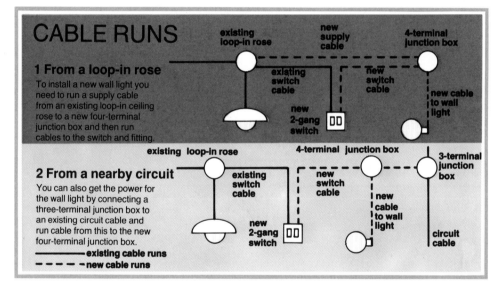

CABLE RUNS

1 From a loop-in rose
To install a new wall light you need to run a supply cable from an existing loop-in ceiling rose to a new four-terminal junction box and then run cables to the switch and fitting.

existing loop-in rose · new supply cable · 4-terminal junction box · existing switch cable · new switch cable · new cable to wall light · new 2-gang switch

2 From a nearby circuit
You can also get the power for the wall light by connecting a three-terminal junction box to an existing circuit cable and run cable from this to the new four-terminal junction box.

existing loop-in rose · 4-terminal junction box · 3-terminal junction box · existing switch cable · new switch cable · new cable to wall light · new 2-gang switch · circuit cable

——— existing cable runs
— — — new cable runs

where space is limited – in a hallway, perhaps – and since many are weatherproof, they are an excellent choice for the humid atmosphere of a bathroom or an outside porch.

More useful still are the spotlights. Usually mounted on adjustable arms away from the wall, they can be used to send a strong beam of light almost anywhere – back onto the wall, say, to light a picture, or out into the room to illuminate a desk or sitting area. Their only real snag is that they need careful shading, if they are not to dazzle you. Mounting them on the ceiling may overcome this problem.

And finally, don't forget fluorescent lights. Slimline fluorescent tubes, though inhospitable looking, give off little heat and are easily concealed. Use them to spread a sheet of light over a wall. The light assembly can be mounted on a wooden batten and

shaded by a pelmet or baffle. If you wish, the pelmet can be painted or papered to match the wall. Miniature fluorescents are also handy for lighting pictures and shelves, but whatever the size, be sure to use a 'de luxe' warm white' tube, or the light will look cold and harsh.

Positioning the fitting

Choosing a light is only half the battle. To give of its best it must be carefully positioned. With the exception of enclosed fittings, which stand very well on their own, most need to be arranged at least in pairs, and sometimes even in a group. Traditional wall lights and mock candelabra, for example, tend to look best when arranged symmetrically in pairs – say, on each side of a chimney breast. Spotlights, on the other hand, are often most effective in a cluster.

Of course, there are no hard and fast

INSTALLING THE FITTING

1 Mark the position of the BESA box on the wall where the light is to go. Use a through box if the light's switch is to be immediately below the BESA box.

2 With a club hammer and bolster chisel, chop out the hole to take the box, and channels to take cables up to the ceiling and down or across to the switch.

3 Fix the box in place with screws and wall plugs, then run in the cables for the light and switch. Note that the switch cable passes straight through the box.

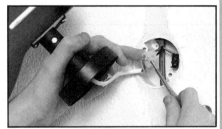

4 Connect the light cable to the light with insulated cable connectors Tuck the earth wire out of the way if it is not needed.

INSTALLING A SWITCH

1 To install a new switch, mark out the position of the switch mounting box (a plaster-depth box) and chop out the hole to receive it.

2 Drill and plug the wall, then screw the mounting box in place, checking it is level. Next, feed in the cable coming from the new circuit's junction box.

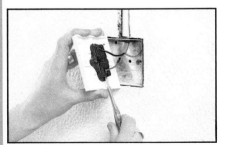

3 Connect the cable to a one-gang one-way switch. Ensure the terminal marked 'TOP' is at the top. Connect the earth wire to the box terminal.

4 If using an existing switch position, insert a new two-gang plate switch. Connect existing cable to one set of terminals, new cable to the other.

Ready Reference

POSITIONING WALL LIGHTS
● fix ordinary wall lights about 1.5m (5ft) above floor level
● bedside lights are best set about 1.2m (4ft) above floor level.

WHAT SWITCH TO USE
Use a one-way plate switch for the wall light. Set it on a metal mounting box sunk into the wall or on a plastic box mounted on the surface.
● a separate switch is needed to isolate a wall light from the main circuit even if it has a built-in switch of its own

● alternatively you can use an existing switch position to control an extra wall light by replacing a one-gang switch unit with a two-gang unit.

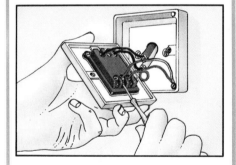

FITTING THE WALL LIGHT
The wires of the fitting are linked to the circuit cable using insulated cable connectors. These are housed in a BESA box or an architrave box which is sunk into the wall and hidden by the light fitting.

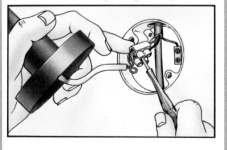

ALTERNATIVES

1 If the light switch is not to be vertically below the light position, use a single entry BESA box instead of a through one, fitting it in the same way.

2 If the light cannot be mounted on a BESA box, connect the wires in an architrave mounting box. Knockouts let this act as a single entry or through box.

LIGHTING CIRCUIT CONNECTIONS

1 Turn off the power at the mains, unscrew the rose and ease it away from the ceiling so you can pull through new 1.0 or 1.5mm² cable.

3 Run the cable to a junction box between the switch and light. Then run one cable to the light, another to the switch position.

2 Connect the cable to the rose's loop-in terminals; the red wire to the centre terminal block, the black to the neutral block, and the earth to the earth block.

4 If you can't connect to the rose, insert a junction box at some point along one of the rose's feed cables. Run cables down to the light and switch as before.

CONNECTING TO A RING CIRCUIT

1 The easiest way to link a lighting spur to the ring circuit is to connect a 2.5mm² cable to the back of a socket. Ensure the socket isn't already on a spur.

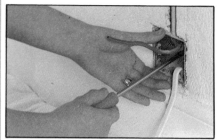

4 Fix the mounting box for the connection unit into the whole, and then run the cable into it from the power socket or three-terminal junction box.

2 Alternatively, cut the ring circuit cables and connect them to a three-terminal junction beneath the floor; then run the spur cable into that.

5 Having run the cable to the light position (or four-terminal junction box), fit the connection unit with a 5A fuse and connect it up.

3 Mark the position of the fused connection unit. Cut through the wallpaper with a sharp knife before you chisel out the hole for the mounting box.

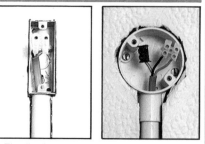

6 Finally, fit an architrave box or a stopped BESA box at the light position and install the light as before. Note the cable will now enter from below.

rules. In the end, it's all down to what looks and works best in your particular situation. Try to imagine how the lights will affect the room – not only the lights themselves and their position, but also the direction of the light they will give out.

You ought to pay particular attention to the light's height above the floor. The general rule is to place the light at just below eye level – about 1,500mm (5ft) – but you can vary this as necessary to stop the light getting in your eyes or to help direct it where it's needed. Wall lights used as bedside lamps, for example, should be about 1,220mm (4ft) above the floor and positioned so they can't get knocked as someone walks past them.

Installing the light

Having mastered the basic electrical techniques (see Chapter 2 pages 23-26 and 31-35), you shouldn't find it difficult to fit the light. But remember electricity can be dangerous if abused, so follow the instructions to the letter. If they don't tie in with your home's existing wiring, or if you're unsure about what you're doing, don't take chances – get expert advice.

The first step is to find a power source, though it is best to leave the connections into the existing circuit until last. That way, you can do almost all the work with your home's electrics working normally; you'll have to turn off the power at the mains only for the few minutes needed to make the final connection.

In most cases, taking a spur off the existing lighting circuit is your best bet. Do check, though, that the wall light will not overload it. Isolate the circuit in question by removing the fuse carrier from the consumer unit, or by turning off its MCB, and add up the total wattage of the bulbs it feeds – those that are now dead, in other words. Bulbs rated at 100W or more count at face value; less powerful bulbs count as 100W. When you've done that, add on the wattage of the new light and make sure the grand total is less than 1,200 watts.

Assuming this is so, there are two ways to break into the circuit. In theory, the simplest is to connect a 1.0 or 1.5mm² two-core and earth cable to a loop-in ceiling rose, and run it to a four-terminal junction box above the ceiling. In practice, it's often hard to fit the extra wires in, so, as an alternative, trace a mains feed cable out of the rose, and connect the junction box into this cable.

Once you've got power to the junction box, wire up the wall light and its switch on the conventional junction box system (see Chapter 2 pages 23-26 again) with one cable going to the light, and another to the switch. The switch can be anywhere convenient, either close to the light or away from it. You can use the switch position by

the room's door if you wish. It's a simple matter to convert the existing one-gang switch there (for the ceiling light) to a two-gang (for ceiling light and wall light).

Many wall lights have a built-in switch, so you may wonder why a switch is necessary. Although these are fine for everyday use, you ought to be able to isolate the wall light completely so an additional ordinary plate switch is required.

Though fitting a wall light is not complicated there are two problems you may meet. The first is in fixing the light to the wall. Many can be screwed to the holes provided in the BESA box housing connections between light and cable. Failing that, you can fix the light to the wall using screws and wall plugs, and house the connections in a metal architrave mounting box sunk into the wall behind it.

The second problem is earthing. Even if the wall light doesn't need to be earthed, the earth wire in the new cables must be linked to your home's main earthing point at the fuse box or consumer unit. (Never connect earth wires to water or gas pipes.) You can, of course, do this by connecting it to the earth wire in the existing wiring, but, if the existing wiring is old, it may not have an earth wire. In this case, you should run a single sheathed earth core from the new junction box back to the earthing point.

Connecting to a ring circuit

If it's inconvenient or impossible to take power from the lighting circuit, you can connect the wall light to a ring circuit. Essentially, you run a spur to the wall light's junction box in the usual way. You then have to break into the ring either by connecting a 2.55mm² two-core and earth cable to the back of a power socket, or by joining it to a three-terminal junction box and connecting this to the ring circuit cable beneath the floor.

However, there is a snag. The ring circuit fuse has too high a rating for a lighting circuit (remember, these need a 5A fuse). To get round this, you have to run the 2.5mm² cable into a fused connection unit fitted with a 5A fuse, and continue the circuit to a four-terminal junction box and then on to the light and switch junction box with 1.0 or 1.5mm² cable.

Obviously, this will involve considerable extra work and expense; but there is a short cut. You can do away with the junction box and separate switch, and use a switched fused connection unit to control the wall light. It sounds appealing, but it too has its drawbacks. The connection unit will not match the other light switches in the room, and it needs to be as close as possible to the light – an unnecessarily complex cable run would be needed to control the light from the far side of the room.

WIRING THE CIRCUIT

The easiest way to provide wall lights with power is to run a 1.0mm² two-core and earth, PVC-sheathed and insulated cable from a loop-in ceiling rose.

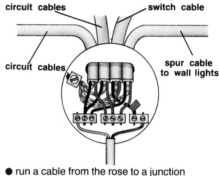

● run a cable from the rose to a junction box. Two cables then run from the box – one to the light and one to its switch (A)
● rather than connecting into the main lighting circuit at a rose, you can break into the main feed cable and install a junction box (B).

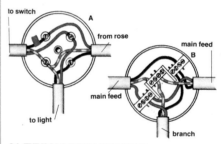

ALTERNATIVE WIRING

Wall lights can also take their power from a ring circuit.
● install a three-terminal junction box (A). Then run a 2.5mm² cable to a fused connection unit fitted with a 5A fuse (B). Continue the wiring to the light (C) and a switch (D) as if the power had been taken from the lighting circuit (ie, use 1.0mm² cable)

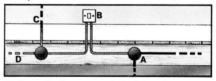

● alternatively use a switched fused connection unit (A), and run the 1.5mm² cable straight to the wall light. The unit then acts as an isolating light switch.

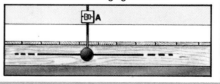

INSTALLING RECESSED LIGHTING

If you want an efficient lighting system that can provide both general and specific illumination without exposed fittings you should fit recessed lighting. It is stylish, practical and easy to install.

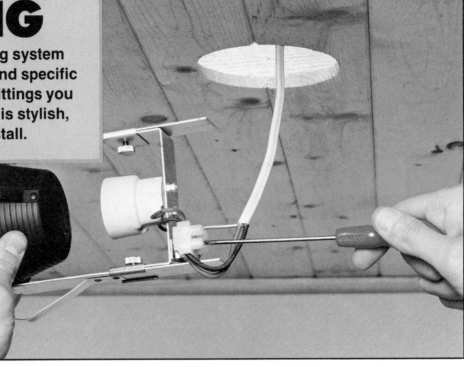

Choosing a lighting system that is both efficient and good looking is no easy task. You'll often find that lamps which provide perfectly adequate light have unattractive fittings out of style with the rest of your decor. Faced with this stark reality, people are beginning to realise that it's the light rather than the associated fittings which is important. For although there are numerous fittings which are attractive ornaments when unlit, their function is, after all, only as lampholders for the light source.

This is why recessed lighting has become so popular. It is the name for any type of light which has its fittings concealed above the ceiling surface, yet still adequately illuminates the room below.

Most homes are suitable for some form of recessed or hidden lighting, but which you install depends largely on the structure of your home. If, for example, you live in a flat where the ceilings are concrete, and therefore solid, you will be unable to fit lights recessed into the ceiling. Since, however, ceilings in flats are usually higher than those in a conventional house or bungalow, there is considerable scope for fitting a suspended ceiling and recessing the fittings into the void above it.

Similarly, the old country cottage with its oak beams and almost non-existent void between the ceiling and the floor above is hardly the ideal situation for recessed lighting. Here, the traditionally low ceiling rules out the addition of a false ceiling. However, even in situations like this there is some scope for hidden lighting or semi-recessed fittings as an alternative to fully recessed lighting.

Types of recessed lighting

You'll probably find that you're familiar with recessed lighting in such places as restaurants, airports and reception rooms, where, no doubt, the lighting was planned at the design stage and incorporated into the original building. However, there is now a wide variety of recessed lighting which you can successfully install in your own home. Perhaps the most popular form is known as the downlighter or the highlighter. This consists of a tube-like fitting that's installed so

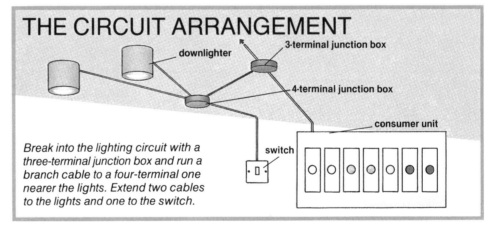

THE CIRCUIT ARRANGEMENT

Break into the lighting circuit with a three-terminal junction box and run a branch cable to a four-terminal one nearer the lights. Extend two cables to the lights and one to the switch.

downlighter · 3-terminal junction box · 4-terminal junction box · consumer unit · switch

that its edge sits flush with the ceiling surface. Other models can be installed so that they are, in effect, only semi-recessed, or, if you are stuck for space you could fit a model which has the lamp mounted on its side so the fitting takes up less vertical space. They usually house special light bulbs known as internal silvered lamps which reflect the light from the filament in a fairly wide beam. And different lamps can be fitted so you can select whichever type of beam you like. The particular advantage of the downlighter is that as all the light is directed downwards very little is wasted.

Another version of the downlighter is the wallwasher and, as its name implies, this fitting directs light an an angle of about 45° to illuminate a feature on the wall. However, its beam is usually somewhat less concentrated than that of a conventional spotlight. Similar

to the wallwasher is the eyeball spotlight; but this can be adjusted through a full 360° to direct light onto a specific surface or feature.

Recessed fluorescent lighting

Fluorescent tubes are extensively used in recessed lighting and, in particular, in illuminated ceilings. This is a very popular way of concealing the tubes and their fittings, yet at the same time making use of their even light: a number of tubes are fixed to the existing ceiling and beneath them a grid of aluminium strips is used to support sheets of translucent diffusing panels (for further details, consult the manufacturers). In most homes, a completely illuminated ceiling is usually confined to the kitchen or bathroom. It is more usual in a reception room or living room to fit one or two panels of illumi-

58

OBTAINING THE POWER

1 After lifting a floorboard to gain access to the lighting circuit, mount a three-terminal junction box on a batten between the joists.

2 With the mains switched off, cut the lighting circuit and connect the two sets of cores to the junction box. Sleeve the earth core in green/yellow PVC.

3 Run a branch cable in 1.0mm² two core and earth cable to take power to a four-terminal junction box that should be sited nearer the lights.

4 Fit the box to a batten and run a switch cable and one or two power cables to the lights. Clip them neatly to the batten.

5 After sleeving the earths in PVC, connect all the cores to their respective terminals. Remember to flag the black switch core with red tape as it's live.

6 Finally replace the lid on the junction box and tighten it up, making sure that the cable insulation reaches right into the box.

Ready Reference

TYPES OF RECESSED LIGHTING

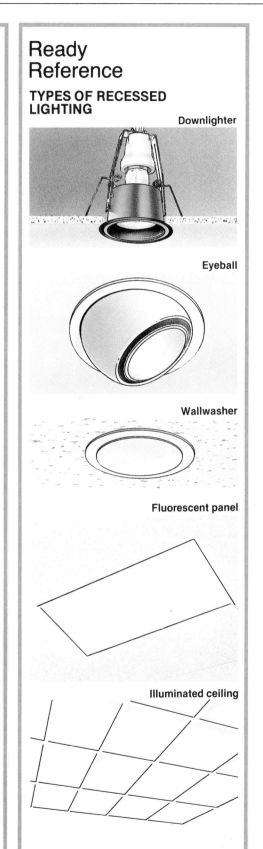

Downlighter

Eyeball

Wallwasher

Fluorescent panel

Illuminated ceiling

FITTING A DOWNLIGHTER IN A SUSPENDED CEILING

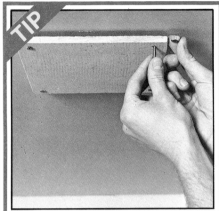

1 Fix a heat-resistant pad to your old ceiling before installing the new one. Use spacers to provide a gap so air can circulate.

2 You should drill a hole in the ceiling to check the new light won't be obstructed in any way. The whole section will eventually be cut out.

3 After checking with the manufacturer's instructions, you should mark on the ceiling the size of the hole required for the light.

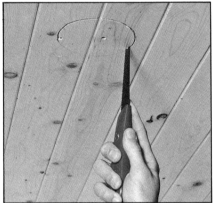

4 Drill a small hole just inside the circle and use a pad saw to cut it out. Don't worry if the edges are rough as the light trim will cover them.

5 Pull the mains cable through the hole. If it isn't heat-resistant, you should sleeve the individual cores with special heat-resistant sleeving.

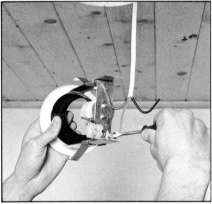

6 Make the connections before you recess the light. The earth can be sleeved in ordinary green/yellow PVC and then connected.

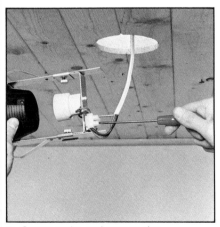

7 Connect the red core to the terminal that has brown flex linking it to the lampholder and the black to the one with blue flex.

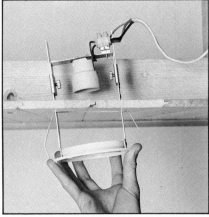

8 Remove the detachable trim and recess the light into the ceiling. Check that the butterfly clips are correctly positioned.

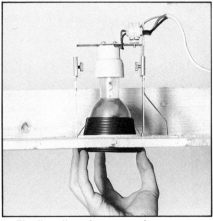

9 Finally adjust the cross piece so the lamp is at the correct level. Fit the detachable trim, screw in the lamp and test the light.

nated ceiling. This involves cutting away a small section of the existing ceiling and is an excellent way of supplementing a room lit by downlighters.

Installing a downlighter

Before buying downlighters to install in your home, it's a good idea to check the depth of the ceiling void where you want to fit them. A typical downlighter designed for domestic installation is about 170mm (6½in) deep and so can be readily accommodated in most ceiling voids. In fact, the depth of joist is not usually the limiting factor when you install a downlighter in the ceiling below the roof space; the real danger is the possibility of mechanical damage when the top of the fitting projects above the joists. There are two solutions to this problem: firstly, you could install a semi-recessed downlighter so the problem won't arise or, secondly, you could construct a box round the fitting to give it adequate protection (see Ready Reference). Having decided on the approximate position of your new downlighter, you should pierce a small hole in the ceiling to check that its position will be completely safe. Lift a floorboard in the room above, if you have access, so you can check that the light will clear the nearest joist and also that there are no cables or pipes obstructing it.

Once you've decided exactly where you want to fit your downlighter, you'll have to cut a hole in the ceiling to enable you to recess it. The size of hole needed varies between models, but it'll be made clear in the manufacturer's instructions.

Using a pair of compasses, mark the hole on the ceiling and then cut it out carefully with a pad saw. If your ceiling is merely plasterboard fixed to the joists, then you can simply cut through it and remove the section. However, if you've a lath-and-plaster ceiling then you should reinforce the ends of the lath after you've cut them. This is simply done, and requires you to fit a batten between the joists on either side of the hole and two battens between them to support the ends of the laths. You should then draw the power cable through the hole in the ceiling so you can make the connections before you actually recess the light itself. Because of the proximity of the lamp, it's a good idea to use heat-resistant cable, but if you can't obtain this at your local DIY or electrical shop, you can instead use heat-resistant sleeving round the individual cores.

Most downlighters have special terminal blocks which are connected to the lamp fitting at the time of manufacture, so the cable's red core should be connected to the terminal which has a brown flex leaving it and the black should go to the terminal with blue flex. You must remember to sleeve the earth core (ordinary green/yellow PVC will

be adequate) before connecting it to the earth terminal. You should then push the downlighter through the hole and adjust the butterfly clips at either side so it sits flush with the ceiling. But before fitting the lamp it's wise to adjust the position of the cross piece so you can have the lamp at whichever level you like best.

Internally silvered lamps direct most of the light and heat downwards and, therefore, out of the ceiling void. However, it is still advisable to fit a pad of heat-resistant material – a mineral fibre ceiling tile, for example – to the underside of the floorboards above. If you're fitting a downlighter in a suspended ceiling, then this pad is often not necessary. However, if you're fitting your lights at the same time as a suspended ceiling you can fit pads onto the original ceiling surface.

Obtaining the power

Connecting your new recessed lighting to the existing lighting circuitry poses no extra problems. However, there are a couple of options open to you. Provided your lights are to be installed close to where the main lighting circuit runs, you can simply break into it at a convenient point using a four-terminal junction box. All you then have to do is add an extra cable to take power to the lights and one to act as a switch feed and return. The wiring is not complicated and it's all done in 1.0mm² two-core and earth cable. But do remember to flag the black switch neutral core with red tape as it's really live.

Alternatively, if your lights are going to be fitted some way from the circuit, you could interrupt it with just a three-terminal junction box and run a spur cable to a four-terminal junction box sited near the new lights; that way you save yourself money on the cable runs. If you are fitting two downlighters, run a cable to each from the junction box – see step-by-step pictures on page 59.

If you are installing several downlighters you can loop the mains cable into and out of each light. All can still be controlled by one switch connected to the four-terminal junction box. But, remember, if you have a suspended ceiling you'll have to drill a hole in the original ceiling to let through the mains cable.

Fitting other recessed lights

Most small recessed lights are fitted in much the same way as downlighters. Both eyeball and wallwasher lights do not require as much depth but nevertheless it's still wise to check your joist size beforehand. If you want to fit a fluorescent panel in your ceiling, you'll have to cut out a section of ceiling plaster and fit battens between the joists to hold the light fittings. You should then replace the section of ceiling with a sheet of diffusing material and finish off the edges with plastic beading.

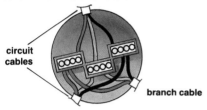
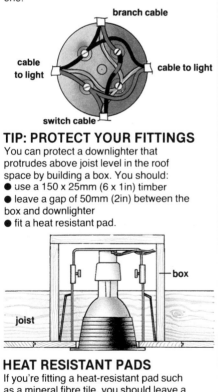

INSTALLING TRACK LIGHTING

Track lighting allows you plenty of scope in lighting your home. It's efficient, versatile and attractive and, what's more, extremely easy to install.

The time is bound to come when you want to alter the lighting in your home. You may want to highlight certain features, such as paintings, or merely provide yourself with extra light. You may want to change your wall lights or depart from the traditional concept of a ceiling rose and pendant light. In all these cases you should think about installing track lighting.

What is track lighting?

Track lighting consists of individual light fittings of various types that are mounted on special tracks fixed to ceilings or walls. This enables you to move the lights into whatever position you like and, in addition, to adjust them so their light is thrown in whichever direction you want.

The track itself is a metal casing, usually square or tubular in cross-section, that contains twin electrical conductors. These live and neutral conductors are bare and extend from one end of the track to the other. They function in much the same way as the conductor rails of an electric railway, with the light fittings instead of the trains picking up electric current from the live rails. The conductors are shielded from touch, while the lights are fitted with special adaptors for making contact with the conductors inside the track and which also serves to hold the lights in place.

Once the track has been fixed in position and the electrical connections made, then the adaptors are placed on to the track and the spotlights moved along to exactly where you want them. You can then lock them into position.

Obtaining the power supply for your track lighting is very simple. You're really faced with two options. On the one hand you can simply connect the 'live' end of the track to the existing ceiling rose, after removing the flex of the original lampholder, or you can run in an entirely new lighting circuit. For track lights mounted on the wall, power can be supplied either by an existing light circuit or the room's socket outlet circuit. The best method, however, is to wire the lights through a fused connection unit, as if it were a wall light linked to the power circuits.

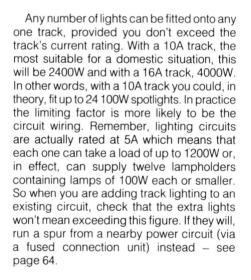

Track and fittings : Rotaflex

Any number of lights can be fitted onto any one track, provided you don't exceed the track's current rating. With a 10A track, the most suitable for a domestic situation, this will be 2400W and with a 16A track, 4000W. In other words, with a 10A track you could, in theory, fit up to 24 100W spotlights. In practice the limiting factor is more likely to be the circuit wiring. Remember, lighting circuits are actually rated at 5A which means that each one can take a load of up to 1200W or, in effect, can supply twelve lampholders containing lamps of 100W each or smaller. So when you are adding track lighting to an existing circuit, check that the extra lights won't mean exceeding this figure. If they will, run a spur from a nearby power circuit (via a fused connection unit) instead – see page 64.

Choosing your lighting track

Lighting track for commercial purposes comes in various standard lengths. The domestic variety usually only comes in two lengths, 1000mm (39in) or 1500mm (59in). Once you've decided on the approximate lengths of track that you'll need, visit your local stockist to see exactly what is available. When making your choice of track, it's a good idea to check what type of light fittings are available

with it and whether they'll meet your requirements. After all, the track itself is usually available in only a few finishes – white, brown, polished brass and polished silver are the commonest – while there are probably over a hundred different types of light fitting available. If you find that you can't get the exact length you require, don't worry; it can easily be cut to size with a hacksaw and if longer lengths are required, special connectors are available. And there are 90° angle connectors for when a track is required to turn a corner.

Choosing the lights

There are so many different types of fitting available that you're bound to find one that will suit the decor of your home and do the job you want it to. The number you fit on any one track will depend largely on what you want to light. As a rule, though, track lighting would prove expensive for just one or two fittings.

Installing the track

There are a number of ways of fixing the track to your ceiling or wall. It can be fixed almost flush to the surface with the help of small clips. Alternatively, you can use a special mounting canopy that will fit conveniently and neatly over an existing ceiling rose or

PREPARING THE CEILING

1 *Switch off the electricity supply at the mains and unscrew the existing ceiling rose cover. You can then remove the old pendant flex and lampholder.*

2 *Site the first surface clip so that the live end of the track will sit close to the power source. Make sure the clip has a secure fixing.*

3 *Measure the position of the second clip: with a 1m (39in) track it should be 600mm (2ft) away; with a 1.5m (5ft) track it should be 800mm (32in) away.*

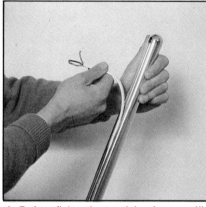

4 *Before fixing the track in place you'll have to free the flex. This is housed in a channel on the top side of the track and can be pulled clear.*

you can use mounting stems, which are merely short rods on backplates. You'll probably find that your lighting track will have a length of special flex already connected to its live end. This is likely to be the same length as the track. An advantage of these mounting methods is that in addition to providing a simple means for fitting the track itself, they help to conceal the track flex – so you won't have to cut it to length. The flex is fitted into a channel on the ceiling face of the track and you may well have to remove the shorter plastic end piece so you can free it. If you're going to use a mounting canopy and obtain power from an existing ceiling rose then the excess flex can be simply tucked into the canopy. Using surface clips will enable you to thread the flex up into the ceiling so that it can be neatly connected to a BESA box or a junction box. Only the mounting stems don't actually conceal the flex. But in their case all

you do is run the flex in its channel and leave only a short section exposed where it runs up to the ceiling rose or BESA box.

Before installing the lighting you'll have to finalise the position for the track on the ceiling or the wall. Ideally you should make sure that the mains outlet of your existing light coincides with the live end of the track. This could mean altering the position of the outlet, or even installing some new wiring, and if this is the case it should be done before you fix up the track.

Mounting track on the ceiling is perfectly straightforward but it will require solid fixings. It's best to use the joists, but if these don't coincide with the fixing holes drilled in the square cross-sectioned track you can easily drill some new holes in it to match your joist spacings. Alternatively, secure a piece of chipboard between the relevant joists and fix the track to this. Most mounting canopies

Ready Reference

MOUNTING METHODS

There are three methods of fixing lighting track to a ceiling:

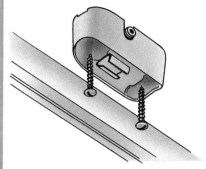

● surface clips – also suitable for use with wall-mounted track

● mounting canopies – designed to fit neatly over an existing ceiling rose and to also conceal any excess flex

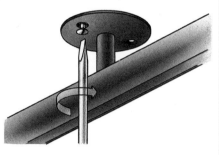

● mounting stems – also suitable for use with wall-mounted track.

TIP: USE A COVER PLATE

An existing BESA box and the connections within it can be neatly concealed by a cover plate with the surface clip fixed on top. You might well find that the mains outlet point is not immediately above where you want to position the lighting track. One solution is to use a cover plate and to run the connecting cable to the track in mini-trunking.

MAKING THE CONNECTIONS

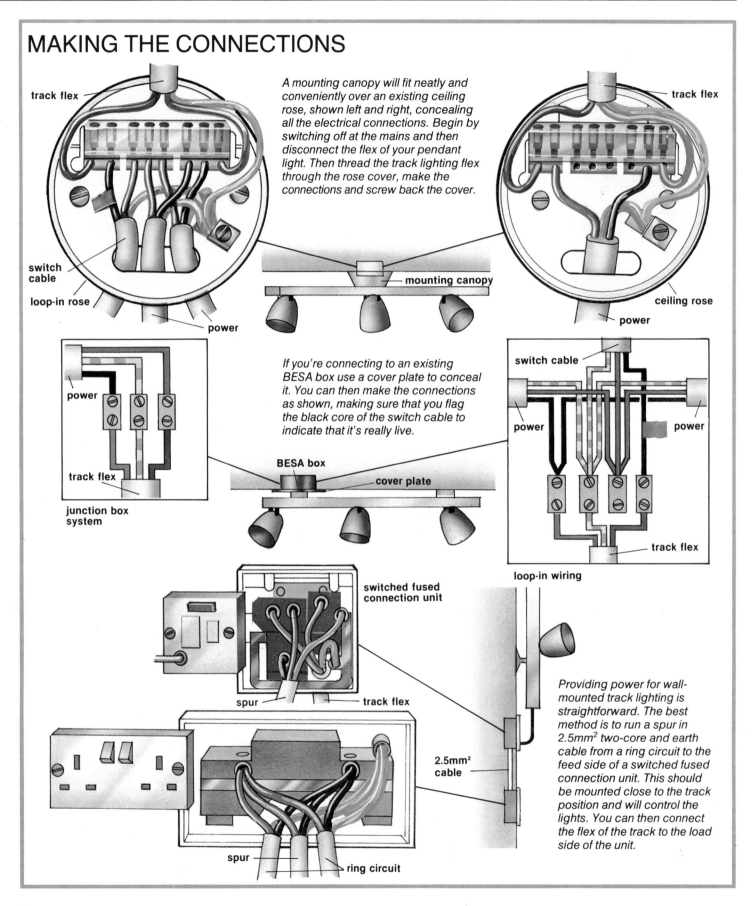

track flex

A mounting canopy will fit neatly and conveniently over an existing ceiling rose, shown left and right, concealing all the electrical connections. Begin by switching off at the mains and then disconnect the flex of your pendant light. Then thread the track lighting flex through the rose cover, make the connections and screw back the cover.

track flex

switch cable

loop-in rose

mounting canopy

ceiling rose

power

power

power

If you're connecting to an existing BESA box use a cover plate to conceal it. You can then make the connections as shown, making sure that you flag the black core of the switch cable to indicate that it's really live.

switch cable

power

power

track flex

junction box system

BESA box

cover plate

track flex

loop-in wiring

switched fused connection unit

spur

track flex

spur

ring circuit

2.5mm² cable

Providing power for wall-mounted track lighting is straightforward. The best method is to run a spur in 2.5mm² two-core and earth cable from a ring circuit to the feed side of a switched fused connection unit. This should be mounted close to the track position and will control the lights. You can then connect the flex of the track to the load side of the unit.

INSTALLING THE TRACK AND FITTINGS

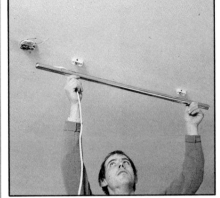

1 Offer up the track to the surface clips, making sure that it will be centrally positioned and that the clip grub screws are slackened.

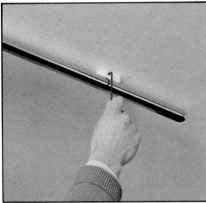

2 When you have the track precisely in position, secure it in place by tightening up the clip grub screws with the hexagonal key provided.

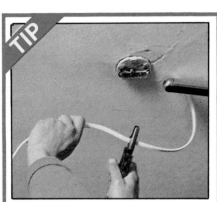

3 Before making the electrical connections, cut the flex to length. If you're using a mounting canopy, you can safely tuck the excess inside.

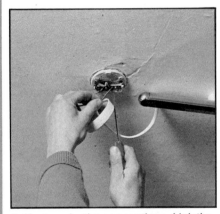

4 Next, make the connections. Link the brown core to the bank of live terminals, the blue core to the neutral bank and the green/yellow core to the earth terminal.

5 Most track lights are stepped on one side so you can't fit them incorrectly. Move the lever through 90° to retract the contacts and fixing levers.

6 Then fix the lights onto the track. Simply hold them in place, reposition the lever and lock the lights in the desired position on the track.

have fixing holes 51mm (2in) apart. In other words, the canopy will be able to fit over an existing rose, and the connection to the circuit can then be completely concealed. However, where the existing rose is old and has different spacings between its fixing holes you'll have to discard it and use an alternative method of connecting to the circuit.

This method involves fixing a BESA box flush with the surface of the ceiling. Inside the BESA box the flying leads of the lighting track are connected to the existing circuit wires with insulated cable connectors. The box itself has two screwed lugs that are spaced at 51mm (2in) centres, so the canopy will fit perfectly in place. If you're using stems, you'll find that the procedure is virtually the same although there could well be slight differences between the various systems currently on the market. Fixing track to walls is much the same as fixing it to the ceiling.

However, you'll probably find that you have to drill and plug the wall to get a really secure fixing, and you'll also have to cut a channel in the plaster to run in the cable unless your track reaches right up to the ceiling and the cable can be concealed within it.

Obtaining power for track lighting

One of the major advantages of track lighting is that it can often be connected to an existing lighting point without any alteration of the circuitry. However, new wiring will be necessary when there is no convenient lighting which can be used to supply the track; where the addition of track lighting is likely to overload the lighting circuit, and where track lighting is to be used in addition to the existing lighting. If you're going to have to run in a new circuit for the track you should use 1.0mm^2 two-core and earth cable rated at 5A. This will be able to supply power for up to 12

spotlights on three or four tracks. The circuit will be the same as an ordinary lighting circuit and you'll probably find it easiest to use junction boxes as each track will need to be controlled by a wall switch. That way you can use BESA boxes in which to make the connections to the track. For further details on running in a new circuit see Chapter 4 pages 72-75.

Track lighting fixed to the wall will be able to obtain its power supply from the existing lighting point if it is replacing wall lights. However, if you're mounting new lights then you're faced with two options. You can either break into the lighting circuit in the ceiling void above and run cable down to the track or you can break into the socket outlet circuit. In the latter case you should take a spur to a switched fused connection and then run 1.0mm^2 two-core and earth cable to the track itself.

TWO-WAY SWITCHING

In a room lit by a single pendant light, controlling that light from a single switch is no great hardship. But if the room contains wall lights it's useful to be able to control them from different parts of the room and that's exactly what two-way switching lets you do.

In most rooms, lights or groups of lights are controlled by just one switch. It's the standard set-up, and electricians call it one-way switching. However, there are situations where a one light, one switch arrangement isn't very convenient.

Take the light over a flight of stairs as an example. Having the light switch at the bottom of the flight is fine if you want to go upstairs. You can turn on the light before you go up without difficulty. But what happens when you reach the top? You can't turn the light off again. And suppose you want to come downstairs and the light is turned off? You can't switch it on without negotiating the stairs in the dark, which rather defeats the object of having a light there at all.

Obviously, what's needed is another switch at the top of the stairs and a system of wiring that allows either switch to turn the light on and off independently of the other. This system is called two-way switching.

Where it can be used

The example of the light above the stairs is such a common one that providing two-way switching for stair lights is now more or less standard procedure. There are, however, many other situations where two-way switching may be useful.

Think of the advantages of having a switch at both ends of a long hallway. And what about rooms with more than one entrance? It makes sense to have a switch beside each of the doors. The same applies to a garage with a side door in addition to the main one.

There are also situations where two-way switching is not vital but still worth considering. For example, where you have installed wall-mounted bedside reading lamps: it is a great advantage when you can control these from the door, as well as from a switch by the bed. You might also want to install a two-way switch for the main bedroom light so you can turn it on and off without getting out of bed.

And don't forget the hall light: in many homes this is one-way switched despite the fact that it often serves as a stair light by illuminating the bottom steps of the staircase as well as the hall itself. It's all too easy to go upstairs having forgotten to switch it off.

How it works

The key to two-way switching lies in using a special switch at both switching positions.

An ordinary one-way switch has two terminals and when you operate it you either make or break the electrical connection between them. For the current to reach the lightbulb and make it work, it must pass down one of the cores in the switch-drop cable, and back up the other. Making or breaking the link between terminals also makes or breaks the link between the two cores and therefore switches the light on or off.

A two-way switch works in a completely different way. It has three terminals, marked 'Common', L1, and L2, and when you operate it, flicking the switch one way provides a link between L1 and Common; flicking it the other way provides a link between Common and L2. If you link the terminals of two two-way switches in a certain way, then one switch can complete the circuit (and turn the light on) while the other can over-ride it and turn the light off again. The reverse also applies.

So, what is this remarkable wiring arrangement? Well, in its traditional form – the one normally illustrated in text-book wiring diagrams – the switches are linked with a pair of single-core cables called straps. Each joins the L1 terminal in one switch to the L2 terminal in the other. The switch drop from the light is

Ready Reference

SWITCHING SYSTEMS

A switch is able to turn a light on or off by completing or breaking a circuit. The one-way switching system, where the light is controlled by a single switch, is the usual system, but the two-way switching system, when two special switches are linked, allows you to control your light from two switches that are independent of each other.

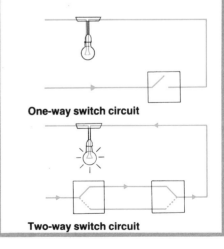

One-way switch circuit

Two-way switch circuit

THE THEORY OF TWO-WAY SWITCHING

How a two-way switching circuit works can be seen in the way in which the switches are linked and how the power flows between them.

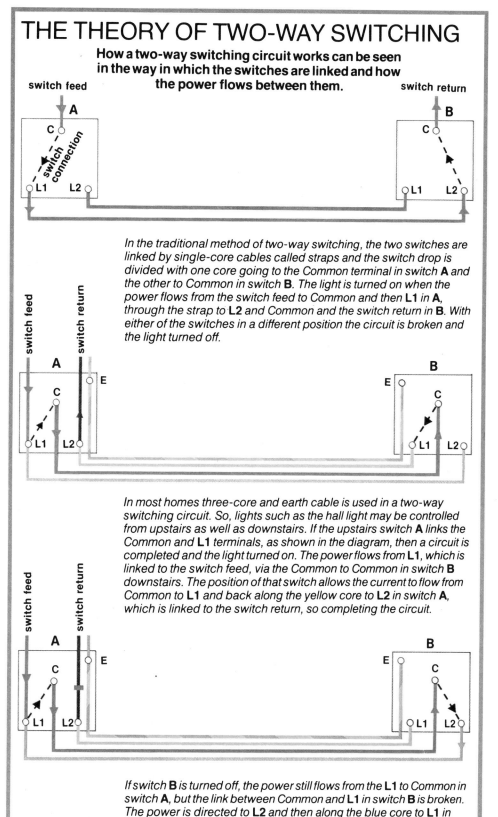

In the traditional method of two-way switching, the two switches are linked by single-core cables called straps and the switch drop is divided with one core going to the Common terminal in switch A and the other to Common in switch B. The light is turned on when the power flows from the switch feed to Common and then L1 in A, through the strap to L2 and Common and the switch return in B. With either of the switches in a different position the circuit is broken and the light turned off.

In most homes three-core and earth cable is used in a two-way switching circuit. So, lights such as the hall light may be controlled from upstairs as well as downstairs. If the upstairs switch A links the Common and L1 terminals, as shown in the diagram, then a circuit is completed and the light turned on. The power flows from L1, which is linked to the switch feed, via the Common to Common in switch B downstairs. The position of that switch allows the current to flow from Common to L1 and back along the yellow core to L2 in switch A, which is linked to the switch return, so completing the circuit.

If switch B is turned off, the power still flows from the L1 to Common in switch A, but the link between Common and L1 in switch B is broken. The power is directed to L2 and then along the blue core to L1 in switch A. This leaves the power 'shunting' between the switches but doesn't allow a circuit to be completed so the light is off.

then divided in two: the first core goes to the Common terminal in one switch, the second to the Common terminal in the other. It's all run in single-core cable, and is designed for use where your home's wiring is run entirely in conduit – as it may well be if you live in a flat.

In most homes, though, the wiring takes the form of multi-cored PVC-sheathed cables, and in this case, a different two-way switching circuit is generally more convenient. What happens is that the switch drop, run in two-core and earth cable, is connected to only one of the two-way switches: one core to L1, the other to L2. This switch is then linked to its partner with three-core and earth cable, a cable which has rather oddly colour-coded wires – one red, one yellow, and one blue. However, this doesn't make the wiring up any more complicated. The yellow and blue cores are connected in the same way as the straps in the traditional system, and the red core is used to link the two Common terminals.

Converting an existing switch

That's the theory, but how does it work in practice? How do you convert an existing one-way switching circuit to two-way switching? You may be surprised at just how simple it is. Using a club hammer and cold chisel, make a hole in the wall to take a one-gang, plaster-depth mounting box at the spot where you want the new switch to go. This should be secured to the wall with a couple of screws and wallplugs.

Then, before running a length of 1.0 or 1.5mm² three-core and earth PVC-sheathed cable to the original switch position, connect up the new switch in order to minimise the time the power has to be switched off at the mains. The red core should go to the Common terminal with the yellow and blue cores acting as strap wires. The running of the cable shouldn't pose any difficulty. The cable is taken up the wall, above the ceiling and back down the wall to the old switch.

Chop a channel in the plaster at the wall sections of the run, insert a length of PVC conduit and pass the cable through that. Above the ceiling, if the cable runs at right angles to the joists, feed it through holes drilled at least 50mm below their top edge.

If the cable runs parallel to the joists, simply rest it on top of the ceiling, unless it is likely to be disturbed – as in a loft, for example. In that case it must be secured to the sides of the joists with cable clips. Turn off the power at the mains before removing the fixing screws. Then, ease the original switch from the wall so you can pass the cable into the mounting box.

With the cable in position, all that remains to be done is connect it up to the new two-way switch at the original switch position. Finally, connect the two cores of the switch drop to terminals L1 and L2, screw the switch securely to its mounting box and restore the power.

CHANGING THE DOOR SWITCH

1 Turn off the power at the mains and remove the screws in the old switch's faceplate. Ease the switch from the wall until you can disconnect it.

2 Run one three-core and earth cable per light from the RB4 box to the switch mounting box, using an existing conduit to carry it down the wall.

3 For two wall lights, install a three-gang, two-way switch. Use two gangs to connect the three-core cables – yellow to L1, blue to L2 and red to Common.

FITTING THE BEDSIDE SWITCHES

1 Using a club hammer and bolster chisel, chop a channel in the wall from the ceiling down to the new switch position ready for the cable.

2 Mark the exact position of the switch on the wall, then chop out a recess, taking care to ensure that it is deep enough to take the metal mounting box.

3 Before running the cable, insert a length of PVC conduit into the channel; where possible poke it through into the void above the ceiling.

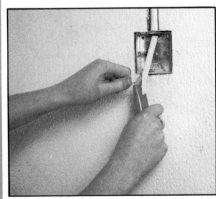

5 Strip the ends of the three-core and earth cable from the RB4 ready for connection, remembering to fit the earth wires with green and yellow sleeving.

6 Next connect the cable to a one-gang, two-way switch, linking the yellow core to the L1 terminal, the blue core to L2 and the red core to Common.

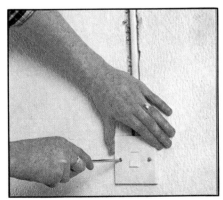

7 Having connected the earth core to the terminal on the mounting box, screw the new switch securely into place and check that it is level.

4 *Connect the switch drop from the room's main light to the third gang to give one-way switching. One core goes to L2, the other to Common.*

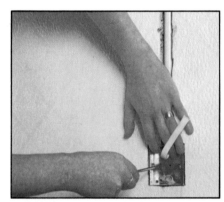

4 *At the second switch position of each light, use screws and wallplugs to fix a one-gang, plaster-depth mounting box in a hole cut into the wall.*

8 *Finally, join up all the cables in the RB4 junction box. It's much easier than it looks and the connections can be seen in detail on page 70.*

New circuits

The same system can also be employed in new work where you require two-way switching. For example, if you are installing a new wall light and want to be able to control it from a switch at the door of the room, as well as from a switch near the light itself, all you need to do is install the light and a new two-way switch in the normal way (see Chapter 2 pages 23-26) and then run a length of three-core and earth cable from this switch to the switch by the door (the one controlling the room's main light). Here, you replace the old one-gang, one-way switch with a two-gang, two-way switch and connect the three-core and earth cable to one gang for two-way switching. Then connect the switch drop belonging to the room's main light to the other gang, this time connecting it up for one-way switching with one of the cores going to the L2 terminal and the other to the Common.

This method is quite straightforward, but it is not necessarily the most convenient way of setting about the job. Suppose you were installing not one new wall light, but two or more. If they are all to have two-way switches then you'll be involved in a great deal of cable running and, therefore, a great deal of work. After all, for each light you have to run a cable down to the new switch, back up above the ceiling, then back down the wall again to the second switch position.

This extra work can be avoided by using a junction box and a variation on the traditional two-way switching circuit. You run the circuit using three-core and earth PVC-sheathed and insulated cable. Doing this you are using the cable's red core as one half of the switch drop and the yellow and blue cores as straps. Then connect them up, together with the cables to the wall lights and the cable supplying the new circuit with power (taken from a loop-in ceiling rose, or from a junction box inserted into one of your home's main lighting circuits) in a large multi-terminal joint box called an RB4. The step-by-step photographs will explain what is happening but note that only one cable need be run to each wall-light.

Intermediate switching

There is one other kind of two-way switching that could be useful in your home. It's called an intermediate switching circuit and it means that a light or group of lights can be controlled by three or more separate switches.It's easy to install because all you do is introduce one or more additional switches into the circuit between the two two-way switches. This can, of course, be very convenient because you can then control a light from as many positions as you like. For example, you could control a hall light from a switch near the front door, from one near the living room door and from another switch on the landing upstairs.

There are two ways of carrying out the wiring but with both methods a special switch called an intermediate switch is needed. This has four terminals: two marked L1 and two marked L2. To install an intermediate switch in a two-way switching circuit all you do is use the switch to interrupt the three-core and earth cable – or the strap wires in a traditional circuit that has been installed in a flat or where the cables are all run in conduit.

The cores from the L1 terminals and L2 terminals in one two-way switch go to the L1 terminals on one side of the intermediate switch and the L1 and L2 cores from the second two-way switch go to the L2

terminals on the other side. However, with a three-core and earth circuit this leaves a break in the core linking the two-way switches' Common terminals. One way of solving this problem is to join the ends of the two cores with a cable connector. Once the two red cores have been joined the connector unit is then placed in the space behind the intermediate switch. However, it's better to interrupt the three-core and earth cable with a multi-terminal junction box above the ceiling near the intermediate switch position. You need six terminals in the junction box: one for the earth cores, one for both the red cores from the Common terminals and one each for the remaining

yellow and blue cores.

At this stage you should introduce two lengths of two-core and earth cable which, by connecting up to the appropriate terminals, are used to extend the yellow and blue cores from each two-way switch. When that's done, run the two two-core and earth cables down to the intermediate switch and connect them up just as if they were the two pairs of yellow and blue cores in the three-core and earth cable. It is worth remembering that if one of the switches in an intermediate circuit is to be cord-operated then it should be one of the end switches. There are no cord-operated intermediate switches available.

INSTALLING A NEW TWO-WAY CIRCUIT

Using an RB4 multi-terminal junction box can save you running extra cable when you install a new two-way circuit with more than one light. Here it has been used to install a bedside lighting circuit, shown diagramatically. Page 68 shows how the circuit is wired up, step by step.

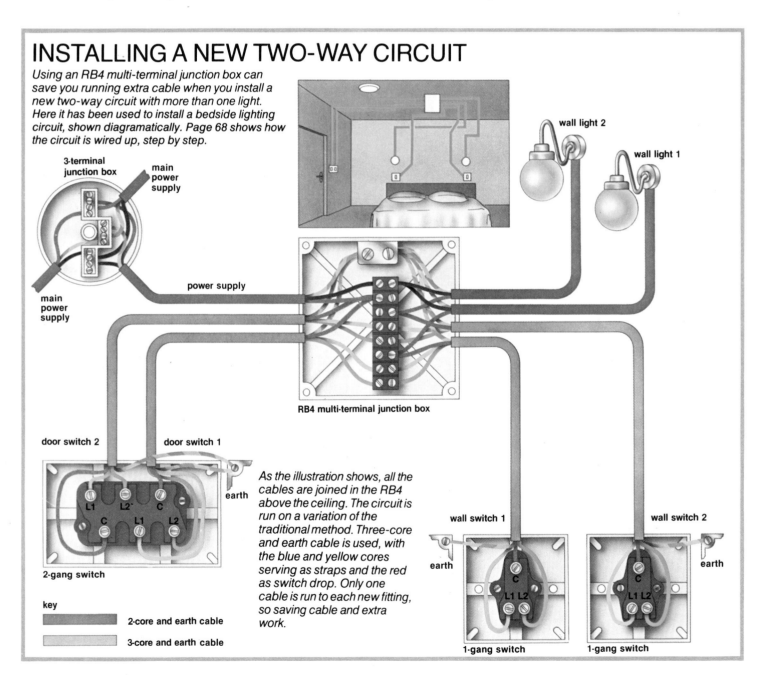

3-terminal junction box

main power supply

main power supply

power supply

wall light 2

wall light 1

RB4 multi-terminal junction box

door switch 2   door switch 1

earth

L1   L2   C
C   L1   L2

2-gang switch

As the illustration shows, all the cables are joined in the RB4 above the ceiling. The circuit is run on a variation of the traditional method. Three-core and earth cable is used, with the blue and yellow cores serving as straps and the red as switch drop. Only one cable is run to each new fitting, so saving cable and extra work.

wall switch 1

earth

C
L1 L2

1-gang switch

wall switch 2

earth

C
L1 L2

1-gang switch

key

▬▬▬	2-core and earth cable
▭▭▭	3-core and earth cable

CHAPTER 4

POWER CIRCUITS

With a never-ending stream of apparently indispensable electrical
appliances reaching the high street, the demand on your home's
power circuits seems set to grow and grow. Making provision for
an adequate number of power points in every room makes it much
easier – and safer – to use appliances wherever they are wanted.

ADDING NEW RADIAL CIRCUITS

A radial circuit can provide power for individual appliances such as cookers, immersion heaters and freezers, or can give you extra socket outlets for plug-in equipment. It's an easy job to install one.

switchfuse unit from Wholesale Fittings Co

Radial circuits have only one cable running from the consumer unit (fuse box) to the power outlet because the circuit terminates at the last outlet. In this way they differ from the more common ring circuit as their cable doesn't have to return to the consumer unit. Installing one can therefore save you both cable and extra work (see Chapter 1).

Before ring circuits were introduced the radial circuit was the standard domestic power circuit. There were fewer sockets and electrical appliances to be supplied than nowadays and a number of radial circuits each supplying an individual outlet usually proved adequate. As more and more electrical appliances came on the market, so the ring circuit was developed to cope with the greater current demands in the modern home. Nowadays, the ring circuit is the more common power circuit.

However, a new radial circuit is especially useful when you want to fit extra fixed electrical appliances such as a deep freeze or immersion heater, supply a couple of new sockets or else provide power for an extension to your home. That way you don't have to run spurs from an existing ring circuit and you avoid the possibility of overloading that circuit through heavy demand.

Types of radial circuits

There are two basic types of radial circuit. These are the 'solo' circuit, which provides power to one fixed appliance such as an immersion heater, cooker or freezer, and the power circuit which can help out a ring circuit or provide power to new sockets and appliances. The second type is itself divided into two kinds. The first is the 20A circuit. This uses 2.5mm^2 cable and can supply an unlimited number of 13A socket outlets (or fixed appliances using up to 3kW of power) – provided they are all within a floor area of 20 sq m (about 215 sq ft). The second type is the 30A radial circuit, which uses 4.0mm^2 cable and can carry power to a floor area up to 50 sq m (540 sq ft). If you look round your home you will see that these restrictions

POWER SUPPLY FOR RADIAL CIRCUITS.

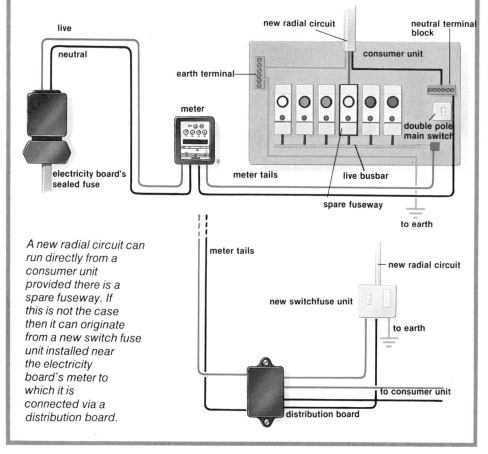

A new radial circuit can run directly from a consumer unit provided there is a spare fuseway. If this is not the case then it can originate from a new switch fuse unit installed near the electricity board's meter to which it is connected via a distribution board.

USING A SPARE FUSEWAY

1 *After you've had the mains supply cut off, remove the consumer unit cover, lift the mounting plate forward and remove the live busbar.*

2 *Slide the units along the busbar to make space for the new MCB or fuse. Remember to arrange the units in the correct current rating sequence.*

3 *Fit the new MCB unit onto the mounting plate, making sure that it's in the right place. Then screw back the live busbar underneath the units.*

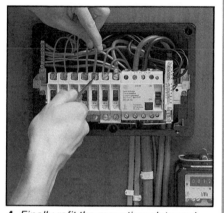

4 *Finally refit the mounting plate and connect the cable to the correct terminals. Get the electricity board to reconnect and test the circuit.*

mean that several radial circuits would have to be installed to supply power to all the sockets and appliances supplied by a normal ring circuit. So radial circuits really come into their own when you want to supply power to fixed appliances. And radial circuits can be modified to cope with heavy demand. So, if you want to have a large cooker you will probably have to run a radial circuit that has been 'beefed' up and will use a 45A fuse and 6.0 or 10.0mm² cable.

Obtaining the power

If you want to install a new radial circuit you'll need a circuit fuseway. First check whether you have a spare (unconnected) one in the consumer unit. If so, check its current rating (see below). If not, you'll have to install a new main switch and fuse unit near the consumer unit and connect it separately. If you have to do this then it might be an idea to install one

with two or more fuseways to save work if you are planning any future extension to your domestic wiring. If you decide to do this it is a good idea to blank off the fuseway you are not using or else fit another MCB or fuse unit without connecting it. Whatever you do, before inspecting or working on the consumer unit you must turn off the main switch.

If there is a spare fuseway it may well be sealed off with a blanking plate or else there might be a fuse unit or MCB without any circuit connections. If you use offpeak electricity for heating then you will have two consumer units and it's very important to make sure that you use the correct one. The unit supplying the night storage heaters will be on a restricted time switch and if you connect to that, you will only get power to your circuit at night (not a very good idea if it is supplying a freezer, for example).

Ready Reference

WHAT ARE RADIAL CIRCUITS?

Radial circuits were the original domestic power circuit, starting at the consumer unit (fuse box) and terminating at the last socket.

Nowadays ring circuits supply most domestic appliances. Radial circuits supply either fixed appliances, such as a cooker:

or a number of sockets.

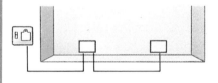

They are very useful for providing power to an extension to your home or supplementing a ring circuit.

CONNECTING THE MAINS

You can connect to a spare fuseway in the consumer unit or else fit a new switchfuse unit. Your fuse must have the same current rating as the new circuit. Modern fuses have a colour coding.

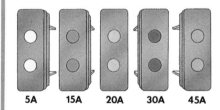

| 5A | 15A | 20A | 30A | 45A |

If you have to buy a new fuse, get a cartridge type. These are safer, more effective and it is impossible to fit the wrong sort.

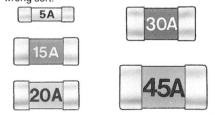

consumer unit and meter from Mk

USING A NEW SWITCHFUSE UNIT

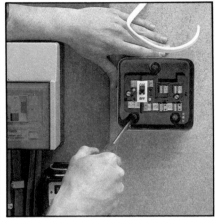

1 The new switchfuse unit should be mounted on a sheet of non-combustible material such as fire-resistant chipboard.

2 Knock out a panel at the top of the new unit and fix a protective grommet before running in the new circuit cable and making the connections.

3 You will have to use extra single core cable (6.0mm²) to connect the unit to the distribution board as you are allowed only two tails to the meter.

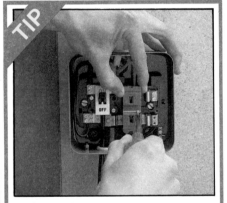

4 Screw on the colour-coded shields for the new MCBs. It's an idea to fit a new unit with a spare fuseway for an extra circuit in the future.

5 Fit the cover over the unit and then slot in the new MCBs or fuse unit. You can fit a blanking plate until you decide to use the spare fuseway.

6 Screw on the smaller shield to protect the new MCBs. Remember, you'll probably have to knock out its lid to allow access to the MCBs.

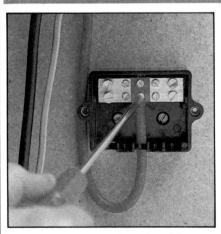

7 Fix the distribution board and then connect the live core from the switchfuse unit and the live meter tail to the live terminal block.

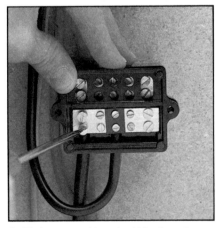

8 Fit the neutral terminal block and base plate which hold the live block in place, and then connect the remaining neutral cores to the block.

9 Connect the earths and then get the electricity board to connect the old meter tails to the distribution board and the new tails to the meter.

Using a spare fuseway

If you are connecting to a spare fuseway, you must check that it has the equivalent current rating to the circuit running from it. Most modern fuses have two spots on their cases to indicate their current rating: white indicates a 5A rating; blue 15A; yellow 20A; red 30A and green 45A. If it's not the correct rating for the circuit you're installing, you'll have to insert a new one. There is the chance that your consumer unit is so old that it could be obsolete. In that case, if you have a spare fuseway in it you will be able to use it only for a new circuit that has the equivalent current rating. Circuit fuses are either the rewirable type or the cartridge type and when buying a new one it is best to get the latter as they are safer and more effective.

The new radial circuit starts at the fuse unit and runs in two-core and earth PVC-sheathed cable, the size of which is determined by the circuit's current rating. A 5A circuit should be run in 1.0mm² cable, 15A in 1.5mm², 20A in 2.5mm² and 30A in 4.0mm² (the 30A circuit fuse must be a cartridge type or an MCB, not a rewirable one). Any circuit with a higher rating should be run in 6.0mm² or 10.0mm² cable.

For detailed advice on how to run cable under floors, in ceiling voids and down walls (see Chapter 2 pages 31-35). Where you are using larger cable for a beefed up circuit, it might be a good idea to measure fairly precisely the length of the cable required as the larger the cable, the more expensive it is. Allow sufficient for connecting the cable within the consumer unit and in the mains outlet, plus extra for contingencies such as hidden obstructions. The choice of mains outlet depends upon its situation and the appliance supplied. For example, a 13A socket is fine for any appliance up to 3kW, but cannot be used in the bathroom where the only socket permitted is one for a shaver. An immersion heater with a dual element, say, should have a 20A dual switch as its outlet. More information on all these can be found in other sections.

Connecting to the spare fuseway

The spare fuseway in the consumer unit will usually be at the end of the row of units and furthest away from the main switch. Units should be placed in the correct rating sequence, with those of the largest current rating (45A) next to the mainswitch, and those of the lowest, (5A) at the other end. The new circuit should be located in sequence, and this might well entail moving the units. With some boxes the fuses slide along a 'top hat' bar after the screws have been released, and in others, the units are simply removed and refixed in their new positions. Turning off the main switch renders all live parts dead, but in some units, where the

mains terminals (to which the meter leads connect) are not recessed, there is still a shock risk even if those main terminals are shrouded. So, in addition to turning off the main switch, it is sometimes advisable to get the electricity board to cut off the mains supply before you work on the consumer unit. Then, when they restore the power, you can ask them to test the new circuit. After you've rearranged the fuse units, thread in the circuit cable and strip off the outer sleeving, leaving about 25mm (1in) within the unit. Trim the cores by stripping off 10mm (⅜in) of insulation, and connect the red core to the fuseway terminal of the new unit and the black to the neutral terminal block. The earth should be sleeved in green and yellow PVC and connected to the earth terminal block. The cable can now be run to the circuit outlet, but remember, it is best to complete all the work at the outlet end of the circuit before connecting up. That way power is off for the shortest possible time and causes least inconvenience.

Unless there is plenty of room on your backing board you will have to fit a sheet of non-combustible material, such as treated chipboard, to your wall to provide a base for the unit and prevent fire risk.

Installing a switchfuse unit

After choosing a switchfuse unit containing an MCB or cartridge fuse of the same current rating as the new circuit, fix it to the wall using No 8 wood screws with wall plugs. The unit should be sited close to the electricity board's meter so that the meter leads bringing power to the new unit are as short as possible. When the electricity board come to connect the new meter leads they might well require a distribution board to be fitted so that the power coming through the meter can be divided up and fed to both units. For the mains leads use 16mm² single core PVC-sheathed cable – one red and one black. They should be connected to the live and neutral terminals of the unit respectively, and you should use 6.0mm² green-and-yellow-sheathed cable for the connection to the earth terminal.

Sections of thin plastic will have to be knocked out to admit these cables and a blank will also have to removed at the top of the unit to allow for the entry of the circuit cable. It's a good idea to connect this cable before fitting the unit to the wall. Connect the red core of the circuit cable to the fuseway terminal, the black to the upper neutral terminal and the sleeved earth conductor to the earth terminal. If you are using a fuseway and an MCB, double-check that you have the correct one and then replace the cover. Finally, call the electricity board to connect the meter leads to the mains and test the circuit.

INSTALLING AN RCCB

A residual-current circuit breaker (RCCB) will protect your home from the risk of electrical fires and its occupants from the danger of electric shocks. It's comparatively easy to add one to your existing installation, to protect some or all of the house's circuits.

A residual current circuit breaker is a form of double-pole on/off switch that automatically cuts out (switches itself off) when there is a leakage of electric current to earth from a circuit or from an appliance plugged into the mains. There are two types in use. The residual current circuit breaker (RCCB), formerly called a current-operated ELCB, is now the only type fitted in new installations. The other type is the voltage-operated ELCB, which is now obsolete but still found on older systems.

Voltage-operated ELCBs
With the voltage-operated type, earth-leakage current from the circuit or appliance flows through the earth conductor into a trip coil, and provided the coil is energised at about 40 volts it operates and cuts off the current. Before the cut-out operates, earth-leakage current flows to earth via an earth connection; this is normally a copper-sheathed steel rod driven into the ground outside the house. An earth conductor links the consumer unit to the ELCB and the ELCB to the rod – see *Ready Reference*.

In fact, the earth-leakage current does not necessarily all pass through the trip coil of the ELCB, but may follow a parallel path via the water or gas mains. Deprived of adequate energy to trip the coil, the ELCB does not operate and unearthed metalwork can remain 'live' and dangerous to touch.

What is more, a voltage-operated ELCB may trip for no obvious reason – a fault in a neighbour's installation has been known to cause tripping, usually because earth rods are too close together. So although voltage-operated ELCBs have been fitted extensively in home installations when an electricity board is unable to provide conventional methods of earthing, there has been a growing tendency to fit residual current types instead.

Residual current circuit breakers
Residual current circuit breakers work on the principle that there is normally a balance between the current flowing into the circuit on the live pole and the current returning to the system via the neutral pole. When an earth-leakage fault occurs, the earth-leakage current is lost to the system via the earth conductor and the amount of current returning via the neutral pole is that much less. The current flowing through the RCCB is therefore out of balance. This out-of-balance current causes a trip coil to be energised and cuts off the current to the circuit.

There are no direct connections of the earth conductors to the RCCB in this case; none are needed, as the circuit current operates the RCCB. The earth conductor from the consumer unit goes directly to the terminal clamp on the earth rod – see *Ready Reference* again.

A snag with residual current devices had been that early models were not very sensitive. If the earth resistance was high, the earth rod was unable to pass sufficient earth-leakage current to trip the RCCB. The standard 60 amp version needed an earth-leakage current of 0.5 amp to trip it and the 100 amp version required 1 amp. The usual practice was to fit a residual current circuit breaker where the soil resistance as measured by the electricity board was no more than 40 ohms, and to fit a voltage-operated ELCB where the electricity board's test showed the soil resistance to be 40 ohms or more. There are numerous voltage-operated ELCBs still in use, and also many of the old type current-operated ones, but the situation is now changing.

Modern current-operated devices
The modern current-operated residual current circuit breaker (RCCB) is of the high-sensitivity type. Some models are used to protect individual socket outlets or appliances and power tools, or circuits supplying socket outlets only. Those used to protect the whole installation usually have a trip current rating of 100mA (milliamps). Those used to protect individual socket outlets have a trip current rating of only 30mA. Some special versions designed for use in hospitals have a trip current rating as low as 10mA, which is too sensitive for general domestic use.

You can buy a consumer unit fitted with a residual current circuit breaker, or you can add one to your existing installation and retain the present consumer unit fitted with a double-pole isolating main switch.

Replacing the consumer unit
If you install a new consumer unit fitted with an RCCB you simply have it connected to the mains by the electricity board, using the appropriate size and type of meter leads and the correct earth conductor.

The RCCB fitted to a consumer unit is made in various current ratings up to 100 amps, and the trip ratings are from 30mA upwards. As the RCCB will trip whenever a live/earth fault occurs, it is wise to choose one having a trip current rating of 100mA. One of this rating is unlikely to be subjected

ADDING AN RCCB AT THE FUSEBOX

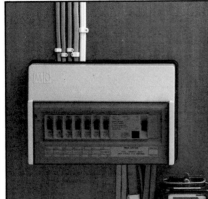

1 *If you're installing a new consumer unit, choose one that's big enough to incorporate an RCCB as well as enough fuseways for all your circuits.*

2 *Alternatively, you can install an RCCB near to the existing consumer unit, in its own enclosure. Screw the baseplate in place and clip on the RCCB itself.*

3 *Connect new live and neutral meter tails to one pair of terminals. They should be long enough to reach to the main terminals on the consumer unit.*

4 *Call in the electricity board to disconnect the existing meter tails, link them to the RCCB and reconnect the consumer unit. Then fit the cover.*

Ready Reference

WIRING UP AN RCCB
When an RCCB is installed between the electricity meter and the consumer unit, the electricity board must be notified first so they can remove the main service fuse and disconnect the meter tails.

The actual connections are extremely simple, and are made using meter tails of the appropriate size – usually 16mm^2.

● with the older voltage-operated type, the connections look like this:

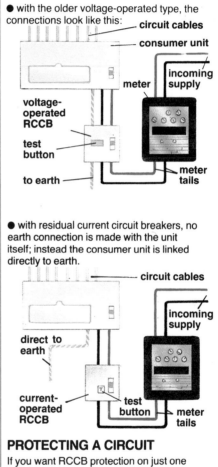

● with residual current circuit breakers, no earth connection is made with the unit itself; instead the consumer unit is linked directly to earth.

PROTECTING A CIRCUIT
If you want RCCB protection on just one circuit, the device is wired into the circuit cable close to the consumer unit. The earth conductors are linked via an external connector block to ensure earth continuity.

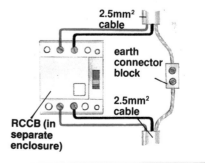

---

to 'nuisance' tripping that could cut off all lighting and power circuits.

Although the 100mA version does not give the same level of personal protection as does one of 30mA trip rating, the manufacturers have stated that no cases of electrocution have occurred where the 100mA version is fitted.

Adding an RCCB to an installation
Where the new RCCB is added to the installation and the existing consumer unit with its double-pole mainswitch is retained, the RCCB is connected into the meter leads between the consumer unit and the board's meter. To make the connection it is first necessary to ask the electricity board to remove its service fuse while the connections are made. Then the leads from the consumer unit are run into the RCCB and another pair are linked to the RCCB for the

board to connect to its meter.

The meter leads are usually 16mm^2 single-core circular PVC-sheathed cable, colour-coded red for the live conductor, black for the neutral conductor, plus green/yellow striped cable for the earth conductor. The size required for the earth conductor is usually 6mm^2, but the board may require a larger size. The board may also require the meter leads to be 25mm^2 so it is best to check with them before starting the work.

Protecting socket outlets
One or more 13A socket outlets can be protected by an RCCB by inserting one into the appropriate circuit. The circuit can be a radial or ring circuit and the RCCB is connected to the appropriate fuseway of the consumer unit – see *Ready Reference*.

The new RCCB used should be of 40A current rating with a trip current rating of

USING SOCKETS AND PLUG-IN RCCBS

1 You can fit a combined socket outlet and RCCB in place of an existing double socket outlet. Isolate the circuit, undo the faceplate and disconnect the cables.

2 Fit a deeper box if necessary to accept the unit. Then connect the cable cores to the three terminals on the back of the new RCCB socket faceplate.

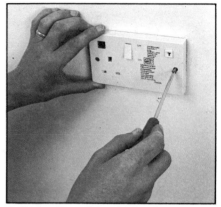

3 Screw the unit back into place over the mounting box. Then plug in an appliance, switch on and test the unit, following the manufacturer's instructions.

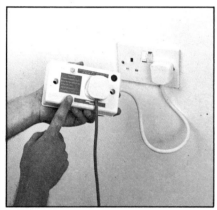

4 An alternative to the wired-in RCCB socket is this self-contained unit. Simply plug it in to any socket outlet, then plug in the appliance and test.

5 For high-risk appliances such as lawnmowers and hedgetrimmers, fit a plug-in RCCB. This is simply connected to the flex in place of the plug.

6 If this type of RCCB trips while the appliance is being used, it cannot be reset until the plug is removed from the socket, as the button is concealed.

30mA. All socket outlets on the circuit will be protected by the RCCB and users of any appliances and tools run off them will be protected from the risk of electrocution.

Socket-outlet RCCBs

One of the latest developments is a combined 13A socket outlet and RCCB. Its purpose is to meet the requirements of the 15th edition of the IEE Wiring Regulations; a new socket outlet (whether installed inside or outside the house) that will supply a power tool or appliance used out of doors must be RCCB-protected. The version having a tripping current rating of 30mA is chosen, for experience has shown that a current of 30mA passing through the human body for a period of up to 30 milli-seconds is unlikely to cause a fatal shock to the normally healthy person.

Some combined 13A socket outlets and RCCBs will fit a standard 2-gang socket box,

flush or surface-mounted. The unit has an on/off switch, and a test button and neon indicator. The new socket can either replace an existing double 13A socket outlet or a spur of 2.5mm² two-core and earth cable can be run from a ring circuit socket outlet to the new protected socket.

Plug-in RCCBs

There is also available an RCCB which plugs into any 13A socket outlet and has an integral 13A socket for plugging in a power tool or appliance, but the latest and most portable RCCB is one made in the form of a 13A fused plug that will fit any 13A socket outlet. The cover is removed and the appliance flex is connected to a readily accessible terminal block. On the outside face of the plug is a test button. If this is pressed, or if the RCCB trips due to a fault, it is necessary to remove the plug from its socket and press a reset button.

Many people believe that a double-insulated tool such as a lawnmower or hedge-trimmer fitted with two-core flex needs no RCCB, and that if one is fitted it will not operate since there is no means of current leaking to earth. This is not so, for the double-insulated tool needs RCCB protection at least as much as an earthed tool. Fatal accidents occur if the flex is cut and the unearthed (and now live) metalwork is being touched; the user will receive a severe electric shock if he is in contact with the ground. A 30mA RCCB will prevent such a shock.

Flex extension leads

Instead of connecting the fused-plug type RCCB direct to the flex of a power tool or appliance, it is better to connect it to a short three-core flex with a trailing 13A plug on the other end, into which a variety of power tools can be plugged in turn.

FITTING AN ELECTRIC SHOWER

If you would like to install a shower but think you can't because there's insufficient water pressure, you might like to consider an instantaneous electric shower. It's connected directly to the mains cold water supply, so you are guaranteed a good jet of water. And as you heat only the water you use, it's very economical to run.

shower from Walker Crosweller; tile – effect wallboard by Laconite

Until quite recently a properly functioning shower was all but an impossibility in many homes. Either it lacked the cylinder storage hot water system needed to supply a conventional shower, or the system that existed wouldn't permit a successful shower installation. For example, the main cold water storage cistern might have had insufficient capacity to supply the cold side of the shower mixer as well as feeding the hot water storage cylinder, or it may have been situated at too low a level to give adequate pressure at the shower rose.

The increasing popularity of showers has led to two new developments: the electric shower pump which increases pressure at the shower rose where this is inadequate; and the instantaneous electric shower, which uses mains-pressure water heated up within the shower unit.

Going back to geysers

There is nothing particularly new about appliances which heat water 'instantaneously' as it flows through them. The Edwardian geyser, installed over the bath in many a turn-of-the century middle-class home, was an early example. The modern single-point or multi-point instantaneous gas water heater – which can provide hot water for the whole house – is its direct descendant. Instantaneous water heaters were designed for connection directly to the rising main so they could operate under mains pressure. They needed no cold water storage cistern or storage cylinder and they had the advantage that heat energy was expended only to heat water that was actually to be used at that time.

However, until a couple of decades ago, the only instantaneous water heating appliances that were available were – like the early geysers – gas-operated. It just wasn't possible to devise an electric appliance that could 'instantaneously' heat a sufficiently large volume of water to fill a sit-down bath, a sink or even a wash basin. It still isn't. But

manufacturers have now produced electric water heaters powerful enough to provide a steady flow of hot water for spray hand-washing over a washbasin in a WC compartment and for the provision of a shower. In neither case is very hot water needed in large volumes.

An instantaneous electric water heater is a relatively compact appliance that needs only to be connected – by means of a 15mm (½in) branch water supply pipe – to the main supply, and to a suitable supply of electricity. It is normally operated by a flow-switch which ensures that electricity is switched on only when water is flowing through the appliance. As it does so, it passes over powerful electrical heating elements.

Temperature control was originally obtained solely by controlling the volume of water flowing through the heater. Opening up the tap or control valve produced a heavy flow of cool water. As the control valve was closed down and the flow diminished, warmer and warmer water was obtained from the shower spray.

The crude, early models were something of a disaster and were frowned on by water authorities and electricity boards. They rarely provided a satisfactory shower. The flow was markedly less than that from a conventional, cylinder-supplied shower. Flushing the WC or opening up any other tap in the house would reduce the pressure of the water entering the heater, so reducing the flow and raising the water temperature from the shower spray. Such unpredictable temperature changes could cause serious scalding to an unsuspecting user. Other problems arose from the hard water scale that tended to form on the heating elements.

Instantaneous showers today

However, an unhappy experience a decade or so ago with one of the early instantaneous electric showers need not deter you from having a modern one installed today. There have been some tremendous advances in design and construction and you can be confident that a modern model will work

79

WHAT'S INSIDE THE CASING

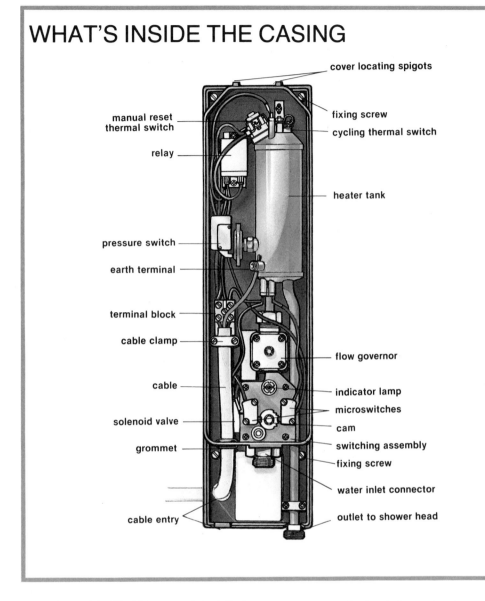

cover locating spigots

manual reset thermal switch

fixing screw

cycling thermal switch

relay

heater tank

pressure switch

earth terminal

terminal block

cable clamp

flow governor

cable

indicator lamp

microswitches

solenoid valve

cam

switching assembly

grommet

fixing screw

water inlet connector

cable entry

outlet to shower head

have a trapped outlet and the branch waste pipe can discharge by the same route as basin or bath wastes already in existence in the bathroom.

Plumbing connections should be straightforward. It's best to connect the supply pipe to the shower heater first and then work backwards to the main supply, making this connection last of all. In this way you will interrupt the supply to the rest of the house as little as possible.

The connection to the shower may be a simple compression coupling or it may have a screwed male thread. In which case you'll need a compression fitting with a coupling at one end and a female screwed connector at the other. To connect into the rising main you should use a compression tee; if you're confident of your plumbing skills, you can use capillary fittings instead.

Obtaining the power

Instantaneous showers get their power from a separate radial circuit (see Chapter 4 pages 72-75). As most models of shower have a loading of either 6 or 7kW they can be supplied safely by a circuit that has a current rating of 30A and is run in 6mm^2 two-core and earth cable. Recently, however, an 8kW shower has been introduced on the market by some manufacturers. This shouldn't pose extra problems for anyone intending to install it: provided the radial circuit originates at either a cartridge fuse or MCB – which both have the effect of uprating the circuit by one third – then a 30A circuit will be adequate. Should you decide to install one of these larger showers then it's still probably a good idea to check their requirements with the makers beforehand.

Showers should be controlled by a 30A double-pole cord-operated switch. From this a length of 6mm^2 two-core and earth cable will run to the shower unit. There is one type that requires a slightly different method of connecting up. If you're going to fit a shower that has a control unit already connected to a length of three-core flex then you'll have to fix a flex outlet unit on the wall near the shower unit so you can connect the flex into the circuit.

Fitting the switch

Ceiling switches can either be surface or flush mounted. If you're going to surface mount one, you'll have to pierce a hole in the ceiling so the cables can be drawn through into a plastic mounting box. Before fixing this in position with No 8 wood screws, you should knock a thin section of plastic from the base to align with the hole in the ceiling. Ideally the box should be fitted against a joist, but if there isn't one suitably placed, you'll have to fix a support batten between the joists made from 75 x 25mm (3 x 1in) timber with a hole drilled in it big enough to let two lengths of

properly provided that it is properly installed according to the manufacturer's instructions.

Most instantaneous showers must be supplied with water at a minimum pressure of 1.05kg per sq cm (15lbs per square inch). They are intended for connection direct to the mains supply, though they can be supplied by a cistern if it is at least 10.75m (35ft) above the level of the shower spray. In most cases mains water pressure will be adequate, but those who live in an area where mains pressure is low should check the actual pressure with their local water authority before incurring the expense of installation.

Modern electric showers usually have an electrical loading of 6kW to 7kW and it is often possible, for the sake of economy, to switch to a low setting of 3kW or 4kW during the summer months. Choose a model that incorporates a temperature stabiliser. This is an anti-scald device that maintains the water

temperature at the level chosen by the user of the shower, despite any fluctuations in pressure which may result from water being drawn off from taps or by flushing the WC. Should there be a drop in pressure beyond the capacity of the stabiliser, a safety sensor turns the shower off completely.

When choosing your instantaneous electric shower, look for evidence that it has been approved by such national safety committees as the B.E.A.B., the National Water Council and the A.N.T. (Assessment of Techniques) Committee of the Institute of Electrical Engineers.

Fitting a shower

Although instantaneous electric showers can be fitted over a sit-down bath, they are usually installed in a separate shower cubicle which may be in a bathroom, in a bedroom or even on a landing. The shower tray must

INSTALLING THE SHOWER UNIT

1 First take the shower spray support assembly and fix it to the wall. It is important to follow the manufacturer's recommendations as to height.

2 Remove the control knobs and any other fittings from the shower unit to enable the faceplate to be taken off before further installation takes place.

3 Carefully position the unit on the shower cubicle wall and mark the screw fitting holes, water and power channels; drill out the fixing holes.

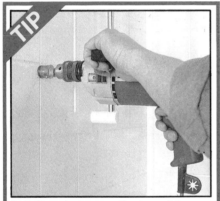

4 Using a hole saw attachment for your drill, cut holes in the cubicle wall for the water and power supplies, then fix the unit to the wall.

5 Make a tee junction with the main, and run a length of pipe to the water access; then add an elbow and length of pipe to go through the wall.

6 Use a swivel tap connector to attach the cold water feed to the unit; this is linked to the inlet pipe by a soldered capillary joint.

7 Make sure the fibre washer in the connector is in place; then screw it up and tighten. Don't use any sealant on the nylon inlet.

8 Attach the shower hose to the screwed outlet, making sure that the rubber washer is in place. Then make the electrical connections (page 82).

9 Turn on the water supply and also the electricity to make sure that the unit works. Finally, replace the cover and control knobs.

6mm² cable pass through. When you're feeding the cables into the mounting box, it's a good idea to write 'mains' on the end of the circuit cable and 'shower' on the end of the shower feed cable. This could be surface mounted on the ceiling and wall, but it's neater to conceal it in the ceiling void and chase it into the wall (for more information see pages 31-35).

You can now strip back the insulation and make the connections. The mains cable should go to the 'supply' side of the switch, with the red core going to the terminal marked L and the black to the one marked N, and the shower cable to the equivalent terminals on the 'load' side. Remember to sleeve the earth cores in green/yellow PVC and connect them to the earth terminal in the switch. Place the six cores neatly in the box and screw the switch to it.

If you're going to flush-mount the switch you'll have to mark the size of the mounting box on the ceiling and, using a pad saw, carefully cut out an equivalent size hole. Then cut a piece of timber to fit between the joists, lay it across the hole and mark the square on it. Knock out a blank from the base of the metal box and drill a hole in the corresponding spot in the timber. Then screw the box to the timber and fix the timber to the joists at a height above the ceiling that allows the box edge to sit flush with the ceiling surface. This can be checked by holding a straight edge across the hole in the ceiling. You should then thread in the two marked cables and make the connections. If you want to fix the switch at a point where there is a joist you can always cut away a section of it. This is best done by using a drill fitted with a 25mm (1in) wood bit to remove most of the wood and then chiselling the remainder away. That way you won't need access to the ceiling void as long as you can 'fish' the cable across the ceiling (see pages 31-35 again).

Connecting into the shower

The cable to the shower can be run down the wall on the surface, using plastic cable clips or mini-trunking, or buried in a chase chopped in the plaster. The cover of the control unit must be removed to allow you access to the terminal block, but do read fully the manufacturer's instructions before going any further. Thread in the cable and strip off some of the sheathing and insulation before connecting the red core to the L terminal and the black to the N terminal. Before connecting the earth core to the earth terminal make sure you've sleeved it in green/yellow PVC. If the unit has a cable clamp, fix the cable in it, double checking that it's the whole, sheathed cable that is held by it and not just individual cores. This is very important as it serves to protect the con-

CONNECTING THE POWER

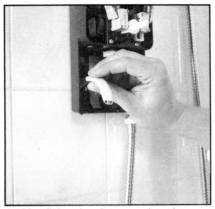

1 *After fixing the shower unit to the bathroom wall and making the connection from the rising main, thread in the circuit cable.*

2 *Feed the cable up the unit and strip it before connecting the red and black cores to the L and N terminals respectively.*

3 *Remember to sleeve the bare earth core in green/yellow PVC before feeding it into the earth terminal and connecting it up.*

4 *Then make sure that the clamp plate will bear down on the cable sheathing before tightening it up to protect all the connections.*

nections. Finally, refit the unit cover, finish off the radial circuit connections at the consumer unit, switch on at the mains and test the shower.

Fitting a flex outlet plate

You'll have to use a flex outlet plate only if there is already a flex connected to the shower unit. This can be fitted on either a one-gang moulded plastic box for surface mounting, or else in a 35mm (1½in) metal box for flush mounting, in which case you'll have to chop a hole. After fixing one or other of the boxes to the wall, run the cable into it through a knockout hole, which, in the case of the metal box, should be fitted with a grommet. The unit has three banks of terminals with two terminal screws per bank and you should connect the green/yellow sleeved earth core to a terminal of the non-shielded bank marked 'E'. Then connect the red insulated core to a terminal of one of the shielded banks and the black to a terminal of the other bank.

Prepare the end of the flex by stripping off approximately 12mm (½in) of insulation from the end of each core. Remember to thread the flex through the hole in the unit's cover before you connect the flex to the unit as you won't be able to fit it after you've made the connections. Then connect the earth core, which should be already sleeved in green and yellow PVC, to the other terminal in the 'E' bank, the brown core to the bank containing the red core and the blue core to the bank containing the black circuit core. Tighten the cord clamp, again making sure that it's the flex sheath that it grips and not the unsheathed cores as this protects the connections. Lay the six cores neatly in the box and fix the unit to the box with the two screws supplied. You can then switch on the power and test the shower.

THE ELECTRICAL CONNECTIONS

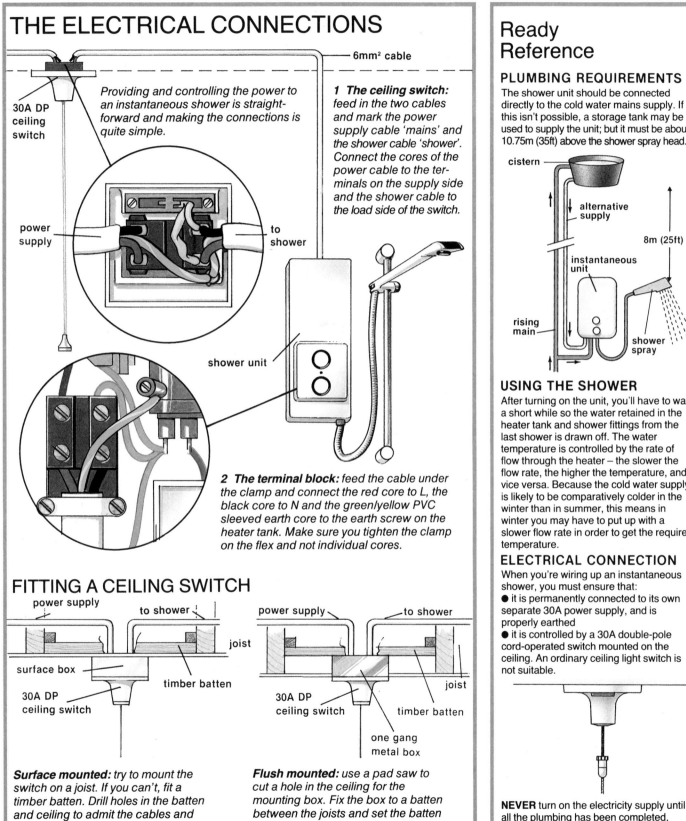

— 6mm² cable

30A DP ceiling switch

Providing and controlling the power to an instantaneous shower is straightforward and making the connections is quite simple.

power supply

to shower

1 The ceiling switch: *feed in the two cables and mark the power supply cable 'mains' and the shower cable 'shower'. Connect the cores of the power cable to the terminals on the supply side and the shower cable to the load side of the switch.*

shower unit

2 The terminal block: *feed the cable under the clamp and connect the red core to L, the black core to N and the green/yellow PVC sleeved earth core to the earth screw on the heater tank. Make sure you tighten the clamp on the flex and not individual cores.*

FITTING A CEILING SWITCH

power supply

to shower

joist

surface box

timber batten

30A DP ceiling switch

power supply

to shower

joist

30A DP ceiling switch

timber batten

one gang metal box

Surface mounted: *try to mount the switch on a joist. If you can't, fit a timber batten. Drill holes in the batten and ceiling to admit the cables and remove a knockout from the base of the box. Fix the box to the ceiling and make the connections.*

Flush mounted: *use a pad saw to cut a hole in the ceiling for the mounting box. Fix the box to a batten between the joists and set the batten so the box is flush with the ceiling. Feed the cables through and make the connections.*

Ready Reference

PLUMBING REQUIREMENTS

The shower unit should be connected directly to the cold water mains supply. If this isn't possible, a storage tank may be used to supply the unit; but it must be about 10.75m (35ft) above the shower spray head.

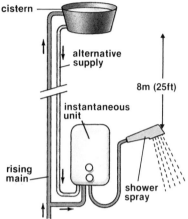

cistern

alternative supply

8m (25ft)

instantaneous unit

rising main

shower spray

USING THE SHOWER

After turning on the unit, you'll have to wait a short while so the water retained in the heater tank and shower fittings from the last shower is drawn off. The water temperature is controlled by the rate of flow through the heater – the slower the flow rate, the higher the temperature, and vice versa. Because the cold water supply is likely to be comparatively colder in the winter than in summer, this means in winter you may have to put up with a slower flow rate in order to get the required temperature.

ELECTRICAL CONNECTION

When you're wiring up an instantaneous shower, you must ensure that:
● it is permanently connected to its own separate 30A power supply, and is properly earthed
● it is controlled by a 30A double-pole cord-operated switch mounted on the ceiling. An ordinary ceiling light switch is not suitable.

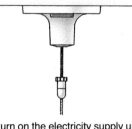

NEVER turn on the electricity supply until all the plumbing has been completed, including mounting the handset and hose, and the power supply and earthing connections are made.

cooker control unit from MK Electric

WIRING FOR COOKERS

Installing the wiring for a new electric cooker is not such a daunting task as it seems. The mains circuitry is similar for freestanding and built-in cookers, and the final connection is simplicity itself to make.

There are two main types of electric cooker which you will come across in the show-rooms. The first is the traditional, freestanding electric cooker which consists of an oven, a hob with three or four boiling rings or hot plates, and a grill that is either at eye-level or else just above the oven. This type is self-contained and usually stands against a wall in the kitchen. The second type is the split-level cooker, and a separate hob and oven are normally built into the kitchen units. In addition to these two there are smaller, table-top models which have only two hot plates, and the increasingly popular micro-wave ovens.

Cooker circuits

Because cookers are heavy current con-suming appliances, they require a radial circuit for their exclusive use. This will run from the consumer unit, provided there is a spare MCB or fuseway, or else from a separate switch fuse unit. A circuit like this may already exist, but it is more likely you will have to install it.

Small cookers that can rest on top of a kitchen unit, and micro-wave ovens, can be run without a special circuit. This is because they have an electrical loading of 3kW or less and when that is converted into current rating (see below) you will find that they can safely get their power supply from a 13A socket outlet. But before you install a new radial circuit (see pages 72-75 for further details) you will have to make sure that it is of the correct current rating.

Circuit current rating

A small electric cooker with, say two boiling rings, a grill and an oven, is likely to have an electrical loading of around 10kW, while a fully equipped cooker with a double oven will probably have a rating of 14kW or more. A cooker that rates up to 11kW is usually supplied by a circuit controlled by a 30A fuse, while one with a higher rating is supplied by a 45A circuit. The current rating of the circuit is determined by the maximum current demand from the cooker. To determine that, the total wattage is divided by the voltage of the mains electricity

CHOOSING CABLE RUNS

The cable and switching arrangements for cookers differ depending on whether you have a freestanding cooker or separate hob and oven sections.

1 Freestanding cooker

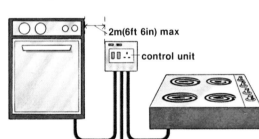

Above: A connection unit allows the trailing cable to join the chased cable, protects the connections and allows the cooker to be easily disconnected for repairs.

2 Separate hob and oven

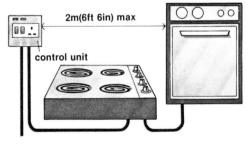

If you want the control unit centred between the sections, run two cables from the control unit, using 6mm^2 cable; the circuit must originate at a cartridge fuse or MCB.

Another method is to run just one cable from the control unit and loop it in and out of one section and then run it onto the second section.

INSTALLING A COOKER CONTROL UNIT

1 Using a club hammer and cold chisel, chop a recess for the mounting box and chases for the circuit cable and the cable to the connection unit.

2 Drill and plug holes in the wall before fitting the box. Remember to put grommets on the knockout holes and run the cable inside conduit.

3 Detach the unit from its faceplate to make the connections on the mains side. Earth the box by linking its earth screw with the earth terminal.

4 Then make the connections on the cooker side. Remember to sleeve all the earth cores in green/yellow PVC before connecting them.

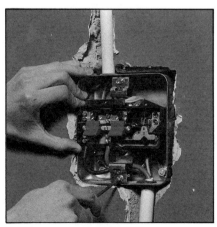

5 When you've made all the connections, make sure the unit is square to the wall and then screw it securely onto the mounting box.

TIP

6 You can now fix the centre part of the face plate. Before fixing the rest, make good and redecorate the surface of the wall.

Ready Reference

SIMPLE COOKER REPAIRS

You can carry out several simple repairs on most electric cookers. However, before starting work, isolate the cooker circuit at the main consumer unit by removing the circuit fuse or switching off the MCB.

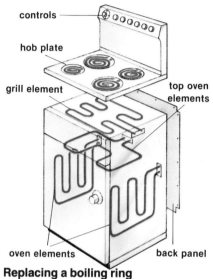

controls
hob plate
grill element
top oven elements
oven elements
back panel

Replacing a boiling ring

Double check that you have bought the correct ring to install. Then:
● remove the faulty boiling ring
● lift off the hob or prop it up
● undo the fixing nuts and bolts in the correct channel
● lift out the faulty ring
● detach the wires, remembering to take note of their positions
● fit the new boiling ring.

Replacing a grill element

When replacing this:
● remove hob spillage tray and grill tray
● lift hob
● disconnect terminal leads to the grill
● disconnect cable leading to the earth
● remove screws holding element supports
● push supports inwards to free element
● replace new element in reverse order.

Replacing an oven element

This can usually be done from the front of the cooker. In some cases, the panels within the oven will have to be removed:
● disconnect the leads and earth to remove the old element or,
● to prevent them slipping back, immediately transfer the leads one by one to the new element with the old one only partially withdrawn
● make sure all parts are replaced in the same positions.

THE CONNECTION UNIT

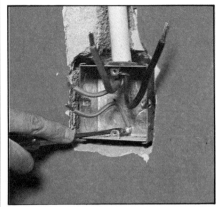

1 *Chop the recess for the box and the chase for the cable. Then run in the cable and earth the box to give it extra protection.*

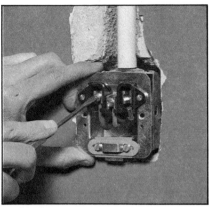

2 *Connect the earths to the centre terminals and other cores to the outer two. If you aren't connecting the cooker yet, fit the unit's cover.*

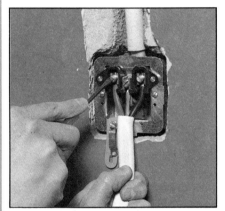

3 *Undo the clamp and hold in place the trailing cooker cable while you connect it. Remember, it should be the same size as the circuit cable.*

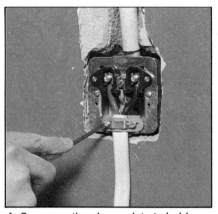

4 *Screw up the clamp plate to hold the cable and protect the connections. Make good before fitting the cover, which should cover any ragged edges.*

supply. So, if you have a 12kW cooker, dividing 12,000 by 240 indicates that, in theory at least, the cooker should be supplied by a 50A circuit. In addition, if the cooker control unit incorporates a 13A socket outlet, the total current demand reaches 63A. However, in practice allowance is made for the fact that the boiling rings, the oven, and the grill will rarely be used all at the same time. And, even if they are, the current demand will still be less than 63A because peak demand is reduced by thermostatic devices incorporated in the cooker.

In fact, when calculations are being made for the current demand of a domestic electric cooker, the wiring regulations take account of this. Therefore, the 12kW cooker, theoretically rated at 63A, is actually reckoned to have a current demand of 27A. That means it can be supplied safely by a circuit controlled by a 30A fuse or MCB.

The new circuit

Cooker circuits are normally run in two-core and earth PVC-sheathed cable. It's best to use 6mm² cable for a 30A circuit and 10mm² cable for a 45A one. The circuit cable runs from the consumer unit to a cooker control unit or control switch, taking the shortest possible route. This could be under the floorboards or in the ceiling void. You could either run the cable in a chase chopped in the wall or else surface mount it by using either mini-trunking or cable clips. Obviously it looks much neater to have your cable concealed within conduit beneath the surface of the wall. For more detailed information on running cable see pages 31-35.

Do remember that this larger size cable can be quite expensive and before buying it, it's a good idea to measure fairly precisely the length you will require, and to aim for the most economical cable run in your planning.

However, you ought to allow a surplus for contingency purposes should you encounter obstacles when you run the circuit.

Cooker control units and switches

You will be able to control the power for your electric cooker from a cooker control unit or a cooker switch. A control unit has two switches, one of which controls the power to the cooker, while the other controls the power supply to a 13A socket outlet that is incorporated in the unit. A cooker control switch is an alternative to this sort of unit and is merely a double-pole switch marked 'cooker'. While it's more convenient to fit a control unit with an extra socket, there is the danger of having the kettle flex trailing across a switched on boiling ring and so risking fire. If you're planning to install a free-standing cooker, a special connector unit is fitted at the end of the chased cable run and from it cable is run on to the cooker. The advantage of this is that if you want to repair or replace your cooker all you have to do is disconnect it at the unit after switching off at the control unit or cooker switch. A connector like this also provides special clamps to prevent any unnecessary strain being put on the terminals when the cooker is moved out from the wall.

An alternative is to use a cable outlet unit which clamps the cable and allows it to run to the cooker without a break.

Position of the control unit

The traditional height for a cooker control unit is about 1.5m (5ft) above the floor so that it can be reached easily. It shouldn't be any closer than 300mm (1ft) to the cooker but mustn't be more than 2m (6ft) away from it. One control unit or switch may supply both sections of a split-level cooker, provided that both of them are within 2m (6ft) of the unit. As the control unit is usually sited midway between the two sections it means that they can be up to 4m (13ft) apart – which allows for considerable scope in kitchen planning. When the control unit is fixed between the two cooker sections, two cables can be run from the unit supplying the oven and hob sections respectively. But if the unit is fixed at the side of one of the sections then one cable is used to connect that and another links into it to provide power for the second section. However, the same size cable is used throughout. Another alternative is to install both a cooker control unit and a cooker switch. The main cooker circuit will still run from the consumer unit or switchfuse unit to the cooker control unit, and from there a cable of the same size will run to one of the sections. Another cable will loop out of the control unit and link the cooker switch into the circuit. Finally, a cable from the switch will then run to the second section. If you are installing an island hob unit, then this is

CONNECTING UP THE COOKER

1 *After removing the cooker's back plate, sleeve the earth core in green/yellow PVC and then connect the cores to their respective terminals.*

2 *Fix the cable under the clamp plate to give the connections extra protection. Then put on the back plate and switch on at the mains.*

obviously a more convenient circuit arrangement than running two new radial circuits to the units.

Connecting to the control unit

If you are fitting a flush-mounted unit you will have to sink a metal mounting box into a chase chopped into the plaster and masonry. Obviously the size and depth of the box depends on the type and model of unit you decide to use. Because the mounting boxes are quite deep, chop the recess out carefully on internal walls, or consider using a surface-mounted box instead. Before finally fixing the box into the wall, do remember to remove the necessary knockout blanks to allow in the various cables – usually two for a freestanding cooker and three for a split-level one – and to fix with plastic grommets into the holes to protect those cables.

For surface mounting a control unit, a plastic mounting box has to be fixed to the wall with wood screws. The circuit cable should run down from the ceiling or up from the floor and should be chased into the wall. Take it into the box and strip off the sheathing, leaving about 25mm (1in) within the box. If you're fitting a surface-mounted box unit it's easier to take the unit out of its box to make the connection. Trim the wires to about 18mm (¾in) and strip 12mm (½in) of insulation from the end of each core. The earth cores should be enclosed in green/yellow PVC sleeving and connected to the earth terminal. The two insulated cores are connected to the terminals marked MAINS, with the red going to L and black to N. The cores of the cable, or cables, running to the cooker are connected to the equivalent terminals, marked COOKER, on the lower side of the control unit. These cables should be

secured under the clamp (ie, incorporated in the unit). After you've connected the cables to the control unit, refit it in its box and fit the cover.

Wiring up the connector unit

The cable from the cooker control unit should be chased into the wall and run to the connector unit. Insert both the cable from the control unit and that leading to the cooker itself into the box. After preparing the ends, connect the sleeved earth cores to the centre terminal, the red insulated cores to one of the outer terminals, and the black insulated cores to the other. Then tighten the clamp screws that secure the trailing cable and replace the unit's cover. Double check this because if the clamp is on the individual cores and not the sheathing it could damage the connections.

Connecting to the cooker

At the back of a freestanding cooker there is a panel which must be removed to allow entry for the cable through the grommetted entry hole. Prepare the cable as you did when you connected to the cooker control unit, not forgetting to add an extra sleeve of green/yellow PVC to insulate the earth core. Then connect the red core to the terminal marked L, the black to the one marked N, and the earth core to the terminal marked E. Again, remember to secure the cable under the cable clamp before refitting the panel as this gives vital protection to the connections if the cooker is moved away from the wall at any time. If you are installing a split-level cooker the connections are basically the same as for a freestanding model, although the position of the terminal blocks may well vary from model to model.

Ready Reference

COOKER HOODS

There are two main types of cooker hood that you can fit easily above your electric cooker and so get rid of unpleasant cooking smells:

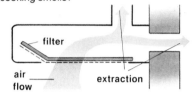

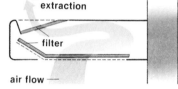

● re-circulating hoods, which contain a replaceable filter that purifies the air before returning it to the kitchen without heat loss

● ducted hoods, which carry the air to the outside. Ideally your cooker should stand against an outside wall, otherwise you'll have to use flexible ducting.

OBTAINING THE POWER

There are three sources of power for a cooker hood:
● from a 13A socket outlet in the cooker control unit
● from the lighting circuit, in which case you should use a 20A double-pole (DP) switch with a flex outlet
● from a spur on the ring circuit, in which case the outlet should be a 13A switched fuse connection unit with a 3A fuse.

TILED WALLS

To fit a cooker control unit or switch on a tiled wall you should centre the box at the join of four tiles for a neater finish.

For flush mounting:
● score the area of tiles to be removed with a tile cutter
● gently tap the scored lines with a bolster chisel, taking care not to crack the rest of the surface
● remove the pieces of tile, chop a hole for the box, then fit it in position.

For surface mounting:
● make a cross of masking tape and mark the point at which you want each hole
● drill through, being careful not to use too high a speed otherwise you risk crazing the tile
● fit the mounting box in the usual way.

INSTALLING SHAVER SOCKETS

If you want to use an electric shaver you'll have to install a special shaver socket. There are a number of different models available, some of which can be installed in a bathroom.

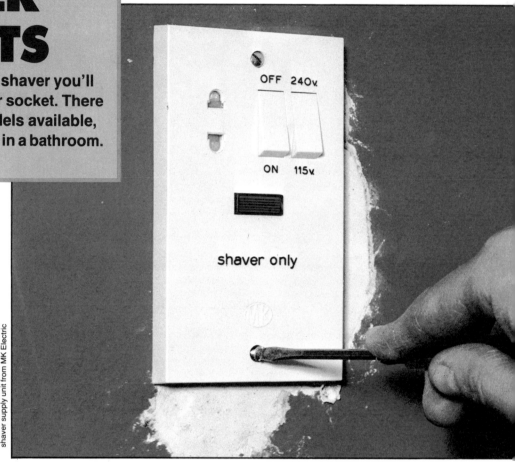

shaver supply unit from MK Electric

A shaver socket is merely an outlet point designed to accept the kind of two pin plugs that are fitted to electric shavers. You'll find that the two-hole socket is virtually universal and accepts a variety of different plugs, including those fitted to British, Australian, American and European shavers.

Types of shaver sockets
There are two principal types of shaver socket – the shaver supply unit and the shaver socket outlet. In addition, there are some models of shaver striplights, which are designed to fit next to a mirror, that include shaver sockets and there are fused shaver adaptors which are similar to 13A plugs except that they have a shaver socket on their backs.

The *shaver supply unit* is designed specially for safe operation in the bathroom. As such, it's the only socket outlet that's allowed there, which means that the shaver is the only mains-operated, portable appliance that should be used in the bathroom.

The reason why the unit is safe for a bathroom is quite simple: it incorporates an isolating transformer which has the effect of providing an earth-free electricity supply at the outlet. This means that there is no direct link between the appliance or socket and the mains supply, so that if your shaver does go wrong, there is virtually no chance of you getting a shock. And, with a maximum current output of 20W, a shaver supply unit is restricted to use for shavers only. If, for example, you try to fit a shaver plug onto some other sort of portable appliance, such as an electric fire or television, a self-resetting overload device will operate.

The usual voltage of the supply unit is 240V, but dual voltage models are available for use with both 240V and 115V shavers. These usually have a switch enabling you to select which voltage you want, but some models have a three-hole socket and the shaver plug is inserted into the centre hole and one of the others according to the voltage required.

The *shaver socket outlet* is similar to the supply unit and performs the same function. However, there is one major difference: because it does not incorporate an isolating transformer it cannot be installed in a bathroom or washroom. Most shaver socket outlets, however, do incorporate a self-resetting thermal overload device that limits the current to 0.2A and is protected by a 2A fuse. Some poorer quality units have only a fuse to protect them, so it's a good idea to check that you have the safest model before installing one.

Shaver strip lights, which have a built-in shaver socket, have either miniature fluorescent tubes or tungsten filament strip lamps. There are two main types. The first contains an isolating transformer and is designed for use in bathrooms, while the other has no transformer and is suitable for any other room. Like the shaver supply unit, some models have a three-hole, dual voltage shaver outlet, while others have just a single 240V outlet. Both types have a self-resetting thermal overload device for the shaver socket, while the light itself is controlled by a cord switch.

A *shaver adaptor* is merely a standard 13A three-pin plug that has a two-hole socket on its back into which a shaver's two-pin plug will fit. Like all shaver socket outlets, the holes are shuttered and as a precaution marked 'shavers only'. These adaptors are certainly convenient if you're travelling in the UK, but it's not really a good idea to use them as a permanent substitute for a shaver socket as they don't have a thermal overload cut out. And, of course, as no mains socket outlets are allowed in a bathroom, shaver adaptors can't be used there.

Obtaining the power
The best method of obtaining power for your supply unit is to use a non-fused spur from the ring circuit.

You should use 2.5mm² two-core and earth PVC-sheathed cable and link into the nearest socket to the bathroom. Before doing this, however, you must switch off the mains. Then remove the socket from its mounting box to check that it's on the ring circuit.

This is quite easily done. If you're dealing with a single gang socket outlet, one cable entering means that it's on the end of a spur; two cables show that it could be either on the ring or else be an intermediate socket on a spur, and three cables entering the socket indicate that it is on the ring and already has a spur from it. With a double socket, one cable shows it's on a spur and therefore you can't connect a new socket from it, two that it's on the ring and therefore suitable for a spur,

FOUR WAYS OF OBTAINING POWER

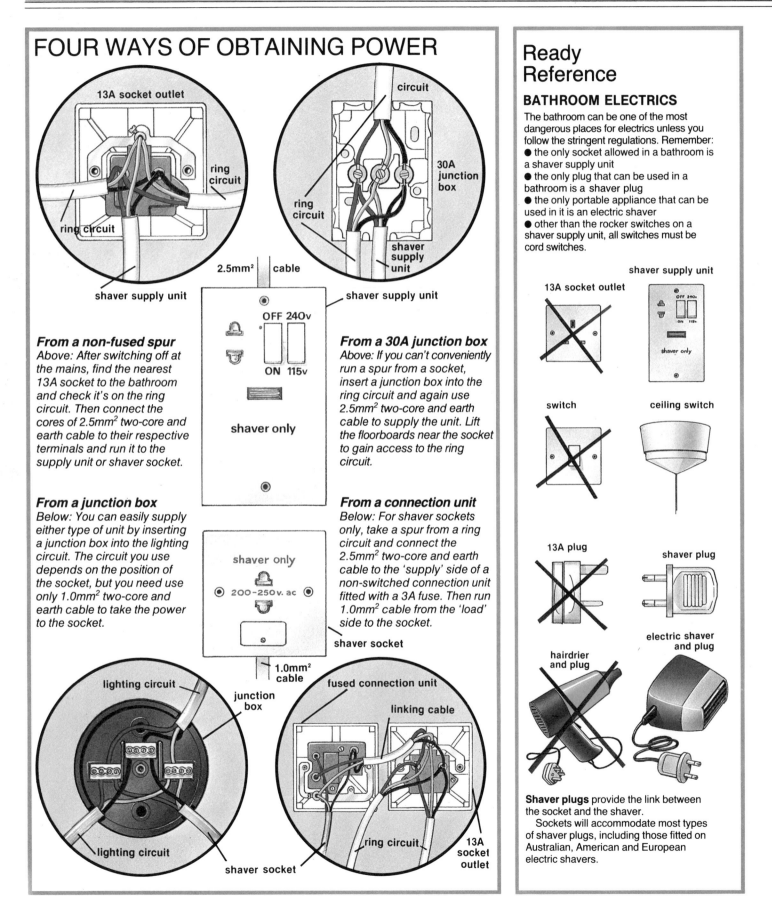

13A socket outlet

ring circuit

ring circuit

ring circuit

shaver supply unit

circuit

30A junction box

ring circuit

shaver supply unit

2.5mm² cable

OFF 240v
ON 115v

shaver only

shaver supply unit

From a non-fused spur
Above: After switching off at the mains, find the nearest 13A socket to the bathroom and check it's on the ring circuit. Then connect the cores of 2.5mm² two-core and earth cable to their respective terminals and run it to the supply unit or shaver socket.

From a junction box
Below: You can easily supply either type of unit by inserting a junction box into the lighting circuit. The circuit you use depends on the position of the socket, but you need use only 1.0mm² two-core and earth cable to take the power to the socket.

shaver only
200-250v. ac

From a 30A junction box
Above: If you can't conveniently run a spur from a socket, insert a junction box into the ring circuit and again use 2.5mm² two-core and earth cable to supply the unit. Lift the floorboards near the socket to gain access to the ring circuit.

From a connection unit
Below: For shaver sockets only, take a spur from a ring circuit and connect the 2.5mm² two-core and earth cable to the 'supply' side of a non-switched connection unit fitted with a 3A fuse. Then run 1.0mm² cable from the 'load' side to the socket.

shaver socket

1.0mm² cable

lighting circuit
junction box
lighting circuit
shaver socket

fused connection unit
linking cable
ring circuit
13A socket outlet

Ready Reference

BATHROOM ELECTRICS
The bathroom can be one of the most dangerous places for electrics unless you follow the stringent regulations. Remember:
● the only socket allowed in a bathroom is a shaver supply unit
● the only plug that can be used in a bathroom is a shaver plug
● the only portable appliance that can be used in it is an electric shaver
● other than the rocker switches on a shaver supply unit, all switches must be cord switches.

shaver supply unit
13A socket outlet
OFF 240v ON 115v
shaver only
switch
ceiling switch
13A plug
shaver plug
hairdrier and plug
electric shaver and plug

Shaver plugs provide the link between the socket and the shaver.
Sockets will accommodate most types of shaver plugs, including those fitted on Australian, American and European electric shavers.

INSTALLING A SHAVER SUPPLY UNIT

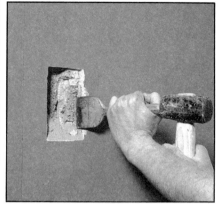

1 *Check your wall is thick enough to take the unit's mounting box. Then mark its position and use a club hammer and chisel to make the hole.*

2 *You can then chop out the chase for the conduit and cable. Drill holes for the mounting box to the back of the recess and insert wall plugs.*

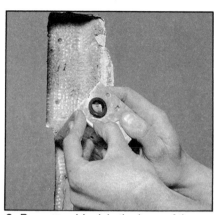

3 *Remove a blank in the base of the mounting box to admit the cable. Remember to fit a grommet to protect the cable from chafing.*

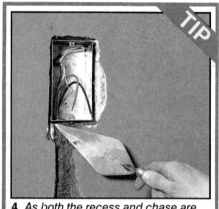

4 *As both the recess and chase are almost 50mm (2in) deep, making good should be done in two stages: use mortar first and then filler.*

5 *You should then connect the cores to their respective terminals. Make sure you add an extra earth core to earth the box and unit completely.*

6 *You can now screw the shaver supply unit to its mounting box. If you wish to, you can repaint or repaper before putting the unit back.*

and three that it's on the ring and already has a spur from it. If you're in any doubt as to which cable is which you'll have to trace the cable runs.

Most terminals should be able to accommodate a third cable core, but if you have any difficulty in running a new cable into the existing socket then it's probably better to lift a floorboard adjacent to the nearest socket and insert a 30A junction box into one of the ring cables. Another alternative is to use a suitable loop-in ceiling rose or junction box in the lighting circuit. In this case you would only have to use 1.0mm² two-core and earth PVC cable.

Whichever way you pick up the power, the cable should run either under the floor or in the ceiling void to a point below or above the unit (for further details see Chapter 2, pages 31-35). It should then be chased into the wall and run to the unit itself.

Installing a shaver supply unit

Supply units can be either flush or surface-mounted. If you intend to flush – fit the unit in a metal mounting box recessed in the wall you must make sure that your wall is thick enough to take it. When you're sure that it is, you can cut a chase in the wall so that the front edge of the box is flush with the wall surface. If the wall is tiled, it's a good idea to centre the box at the junction of four tiles and cut a section from the corner of each to give a neater finish. You should then drill and plug the necessary holes before fixing the box to the wall with wood screws.

Before you actually fit the box, however, don't forget to remove a blank from one of the knockout holes so you can insert the cable. It's also wise to fit a grommet onto the sharp edges of the holes so the cable can't chafe against them. Having cut a chase for the cable and prepared it (not forgetting to

sleeve the earth in green/yellow PVC), connect the cores to their respective terminals and fit the unit to the box with the screws provided. The procedure for fitting a surface-mounted supply unit is exactly the same except that the plastic mounting box is screwed to the wall surface.

Shaver socket circuit

A shaver socket is supplied from the lighting circuit, so all that's required is to run 1.0mm² two-core and earth PVC cable from either a loop-in celing rose or a lighting circuit junction box. Which lighting circuit you choose to extend depends on the position of the shaver socket. But it's worth remembering that an unlimited number of shaver sockets may be supplied from one cable – which means that you can install one in each bedroom merely by looping in and out of each socket in turn. In fact, the back of the socket has

INSTALLING A SHAVER SOCKET

1 *Using a club hammer and cold chisel, cut a recess and chase approximately 30mm (1¼in) deep to take the mounting box and conduit.*

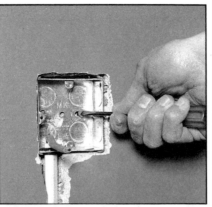

2 *Drill the holes and plug them. Before fixing the box to the wall with wood screws, put a grommet into the knockout hole.*

3 *Do the making good and make the connections. In the case of a shaver socket the earth core is connected directly to the mounting box.*

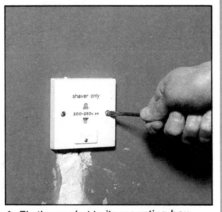

4 *Fix the socket to its mounting box. Remember that you can fit other sockets easily by looping in and out of each one of them.*

Ready Reference

SITING THE SUPPLY UNIT
Shaver supply units must be easily accessible and at a convenient height. You should fit them:
● about 1.5m (5ft) above the floor
● near a source of light
● near a mirror.

Rechargeable shavers can usually be plugged into the unit. It's a good idea to make sure there is a shelf nearby on which the shaver can rest while its batteries are charged.

SHAVER STRIP LIGHTS
These units provide both light and power for an electric shaver. They are ideal for installation in the bathroom and are best fitted next to a mirror. Shaver strip-lights incorporate:

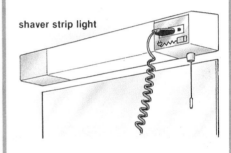

shaver strip light

● a tungsten or fluorescent strip lamp
● a dual voltage, three hole safety socket that in some models is protected by an isolating transformer
● a cord switch to control the light
● a terminal block to make installation safer and easier.

SHAVER ADAPTORS
Shaver adaptors allow an electric shaver to be used from a 13A socket outlet without the need for extra wiring. They have a number of disadvantages:

shaver adapto

● they have no thermal overload device and are only protected by a 1A fuse.
● they cannot be used in bathrooms
● they cannot serve as a permanent substitute for a shaver socket.

---

extra cable holes expressly for this purpose. The sockets can be fixed at whatever level you find most convenient. If you want to fit one low on the wall, it's best to tap into the circuit supplying the lights in the room below – as the cables are likely to be under the floorboards. But if you want one at a higher level, tap into the lighting circuit in the same room – as the cables will be in the ceiling void or roof space.

You'll have to make sure that you have a ceiling rose with a loop-in system and if you don't, look for a junction box. If you have neither then you'll have to insert a new junction box in the circuit feed cable.

There is another option. This involves replacing the one-gang box of a single 13A socket outlet with a dual mounting box. Using 2.5mm² cable you can then join the original socket to the 'supply' side of a non-switched, fused connection unit (fitted with a

3A fuse to add greater protection). Then run, 1.0mm² cable from the 'load' side of the unit to the shaver socket.

The socket itself is fixed to the wall and connected in much the same way as a conventional 13A single socket outlet (for further details see pages 27-30).

Shaver strip light
A shaver strip light is supplied by 1.0mm² two-core and earth PVC-sheathed cable run from a loop-in ceiling rose or junction box in the lighting circuit or else from a fused connection unit on the ring circuit. It should be fixed either at the side or above a shaving mirror in the bathroom or bedroom. The end of the cable should be prepared in the normal way and then passed simply through the cable entry hole so it can be connected to the live, neutral and earth screws on the terminal block.

REPLACING AN IMMERSION HEATER

Immersion heaters are a versatile way of heating water, but can be expensive if used carelessly. They are also a useful back-up for conventional heating systems.

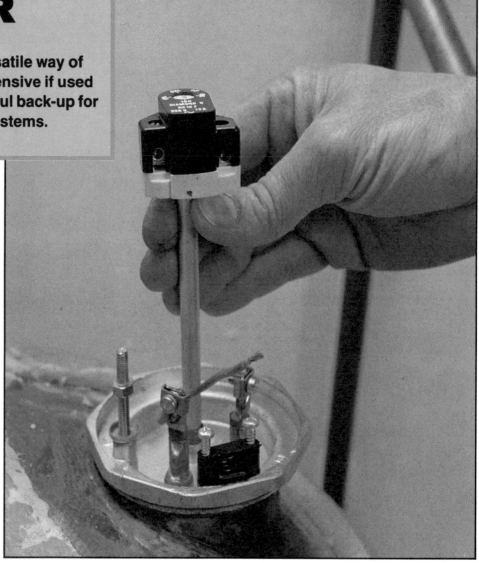

An electric immersion heater may be used either as the sole means of providing domestic hot water, or as a supplement – perhaps during the summer months – to a solid fuel, gas- or oil-fired boiler. It provides the simplest means of heating water and is the cheapest to install. However, with constantly rising electricity prices an immersion heater can prove to be prohibitively expensive to use, unless it is operated intelligently in a carefully designed and insulated hot water system.

Immersion heaters raise the temperature of the water in the storage cylinder or tank in which they are installed by conduction and convection. Water in direct contact with the element is heated by conduction. Since warm water is lighter than cold, it rises to 'float' on top of the cold and other, cooler, water takes its place in contact with the element and is heated in its turn. This has the effect of setting up convection currents within the cylinder, and circulation continues until all the water above the level of the immersion heater has been raised to the required temperature. The thermostat then switches the immersion heater off.

Consequently, only water above the immersion heater element is heated. This is an important fact that must be borne in mind when deciding whether an immersion heater is to be fitted horizontally or vertically, and, in the latter case, the length of the heater required. You can buy the heating elements in lengths ranging from 275 to 900mm (11 to 36in) and these are provided with a thermostat. In soft water areas this should be set at 70°C (160°F), but in hard water areas a setting of 60° (140°F) is quite adequate for normal domestic use and will not cause water scale or 'fur' to precipitate.

Purpose-made immersion heaters

These heaters are known as 'whole house' electric water heaters because they can supply hot water for all domestic needs, and they are used when the sole means of heating water is by electricity. They are sometimes called under-draining board or UDB heaters because of the position in which they are usually situated. They are heavily insulated and look like rather squat hot water storage cylinders with a capacity of some 113 litres (25 gal). Inside there are usually two immersion heaters fitted horizontally, one above the other. The upper one is positioned about one quarter of the distance from the top of the cylinder and is intended to be kept switched on throughout the period during which hot water may be required. This ensures that there are always about 15 litres (3½gal) of hot water available for personal washing, washing-up, household cleaning and so on. The lower element is fitted a little way up from the base of the cylinder and you have to use this when you need larger quantities of hot water say for a bath or washing laundry. Normally you have to turn it on about half an hour to an hour before you need the water; but it's worth keeping a close eye on the time needed to heat your water, as this could save money.

Immersion heaters in hot water cylinders

Modern hot water storage cylinders, both direct and indirect, intended for use with a boiler as the primary source of heat, are usually fitted with an immersion heater boss in the dome of the cylinder. This means you can fit an immersion heater so it protrudes downwards into the water. And, if it is to heat all the water in the cylinder, when the boiler is off, it must extend almost to the base of the cylinder. Some immersion heaters, intended for vertical fitting, have two elements. A short one performs the same function as the upper element in a UDB; it ensures that there is always a basic amount of hot water stored in the upper part of the cylinder. Similarly, like the lower element of a purpose-made electric water heater, the longer element is switched on prior to a demand for a larger volume of hot water.

TAKING OUT THE OLD HEATER

1 *Try to unscrew the immersion heater boss. If it's stiff then remove any insulating material in the immediate vicinity.*

2 *Use a blow-torch to heat the boss and screw fitting; the differing expansion between the materials should loosen the thread.*

3 *Use the special immersion heater spanner to unscrew the boss gently. Don't wrench too hard or the cylinder may get dented.*

4 *Remove the old heater and clean up the screw thread. Make sure it isn't damaged or else you may have to replace the cylinder.*

Using immersion heaters efficiently

As an immersion heater is the most expensive means of heating water, it is worth bearing a few things in mind. Perhaps the most important factor in making it economical to use is the amount of insulation packed round the cylinder in which it is fitted. A 130 litre (30gal) copper cylinder will, if it is unlagged and the water temperature maintained at 60°C (140°F), waste no less than 86 units (kWh) of electricity a week. If it is provided with a 50mm (2in) thick lagging jacket, the loss will be cut to only 8.8 units per week. Increase the thickness of the insulation to 75mm (3in) and the weekly heat loss will be reduced to 6 units. In fact, 75mm (3in) is the optimum thickness of a lagging jacket. Further increases in thickness do not produce commensurate savings.

Some people remove, or partly remove, the lagging jacket for clothes airing, but it's not cost effective to do this, and in any case enough warmth will still escape from the cylinder and its pipework to warm the average airing cupboard. If more heat is needed, you will find it far more economical to provide a low powered electric airing cupboard heater.

Water heated by an electric immersion heater must never be allowed to circulate through the central heating system. Electrically-heated water at 60°C circulating through 15mm (½in) copper tube will waste 1.36 units of electricity for each 300mm (1ft) of pipe run per week. It sometimes happens that pipework to a towel rail is run from a direct hot water system. If the system is sometimes heated by an electric immersion heater, the towel rail pipework should be kept wholly below the level of the heater, or alternatively, a gate-valve must be provided and must be turned off to prevent circulation whenever the heater is switched on.

CHOOSE THE RIGHT HEATER
There are several types of immersion heater available, and it's important to select the type that matches your needs.

For straightforward water heating, or as back-up for a conventional central heating system, install a single-element heater.

For the most economical use, link the heater to a timeswitch. This will turn it on a short while before you want to use the hot water, usually first thing in the morning and in the early evening.

To cope with variable demand, you can either:

● fit a dual-element heater (A) in the usual position, or

● install two short heaters (B) through holes cut in the side of the cylinder.

When only small quantities of hot water are needed, you switch on the short element or the upper heater only; for heavy demand, both elements or heaters are on.

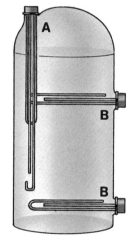

TIP: RESCUE THE CUT-OUT
If you have to cut a hole in your cylinder to install your heater, drill a series of holes in a circle and complete the cutting with a hacksaw blade. To stop the cut-out falling into the cylinder:

● drill a hole in its centre before cutting round it.

● insert a toggle (nail or dowel, for example) tied to a piece of string, so you can retrieve the cut-out when it's severed.

Alternatively use a hook made from something like coat-hanger wire.

The cylinder, with its immersion heater, should be positioned as closely as possible to the hot water tap in most constant use, not the one from which the greatest volumes of hot water are drawn. This will normally be the hot tap over the kitchen sink. Where the position of a hot water draw-off point, over a cloakroom washbasin for example, involves a run of more than 7m (20ft), you ought to consider installing a small instantaneous water heater to serve that particular fitting.

Finally, if an immersion heater is to be used economically, it must also be used intelligently. No matter how thoroughly a cylinder is lagged, the water stored within it will slowly lose heat. It's rare that hot water is required in any amount between, say 11.00pm and 7.00am. It's sensible therefore to switch off the immersion heater at about 10.00pm and to switch it on again at about 6.30am. When a house is empty for most of the day, it's also wise to switch off the immersion heater during the period that the house is usually unoccupied.

This doesn't have to be done manually. Nowadays there are clock-controlled time switches available that will switch the immersion heater off and on again at pre-determined times. These controls normally have a manual over-ride for use at weekends or other occasions when the house is occupied throughout the day.

Replacing or installing an immersion heater

When you're dealing with an immersion heater, one tool you will have to get hold of, (and it's worth hiring it for the day rather than buying), is an immersion heater spanner. No other use has been found for this dinosaur amongst spanners, as you'll understand when you see its gigantic proportions. (If there were another purpose, it would probably be in connection with constructing marine diesel engines for oil tankers!)

Before starting work you must turn off the heater, if you already have one, and drain the cylinder by attaching a length of hose to the drain cock near the base of the cylinder. You don't actually need the whole cylinder drained but because of the way they are constructed it's all or nothing, unless you want to go to the trouble of siphoning a small quantity out through the vent pipe hole in the top.

If you're installing an immersion heater in a cylinder that doesn't have one, there should be a boss plug in the top to take it. If not, then you may have to think about buying a new cylinder. However, you can carefully cut out a hole using a hole cutter. If all you've got is a drill then you'll have to draw a circle on the cylinder the same diameter as the screw boss and then drill a series of holes on the

PUTTING IN THE NEW HEATER

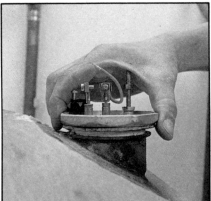

1 *Take the new heater and remove the cap. Put some plumber's sealant on the metal washer and run some PTFE tape round the thread.*

3 *When the nut has been fully tightened, fill the cylinder with water and check for leaks, then insert the thermostat in its housing.*

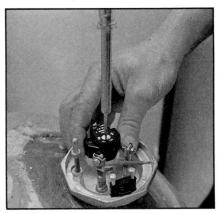

2 *Put the heater element inside the cylinder and gently screw up the boss nut, ensuring the thread doesn't cross, then tighten with the spanner.*

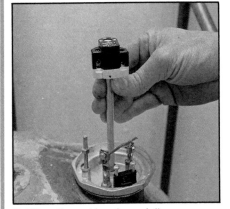

4 *Adjust the thermostat to the temperature you require, and then complete the electrical connection and replace the cap.*

inside of this circle. Once you've done this you can cut out the circle of the metal with a hacksaw blade and smooth off the inside edges of the hole with a half-round file. You then have to insert a solderless flange into which the immersion heater can be screwed.

If there is a boss plug or an old heater, then you will need the special immersion heater spanner to remove it before you can put the new heater in. With an old heater it's quite likely that you'll have to play a blow-torch over the fitting to make it easier to loosen the screw, but make sure there is no combustible material around. If it doesn't turn after you've heated it you'll have to leave it for a few moments to cool and then try again. Applying heat once or twice should do the trick.

You must get the right length of heater to extend almost to the base of the cylinder.

When you fit it you'll need to bind PTFE tape round the thread of the new heater boss and put some plumbers' sealant between the metal washer and the boss head. Then insert the heater into the body of the cylinder and gently screw it up tight.

Once you've done this you can fill the cylinder with water and check for any leaks round the boss. When you're satisfied that everything is in order you can deal with the electrics (see opposite). This entails running a flex from the heater to a double-pole isolating switch, which in turn is connected to a separate radial circuit. Most switches are sited in the cupboard which houses the heater or just outside the door, but for greater convenience you could install a second switch, say, in the kitchen. Finally, you'll need to insert the thermostat and adjust it so that it heats the water to the temperature which you require.

CHECKING THE ELECTRICS

When replacing an immersion heater it's a good idea to check that the existing cable runs and switch are not worn or poorly installed. It is quite likely that if the heater has been in for some time the cable may need replacing, and a more modern switch may be desirable. If you are installing an immersion heater from scratch, you will have to install new wiring, and it is vital that this meets Wiring Regulations requirements.

An immersion heater must be controlled by an isolating double-pole switch fitted close to it. This is usually a double-pole 20A switch, which may have a neon indicator. The normal way to provide the supply is by

a 15A radial circuit connected to a spare fuseway in the consumer unit, or to a separate switchfuse unit if no spare fuseway is available. For heaters rated at 3kW or less, the connection can also be via a socket-outlet connected to a radial or ring circuit, or via a fused connection unit looped off a suitable ring circuit or radial feed from the consumer unit (as shown below).

A special switch is needed for a dual immersion heater and this may be sited elsewhere in the house for convenience – usually in the kitchen. Alternatively, there may be a change-over switch on the heater head itself.

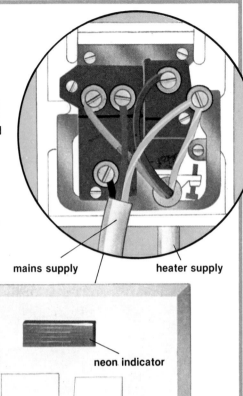

mains supply

heater supply

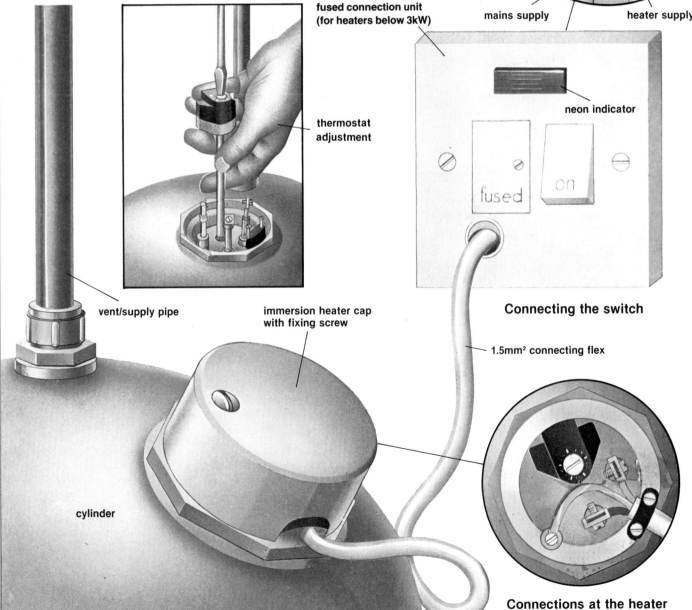

thermostat adjustment

fused connection unit (for heaters below 3kW)

neon indicator

fused

on

Connecting the switch

vent/supply pipe

immersion heater cap with fixing screw

1.5mm² connecting flex

cylinder

Connections at the heater

FITTING A WASTE DISPOSAL UNIT

Unwanted food – everything from potato peelings to leftovers – usually ends up in a smelly kitchen bin. It can be got rid of more quickly and hygienically with a waste disposal unit.

Waste King disposal unit by Wilec Ltd

Waste disposal units are an excellent means of getting rid of waste food and the like. Potato and vegetable peelings, cabbage stalks and outer leaves, food scraps, apple cores, tea leaves, dead flowers and so on are simply washed down the kitchen sink, ground to a slurry and flushed into the drainage system. Disposal is instant and hygienic, so it removes the need for constantly emptying smelly bins of rotting food. Whether you live in a house, flat or apartment, one of these units can be a tremendous labour-saving device which makes keeping the kitchen clean that much easier.

Of course there are limitations to what a waste disposal unit can do: it can't deal with all household waste. Broken china, tin cans, bottle caps and large bones will only clog and possibly damage the appliance, so you must be careful not to put them in with other waste. Indeed, jamming is the most common problem with these units, and it usually occurs as a result of misuse. Many modern units have a reversible action motor which enables the jammed material to be cleared by flicking the reversing switch and restarting the motor. Jamming is likely to give rise to over-heating and may cause a thermal cut-out, automatically turning off the motor. In a case like this, it may take some five minutes for the motor to cool sufficiently for it to be restarted. Models without a reversible motor are usually supplied with a key to free the jammed unit. But remember, the electricity supply must be cut off before using it.

When waste disposal units were first introduced, the sewage authorities were concerned that the slurry produced by them could result in sewers becoming choked with silt. Although these fears have proved unfounded, you must make sure that any sediment produced is flushed safely through the household drainage system. It's therefore important to leave the cold tap running while the unit is in operation. This will also help to prevent jamming.

Installation requirements

Waste disposal units have to be plumbed permanently into the waste outlet of the kitchen sink. They are driven by a relatively powerful motor which turns a set of steel blades. It's these blades that grind the waste into the slurry that's washed into the drainage system.

In order to operate effectively the unit needs to be connected to an 89mm (3½in) diameter sink waste outlet instead of the usual 38mm (1½in) hole, although some models can be adapted to fit this size. You can usually buy a sink with this larger sized opening, but if you already have a stainless steel sink the outlet can be enlarged using a special cutting tool which is rather like a hacksaw with a saw file as a blade.

If you have a sink top made of ceramic or plastic material, or enamelled pressed steel, you can't fit a waste disposal unit unless you're prepared to renew the sink top at the same time.

The outlet from the unit itself is 38mm (1½in) diameter and, like any other waste outlet, must be connected to a trap to prevent smells from the yard gully or the main soil and waste stack entering the kitchen. It's best to use a simple tubular P-trap which will allow the waste and slurry to pass through without leaving any sediment behind. Bottle traps should not be used as they are more likely to block and they also discharge more slowly.

Where the waste pipe from a waste disposal unit situated on the ground floor of a house is taken to a yard gully, it is particularly important that the waste pipe should discharge into the gully above the water level but below the level of the gully grid. In this way the grid will not become fouled by the slurry and, more importantly, the full force of the water discharged from the sink waste will be available to ensure that the slurry will be flushed through the gully and then out into the sewer.

Back or side inlet gullies are available and these are to be preferred when a new drainage system is being installed. However, there are also slotted gully grids on the market and these are highly suitable for converting existing drainage systems. The branch waste pipe from the kitchen sink is simply extended to discharge just below the slot in the gully.

Fitting a waste disposal unit

An existing stainless steel sink can be adapted by using a special cutting tool, after removing the existing waste outlet. When you are trying to remove the outlet, use a pair of pliers to hold the waste grid while turning the back-nut with a wrench. If this proves difficult, try heating it with a blow-torch. If this still doesn't do the trick, try burning out the washer between the base of the sink and the back-nut with your blow-torch and cutting through the old waste with a hacksaw. When

MAKING A NEW WASTE OUTLET

1 *Disconnect the waste trap from your waste outlet. If the trap is plastic this should be easy; for metal traps a little more effort may be required.*

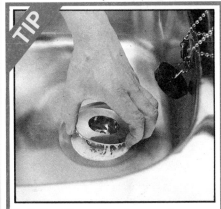

3 *Pull out the outlet when you have detached the back-nut. If the mastic or putty holds it tightly in position, lever it out with a screwdriver.*

5 *Lift out the metal section carefully as it will be ragged and sharp where you have cut it. Check that the hole is the right size.*

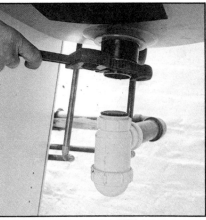

2 *When you have detached the waste trap, use a wrench to unscrew the back-nut which holds the outlet in position. Remove it and the washer.*

4 *When you have removed the waste outlet, measure the hole you need, mark it out in the sink and cut it with a saw file cutting tool.*

6 *Take the new outlet flange supplied with the unit and put a bead of plumber's putty underneath it before placing it in the opening.*

Ready Reference

OPERATING A DISPOSAL UNIT

ALWAYS
● grind food waste with a strong flow of cold water
● grind all soft waste including paper napkins, paper towels, cigar and cigarette butts, tea bags provided they don't have strings, and also small bones such as chicken bones
● flush the unit regularly to aid thorough cleaning
● turn the power switch off before attempting to clear a jam or remove an object from the disposer
● use a long piece of wood to clear jams
● leave the outlet cover in place to reduce the risk of objects falling into it when not in use
● make sure the unit is earthed.

NEVER
● put your fingers or hands into the unit to clear a jam
● let children operate the unit
● use hot water when grinding waste – but you can drain it out between grinding periods
● feed in large quantities of fibrous waste at once – instead, this should be well mixed with other waste and fed in gradually
● grind cans, bottles, bottle caps, glass, china, leather, cloth, rubber, string, feathers, newsprint, or large bones
● pour any drain-cleaning chemicals through the unit
● turn off the motor or water until grinding is completed (ie, only when you can hear the motor running freely).

FAULT FINDING
Problems may occur with your unit:
● if there is a water leak round the sink flange: the seal will have to be remade
● if the water drains slowly when the unit is in operation and the waste is clogging up the outlet: keep on grinding and flushing through
● if the disposer won't start. There may be an electrical fault or the motor may have been overloaded: check the cut-out and reset if necessary
● if the unit doesn't function properly immediately after installation. It is likely that the drain line is blocked or can't cope with the outlet discharge – unless there is a problem with the unit itself
● if there are loud noises from the unit when it's in operation: switch off and check for foreign bodies
● if the unit jams: turn it off and follow the manufacturer's instructions for cleaning blockages.

INSTALLING THE WASTE DISPOSAL UNIT

1 Take the basic flange components supplied and check the assembly order. There will be a gasket ring, a spacer ring, and a protector ring.

2 Hold the sink flange down, slide the assembly into place, and tighten the screws evenly to make sure there is a watertight seal.

TIP

3 Lubricate the inner lip of the rubber flange on the top of the unit with a small amount of petroleum jelly or household oil.

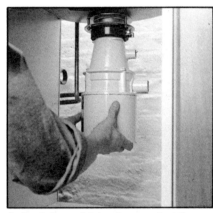

4 Push the unit into place so that the rubber lip engages the sink flange and is held in place by it, leaving the unit hanging by itself.

5 Rotate the unit to align it with the waste outlet and tighten the screw clamp evenly all round to hold the whole assembly firmly in position.

6 Fix on the waste outlet elbow and attach a P-trap 38mm (1½in) in diameter. Check that the trap is tight and connect it to the waste pipe.

the outlet has been removed, check the size of the enlarged hole you need with the new outlet as a guide, then use the cutting tool to cut it out.

With your aperture cut, or with your new sink, bed down the new waste outlet with plumbers' putty, and screw up the backnut and washer. Then attach the suspension plate for the unit, and finally the unit itself. The manufacturer should provide full instructions for the whole operation; follow them carefully.

A tubular P-trap should be attached to the unit via pipe connections which will be supplied. If there is no convenient way of attaching a sink overflow to a disposal unit, you can either seal it off or pipe it down to a socket fitted above the trap in the waste outlet.

PARTS OF A WASTE DISPOSAL UNIT

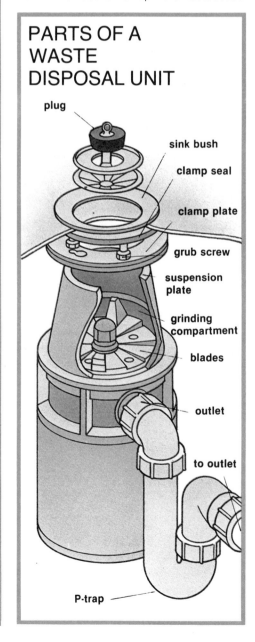

- plug
- sink bush
- clamp seal
- clamp plate
- grub screw
- suspension plate
- grinding compartment
- blades
- outlet
- to outlet
- P-trap

WIRING UP THE UNIT

Providing power for a waste disposal unit is simple. You can plug it directly into a 13A socket outlet, but it's better to run a spur and use a connection unit.

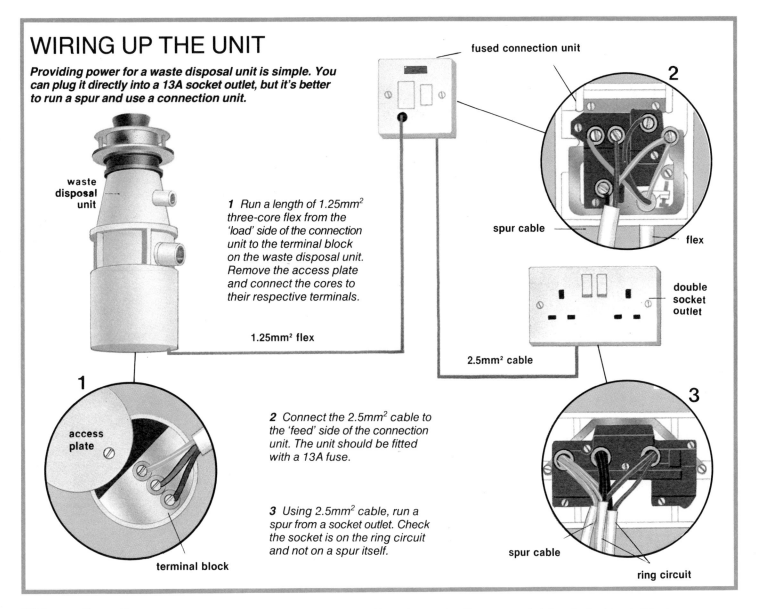

waste disposal unit

1 Run a length of 1.25mm² three-core flex from the 'load' side of the connection unit to the terminal block on the waste disposal unit. Remove the access plate and connect the cores to their respective terminals.

1.25mm² flex

1

access plate

terminal block

fused connection unit

2

spur cable

flex

double socket outlet

2.5mm² cable

2 Connect the 2.5mm² cable to the 'feed' side of the connection unit. The unit should be fitted with a 13A fuse.

3 Using 2.5mm² cable, run a spur from a socket outlet. Check the socket is on the ring circuit and not on a spur itself.

3

spur cable

ring circuit

Wiring up the unit

Most waste disposal units are powered by an electric induction motor. This sort of motor is constructed differently to the motor found in most other home electrical appliances. It starts immediately on full load, the starting current needed being much less than that of other types of electric motor. As a result a waste disposal unit needs only a 13A electricity supply, which can conveniently be provided from a nearby circuit.

There are a number of models on the market, and the differences between them can affect the electric wiring you have to provide. The principal difference is whether the unit has reversing facilities or not. The simplest type has no reversing facilities – it runs in one direction only. Should the unit become jammed the electricity supply must be switched off before a release key is inserted to engage the impeller and release the jam. Such one-way

motors are protected from the overloading a jam causes by a thermal cut-out; after clearing the jam you will have to re-set this by depressing a button on the motor frame before the motor can be re-started.

Other versions have special switch-gear which reverses the direction of the electric motor every time it is switched on. With these types the reversing controller, which incorporates a double-pole switch and 13A fuse, is either mounted on the unit as an integral unit, or fixed to the wall in the kitchen some 300mm (12in) above the work surface.

A waste disposal unit should ideally be connected to a 13A switched fused connection unit (often called a fused spur unit). This unit has the required double-pole isolating switch and 13A cartridge fuse; it might be best to choose the version with a neon indicator light.

A possible alternative outlet is a 13A fused plug and switched socket outlet, but as the

switch is only single-pole it is always necessary to remove the plug to isolate the unit and there is also a likelihood that the socket may be used temporarily for other appliances. The circuit wiring required to supply a waste disposal unit is simply a spur cable branching off the ring circuit cable. The connection at the ring circuit is usually more conveniently made at an existing 13A socket outlet than at a junction box inserted into the ring cable. You should use 2.5mm² two-core and earth cable and run it from the socket to the point where you intend to fix the switched fused connection unit or special reversing controller.

Connect a length of 1.25mm² three-core flex to the 'load' side of the connection unit and run it to the terminal block of the waste disposal unit. The brown core should then be connected to the 'L' terminal, the blue to the 'N' and finally the green/yellow to the 'E' terminal.

FITTING AN EXTRACTOR FAN

Stale air, poor ventilation and the build-up of condensation are potential problems in the modern home, particularly in the kitchen and bathroom. Extractor fans can help; they're easy to install, cheap to run and, most important, extremely efficient.

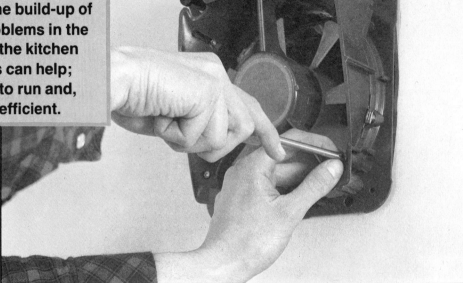

extractor fan from Xpelair

Every home experiences the unpleasantness of lingering cooking smells and poor ventilation. With draught-proofing, double glazing and central heating, the result, in the long term, is likely to be the constant presence of condensation which can eventually damage both the decor and the structure of the home. And in the kitchen persistent condensation is not only unsightly but also unhygienic.

There are a number of measures that can temporarily relieve the problem, but in the long run the only way to deal with it is to get rid of the stale air completely and replace it with fresh. To do this you need to install an extractor fan.

Types of fans
There are three types of extractor fan commonly used in the home and all are comparatively easy to install.

Perhaps the most common is the window fan which is fitted in a hole cut in a fixed pane of glass. These fans can be controlled by an integral switch, usually cord-operated, or else by a separate wall-mounted, rocker switch. The installation involves no structural work; just ask your glazier to replace the pane with one in which a hole has already been cut.

A wall fan, controlled by similar switches, is fitted in a hole made in an external wall or in an air brick vent. This sort of fan takes a little longer to install, as a hole has to be made in the external wall. However, by installing a wall fan in preference to a window-mounted fan you avoid restricting the view from a window and the inconvenience of having to have that window permanently closed.

There's one other common kind of extractor fan and that's the self-actuating, window-mounted plastic ventilator. But although the easiest to install and cheapest to run – no further expenses after installation – this type is also the least effective.

There are other, more specialised, types of extractor fans such as cooker hoods and timed fans for the bathroom or toilet which are variations on the three main types already described. Cooker hoods either

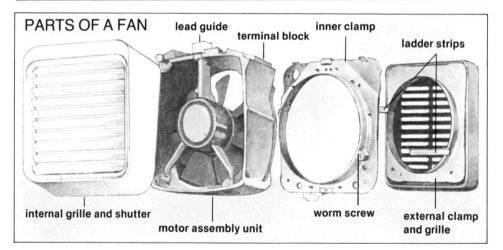

PARTS OF A FAN — lead guide, terminal block, inner clamp, ladder strips, internal grille and shutter, motor assembly unit, worm screw, external clamp and grille

recirculate the air in a kitchen after filtering it, or else extract it. Timed fans in the bathroom or toilet are activated by the lightswitch and are particularly useful when these rooms don't have external walls. Obviously, they will require ducting to enable the air to be expelled outside, but the timed switch poses no extra problems as it's connected up to the light switch when the fan is linked to the lighting circuit. Ceiling-fitted extractor fans are also available. They require an unobstructed space of 300mm (12in) between ceiling joists, and may also require ducting to an external wall if you have glass fibre roof insulation.

Calculating your needs
Which type of fan you install is obviously determined by the size of the room but also by whether there is an accessible external wall available.

It's simple to work out the size of fan required for a particular room. All you do is work out the volume of the room in cubic metres or feet by multiplying the length by the breadth by the height. Then multiply that volume by the number of air changes (see *Ready Reference*).

Siting your fan
If your home has already been fitted with an extractor fan, and it has proved to be less than satisfactory, the chances are that it has been sited in the wrong place.

The most common sign of that is poor ventilation – the result of the short circuiting of air movements between the fan and the air inlet. The extractor fan should be sited as far away from and, if possible, opposite the main source of air replacement.

In a kitchen, fans should always be fitted as high up as possible on a wall or window,

CHOPPING THE HOLE

1 *Drill a hole through the wall and, using a length of string and the drill bit as a compass, accurately mark out the hole to be cut.*

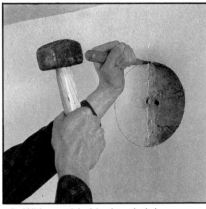

2 *With a cold chisel and club hammer chop round the circle perimeter and then move inwards to dislodge the surface layer of plaster.*

3 *Once you've done this you can use the same chisel to chop away the bricks. Try to leave a brick in the middle of the hole for leverage.*

4 *The hole should be trued up outside. It doesn't matter if it's slightly inaccurate as the clamp plates will cover and seal any rough edges.*

Ready Reference

TYPES OF FAN
There are three main types of extractor fan:

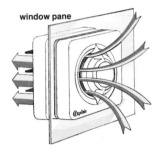

window pane

● the window fan fitted to a window with a hole cut in it

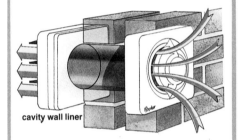

cavity wall liner

● the wall fan fitted in a similar way to a wall with a hole chopped through it

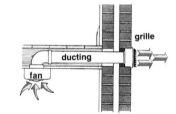

grille

ducting

fan

● the ducted fan fitted to an internal wall or ceiling, with ducting to carry the stale air outside.

CALCULATING YOUR NEEDS
To calculate the size of fan you require, multiply the volume of your room by the number of air changes needed per hour. Therefore, length x breadth x height x changes per hour = capacity.

Examples of air changes. Manufacturers recommend the following number of air changes per hour:
bathroom 15 – 20
kitchen 10 – 15
toilet 10 – 15
living room 4 – 6
Remember, always use the higher of these two figures to avoid any possibility of unsatisfactory ventilation.

but it is advisable not to install one immediately above a cooker or grill where temperatures are likely to exceed 40°C. So, the best place for it to be located would be on the wall or window adjacent to the cooker and opposite the door or main air inlet.

It is vital to make sure there is an adequate source of fresh air. If you have natural gas or smokeless fuel heating and your house is well sealed, but with no air inlet, an efficient extractor fan might cause a reversal of flow in the flue gases, which would prove extremely dangerous.

In addition, without an adequate inlet, the air pressure might drop and so impair the efficiency of your fan.

If you intend to fit a wall fan, it shouldn't be placed any closer than two brick lengths to a wall edge for fear of causing structural weakness. So, working out where to fit the fan is crucial to its ultimate success in ventilating your home. If you have any doubt about the supply of fresh air it might be an idea to fit an air brick.

Installing a wall fan
As only the very high capacity extractor fans rate over 100W, your fan can take its power from the lighting circuit. However, you should check that, including the wattage of the fan, the light circuit does not exceed the safety level of 1200 watts (counting each light as rated at 100 watts).

Before breaking into the lighting circuit for power a hole must be made in the wall to accommodate the fan. If you have to go through a cavity wall, it must be sealed with a special sleeve that can be obtained from the manufacturer. This will prevent unpleasant air leaking into the room from the cavity. The fan is connected to the circuit wiring by $1.0mm^2$ two-core and earth PVC –

INSTALLING THE FAN

1 *Attach the ladder strips to the outer clamp and position it in the hole. The ladder strips should run inside any cavity liner.*

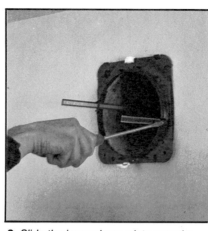

2 *Slide the inner clamp plate over the ladder strips and tighten the worm screws to secure the two plates. Then trim the ladder strips to size.*

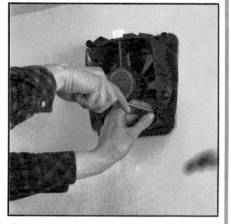

3 *Attach the motor assembly unit by screwing it to the inner clamp plate. Make sure that any exposed ladder strip is left outside the unit.*

4 *Thread the flex through the lead guide hole and connect it to the terminal block (see diagram), which can be temporarily removed for fitting.*

5 *Clip on and secure the external grille to the outer clamp plate making sure you tighten the holding screw on the underside.*

6 *Finally fit the inner clamp and connect the flex to the fuse unit of the clock connector, which is linked directly to the power supply.*

sheathed house wiring cable; the connecting point should be a fused clock connection unit. This makes isolating the fan for repairs easy: all you do is remove the fuse section.

There are three options for obtaining power for the new fan. You can connect into the circuit at an existing loop-in ceiling rose, run the cable to an existing junction box (always present if you have strip lighting in your kitchen), or install a new junction box in the lighting circuit feed cable and run the new cable to that.

At the fan end of the new cable connect it to the fixed section of the fused clock connector unit. With the main switch turned off connect the new cable to the appropriate terminals of the ceiling rose or junction box.

Then connect one end of a length of 1.0mm² three-core circular sheathed flex to

the fan and the other end to the plug part of the connection unit. If your fan is double insulated, as in most cases, you need use only two-core flex.

A wall fan is fixed to the wall in almost exactly the same way as a window fan is fitted to a window, the assembly being straightforward and simply a matter of following the manufacturer's instructions. In some cases ladder strips are used to secure the inner and outer clamp plates, and these may need cutting to length to match the wall depth. Otherwise the two plates are mounted independently of each other on either the wall or a panel that must be at least 35mm (1½in) thick. The rubber gaskets on both inner and outer clamp plates are retained in both cases. All fans have shutters which close automatically when the fan is

switched off and so prevent any draughts.

If your fan doesn't have an integral switch then a separate switch will have to be fitted. A mounting box should be fixed to the wall at a convenient height below the clock connector. From the connection unit run a length of the 1.0mm sq two-core and earth PVC flat-sheathed cable to the switch. Remember that as one of the wires is the live feed this must be joined at the connection unit end to the circuit live conductor with a plastic cable connector. The connector should be placed in the box behind the clock connector.

If you want to fit a speed controller in conjunction with a fan that has an integral cord-switch there is no essential difference in the wiring. It should be located at the same height as the new switch.

MAKING THE CONNECTIONS

Making the connections for a wall-mounted fan is the easiest part of the installation. Cable can be channelled in or run on the surface.

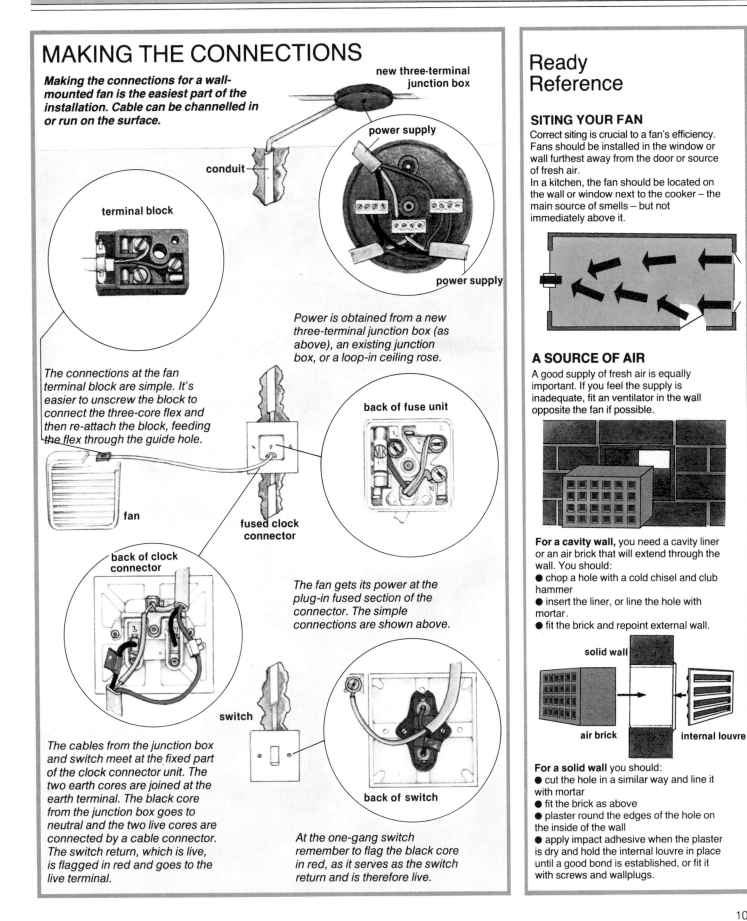

new three-terminal junction box

power supply

conduit

terminal block

power supply

Power is obtained from a new three-terminal junction box (as above), an existing junction box, or a loop-in ceiling rose.

The connections at the fan terminal block are simple. It's easier to unscrew the block to connect the three-core flex and then re-attach the block, feeding the flex through the guide hole.

fan

back of fuse unit

fused clock connector

The fan gets its power at the plug-in fused section of the connector. The simple connections are shown above.

back of clock connector

switch

back of switch

The cables from the junction box and switch meet at the fixed part of the clock connector unit. The two earth cores are joined at the earth terminal. The black core from the junction box goes to neutral and the two live cores are connected by a cable connector. The switch return, which is live, is flagged in red and goes to the live terminal.

At the one-gang switch remember to flag the black core in red, as it serves as the switch return and is therefore live.

Ready Reference

SITING YOUR FAN

Correct siting is crucial to a fan's efficiency. Fans should be installed in the window or wall furthest away from the door or source of fresh air.

In a kitchen, the fan should be located on the wall or window next to the cooker – the main source of smells – but not immediately above it.

A SOURCE OF AIR

A good supply of fresh air is equally important. If you feel the supply is inadequate, fit an ventilator in the wall opposite the fan if possible.

For a cavity wall, you need a cavity liner or an air brick that will extend through the wall. You should:
● chop a hole with a cold chisel and club hammer
● insert the liner, or line the hole with mortar.
● fit the brick and repoint external wall.

solid wall

air brick

internal louvre

For a solid wall you should:
● cut the hole in a similar way and line it with mortar
● fit the brick as above
● plaster round the edges of the hole on the inside of the wall
● apply impact adhesive when the plaster is dry and hold the internal louvre in place until a good bond is established, or fit it with screws and wallplugs.

FITTING A CEILING FAN

If any rooms in your home are difficult to ventilate – such as an internal WC or a bathroom – the answer could be to fit a ceiling fan, with ducting to the outside. Installing one is straightforward.

Installing an extractor fan is an ideal way of dealing with the problems of stale air, poor ventilation and condensation (see pages 100-103 for details). But in some circumstances fitting the normal wall or window mounted fans could prove undesirable or even impossible. In these cases the answer is simple: install a ceiling fan.

When to use a ceiling fan
If either your bathroom or WC are internal rooms, then you'll be familiar with the problems of adequately ventilating them. With no outside wall, it will be impossible to fit either a wall or window fan, and merely opening a door will hardly suffice. In this type of situation a ceiling fan will really come into its own and will simplify the whole business of getting rid of stale air. If you want to ventilate a room beneath a flat roof then the fan can merely take the air straight out into the open. If there's loft space above it, then the air could be discharged directly here, but this is not recommended practice, and in these circumstances ducting should be installed to take the air to an exterior grille or out through the roof.

Choosing a fan
Choosing a ceiling fan is not that difficult as, apart from anything else, there aren't that many different models to choose from. However, the model you choose is likely to be decided by the exact job you want it to do. If you want to ventilate only one room – a bathroom, for example – then the chances are that you'll choose the simplest type of ceiling fan. You'll probably be able to choose between surface-mounted models, partially recessed models and those that are fully recessed so that only the louvred grille inlet is visible. As far as looks are concerned, most fans have rigid plastic casings finished in neutral tones of grey or off-white.

But what if your WC is separate from your bathroom and you want to provide adequate ventilation for both? In this case you'll have to get a fan that can cope with ventilating two or more rooms at the same time. The fan itself is fitted in one room or even in the loft, and linked to other rooms via a system of ducting.

Disposing of the air
Before you buy a fan you must consider how you're going to deal with the air it will expel. It is possible for a fan to release the stale air in the loft. However, in practice, there is a risk of causing condensation if you release a lot of warm and humid air there. Your best bet is to use some form of ducting to carry off air directly outside.

Most fans are designed to fit a PVC soil pipe, which is usually 100mm (4in) in diameter, and this is probably the simplest and best type of ducting to use. If your fan won't fit this the manufacturers might well be able to provide you with special adaptors. However, soil pipe is not suitable for every type of fan and it could prove awkward if your ducting run requires a number of corners. In this case purpose-made flexible ducting offers a better alternative. You'll have to extend the ducting run up through the roof, and finish it off with a special weatherproof collar and cowl that should be available from the manufacturers. Alternatively, you can extend the ducting out through the eaves, via a hole cut in the soffit and covered with a grille, or through a hole in a gable end wall.

With any type of ducting, however, you must always bear in mind the problem of condensation. This is a strong probability where ducting carrying warm, moisture laden air passes through a well insulated, and therefore cold, loft. You must insulate the ducting itself as efficiently as you would cold water pipes, otherwise you risk the condensation finding its way back to the fan. One way of avoiding this extra task is to use double-walled flue pipe in preference to soil pipe.

Controlling the fan
How you will actually control the fan is another important consideration. Some models have a simple on/off switch and this should be perfectly adequate if you're installing the fan in a kitchen, say. However, if the fan is to be installed in a bathroom this will have to be a cord-operated switch, otherwise the switch would have to be mounted outside the bathroom, safely out of reach of anyone in the bath or shower.

In fact, you'll probably find that some kind of automatic switching is your best bet and this is particularly suited to bathrooms and WCs. Two versions are available; one is

FITTING A ROOF VENT

1 Lift off a few tiles from the roof to get at the felt. With a slate roof, you'll have to use a slater's ripper to remove the slates.

2 Cut a hole in the felt to let through the ducting. Use the rafters as a guide so the hole will be in line with a space between the joists.

3 Poke through the ducting and slip the weatherproof apron over it. Shape the apron with a piece of wood so it sits tightly on the tiles.

4 Replace some tiles so that little of the apron is visible. Finally, fit the cowl on top of the ducting so that the rain is kept out.

Ready Reference

ELECTRICAL CONNECTIONS

Fans must be connected to the mains via an isolating switch and you must use a switched fused connection unit. If you're taking power from the mains, run 2.5mm^2 two-core and earth cable to the feed side of the unit. With power from the lighting circuit use 1.0mm^2 or 1.5mm^2 two-core and earth cable.

DOOR SWITCH CONNECTIONS

From the connection unit run a length of 1.0mm^2 two-core and earth cable to the fan terminal block. You should then link the fan terminals and the door switch with 0.75mm^2 PVC sheathed two-core flex.

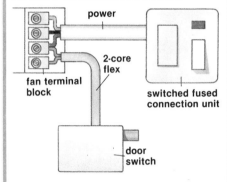

LIGHT SWITCH CONNECTIONS

From the fan's terminal block run 1.0mm^2 three-core and earth cable to the ceiling rose. That way the light will obtain its power via the fan, which works on its timer once the light has been switched off.

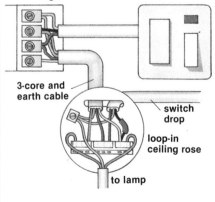

TIP: POSITIONING YOUR FAN

When positioning your fan on the ceiling you should:
● take into account a source of fresh air
● avoid direct water or spray
● avoid siting it so that someone in the bath or shower can touch it
● avoid siting it directly above a heat source producing a temperature above 40°C (104°F).

connected to the door so that the fan will work whenever someone enters the room, the other is connected to a ceiling rose so that it works when you switch on the light. Both types of automatic switch should incorporate timers. That way the fan will stay on for a while after you've turned off the light or left the room. Normally, there's an adjustable screw to allow you to set the timer at almost any limit up to forty-five minutes.

Installing the fan

Once you've decided where you want the fan to go you'll have to get into the loft to check that there are no obstructions such as pipes and cables and that the position corresponds to a gap between the joists. After you've decided your ceiling is suitable, you'll have to make up a timber support for it. Use a piece of 12mm (½in) chipboard fixed to two battens. The template normally provided

by the manufacturers will help you cut out a hole in the timber for the fan exhaust spigot and also a suitable hole for the cables. You can use the timber as a template and make four holes through the ceiling to mark the diameter of the circle. Then return downstairs and use a padsaw to cut out the section of the ceiling.

Next, fix the support in position by screwing the battens to the joists. If the fan is to be surface-mounted, screw the chipboard to a couple of 50x25mm (2x1in) battens and then attach these to the sides of the joists so that the support timber is hard against the ceiling. If you want a recessed or partially recessed installation, then you'll have to fix the support to the top of the joists leaving a gap between the support and ceiling sufficiently deep to accommodate the body of the fan. If the fan is too large then you might be forced to accept only a partially recessed installation.

FITTING THE FAN

1 *Use the ducting to mark out the section of ceiling that will have to be cut away. Then pierce guide holes through the ceiling below.*

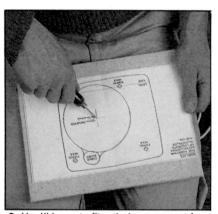

2 *You'll have to fit a timber support for the fan between the joists. Use 12mm (1/2in) chipboard and cut a hole in it with the help of a template.*

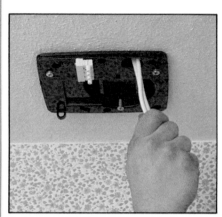

1 *Run in both the power cable from the fused connection unit (see Ready Reference) and the flex for the switch drop. Fit them under any cable clamps.*

3 *Move downstairs and remove the section of ceiling marked out by the holes from above. Use a padsaw or jig saw to cut it away.*

4 *Return to the loft and screw the chipboard to two 50 x 25mm (2 x 1in) timber battens. Then fix the entire construction between the joists.*

5 *Finish off your work on the fan by fitting its cover. This will protect the fan's mechanism from water or humidity which would cause damage.*

5 *Now fix the fan backplate to the ceiling. Use dome-headed woodscrews long enough to make a secure fixing into the chipboard above.*

6 *Fix the ducting in place. Make sure it fits tightly over the fan spigot so that no humid air can escape. Seal the join with waterproof tape.*

Obtaining the power

Extractor fans can take their power from a lighting circuit or a power circuit. Irrespective of which method you use, however, the fan must be capable of being isolated from the mains. For this purpose all power cables must run to a switched fused connection unit fitted with a 3A cartridge fuse, before being connected to the fan itself. If you are going to get power from a lighting circuit, you have two options. You can either connect directly to a ceiling rose, or else break into the circuit with a new three-terminal junction box. But remember, before working on any of the circuits, switch off at the mains. To obtain power from a ring circuit you can run a spur from a nearby socket outlet, or break into the circuit with a new three-terminal junction box.

What happens now depends on the control arrangements you have chosen. Where the fan has an integral cord switch all you have

CONNECTING UP THE FAN

2 Connect the cable and flex to the shrouded safety terminals. Make sure that you follow the manufacturer's instructions closely.

3 You can now attach the fan itself to the backplate. Hook it onto the special fixing screws and tighten them to hold it firmly in place.

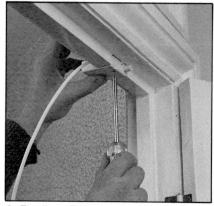

4 With the fan fixed to the ceiling you can complete the electrical connections. Push the connector plug firmly into the terminal block.

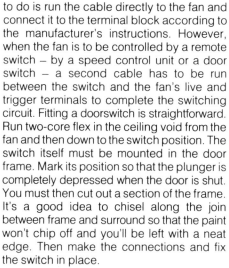

6 Run the two-core flex in the loft and down to the door switch. Remove the terminal block from the switch and make the connections.

TIP

7 Mark the position of the door switch on the doorstop. Make sure that the plunger will be fully pushed in when the door is closed.

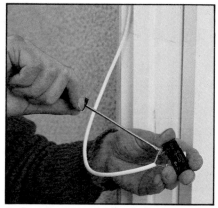

8 Finally, refit the terminal block and screw the switch in place. You can now turn on at the mains and at the fused connection unit to the fan.

to do is run the cable directly to the fan and connect it to the terminal block according to the manufacturer's instructions. However, when the fan is to be controlled by a remote switch – by a speed control unit or a door switch – a second cable has to be run between the switch and the fan's live and trigger terminals to complete the switching circuit. Fitting a doorswitch is straightforward. Run two-core flex in the ceiling void from the fan and then down to the switch position. The switch itself must be mounted in the door frame. Mark its position so that the plunger is completely depressed when the door is shut. You must then cut out a section of the frame. It's a good idea to chisel along the join between frame and surround so that the paint won't chip off and you'll be left with a neat edge. Then make the connections and fix the switch in place.

The wiring gets slightly complicated if you

wish to have the fan controlled by the room's light switch. In this case the room's lighting will still get its power from the normal circuitry, but it will have to be via the fan (see *Ready Reference*). In other words a length of three-core and earth cable will run from the fan's live, neutral and trigger terminals to the loop-in ceiling rose. The switch drop will then be wired up across the rose's live and switch terminals so that when the light is turned on, the fan will start to operate.

Fixing the ducting

Once you've installed all the cable runs you can secure the fan unit to the back of the spigot and then screw on the casing. You'll now have to install the ducting that will direct the stale air outside. Build up the run in the same way as you would a run of soil pipe, solvent-welding the joints where necessary. Make sure that the ducting is adequately

supported along its length, and take extra care where it passes through the roof and along horizontal sections; any sags could trap condensation.

Using flexible ducting is just as easy, only it should be linked to the fan's exhaust spigot and the PVC roof outlet with large worm clips.

Where the pipe is to pass through the roof, carefully lift off a few tiles. Then fit the weather apron by locating it beneath the surrounding tiles and poking the pipe through. With that done, you should complete the ducting's protection by fitting the weather cowl. Once the ducting is securely in place, make the final connections at the fan's terminal block, making sure that the cable is firmly held in any cable clamps. Ease the fan into the casing and secure it there before finishing off by fixing the grille plate to the fan body. Then you can switch on the power at the mains and test your fan.

INSTALLING WALL HEATERS & TOWEL RAILS

Electric towel rails and wall-mounted heaters are straightforward to install, but you must obey the wiring regulations if you're fitting them in a bathroom.

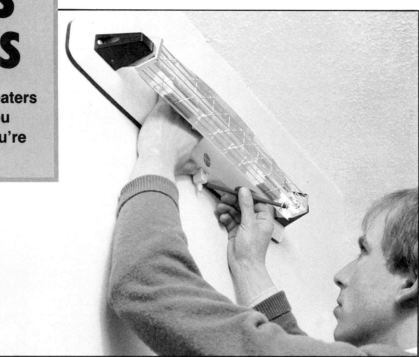

A wall-mounted heater and heated towel rails are two electrical appliances guaranteed to make life in your bathroom that much more civilized. Everyone knows how unpleasant stepping out of a hot bath into a cold bathroom can be, and having to use a damp towel is just as bad. Installing both these appliances will not only increase your comfort, but will also provide help in cutting down on the amount of condensation in the bathroom. While mounting them and obtaining power for these appliances is quite straightforward, bathrooms require special consideration as they are potentially the most dangerous room in which to use electricity.

Bathroom regulations
There are a number of regulations that apply when you're doing any kind of electrical work in your bathroom and these must, of course, be strictly adhered to.

You are not allowed to install any kind of socket outlet other than a shaver supply unit in a bathroom (see pages 88-91 for details). As a result this means that no portable appliance other than a shaver can be used there. Therefore all other electrical appliances, including both heaters and towel rails, have to be securely fixed and connected permanently to the mains. Switches must be cord-operated unless they are safely out of the reach of anyone in the bath or using the shower.

Installing a heated towel rail
There is a wide variety of towel rails available, so select one carefully to match your needs. As rails can be mounted against a wall they are not very obtrusive and you should really choose the largest one that can fit neatly into the space available in your bathroom. That way, of course, you'll be able to dry the whole family's towels at the same time. It's a good idea to get rails that incorporate a pilot light as this will help you not to leave them on when they're not being used – always an easy thing to do. If this is impossible make sure that the mains outlet point is fitted with a neon indicator. After deciding where you're going to mount the rails, make sure that they

can be safely fixed to the walls. Check that they'll be level and mark their position before drilling and plugging the wall. You can then screw the rails in place. Floor-mounted models are also available, and will have to be screwed to the floor surface.

Towel rails obtain their power from a spur on the ring circuit via a switched fused connection unit fixed out of reach of bath or shower. Fix this as close as possible to the towel rail. However, as it's unlikely that the flex already attached to the rail will be long enough to reach the unit, you'll have a run a length of 1.5mm² two-core and earth cable to a flex outlet plate mounted close to the rail, and connect in the flex at that point.

Installing a bathroom heater
There are plenty of different heaters that can be installed in the bathroom. Perhaps the most common is the reflector heater that consists of a rod element that glows while it's in use. Despite its wire guard, it's not difficult to touch the element in this type of heater so it must be fixed high up on a wall away from the bath or shower. Mounting the heater is a simple matter of drilling and plugging the wall before fixing it in place.

To obtain power you'll have to run a spur from the nearest socket outlet to a switched fused connection unit. This incorporates the required double-pole switch to isolate the heater completely when it's switched off. You'll find it more convenient if the model of heater you install has its own cord switch as well, so that you can switch it on and off in the bathroom. You'll probably then have to extend a cable from the switched fused

connection unit to a flex outlet plate mounted close to the heater so that the heater's flex can be connected directly to the circuit. Alternatively, if the heater is not fitted with a length of flex, you'll have to run a cable directly into the heater. If your heater does not have its own cord switch and you want to be able to control it from within the bathroom then you'll have to run the cable from the connection unit up into the ceiling void and connect it to a cord-operated switch.

Other bathroom heaters
Oil-filled radiators that are thermostatically controlled and which include a pilot light can either be fixed to the bathroom floor or by brackets to the wall. If you're installing the radiator within reach of the bath or shower then, like a heated towel rail, it will have to be controlled by a switched fused connection unit outside the bathroom. Then all you'll have to do is run a cable to a flex outlet plate and connect in the radiator's flex. Wall panel heaters that consist of a metal panel containing an element to provide low radiant heat come in numerous sizes and obtain their power in the same way. Skirting panel heaters are very similar but as they're slimmer they can actually replace existing wood skirting or can be fixed above it.

Special heaters for airing cupboards are easy to install. They are basically a cylinder of perforated metal containing a wire element and can be fixed to either the wall or floor of the cupboard. Wall fixing is best as you mount the heater about 300mm (12in) above the floor and therefore away from any article that might fall down and become a fire risk.

MAKING THE CONNECTIONS

Towel rails and heaters installed in the bathroom must be controlled by a double-pole switch, so that they can be safely isolated from the mains.

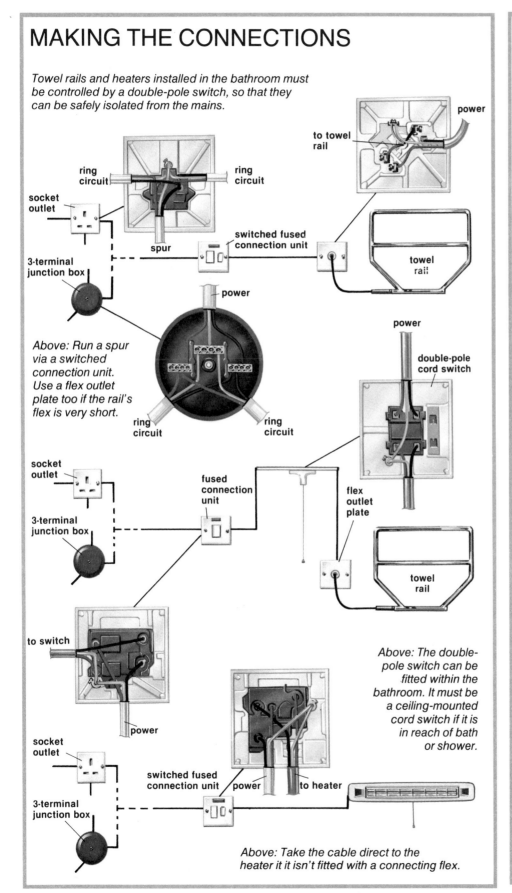

ring circuit

ring circuit

socket outlet

spur

3-terminal junction box

switched fused connection unit

to towel rail

power

towel rail

Above: Run a spur via a switched connection unit. Use a flex outlet plate too if the rail's flex is very short.

power

ring circuit

ring circuit

socket outlet

3-terminal junction box

fused connection unit

power

double-pole cord switch

flex outlet plate

towel rail

to switch

power

socket outlet

switched fused connection unit

power

to heater

3-terminal junction box

Above: The double-pole switch can be fitted within the bathroom. It must be a ceiling-mounted cord switch if it is in reach of bath or shower.

Above: Take the cable direct to the heater if it isn't fitted with a connecting flex.

Ready Reference

SAFETY IN THE BATHROOM

● Don't install any socket outlets. The only permissible type is a shaver supply unit
● don't use portable electrical appliances in the bathroom. The only permissible one is a shaver run from its own supply unit
● don't bring in portable appliances on extension cables plugged into a socket outside the bathroom
● don't fit lights with open lampholders. All lights must be totally enclosed
● don't fit ordinary rocker switches. For safety's sake all switches should be the ceiling-mounted cord-operated type fixed well away from the bath or shower.

INSTALLING A LIGHT/HEATER UNIT

If you're really short of space in your bathroom, installing a combined light and heater could be the answer. This consists of a ceiling-mounted light with a heating element round it. It incorporates a cord-operated switch to control the heater and you should also install a ceiling-mounted switch for overall control of the light. There are two ways of obtaining power. You can
● take a spur from the nearest socket outlet or break into the ring circuit with a three-terminal junction box. Run the cable to a switched fused connection unit outside the bathroom or,
● run in a completely new circuit from a 5A fuseway in your consumer unit, if you have a spare one available. In this case, make sure that the ceiling switch is a double-pole one.

TIP: USE NEON INDICATORS

When installing a ceiling-mounted cord-operated switch in the bathroom it's a good idea to fit one with a neon indicator as a reminder that your heater or towel rail may have been left on when not required. The indicator can be elsewhere in the house if this is handier.

INSTALLING A WALL HEATER

1 When positioning the heater, make sure it's out of reach of anyone using the bath or shower and is at least 150mm (6in) below the ceiling.

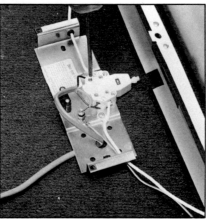

2 Connect a length of 1.5mm² two-core and earth cable to the heater terminals. If it's already fitted with flex, install a flex outlet plate close by.

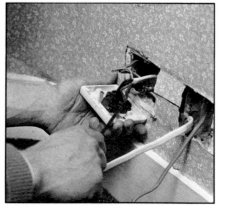

3 Run a spur to the heater from the nearest socket outlet. Alternatively, break into the ring circuit with a three-terminal junction box.

4 Run the spur to the supply side of a switched fused connection unit mounted out of reach of the bath, or else to one outside the bathroom.

5 Connect the 1.5mm² two-core and earth cable from the heater to the feed side of the connection unit, or to the terminals of the flex outlet plate.

6 Finally, drill and plug the wall and fit the heater securely in place. Link its flex to the terminals of the outlet plate if one is being used.

A TOWEL RAIL

1 Connect a length of three-core heat-resisting flex to the terminals of the towel rail. It will eventually get its power from a spur off a nearby power circuit.

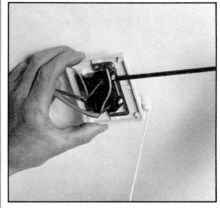

2 Run the spur in 2.5mm² two-core and earth cable to a fused connection unit. Then take a 1.5mm² cable to a ceiling-mounted double-pole (DP) switch.

3 Finally, run the cable to a flex outlet plate mounted close to the rail. Fix the rail securely to the wall (or floor) and connect the flex to the terminals.

CHAPTER 5

ELECTRICS OUTDOORS

One area where the use of electricity has greatly increased in recent years is out of doors, so make sure your outside circuits are safe by installing them properly and providing essential protective switchgear.

RUNNING CABLE UNDERGROUND

The most important part of taking power outside to a garden, a detached garage, or a workshop is running the electricity supply. An overhead cable run is a possibility, but taking it underground is the safer and more secure solution.

There are all sorts of reasons for taking a power supply out of doors. You may want to provide power to a garage so you can work on your car in light and warmth, or to transform your shed into an efficient workshop; you may require power sockets so you can use electrical appliances in the garden, or a circuit to light your pool or garden fountain. Whatever you do involves running cable out of doors and this is bound to be the major part of any outside installation. There are three ways of running cable: overhead (for further details of overhead cable runs see pages 116-120), along a wall or underground. Running the cable underground is probably best, even if it involves the most installation work. That way it is concealed, cannot be disturbed and presents no danger whatsoever. But before you run the power supply, you'll have to decide which type of cable you want to use.

Underground cables

Three sorts of cable are suitable for running underground, and two of them can be laid directly in the ground without the need for further protection. PVC-covered mineral-insulated copper-covered cable (MICC) has a very small diameter and will pass conveniently through an airbrick, so avoiding the necessity of chopping a hole through the house wall. However, as the mineral insulation tends to absorb moisture, the ends of the cable have to be fitted with a special seal to prevent this. It is a complicated job for the do-it yourselfer to fit these seals and several special tools are required. The easiest thing to do is measure the cable run and ask your local electrical contractor for the length of cable with seals already fitted. This cable is usually two-core, as the copper sheathing provides adequate earth bonding and, as the cable run starts and ends in a metal conversion box (see below) which allows you to switch to ordinary PVC two-core and earth cable for indoor sections or for connection to accessories, each end should also be fitted with a screwed compression gland. These glands attach the cable to the box and provide the necessary earth continuity,. The cable usually has an outer

CABLE TYPES AND CONNECTIONS

Only PVC cable run in conduit (1) can be taken directly from the consumer unit to the switchfuse unit. If you use either PVC armoured cable (2) or mineral insulated copper cased cable (3) they must both be fitted with a gland and a seal and then run from a conversion box to another in the garage.

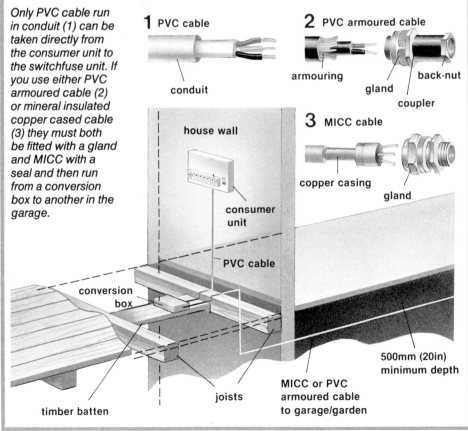

1 PVC cable — conduit

2 PVC armoured cable — armouring, gland, back-nut, coupler

3 MICC cable — copper casing, gland

house wall

consumer unit

PVC cable

conversion box

timber batten

joists

MICC or PVC armoured cable to garage/garden

500mm (20in) minimum depth

covering of PVC, often orange in colour, and is slim enough to be fairly unobtrusive – if run on the surface to wall-mounted light fittings, for example.

PVC-covered wire-armoured insulated and sheathed cable needs no seals, but has to have glands fitted at each end where it, too, enters the conversion box. This cable often comes with only two cores, in which case the armouring serves as an earth, but it may well be better to run three-core armoured cable. If you are using the three-core version, you'll find that the insulation colours will be slightly different to ordinary cable. Live is red, neutral blue, and earth yellow. The cable itself is usually black.

Both these types of cable are protected enough to allow them to be laid directly in the ground. But if you use PVC-sheathed two-core and earth cable then you'll have to run it in either heavy gauge galvanised steel or high impact rigid plastic conduit. You'll undoubtedly find it easier to use the plastic conduit as the steel sort requires stocks, dies and bending equipment that is not normally available to the householder. When using plastic conduit, however, do remember that it's likely to fracture in temperatures of –5°C or below, and also that fairly substantial holes will have to be cut in both the exterior wall and the garage wall to admit the cable.

The indoor section

All power supplies that are run outside are classified as sub-main cables and must originate from a spare fuseway in the consumer unit, or else from a new switchfuse unit. For further details on this and on the size of cable to use see pages 116-120 and Chapter 4 pages 72-75. The section inside the home will normally be run in ordinary PVC-sheathed two-core and earth cable which will be taken to the exit point. Obstructions inside the home can alter the route of the indoor cable but there are a number of straightforward methods (for example, fishing cable through a ceiling void) which can be employed if you don't have access from above. For further details on running cable see Chapter 2 pages 31-35.

When the cable is being taken underground, the exit point is likely to be where the ditch in which it will run starts against the house wall. However, the presence of a concrete terrace or some other obstruction may mean you'll have to change the proposed exit point (although it may be possible to take other measures, such as chopping a chase to protect the cable). It is important to note that only if you're running the outdoor section in PVC two-core and earth cable will it run directly from the switchfuse unit to the outside installation. Otherwise the indoor section must be taken right inside the conversion box.

Laying cable underground

Having drilled the exit point in the house wall, if you are running the power to a garage in the outbuilding, you'll have to dig a ditch in which to lay the cable. This should be at least 500mm (20in) deep, and digging it will probably be the most tiring part of the job! Try to avoid taking the cable under vegetable plots and flower beds where it could be disturbed; and obviously you won't want to dig up your lawn. Probably the best place for a ditch is at the side of a concrete or gravel path; but if you're forced to run it at the edge of a flower bed, dig the ditch somewhat deeper to give the cable extra protection. If you're using either PVC-armoured cable or MICC cable, it's a good idea to place the cable on a layer of sand at the bottom of the trench and also to sift the soil before filling it in; that way you can avoid the slight risk of sharp stones damaging the cable. It's also wise to place a line of slates on top of the cable to give it extra protection, when you fill in the trench. If you're using PVC-sheathed two-core and earth cable, you should first lay the conduit in the trench and cut it to fit. You'll have to buy couplers for lengths that need to be joined; for vertical runs you'll have to fit elbows and you'll need a further elbow to take a short length of conduit into the wall so that the cable has complete protection. Do not use solvent-weld adhesive to assemble the conduit run at this stage, as you'll have to dismantle the fittings to thread in the cable. Start at the house end and, working in sections, thread through enough of the PVC cable to reach the mains switch in the garage to wherever you're running it. An alternative method is to attach the cable to a drawstring; thread it through the conduit and then pull the cable through after it. You can then start fixing the elbows and couplers permanently. Smear the solvent-weld adhesive over the end of the conduit and inside the elbows and couplers with the special brush provided before joining the sections together. Then place the assembled run into the trench, making sure that each elbow is correctly positioned. At the garage end push the end of the cable and the short length of conduit into the hole in the wall and then carefully fill in the trench. If you're using PVC-covered wire-armoured cable it should be laid directly in the trench and the ends passed directly into the house and garage. It will then be taken into a conversion box at each end.

Fitting a conversion box

Extending either PVC-armoured or MICC cable beyond the entry point to the house or garage is pointless. They are both relatively expensive cables, cannot usually be connected to a switchfuse unit and can be awkward to run. That is why you should fit what is called a conversion box. This allows

RUNNING CABLE UNDERGROUND

1 After digging a ditch that is a minimum of 500mm (20in) deep, lay the conduit in it to give you an idea of what length you'll need.

2 Use a hacksaw to cut the conduit to length where necessary, and link it with special couplers; don't weld the joints yet.

3 Use an elbow fitting to join the vertical (above-ground) section of the conduit to the horizontal (underground) part next to the wall.

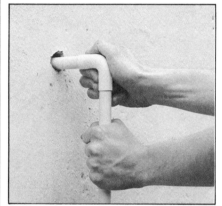

4 Fix a short section of conduit to the top elbow and check that it's long enough to take the cable completely through the garage wall.

5 Thread through the cable from the consumer unit. You can either dismantle the conduit or use a drawstring to pull through the cable.

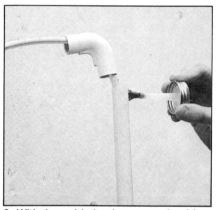

6 With the cable in place, you should use special conduit adhesive to fix the couplers and elbows firmly in position. Then bury the conduit.

you to change the type of cable in your sub-main circuit to ordinary PVC two-core and earth cable.

All that is required is a box containing three terminals and two entry holes. The correct one to use is an adaptable conversion box and lid or alternatively a standard one-gang metal mounting box fitted with a blanking-off plate as a cover. You can use a special three-way terminal block to make the connections, or else ordinary cable connectors. However, if you do use the cable connectors, you must make sure they are large enough for the current.

At the house end, the conversion box should either be fixed with wood screws to a timber batten fitted between the joists beneath the floor, or alternatively to the wall near the entry point of the cable. If you're running power to a garage or shed, the box at that end should be fitted to the wall near the cable entry point. You should remove two knockout holes, one of which must be fitted with a PVC grommet while the other should be large enough to accommodate the PVC-armoured cable. Strip away the outer layer of PVC and slide a PVC sheath and gland nut onto the armoured cable. You should put a back-nut in the knockout hole without a grommet and then prepare the cable by clipping away the excess armouring, leaving enough to carry up to the end of the gland's thread. You can now slide on the gland which will screw into the gland nut and keep the armouring in place. It's a good idea to attach a coupler to the gland as this will allow you more room in the box for the connections. Then feed the cable into the box and attach the back-nut to the coupler. If you are using two-core cable the armouring will serve as the earth so the back-nut must be tightened by a spanner to provide good metal-to-metal contact. Then pull the PVC protective hood over the whole assembly and remove the remaining PVC insulation to expose the red and black cores. If you are using two-core cable you'll now have to earth the box; it's a good idea to do this even if you're using three-core cable. You should link the earth screw on the box (which holds the earth connector) with a length of core that you have sleeved in green/yellow PVC. Feed in the PVC two-core and earth cable, which must be the same size as the sub-main cable, through the knockout hole previously fitted with a grommet, and prepare the ends of the cable in the usual way before joining the cores of the two cables together. From here the PVC cable will run to whatever appliance you want to supply. If it is a garage or workshop, it's likely to go to a switchfuse unit; if in the garden, it might be to well-protected sockets for lawnmowers, hedge trimmers, or lighting for an ornamental fountain.

FITTING A CONVERSION BOX

1 Use an adaptable mounting box to serve as a conversion box. Remove two opposite knockouts and fit a grommet to just one of them.

2 Remove two small knockouts at the back for the screws. Drill and plug holes in the corresponding spots on the wall, and position the box.

3 Fit a back-nut in the knockout hole. without a grommet, and then slide the PVC hood and gland nut onto the armoured cable.

4 Put on the gland and coupler and trim the armouring of the cable so that it ends at the bottom of the thread on the gland.

5 Feed the cable into the box and attach the back-nut to the coupler. Using a coupler allows you more room in the box for the connections.

6 The armouring serves as an earth but you should earth the box too by fitting an extra core to the box and connecting it to the terminal block.

7 Feed in the PVC two-core and earth cable that is to run to the switchfuse unit. Remember, this must be the same size as the armoured sub-main cable to which it is connected.

8 Using a block of three connectors, join the two cores of the armoured cable to their equivalents in the two-core and earth PVC cable and then connect the earth cores.

9 Finally screw on the lid of the conversion box. At the house end, the conversion box can be fitted safely to a timber batten that is fixed under the floorboards.

PROVIDING POWER IN THE GARAGE

If you add power and lighting to a garage, you can make it more than mere storage space for your car: your garage becomes a workshop. Connecting up the electricity supply is not difficult and sturdy accessories are produced specially.

Installing electricity in a garage can completely transform it. No more fumbling in the dark for car keys; or flat batteries on a winter's morning; and car repairs will be carried out in the relative comfort of a well-lit and pleasantly heated garage. Indeed, a garage equipped with a number of power sockets, some lights and a couple of work surfaces can double as an extremely efficient workshop. If your garage is attached to your home, it is likely that it will already have a power supply; if it's detached, it's possible you'll have to install the supply yourself. But running electricity to a garage, or indeed to any other outside building, is not that difficult. It should be done in three stages: work inside the house; work outdoors, and finally the new circuitry in the garage itself.

Inside the home

If you're going to run a power supply to your garage you should remember that the electricity supply to any outbuilding, even if only for a lighting circuit, must be independent of the house circuits. Tempting though it may be, you're not allowed to run the supply in the form of a spur from a ring circuit in the house. The basic requirements are: a separate mains switch and fuse unit in the home, and an isolating switch and fuse unit in the garage. The mains switch at the house end will usually be a switchfuse unit that should be linked to the mains by the electricity board. If there is a spare fuseway in the main consumer unit obviously you can make use of it. However, it's probably better to leave the spare fuseway for another circuit within the house and install a new switchfuse unit for the circuit to the garage or outhouse. Note that outdoor sockets should be RCCB protected – see pages 76-78. The cable running from the new switchfuse unit in the house to the garage is technically not a circuit cable and is classed as a sub-main cable. This is because it supplies a complete installation which has its own mains switch and fuse.

The section inside the house will normally be run in ordinary two-core and earth PVC sheathed cable, the size of which depends upon the circuit requirements in the garage.

The 2.5mm² size is suitable for a 20A supply; use 4mm² for a 30A supply, and 6mm² for a 45A supply. Do remember that if you are using the 4mm² cable for a 30A supply you must make sure that both switchfuse units are fitted with either a cartridge type fuse or MCB so that the circuit is uprated by one third. This is because 4mm² cable controlled by a rewirable fuse has a current-carrying capacity of only 27A and would consequently be a safety risk.

The outdoor section will either be in the same type of cable or else in special cable; which sort you use is determined by whether you run it overhead or underground, and, if run underground, whether or not it is to be in conduit. More details of underground cable runs are given in the previous section. It's best to make the outdoor section as short as possible, so the point at which the cable emerges from the house should be as near as practicable to the garage. This will obviously affect the section run in the home, as will obstructions inside. For further information on running cable procedure see Chapter 2 pages 31-35.

Installing an overhead cable

Where the distance between the house and garage is no more than 5m (about 17ft), an overhead cable attached to a catenary wire is a practical alternative to an underground cable run. A catenary wire is merely a length of galvanised steel-stranded cable similar to that sometimes used for fencing and should be secured to an eye bolt or eye screw fixed into the wall of the house and of the garage. For spans larger than 5m, intermediate supports such as poles are required to prevent sagging. Apart from looking unattractive, there is always the risk of damage in high winds so you may find it better to take the cable underground for long runs.

In theory a span of less than 3.5m (11ft) need not be supported by a catenary wire. If you're running an overhead cable to your garage, you'll have to make sure that there is no danger of it being hit by anything passing underneath. For that very reason the regulation minimum height of an overhead cable run is 3.5m (11ft). However, when the cable is suspended across a driveway the minimum height is increased to 5.2m (17ft).

RUNNING CABLE OVERHEAD

Running power overhead keeps the cable out of harm's way provided you have the catenary wire at a minimum height of 3.5m (11ft). The cable should be taped and clipped and the catenary

wire itself should be bonded to earth. To gain extra height at the garage end use a length of 100x50mm (4x2in) timber which should be bolted securely to the wall with 150mm (6in) coach screws.

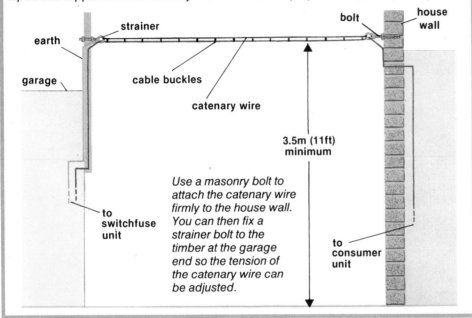

Use a masonry bolt to attach the catenary wire firmly to the house wall. You can then fix a strainer bolt to the timber at the garage end so the tension of the catenary wire can be adjusted.

THE GARAGE CIRCUITS

The lighting circuit can be either a loop-in or junction box system; the power circuit is wired as a radial circuit. Metal-clad sockets and switches are more robust

than plastic ones. Cable should be taken on the surface with vertical runs being clipped every 400mm (16in) and horizontal runs every 250mm (10in).

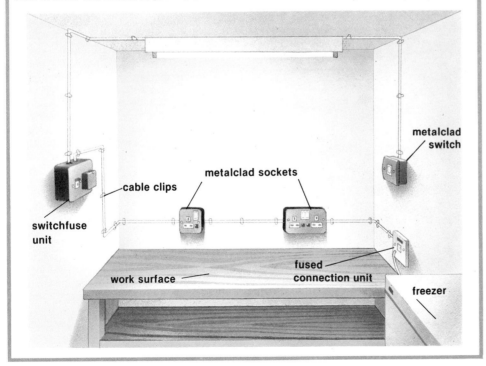

Ready Reference

ATTACHED GARAGES
If your garage is attached to your home you can safely run the power as a spur from a ring circuit.

DETACHED GARAGES
If your garage is detached from your home then it is deemed a separate building and must be:
● supplied by a sub-main cable
● controlled by an isolating switch and fuse unit at each end.

TEMPORARY POWER SUPPLY
The only other form of power supply allowed to a detached garage, other than a sub-main cable, is an extension cable. This can be linked up temporarily while the actual appliance that it supplies is in use.

PERMANENT POWER SUPPLY
Power can be supplied permanently to a detached garage in three ways:
● by an overhead cable
● by an underground cable
● by a cable fixed along a wall. Cable should never be taken along a fence for reasons of safety.

OVERHEAD CABLE RUNS
Points to note:
● the minimum height for an overhead cable run is 3.5m (about 11ft)
● if the cable crosses a driveway the minimum height is increased to 5.2m (17ft)
● with a span of under 3.5m (11ft) the cable need not be supported
● if the span is between 3.5m (11ft) and 5m (about 17ft) the cable should be attached to a catenary wire
● for spans over 5m (17ft) there should be intermediate supports in addition to a catenary wire.

TIP: TAPE THE CABLE

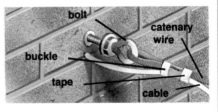

Attach the cable to the catenary wire with tape before fitting the buckle clips. That way the buckles will neither cut into the cable nor slide along it. It's also a good idea to leave a loop in the cable at each end to ease the strain and prevent water from entering the wall.

FITTING THE SWITCHFUSE UNIT

1 *If your garage is situated away from the house, it will need its own mains switch and fuses. Fix the unit to a sheet of treated chipboard.*

2 *Thread in the circuit cable and feed the red and black cores behind the switch so that they can connect to the unit's terminals.*

3 *Strip off some of the insulation from each core and make the connections. Sleeve the earth core in green/yellow PVC.*

4 *Then feed in the cables for the two circuits to provide power in the garage. Connect the lighting circuit to the fuseway nearest the switch.*

5 *When you have made all the connections fit the fuseway covers. Make sure you fit the correct one over each set of terminals.*

6 *Finally fit the cover and shield and slot in the two MCBs. You can then turn on the power in both the house and garage.*

Running the cable

It's a good idea to insert an adjusting device at one end so that the catenary wire can be tightened once the cable has been attached to it. You'll probably have to fix a length of 100x50mm (4x2in) timber to the garage wall to obtain the necessary minimum height at that end. To fix the timber to the garage wall you'll have to drill and plug two holes and use 150mm (6in) coach screws. You should drill a hole in the house wall to serve as an exit point for the cable. This should be at about first floor level in a two-storey house and at eaves level in a bungalow.

You'll also have to drill a hole in the garage wall to enable the cable to enter and run to the mains switch. In addition, it's wise to run a length of green/yellow PVC insulated cable from the catenary wire to the mains switch to bond the catenary to earth. Measure the length of cable required to run from the switch-fuse unit in the house to the mains switch in the garage. Having fixed and tightened the catenary wire to the two eye bolts, pass the end of the cable through the hole in the house and then pull through sufficient to reach the mains switch in the garage. You should connect the bared end of the catenary wire to the bonding earth core by using a cable connector. After temporarily attaching the cable to the catenary wire (so you can make sure that there is sufficient to reach the garage) you can make a permanent attachment by using cable buckles every 250mm (10in). Both the supply and the earth cable should be fixed to the post with plastic cable clips that should be no more than 400mm (16in) apart. Alternatively, you can run the vertical section in metal or plastic conduit that is attached to the timber. You can now make the connections to the switchfuse unit in the house and in the garage.

An alternative method of running cable overhead is to carry it in an unjointed length of heavy gauge steel conduit; in this case the minimum height is reduced to 3m (10ft). You could also run it in rigid plastic conduit, but this will sag and is also likely to fracture at temperatures below −5°C. If you don't want to run the cable either overhead or underground then you may be able to take it along a boundary wall to the garage. Under no circumstances, however, may the outdoor section be fixed to a fence.

Inside the garage

Running cable to the garage is probably the most important and also the most difficult part of installing electricity there. There are, to begin with, certain precautions you must take with the work inside the garage. Remember that a detached garage is classed as a completely separate building and therefore must be fitted with a double-pole isolating switch, enabling the electricity to all circuits

FITTING POWER POINTS IN A GARAGE

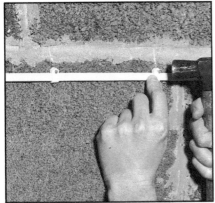

1 To provide current for a garage power point you should use 2.5mm² two-core and earth cable clipped firmly to the wall every 150mm (6in).

2 Fit a grommet on a knockout hole and fix to the wall the special metal box for surface mounting in garages and workshops.

3 Make the connections after sleeving the earth core in green/yellow PVC. It's a good idea to add an extra earth to protect the box.

4 Fit the faceplate with great care. This is necessary because its screws link the box into the earthing of the socket.

Ready Reference

GARAGE ACCESSORIES

It's best to fit metal-clad switches and socket outlets in a garage or workshop. They are tougher than the plastic variety and last longer.

It's a good idea to choose versions which incorporate a neon indicator light. That way you can see at a glance if the power is on or off.

FIXING THE ACCESSORIES

These accessories are usually surface mounted. To install them:
● drill and plug the holes in the wall
● feed the cable into the surface mounting box
● fix the box to the wall with No 8 wood screws
● make the connections in the usual way
● attach the faceplate.

TIP: EARTH THE BOX

The circuit cable earth core protects the socket itself but it's wise to add extra protection for the mounting box. You can do this in two ways:

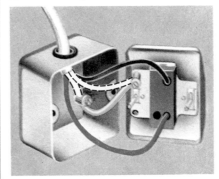

● loop the circuit earth core into the earth screw on the box and then take it onto the socket, or
● add an extra green/yellow sleeved earth core linking the box earth screw to the socket earth terminal.

and equipment to be completely cut off at the flick of a switch. If you're going to run more than one circuit within your garage, it's best to fit a switchfuse unit and the mains switch on this will serve as an isolating switch.

When you fit the new switchfuse unit, it's best to fix it as near as possible to the point where the incoming cable enters. It should be installed in the same way as inside the home and it's important to fit a sheet of fire-resistant material such as treated chipboard to the wall beforehand.

You can obviously install as many circuits as you like, but for most garages two – one for power and one for lighting – should prove ample. Generally, you should fit the new switchfuse unit with a 5A and 15A MCB. If, however, you plan to have a number of power sockets, heaters and appliances, it is wise to fit a 30A fuse for the power circuit. Cartridge fuses will also suffice but it's not advisable to

use rewirable fuses. You should run the lighting circuit in 1.0mm² or 1.5mm² two-core and earth PVC cable, fixed to the wall and roof surfaces, and you can install a loop-in or junction box system. The power circuit will have to be run in 2.5mm² two-core and earth cable and horizontal runs should be clipped every 250mm (10in), while vertical runs need to be clipped every 400mm (16in).

Although the standard plastic fittings can be used safely in a garage, it's probably best to use the special metal-clad versions. Although these are slightly more expensive, they are more robust and therefore safer in an environment where they could be subjected to the occasional knock or blow. It's also wise to choose versions with neon-indicators to show, at a glance, whether the socket is on or off. They are designed specifically for surface mounting and come complete with mounting boxes.

INSTALLING A LAMP AND SWITCH

1 If you're fitting a lamp to a beam, clip the cable along the middle of the beam so it runs to the centre of the battenholder.

2 You'll have to nibble out some plastic knockouts on the pattress block before offering it up to the beam or ceiling.

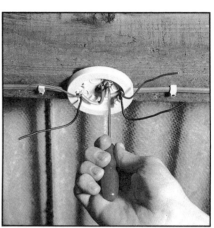

3 Clip the power and switch cables to the beam and run them into the pattress. Then sleeve and connect up the earth cores.

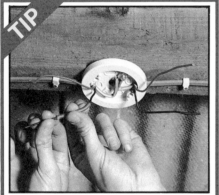

4 Before going any further make sure that you have flagged the black core of the switch cable with red PVC tape: this indicates that it's live.

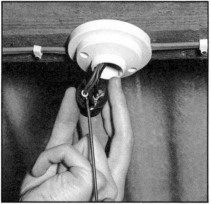

5 Make the connections. The two red cores go to one terminal; the flagged black core to another and the neutral to the third.

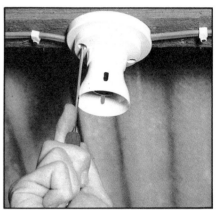

6 Finally screw the battenholder and pattress block to the beam after making holes with a bradawl. You can then connect up the switch.

7 Clip the switch cable onto the wall and run it to the point where you'll mount the switch. Fit a grommet to the knockout hole.

8 Feed the cable into the box and make the connections. Remember to sleeve the earth in green/yellow PVC and also to earth the box itself.

9 Replace the switch in the mounting box and fit the faceplate. You can now switch on the power in the house and in the garage itself.

INSTALLING OUTDOOR LIGHTS

By installing outdoor lighting you can make your home that much more welcoming and secure as well as ensuring that it's easier and safer to approach.

Outdoor lighting can be divided into two groups; the largely decorative and the primarily functional. In the first group you'll find spotlights for various parts of the garden, festoon lights and underwater lights. Further information both on what decorative lighting is available and how to install it will be given in another article. Functional outdoor lighting is the most practical and also the most common. It's used to light front and back doors, patios, paths, drives and gateways.

The advantages of outdoor lighting

Outdoor lighting will make life a lot easier for any visitors arriving in the evening: no longer will they face the prospect of tripping down steps or stumbling blindly along paths to reach your front door. With a porch light installed you'll find that your home seems that much more welcoming and, of course, you'll no longer have to fumble in the dark for your keys. Equally importantly, would-be burglars will be deterred by a well-lit house. And, what's more, really efficient outdoor lighting will enable you to get that much more out of your patio or garden.

Outdoor lighting is usually simple to install and the circuit requirements are quite straightforward. When you are going to install one or perhaps two lights outside your home – in the porch or outside your back door, for example – you can normally run them off an existing lighting circuit. When you want to install a lot of lighting outdoors and away from the house you'll probably find it best to install a new circuit.

If your home has no outdoor lighting then the first areas you're most likely to consider will be the porch, walls and the back door.

Basic outdoor lighting

There are so many different types of lights that can be installed outdoors that the first thing you'll have to do is visit your local showroom and make your choice. For a porch light you could have a close-mounted ceiling fitting such as a globe or cube, a pendant lantern, a wall-mounted light with a bracket or bulkhead fitting or a period-style carriage light. Traditional fittings for a back door are bulkhead or bracket lights.

The former, usually containing either a tungsten halogen lamp or miniature fluorescent tube, is fixed directly to the wall surface. A bracket light is normally fixed to the wall by a backplate with the bracket – usually either a straight stub or what's referred to as a swan neck bracket – extending to the fitting itself. The bracket is likely either to be the type that can be fitted to a flat wall or to an external corner of the house, in which case the lamp will be able to throw light over a wider area – including part of the back and side of the house. The chances are that the light itself will consist of a well glass fitting available in various designs and containing a tungsten halogen lamp, which is particularly bright and long-lasting.

Lighting bricks are also available and are particularly suited to installation on side walls although, of course, they can easily be installed elsewhere. They consist of opal glass lights, normally rectangular or square although circular ones are also available, which are mounted on a die-cast aluminium backplate. The advantage of these lights is that they can either be flush or surface-mounted.

Wiring and controlling the lights

If your outdoor lights are being mounted directly on the external wall then running in the power is normally straightforward. It'll be a question of drilling a hole in the wall of the

Ready Reference

USING MASTIC
If you are running cable on the surface to an outside light then make sure water can't get into the light fitting. To make a waterproof installation:
● seal the cable entry hole with non-setting mastic
● seal round the edges of the fitting's backplate with mastic too (this is particularly important if the cable runs through the house wall directly into the back of the light).

TIP: ANGLE THE CABLE HOLE
If you are drilling through the house wall to run a power cable to an outside lamp, angle the hole so that it slopes slightly downwards to the outside wall. Then there's no danger of water running down the wall, entering the hole and causing any damage to the decorations.

TIP: USE A GRIDSWITCH
If you want to control your path or gate lights from your gateway, then you can use a secret-key gridswitch. It's better to choose a weather-proof type that can be installed on the gate-post or on the wall of the house.

WHERE TO SITE OUTSIDE LIGHTS

1 *Porch lights by the front door*
2 *External corner light to light two walls*
3 *Post top lights at the gateway*
4 *Patio lights above sitting areas*
5 *Bulkhead light above the back door*
6 *Bollard light on the path.*

porch, say, and bringing the power cable out at a point that coincides with the backplate of the light fitting. Running in the cable for a roof or ceiling-mounted light may be slightly more involved but this depends largely upon the height of the porch and how easy it will be to drill through the wall.

You'll probably find it most convenient to mount the switch for a porch light in the hall, close to the front door. That way you'll be able to switch the light on and off as you wish. You might, of course, find it convenient to have a second switch actually in the porch, in which case it is a simple job to drill a hole through the wall, link the switches with a short length of three-core and earth cable and mount them back to back. Wiring in a back door light or wall-mounted light is much the same, although if you're going to install an outside switch you should make sure that it's thoroughly protected against the weather.

Patio lighting
If you're going to install lighting on your patio then you'll discover the range of lights available will be much wider. In addition to the types of fittings mentioned above, you could also fit spotlights, table lamps and standard lamps. While a single light could easily be wired from an existing lighting circuit it's probably best to run a separate circuit specifically for the new lighting. A socket outlet on your patio can obtain its power on a spur from the house ring circuit. However, you should always bear in mind that when added to the area in the house, the patio mustn't exceed the maximum area to be supplied by any one ring circuit. And, of course, you must take precautions to protect the socket from the weather. Probably your best bet is to twin-mount the socket and then fit a hinged plastic cover specially designed for outside sockets in relatively protected positions – such as a patio.

Probably the best way to supply power for patio lighting is to run a new radial circuit. Use a 20A circuit for a patio no larger than 20m^2 and a 30A one where the area is in excess of 20m^2. Once the circuit is installed, it's easy to supply fixed lights via switched fused connection units fitted with a 3A fuse. For further information on running in a new circuit see Chapter 4 pages 72-75.

Gateway lighting
If you want to install lighting on your gate to help people drive in at night then it must, of course, be visible from the road. Post top lamps are particularly suitable. They are robust and as they have only a small area of glass any damage that might be caused by high winds or vandals is likely to be minimal. Glass spheres look extremely attractive when mounted on top of gate posts and they provide considerably more light. However, they are also that much more fragile and shouldn't be installed if there is the slightest likelihood of them getting damaged. Possibly the best type of light to install would be a bulkhead fitting with a vandal-resistant acrylic diffuser in place of the more traditional glass. As your gateway is likely to be some way from the house the cable will have to be taken underground and must either be a specially protected cable or else run in PVC conduit – see pages 112-115.

Drive and path lighting
There's little point in lighting your gateway and then not providing sufficient illumination along the path or drive to your house. There is no reason why you shouldn't continue the style of the gate lighting along the drive.

Alternatively, you may find that small bollard-style lights are the most suitable for lighting your path. These shouldn't be confused with the bollards we find in the streets, as they are attractive, provide a useful amount of light and are available in numerous designs. The bollard is usually a

WIRING OPTIONS

There are several ways of obtaining power for outside lights.

1 For a porch light, break into an existing lighting circuit and run one cable to the light and one to a switch.

2 If the light circuit isn't close by, run a spur cable from a 3-terminal junction box (A) and proceed as above.

3 You can break into a circuit and run a spur. Take the cable to a fused connection unit and on to the lights and switch.

4 If you are installing a number of outside lights, you might find it best to run in a completely new circuit.

Sleeve earth cores with green/yellow PVC and flag the black cores of the cables.

Wiring a new circuit

The new circuit should originate at a spare fuseway in your consumer unit. There are several ways of wiring up the lights. You can:

● *install a 4-terminal junction box in the circuit before the first light (see 2B above) and link it to a master switch)*
● *use a junction-box system with individual switches and a branch cable to each light (see ELECTRICAL TECHNIQUES 2)*
● *use a loop-in system with BESA boxes sunk in the house wall (see ELECTRICAL TECHNIQUES 6).*

Ready Reference

TYPES OF OUTDOOR LIGHTING

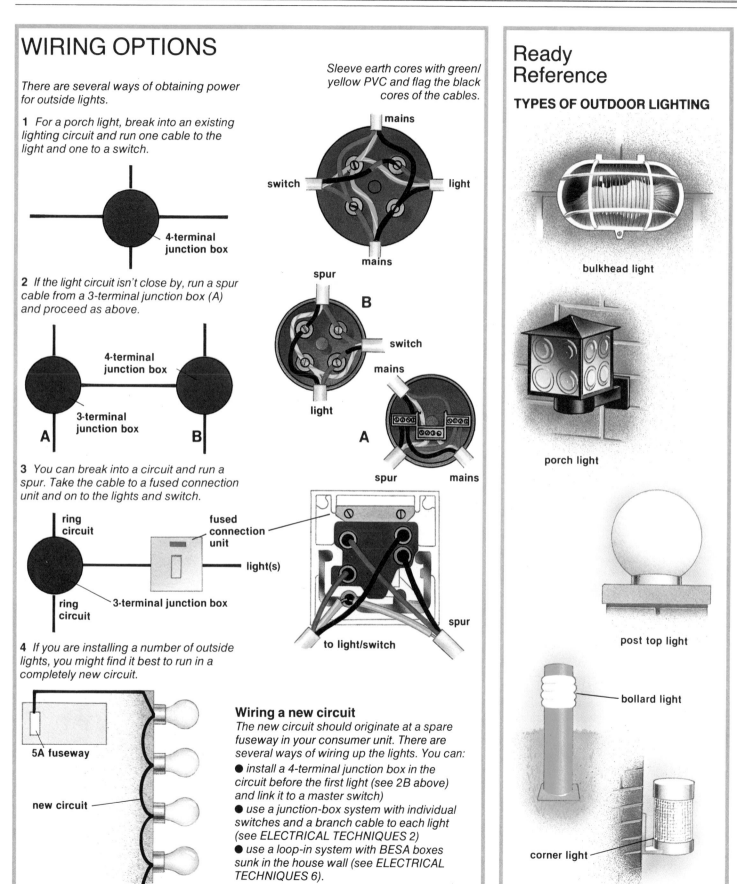

bulkhead light

porch light

post top light

bollard light

corner light

FITTING AN OUTSIDE WALL LIGHT

1 *Drill a hole for the cable or flex at an angle to prevent water penetration. Then mark the positions of the fixing holes, drill and plug them.*

2 *With this fitting the mains cable is linked to the fitting's flex via a connector block. Strip the cores and connect them; no earth is needed here.*

3 *The connector block will be concealed by the fitting's backplate. Wrap the block carefully with PVC tape to make it waterproof.*

4 *Mount the fitting using rust-proof screws, fit the lamp and add the glass dome, checking that it is secure. Then complete the connections indoors.*

5 *Where the cable runs directly into a terminal block within the fitting, feed it through a grommet to prevent chafing before making the connections.*

6 *If you don't mind the cable being on show, clip it neatly to the wall. You can, if you prefer, hide the cable run in surface-mounted conduit.*

black or green-finished aluminium or steel pole with a base plate for a secure fixing. They come in a variety of heights.

Taking power outdoors
The most important thing to remember when installing any outdoor lighting is that all fittings and cable runs must be protected against the weather.

If you're mounting a light on a porch wall or near the backdoor the easiest way of providing power is to break into an existing light circuit with a three-terminal junction box and extend a power cable to a four-terminal junction box near the lighting point. From here you'll have to run a length of 1.0mm² two-core and earth cable through the house wall and to the light's terminals. A similar-sized cable will be run from the junction box to a convenient point for the controlling switch to be mounted. If, however, supplying

an extra light will exceed the limits of the existing circuit then you could run in a new circuit and take it directly to a four-terminal junction box; from here you can run the cables to the light and switch respectively. Remember to sleeve all earth cores with green/yellow PVC sleeving and, at the junction boxes, to flag all switch neutrals with red tape as they're really live.

Wherever possible you should try to avoid running cable along an outside wall. However if this can't be avoided it's best to use PVC-covered mineral-insulated copper-covered (MICC) cable fixed directly to the wall. If you want to use MICC cable make sure you first measure the cable runs. That way you'll be able to get it cut to an exact length as well as having the correct seals and glands fitted to it. For further information on running cable out of doors, see pages 112-118. In fact for short lengths that are unlikely to be

disturbed, PVC cable run in rigid high-impact plastic conduit will be acceptable. When cable is run on the surface to an outside light or switch the cable entry hole must be sealed with mastic to prevent moisture penetration.

Gate lights, drive lights and path lights are inevitably going to be some way from the house and will so obtain their power via cable run underground to them. Whichever cable you use will have to be buried in a trench that is at least 550mm (20in) deep.

Finally, if you want to control your outdoor lights with two-way switching then you'll have to link the switches with 1.0mm² three-core and earth cable. Should you want to provide two-way switching for your gate light, then rather than running two lengths of special cable it's easier and much cheaper to use PVC cable and run both cables in a single length of conduit.

INSTALLING LOW-VOLTAGE LIGHTING

1 *Low-voltage lighting kits contain all the necessary components. Lay them out and connect the brown low-voltage cable to the transformer's output terminals.*

2 *Assemble the lights by feeding the terminal lead in each one up through the extension pole. Then push the pole firmly into the spike base.*

3 *Unscrew the lampholder from the lamp housing. Then feed the terminal leads through the housing and push it onto the other end of the pole.*

4 *Connect the leads to the terminals on the lampholder by pushing them on firmly. Then screw the lampholder back into place in the lamp housing.*

5 *Next, fit the lamp into its holder by turning it in a clockwise direction. Add the translucent shade and snap on the green mushroom top.*

6 *Unscrew the spike base cover to expose the two metal terminal spikes. Decide where the light will go, and lay the cable over the terminals.*

7 *Press the flat side of the cable firmly onto the terminal spikes to drive them into the cable. That way you'll make the necessary connections. Then replace the terminal cover.*

8 *Stand each lamp in position in a hole 200mm (8in) deep and 150mm (6in) diameter, and replace the soil. You can bury the cable if you wish or run it along a conveniently-sited wall.*

9 *Unless the transformer is weatherproof, it must be installed under cover. Place it just inside your house or – if you have power there – in a garden shed. Plug it in and test the lights.*

INSTALLING GARDEN LIGHTING

Apart from its functional value, being able to illuminate your garden after dark will extend the time you can enjoy it. Here's how to plan and install the fittings to get maximum effect.

The first thing to bear in mind when planning to install lighting in your garden is that in the dark, a little light goes a long way. In other words, a 40W lamp used outside will seem considerably brighter than, say a 100W lamp used in your home. This means that you won't have to floodlight the garden like a sports stadium merely to see and, with only a few lights, you'll be able to create some quite subtle effects. This is all due to the eye's ability to adapt to different lighting levels. However, as well as adapting to low light levels, the eye also adjusts to bright lights and if you install very bright lights then you'll view the rest of the garden as nothing more than shades of black.

While this will allow you to create attractive cocoons of light, in which you could enjoy an outdoor meal, for example, it can work against you. Stepping out of the spotlight, you'll effectively be blinded for several seconds, during which time you could easily miss your footing or walk straight into something. Further steps to prevent this happening should be taken by making sure you position the lights so that people can't look directly at them and by using lights with shades and diffusers. Better still, design your lighting scheme so that, where possible, illumination is provided by bouncing light off walls, shrubs or other surfaces.

The final thing to consider is the question of flexibility – whether you want to be able to adjust the level of lighting or even change the position of individual lights. The best guide for this is the thing you are illuminating. If it is a static structure, like a path or drive, then some sort of permanent light fitting giving a predetermined light level is best. Other structural garden features such as swimming pools and barbecues will also benefit from permanent lighting, but a more flexible approach to lighting levels will be required. After all, when you're using them you'll want lighting almost to indoor standards simply to be able to see what you're doing; when not in use, the lighting's role will change to showing off the structure as a feature of the garden as a whole and so won't have to be so bright. You might need a variety of lamps for this situation.

But when lighting foliage, though, with the exception of large, established, slow growing trees, mobility is the key. Install lights that you can move as plants come into bloom and fade or when you introduce new plants. After considering these design principles you'll have to decide just how you want to use the lighting in your garden. There are two categories, the practical and the pretty.

Lighting with a purpose

The main purpose of garden lighting is to allow you to see what you're doing and where you're going – in other words for safety and convenience. Lighting to see what you're doing applies mainly to such things as barbecues and swimming pools. With barbecues the ideal thing is to break the 'low level reflected light is best' rule and direct a couple of spotlights on the cooking or preparation area. However, you should keep this area as small as possible and keep the lights high up so that they shine down on what you're doing, reducing both glare and shadows. You'll have to arrange the lighting of the surrounding area very carefully so that its level gradually diminishes; you'll then avoid the risk of stepping out into pitch darkness. The same approach can be used for lighting a swimming pool, and you may find that by shining light down on the water, you don't need to light the poolside – the reflection could well be enough. Alternatively, you could consider lighting the pool from beneath the water – either with suitable lights built into the sides of the pool or merely with weighted lights lying on the bottom.

Lighting designed to help you see where you're going is more straightforward. With paths or drives, it's best merely to line them with bollards or mount lights on adjacent walls. For a subtler effect, consider lighting trees or shrubs near the path and use the light reflected back to illuminate the path itself. Do take extra care when lighting steps as for safety's sake they require stronger light, especially on the risers. Consider building lights into each riser or light the steps from the side to eliminate shadows. For further information on lighting paths see pages 121-125.

Lighting for looks

How you illuminate your garden to make it look more attractive after dark depends largely on its precise design and style and, of course, your personal taste. It's a good idea to build up a lighting scheme gradually, experimenting with cheap and mobile fittings before going to the expense of installing fixed lights. However, there are a few things to bear in mind. Firstly, aim for the lighting to look its best from a particular vantage point – the patio or a window, for example – that way planning will be a lot easier.

Secondly, remember that reflected light will always look best. Although lights can be expensive and quite attractive in their own right (when positioned within a flower bed, say,) it's the garden you really want to see. Thirdly, you should give thought to lighting levels. Varying the intensity will add interest, and by using progressively dimmer lights as you move away from your chosen vantage

IDEAS FOR GARDEN LIGHTING

Lighting your garden so it looks attractive after dark will require planning, combined with a certain amount of experimentation. Aim to design the lighting so that the garden will look its best from a particular vantage point – a patio or terrace, say. Consider, too, that you won't have to use particularly bright lamps – the light will go that much further in the dark and if parts of your garden are too brightly lit, then the rest is likely to appear just as a black hole.

As a rule, reflected light will look best. Aim to bounce it off walls, shrubs and trees. And, of course, try to conceal spotlights, which are not particularly attractive in their own right; either mount them high on a wall or else fix them within shrubs or a group of plants. When lighting foliage, think twice before using coloured lights as plants will probably turn out looking rather strange. Yellow will turn them pale and wan; red will make the leaves appear brown. Blue light will give plants a curious unearthly quality, while green will bring out the colour, but will make it look somewhat artificial. Coloured lamps could, however, be used to light a swimming pool or patio.

This low-voltage lamp, neatly concealed within the foliage at the side of a patio, gives a diffused light sufficient for any summer evening. Mounted on a spike, it can be easily moved.

Playing a couple of spotlights onto this mixed group of shrubs gives an attractive effect. Note how the illumination is in part produced by light reflected from the lawn in front.

For a really impressive effect spotlights can be positioned behind shrubs or bushes and then directed at a particular feature to give sharp, dramatic shadows.

Bollards on either side of these patio steps have the practical effect of lighting both treads and risers of the steps. And, of course, they highlight the foliage and plants too.

A couple of bollards driven into the soil on either side of this path not only serve to guide the feet but also lead the eye to the area on the other side of the tree arch.

point you can create an artificial perspective so making the garden seem larger.

Finally, think carefully before using coloured lights. They'll look fine when applied to water, statues, barbecues and a patio, lending a sort of party-like appearance. But most plants will look decidedly odd under coloured lights; yellow lights leave plants looking pale and sickly, for example.

Choosing the hardware

There is a tremendous selection of equipment available for installation in the garden. It falls into one of three basic categories. Perhaps the most useful are fittings that provide a general, diffuse light. If you're looking for a permanent fixture and there is a wall or similar structure close at hand then there's nothing to stop you using the same sort of lights as in a porch or a patio, see pages 121-125 for more details. However, these must, of course, be completely weatherproof.

Bollard lights vary considerably in design between the simple and highly decorative, and as a rule they are best suited to lighting paths, drives and other 'traffic' areas. Elsewhere in the garden lantern style fittings mounted on spikes that you drive in the ground are probably the best bet as they are quite attractive without being too obtrusive.

The second category worth considering is spotlights – essential if you want to highlight a particular feature or illuminate a small area very well. Again use spots that you might normally install on a patio or those mounted on spikes specially for fixing in the ground. Finally, there are lights designed to be decorative features in their own right and little else. The simplest type are fairy lights, strung through a tree, which lend themselves perfectly for the occasional party rather than anything more permanent. A host of other styles exist, however, ranging from ultra modern lights of almost every shape and size to full-size, old fashioned lamp posts.

Electricity outside

Finally, you must make sure that your outdoor lighting will be safe. After all, electricity and wet weather are a potentially lethal combination. That's why you must always use purpose-made, fully weatherproof lights and never make up your own from ordinary light fittings, however simple it might appear. Take extra care when running in the power. If your lights obtain their power directly from the mains then flexible cable must be run in conduit and buried at least 450mm (18in) below the soil. If you are using a low voltage system you can merely run the special cable along the ground, although you still need to be careful. Be sure you won't be able to cut through it accidentally when mowing the lawn and that people using the garden won't trip over it.

WIRING UP AND INSTALLING GARDEN

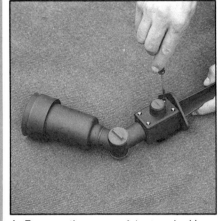

1 Remove the cover of the terminal box by undoing the screws on the side. Work on a smooth surface to avoid the risk of losing small parts in the grass.

2 Next, unscrew the bush on the other side of the light body. Carefully lift out the rubber grommet and the nylon grab ring, and set them aside.

5 Trim back a short section of the flex sheathing. Then carefully remove enough insulation from the cores to allow their insertion into the connector terminals.

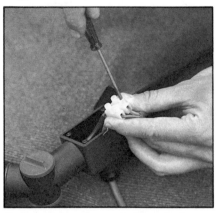

6 Connect each core to its correct terminal. This is indicated by an equivalent coloured core of fixed wiring. Make sure each is securely held in place.

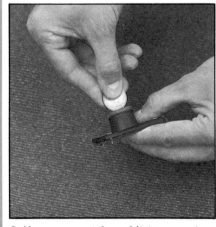

9 You may want the cable to run on to another light connected in series. If so you'll have to remove the red blanking-off plate. Use a coin for this.

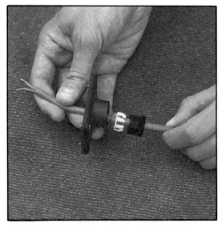

10 Thread in the next section of flex, checking all the components are in the correct order. Strip the flex and make the connections.

LIGHT FITTINGS

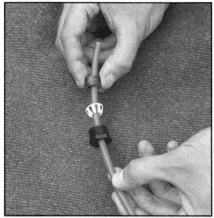

3 Use 0.75mm² two-core coloured flex to run power to the lamp directly from the mains. Thread on the bush, grab ring and grommet in the correct order.

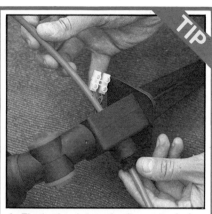

4 Fix the bush into the flex entry hole without tightening it up too much. You can then pull through enough flex to allow you to make the connections.

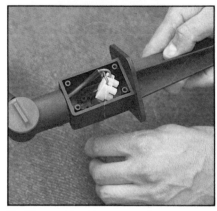

7 After making the connections you can then pull back the excess flex so that the connector sits comfortably in position within the terminal box.

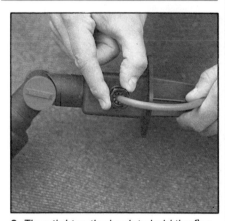

8 Then tighten the bush to hold the flex in place. Make sure the grommet and grab ring sit correctly in place, so guaranteeing a waterproof seal.

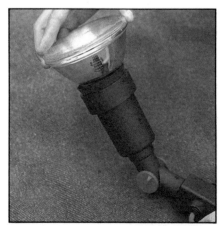

11 With the connections made, refit the cover plate. You can then screw in a PAR lamp, making sure that it sits tightly on the rubber gasket.

12 The flex is led to each light through conduit, buried 450mm (18in) underground. Spike the light into place and plug the cable into the nearest socket.

Ready Reference

TYPES OF GARDEN LIGHTING

spotlight

mini-bollard

bollard

globe light

low-voltage light

ALTERNATIVE GARDEN LIGHTING

If you don't want to have electric lighting in your garden, don't worry; there are alternative methods which can work almost as well. You might consider using
● candles or night lights in flower pots or glass jars
● a powerful weatherproof torch that can serve as a temporary spotlight
● garden flares, which provide a lot of light and burn for over two hours in all weather conditions. However, they tend to be a little too tall for some situations.

TIP: REPELLING INSECTS

Bright lights attract insects, especially outside. It's a good idea to use a special candle that not only provides light but also repels mosquitos and other insects.

WEATHERPROOF CONNECTIONS

If you are connecting any two lengths of cable together outside you must use a special waterproof rubber connector. Link the female section to the live side and the male one to the fitting's flex.

FITTING A POND PUMP & FOUNTAIN

A garden pond can add an extra dimension to any garden. By including a fountain, a waterfall and some lighting as well you can really bring your pond to life.

When it comes to adding interest to a pond, there's nothing to beat the splash and sparkle of moving water. It will turn the pond into the focal point of your garden, as well as giving soothing sounds of moving water. You can use an ornate fountain, a simple spout, a lively cascade or a full-blown waterfall, but first of all you have to get the water on the move.

It's not unknown for people merely to tap into the mains supply via a garden tap and a suitable length of hose. However, before you try this as an easy way to provide a waterfall, it's wise to realise the serious disadvantages associated with this method. While movement of the pond water will aerate it nicely, a continuous supply of tap water is not a good idea because it will reduce the temperature of the pond considerably and will also encourage the growth of algae. In addition, the local authority will probably object to the flagrant waste of water, as well as opposing this method on the grounds that dirty water from the pond could in theory find its way back along the hose to contaminate the mains water supply.

A more sensible method of moving the pond water will be simply to recirculate it, and to do this you're going to need some sort of electric pump. There are a great many on the market, available either from your local garden centre or else specialist suppliers. As their performance varies, with many being designed for a specific installation, you would do well to consult your supplier to make sure that the model you have in mind will actually do the job you want it to do. However, there are a couple of general points to consider before buying one.

Choosing a pump

One of the first things to think about is the pump's power. In simple terms, you'll have to find out how much water it will cope with and how much water you'll need to move in your pond. When it comes to fountains, the necessary calculations could hardly be simpler, as fountainheads and pumps are usually produced by the same manufacturer and a quick glance at the relevant sales literature should give you all the information

you need. You'll have to look at the amount of water the pump will move per hour; the height of the fountain produced and the diameter of the fountain or the falling circle (called the 'sill') of the water lifted into the air. So, for a small pond you're likely to need a pump that will produce a maximum output of about 680 litres (150 gallons) per hour with a maximum fountain height of 1.2m (45in) and a sill of 800mm (30in). It's still a good idea, though, to see the fountain in action before actually buying it. There are other factors, such as the thickness of the individual jets, which will have a marked effect on the way the fountain looks in use.

When it comes to creating waterfalls and cascades, things are not quite so straightforward. Again the volume of water is important, but relating the volume to the effect achieved is quite tricky. Most suppliers sell pre-fabricated waterfalls so they'll know exactly what works and what doesn't. If you want more than one effect – say, a number of waterfalls or fountains, or a combination of the two – then you'll have to make sure that the pump can cope with multiple applications. You'll then have to decide whether you want a surface or submersible one.

Types of pump

For all but the largest fountains and water falls, surface pumps mounted outside the pool and sucking in pond water to redistribute it through a series of pipes are now the

Ready Reference

TIP: A POOL HEATER
If you're worried about your fish surviving a cold winter the answer is to install a pool heater. This will keep an area of the pond surface ice-free and so allow vital oxygen into the water. Heaters are mains-powered and so can be simply plugged into the nearest socket outlet – in your home or an outbuilding.

TAKING POWER OUTSIDE
Extra care must be taken when running a circuit outside to provide power for your pool equipment. You should use:
● PVC-sheathed cable run in conduit and buried in the ground
● mineral-insulated copper-cased (MICC) cable, or
● PVC steel-armoured cable.
Only PVC-sheathed cable can run straight from a consumer unit to an outside socket. With other cables you'll have to
● fit both ends with glands, and the MICC cable with a special seal too
● run them from a conversion box located within the home to another in the outbuilding, and continue the circuit to a socket in PVC cable.

For further information see pages 112-118.

OBTAINING POWER

With a low voltage pump (below), house the transformer close to a socket outlet and run the low voltage cable outside to the pump. It's best to run it underground. With direct mains supply (right) the pump cable connects to flex run underground in conduit from the nearest socket outlet.

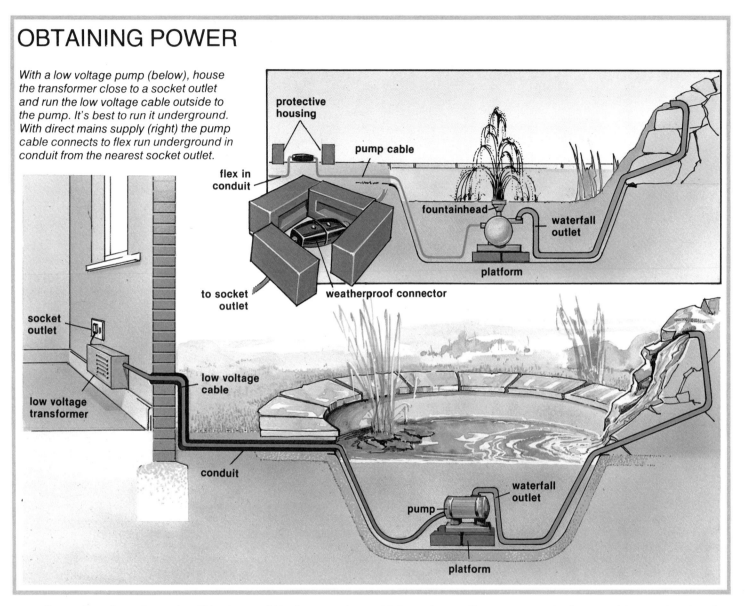

exception rather than the rule. This is because of the complications involved in installing and maintaining them: they cannot stand exposure to the weather and if they are deprived of water when they're in operation, they overheat and burn out.

In practical terms, ensuring an adequate water supply means installing the pump reasonably close to the pond. That way the inlet pipe is kept as short as possible. You can alter the size and length of the outlet pipe if you need, but you risk not achieving the full desired effect. The length and design of the inlet pipe is more critical. Of course, it needs to be the correct diameter, but most importantly it has to be sufficiently robust to resist collapse as the pump begins to suck. Even so, you might get problems if the pipe-work leaks, allowing air into the system, if the strainer fitted to the end of the inlet pipe becomes clogged or, worse, if the impeller

within the pump jams with ice or leaves. To avoid the danger of overheating, it's best to get a pump with a thermal cut-out.

Weatherproofing can create more difficulties. The pump must be housed in a weatherproof chamber where it'll be free from damp. At the same time, however, the chamber must be well-ventilated to stop the pump from overheating.

Finally, you'll have to decide where to position the pump in relation to the water level. If it's below the water level, so it's primed for use at all time, then there's always the risk of the pond overflowing and the chamber flooding. Conversely, if it's above the water level, you'll have to keep it primed – either by fitting a special kind of strainer to the inlet pipe, or by incorporating a header tank in the system. All things considered, a submersible pump is probably a better bet for most ponds. This type usually sits under-

water on the bottom of the pond and works silently, sucking in water and pushing it through a fountain jet or taking it to the top of the waterfall. With some models, however, you'll have to build a simple platform so they sit just below the surface. Most pumps come ready fitted with an integral fountain head so there is no plumbing to be done; all you have to do is connect it to the power source.

Pond lighting

No matter what type of pump, fountain or waterfall you choose, to make the most of moving water you need light. After all, it's really the sparkle of light on water that works the magic; not the water itself. During the daytime the surface will reflect light provided the pond is in a position where it'll catch the sun. However, in the evenings and at night you'll need some sort of artificial lighting.

Ordinary garden lighting certainly has a

MAKING A WATERFALL

1 Test the flow of water down the waterfall where you want to install it. Make sure that it fills the pools and flows smoothly into the pond.

2 Make adjustments to the angle of the waterfall by removing or adding extra earth or sand. This will provide a stable base for the waterfall.

3 You'll have to run a hose from the pump position in the pond up to the top of the waterfall. Protect the hose by concealing it in the earth.

4 When you're happy with the waterfall's position, bed paving slabs or bricks in the earth to provide extra support for the waterfall pools.

5 Replace the waterfall and bed it securely in position. You can then pack round the edges with extra earth or build a rockery round it.

6 Pile up some rocks where the hose runs into the waterfall. These will conceal the water outlet and also disperse the water at its entry point.

part to play (for further information on this, turn to pages 126-129). However, there are a number of attractive effects that can only be achieved by placing lights under the water. These fall into two categories; those that are general-purpose pond lights and those designed specially for use with fountains. The former normally consists of PAR lamps with a variety of coloured lenses that can either float on the surface or be tethered to the bottom of the pond. Fountain lights are more spectacular and the combination of a light and a fountain head, so the spray is illuminated from beneath, is quite striking. Alternatively, the lighting may be built into a submersible pump, complete with a fountain head. Some models even incorporate a rotating plastic filter which alters the lighting colour from red to amber to blue and on to green at a chosen speed – an effect you need to see working to appreciate.

Dealing with the electrics

Another factor to be borne in mind is the question of power supply. The choice is between a mains voltage system and a low voltage one. Mains voltage systems are obviously the more powerful of the two and will probably be necessary for the largest pumps and fountains. The cable supplied with the pumps can be fitted with an ordinary plug and linked to the nearest socket outlet in your home or in an outbuilding. However, it's not always the case that the pump will be sited close enough to the home or shed to do this. In this case you'll have to connect the pump cable to a length of flex run in conduit underground from the nearest socket outlet or else run an exclusive circuit for the pump. This will mean making use of a spare fuseway in your consumer unit or else installing a new switch-fuse unit. You'll then have to run special cable outside to the point where it can connect

to the pump cable. As an additional safety precaution, it's a good idea to equip your home with an earth leakage circuit breaker; that way if for some reason the cable gets cut, damaged or broken the power will cut off almost instantly; certainly before you have received more than a mild shock. Fuses and miniature circuit breakers are not fast or sensitive enough to prevent injury in this situation.

Low-voltage systems consist of a step-down transformer plugged into the ring main at a convenient socket outlet in your home or a spur to a shed. Keep the transformer inside, close to the socket in question. From here you merely run the special low-voltage cable to the pump. You can even leave the cable lying on the ground as long as you can be reasonably sure that no one will trip over it. Alternatively, it can be buried in the ground – ideally in plastic conduit.

INSTALLING A PUMP

1 Before installing the pump, you'll have to assemble it. First of all fix on the plastic T-piece that incorporates the outlet for the waterfall.

2 You can then fit the fountainhead spray unit to the upper outlet of the T-piece. Turn the flow control nozzle so that it's fully open.

3 Before fitting the waterfall hose to the pump outlet, immerse its end in boiling water. This will soften it and make it that much easier to fit.

4 Slip the end of the hose on to the pump outlet on the T-piece. As the hose cools down it will contract and so give a tighter fit.

5 You'll have to make a platform on which the pump should sit. Use bricks and then top them off with a paving slab to provide a level surface.

6 You'll then be able to position the pump on the platform. Make sure that it sits about 150mm (6in) below the surface so the fountainhead just emerges.

7 Slip a length of plastic hosing over the submersed cable to give it extra protection, both from the water and from direct sunlight.

8 Connect this cable to the plug section of a weatherproof cable connector. The socket should be connected to a length of 0.5mm^2 two-core and earth flex.

9 House the connector in a special shelter. Run the flex in conduit underground to the nearest socket – see pages 112-116 for details.

CHAPTER 6

UPDATING & REWIRING

If you have an electrical installation that's sound but can't provide
all the facilities you need, updating it could be a relatively
inexpensive and simple way of bringing it up to scratch.

PLANNING TO UP-DATE YOUR ELECTRICS

Rewiring your home can be very straight-forward but it still requires detailed planning and careful consideration. If you know exactly what you want from your home's circuits and where you want to site your power outlets and lights, then you're halfway to completing the job.

C ompletely rewiring your home is a job that sounds more difficult than it really is. If you've mastered such techniques as running cable, fitting new lights and installing new socket outlets then it certainly won't pose you any major problems.

Making the decision to rewire is perhaps the biggest step you'll have to take and, as with any electrical installation, you should never undertake the job without knowing exactly what you want and where you want it. Detailed planning is crucial to the final results and overlooking one important socket outlet or light can cause considerable inconvenience and, in the long run, extra work. Before making any decision about rewiring your home it's a good idea to examine the existing circuitry thoroughly to make sure that it really does need replacing.

When to rewire

There are two basic reasons for rewiring your home: first, because the existing fixed wiring is past its useful and safe life; and second, because the number of power outlets and lights no longer meets your requirements. There are certain tell-tale danger signs which you might come across when you inspect your circuitry. The use of rubber-sheathed cable ended in the early 1950s, so if you find this used in your circuits you'll know that they're quite old. If the insulation is worn and perished, then it's clear that the cable will have to be replaced to avoid the risk of fire or shocks. And, if you find that fuses in your consumer unit are blowing with alarming regularity, it's obvious something is seriously wrong.

You'll also have to consider whether the existing circuitry provides adequate lighting points and power outlets. Again there are a number of tell-tale signs. If you have to use adaptors to cope with all your appliances you'll know you don't have enough sockets; long trailing flexes will indicate that those existing outlets are not correctly sited. If you find you have to move lamps around to provide yourself with decent lighting, then it's clear that your lighting system is also inadequate.

Having examined your existing power and lighting systems, you're left with two alterna-

tives. You can either adapt the existing circuitry (provided, of course, that the cable is in good enough condition) to give yourself extra power outlets and lighting points, or else you can completely rewire it. If you are in any doubt, then it's best to rewire; the chances are that it'll have to be done at some stage anyway and, by doing so immediately, it's likely to give you a safer and more efficient system cheaply and to increase the value of your home.

The circuitry

Before planning the number of sockets and lighting points you want, you'll have to decide exactly how you're going to run the circuits. Most modern homes are fitted with one ring circuit and one lighting circuit per floor. However, this is not necessarily the best arrangement. It's worth considering dividing your home up vertically, so that you have one ring circuit supplying one half of the house and another the second half. It'll mean a little more work, but, if one of the circuits blows at any time, you'll still have light and power left on each floor. It's a good idea to have your kitchen supplied by its own ring or radial circuit as, of all the rooms in the home, it uses most power.

Remember that certain electrical appliances, such as a cooker or immersion heater,

should be connected exclusively to a separate radial circuit. Whatever you decide, you'll probably find that two ring circuits plus an extra radial or ring circuit for the kitchen, and additional radial circuits for certain fixed appliances, will suffice. Your next step will be the detailed siting of individual power outlets and lighting points in each room.

Living areas

The increase in electrical gadgetry and appliances over the past decade means that the average home now requires many more socket outlets. What with stereos, TVs, digital clocks and video games, as well as standard and table lamps, living rooms are going to need about ten sockets rather than the two or three usually fitted. Dining rooms are unlikely to need as many, unless you are in the habit of using toasters, coffee percolators, food warmers and so on at every meal, but remember that it's better to provide too many rather than too few.

For reasons of economy and convenience it's best to fit switched double sockets throughout, and you can, of course, re-use those from the previous circuits if they are in good condition. Flush-mounted ones are neatest, but require a bit of extra work to fit them.

Most living rooms and dining areas are

REWIRING YOUR LIVING AREAS

When rewiring your home you should carefully plan the wiring so that you have enough socket outlets for all your electrical appliances.

An outside socket (below) gets its supply from the circuit supplying the garage. It should be completely weatherproof and the circuit must be protected by an RCCB (see pages 76-78).

Boiler electrics (left) are linked up via a plug and socket or a switched fused connection unit. A safe alternative is to run them on their own circuit from a spare fuseway in the consumer unit.

Wall lights (above) get their power either from a lighting circuit in the ceiling void above, or from a power circuit via a fused connection unit.

Aerial sockets (above) should be sited near the television. Co-axial cable can run outside the house direct to the aerial, or inside to another socket in the loft.

Porch lights (left) get their power via a spur from the existing light circuit. You have to install a new four-terminal junction box and then run cable outside to the lights and inside to a new switch.

Door bells (left) with a low voltage transformer obtain their power from either the lighting circuit, via a ceiling rose, or the mains, via a fused connection unit. Alternatively, some can be powered by batteries.

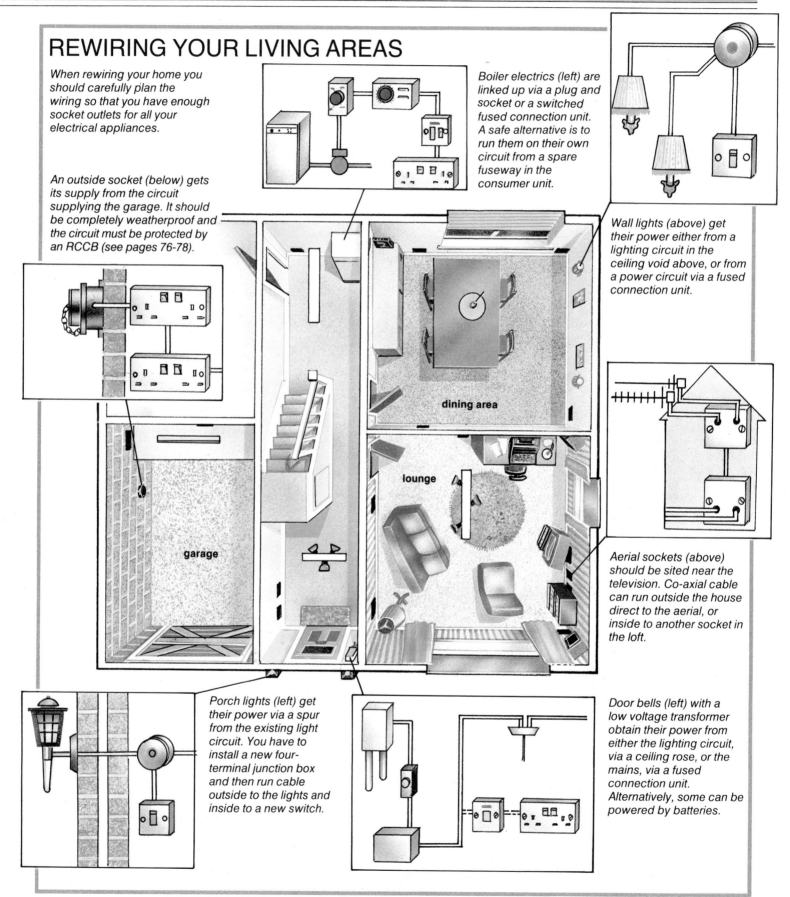

dining area

lounge

garage

REWIRING BEDROOMS AND BATHROOMS

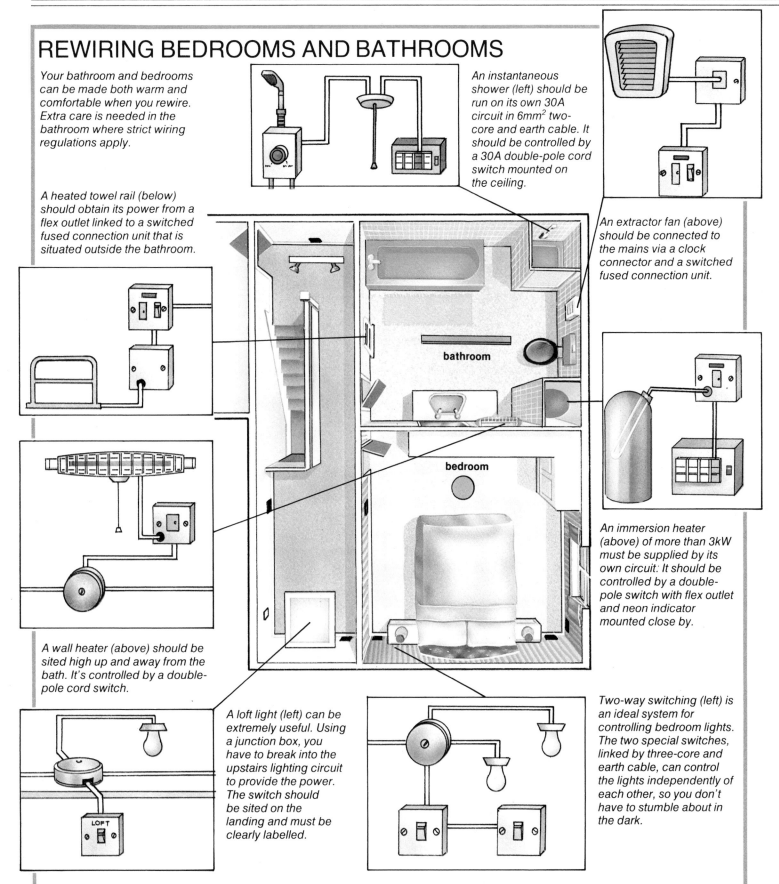

Your bathroom and bedrooms can be made both warm and comfortable when you rewire. Extra care is needed in the bathroom where strict wiring regulations apply.

A heated towel rail (below) should obtain its power from a flex outlet linked to a switched fused connection unit that is situated outside the bathroom.

An instantaneous shower (left) should be run on its own 30A circuit in 6mm² two-core and earth cable. It should be controlled by a 30A double-pole cord switch mounted on the ceiling.

An extractor fan (above) should be connected to the mains via a clock connector and a switched fused connection unit.

An immersion heater (above) of more than 3kW must be supplied by its own circuit. It should be controlled by a double-pole switch with flex outlet and neon indicator mounted close by.

A wall heater (above) should be sited high up and away from the bath. It's controlled by a double-pole cord switch.

A loft light (left) can be extremely useful. Using a junction box, you have to break into the upstairs lighting circuit to provide the power. The switch should be sited on the landing and must be clearly labelled.

Two-way switching (left) is an ideal system for controlling bedroom lights. The two special switches, linked by three-core and earth cable, can control the lights independently of each other, so you don't have to stumble about in the dark.

137

fitted with a central light and if you decide to reposition this you must make sure that the new rose can be fitted securely to a joist or a wooden batten fitted between two joists. If you decide to install a fluorescent fitting instead, you'll have to alter the wiring only if you already have a loop-in system, in which case you'll have to install an extra junction box.

Spotlights or wall lights can provide a more specific light on particular areas of the room, or for special tasks such as reading or sewing. A point to remember, however, is that wall and table lights can be run from the power circuit to avoid the risk of overloading the lighting circuit. They should be connected to a fused connection unit or plug fitted with a 3A fuse.

Halls and passageways
Sockets for plugging in a vacuum cleaner are necessary in the hall or on the landing, but the lighting is likely to be your most important consideration. Adequate lighting over the stairs is vital as every year many people injure themselves by falling down badly-lit stairs. But, whilst lighting should be adequate, it shouldn't be so bright as to dazzle you as you're going up or down the stairs; so it's worth considering the use of downlighters or carefully directed spot-lights. Incidentally, don't forget about two-way switching: it will prevent you ever having to use the stairs in the dark. If you have a cupboard under the stairs it's a good idea to run in power for a light there; it'll make a lot of difference when you're looking for things. Fit the light on its own circuit. As most consumer units are kept under the stairs, it will enable you to replace the fuse without having to work in the dark. At the same time as rewiring the hall, it's also worth installing a porch light. This will make your home that much more welcoming, deter burglars and can be con-nected to an ordinary lighting circuit. Also, as you'll be running cable in the roof space, it's a good idea to install a light in the loft.

Bathrooms
Bathrooms require special consideration as they are potentially the most dangerous room in which to use electricity. However, there are a number of regulations that apply to them and if you bear these in mind when planning the rewiring you shouldn't experi-ence any difficulty.

The only socket outlets permitted in the bathroom are double-isolated shaver sockets so that means the only portable appliance you can use is an electrical shaver. Any other appliance plugged into this socket will trip the thermal overload device and cut off the current.

All switches must be cord-operated and any lights they control must either be completely enclosed, to prevent the use of

the lampholder for any other appliance, or else be fitted with a protective skirt. They must, of course, be out of reach of anyone using the bath or shower.

Fixed appliances may be installed in the bathroom, but again you must proceed with caution. A towel rail, for example, can be connected to a fused connection unit, but the unit itself must be outside the bathroom and you'll have to use a simple flex outlet near the appliance. A wall heater or fire must be fixed high on the wall, away from the bath or shower, and must also be controlled by a cord switch, preferably with a neon indicator. An electric shower requires its own 30A radial circuit, and should be controlled by a double-pole cord switch to isolate it from the mains.

Bedrooms
Along with the living room and the kitchen, the bedroom is likely to be where you'll make most use of electric appliances – after all, you're going to want to make it as comfortable as possible. By the time you've plugged in the tea-maker, the radio/alarm, the electric blanket and two bedside lights you're already up to five sockets, and that's four more than most builders seem to think are necessary! When planning the siting of the socket outlets you should also bear in mind that the needs of a teenager are quite different from those of a young child, while those of an elderly parent staying permanently are different from those of an occasional guest. So you shouldn't necessarily install the same number of sockets in the same position in each room; but it's always better to install more than you immediately need. Once again, two-way switching is a useful way of avoiding stumbling around in the dark and is particularly suited to the bedroom. It's also important to have some kind of bright overall light so that you'll find it easier to look for something, should a small item, like jewellery, drop on the floor.

Outside the house
When you rewire your home you are advised to run a special circuit so you can have power and light in your garden, garage or shed. This will be classified as a sub-main cable and under new wiring regulations must be protected by a residual current circuit breaker (RCCB). This legislation also applies to simple extension cables which are only in use while the appliance they supply is being used. Special waterproof and hard-wearing accessories are available and these should be connected up with great care before being used.

Only after you've carefully considered the state of your home's electrics and deter-mined exactly what your requirements are can you proceed with the actual re-wiring. This is covered in more detail on pages 144-157.

This is covered in more detail on pages 144-157.

Ready Reference

A NEW CONSUMER UNIT
If you're rewiring your home it is advisable to install a new consumer unit at the same time, to cope with the extra circuits that will be needed. You should:
● choose a unit with enough fuseways to allow some to remain spare for future use
● install it where it can be easily and speedily located. You can always site it in a more convenient position, although extending the incoming mains cable can be costly
● include a residual current circuit breaker, and most importantly,
● get your electricity board to make the final connections to the meter.

A LIGHT UNDER THE STAIRS
If your consumer unit is under the stairs it's a good idea to fit a light there. You should:
● run it on its own circuit so you'll have light when other circuits are off
● use a loop-in battenholder
● fix the switch close to the door
● avoid fixing the lamp so it gets knocked by anyone entering the cupboard.

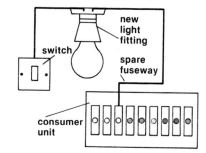

TIP: LABEL YOUR CIRCUITS
When you install your new consumer unit, make sure that you label all the fuseways. Then, in the event of a fuse blowing, you'll be able to identify which is affected almost immediately.

OTHER TECHNIQUES
Other techniques articles to which you can cross-refer include:

Adding ceiling lights and switches 23-26
Fitting extra power points 27-30
Fluorescent lights 46-49
Decorative lights 50-53
Porch lights 54-57
Two-way switching 66-70
Running cable 31-35
Installing a new circuit 72-75
Connecting up a cooker 84-87
Fitting shaver sockets 88-91
Garage electrics 116-120
Underground cable runs 112-115
Instantaneous showers 79-83

IMPROVING LIGHT AND POWER IN THE KITCHEN

An old kitchen can be transformed and updated simply by adding extra socket outlets and additional lighting. Supplying the power is not complicated, and existing circuits can be easily adapted or completely rewired.

The kitchen is one of the most frequently used rooms in the home and as a result should be as efficient and streamlined as possible. A modern one ought really to be able to take full advantage of the growth in electrical appliances and the improvement in artificial lighting that has been seen over the past decade or so. If you cast a critical eye round your kitchen you'll probably find that the electrics certainly leave something to be desired. A couple of socket outlets and a central light are painfully inadequate in this day and age: if you were to equip your kitchen with many of the available labour-saving devices you certainly wouldn't be able to power them from individual socket outlets. And a single central light will mean that you're likely to have to prepare food and wash dishes in your own shadow.

If you're not satisfied with the electrics in your kitchen, to improve them you can either rewire the whole kitchen or else extend the existing circuits.

Planning your needs

Before you start work on your kitchen you must decide exactly what you want from it. You'll have to decide how many socket outlets you're going to need and just what sort of lighting you'll want. The best way of deciding on sockets is to make a list of electrical appliances and tick off those you own, or are likely to own. Then decide upon other things, such as a radio or television, which you might also want to use in the kitchen occasionally. In your calculations you shouldn't forget that some appliances, like a cooker hood or a waste disposal unit, are better connected to a fused connection unit rather than a socket outlet. However, it's still a good idea to allow more socket outlets than you think are necessary. That way you'll do away with the need for adaptors (never, in any case, to be recommended from a safety point of view) and the temptation of trailing flexes for long distances over worktops. And though you may think that you could use one socket for several different pieces of equipment, it's better, in fact, to have one per appliance so that you minimise the amount of plug changing. Moving appliances around is

specially risky in a kitchen where you might be tempted to change plugs with wet hands and so risk getting a nasty shock.

There's only one electrical appliance used in the kitchen which can't get its power from an ordinary 13A socket outlet or fused connection unit and that's the cooker. Both freestanding and split-level cookers must be connected exclusively to their own radial circuits. For further details on installing a new radial circuit and connecting up a cooker see pages 72-75 and 84-87 respectively.

Planning your lighting needs is just as important, and you'll probably find that you'll need two sorts of artificial lighting to make your kitchen completely practical. It's a good idea to have some kind of general lighting and to complement that with more specific 'task' lighting on certain areas.

General lighting will be adequate for the kitchen as a whole, so you can eat and work in comfort, while the specific lighting will provide the more intense local light needed on worktops, sinks and sometimes the cooker. You might find that simply replacing your existing light with a fluorescent tube provides you with adequate lighting, and this will certainly be true if your kitchen is not very large. However, if you've a fairly sizeable kitchen you might well require spotlights or downlighters in addition to two or more fluorescent tubes on the ceiling. And if

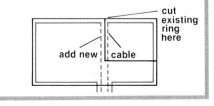

you feel the light from fluorescent lights is too harsh, you might decide to fit an illuminated ceiling or recessed lights. None of this is beyond the ordinary do-it-yourselfer, and will all go towards transforming your kitchen into a modern one of which you can be proud.

Identifying the circuits

When you've decided exactly how you want to modify your kitchen you'll have to turn your attention to the existing circuitry. First of all you must establish whether the kitchen is supplied by its own ring circuit, whether it's part of a larger ring circuit serving a whole floor, or whether it's supplied by a radial circuit. The chances are that it'll be on a large downstairs ring circuit, but if you're not sure, it's quite easy to check. You'll have to switch on an appliance in the kitchen and then remove the fuse for the ring circuit from the consumer unit. Its fuse should be labelled but if it isn't, you can identify it by virtue of the two cables leaving the fuseway. If the appliance still doesn't work, you'll know it's on the ring and if the removal of the fuse doesn't affect electrical appliances in any other rooms you'll know the kitchen has its own ring circuit. If you find the kitchen circuit has only one cable leaving the consumer unit then that shows it is supplied by a radial circuit.

Remember that there are limitations imposed on both types of circuit. There is no limit to the number of sockets and fused connection units you can install on any new circuit, but you must make sure that the non-fused spurs do not outnumber them. However, there are limitations to the area which each new circuit can serve. A new ring circuit must on no account exceed 100sq m (1075sq ft), while an equivalent 30A radial circuit is limited to an area of 50sq m (540sq ft) – although this is still considerably larger than the average kitchen. A 20A radial circuit is restricted to an area of 20sq m (215sq ft). While those referring to the area each circuit supplies are unlikely to restrict you, they are worth bearing in mind, especially if you have a very large kitchen.

Adapting the circuitry

Once you've established exactly what kind of circuit you have you'll find that there are a number of options open to you. If your power needs are not going to be too demanding you simply fit new socket outlets onto your existing circuit. Alternatively you can modify it so you can provide new power outlets or, if you want, replace it completely with a new circuit for the kitchen's exclusive use.

Simply fitting new sockets onto an existing circuit is not difficult and the only inconvenience will involve disturbing the decorations in the kitchen. For further details

PROVIDING POWER FOR APPLIANCES

Electrical appliances in the kitchen can obtain their power from the ring circuit, a spur or a radial circuit. Double socket outlets are best and switched fused connection units provide extra safety and convenience.

Instantaneous water heater

This is useful mounted close to a sink where there is no regular hot water supply. It should obtain its power through a fused connection unit.

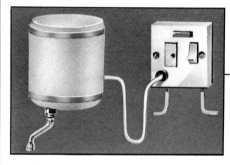

Double socket outlet

This kind of power point is specially suited to use in the kitchen because of the large number of electrical appliances. Switched sockets are safest.

Chest freezer

It's best to use an unswitched fused connection unit as the outlet. That way you avoid the risk of the freezer being accidentally switched off.

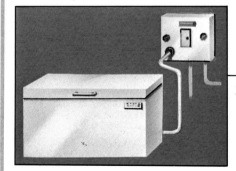

Washing machine

This can be supplied by a spur from the ring circuit. It's a good idea to use a switched fused connection unit so it can't be accidentally disconnected.

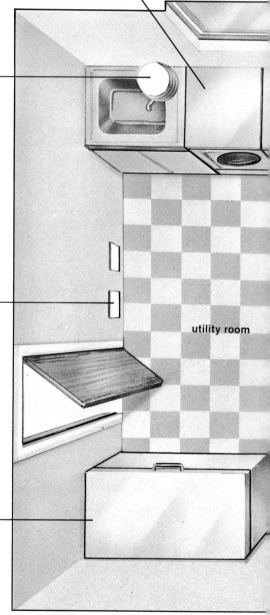

utility room

Dishwasher

A switched fused connection unit on a spur is the best way to provide the power. A neon indicator shows at a glance if the power is on or off.

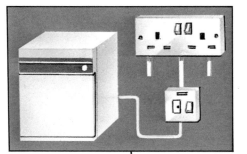

Waste disposal unit

The switched fused connection unit can be sited under the worktop where it will be easily accessible if it is needed, but also neatly out of sight.

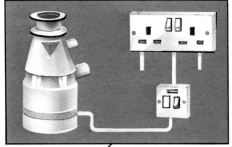

Extractor fan

A switched fused connection unit on a spur from the ring circuit lets you control the fan. A clock connector links the flex from the fan to the spur cable.

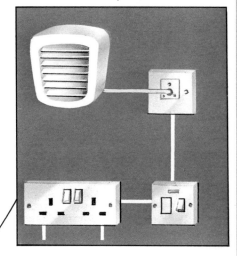

Cooker

This is the only appliance that requires an exclusive radial circuit. This should run from the consumer unit via a cooker switch and connector unit.

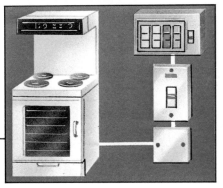

Refrigerator

This can be simply plugged into a socket outlet which should be below the worktop but where it can be easily reached without moving the appliance.

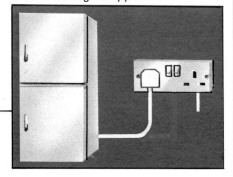

kitchen

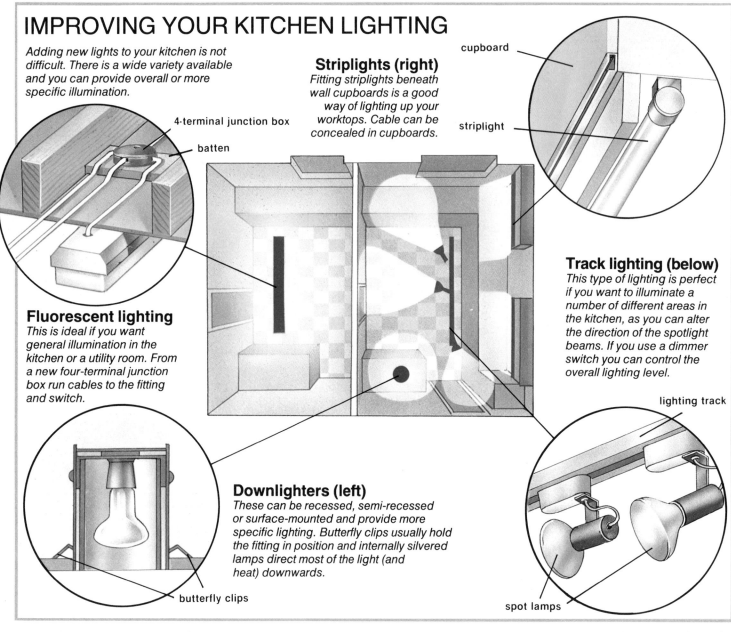

IMPROVING YOUR KITCHEN LIGHTING

Adding new lights to your kitchen is not difficult. There is a wide variety available and you can provide overall or more specific illumination.

Striplights (right)
Fitting striplights beneath wall cupboards is a good way of lighting up your worktops. Cable can be concealed in cupboards.

cupboard

striplight

4-terminal junction box

batten

Fluorescent lighting
This is ideal if you want general illumination in the kitchen or a utility room. From a new four-terminal junction box run cables to the fitting and switch.

Track lighting (below)
This type of lighting is perfect if you want to illuminate a number of different areas in the kitchen, as you can alter the direction of the spotlight beams. If you use a dimmer switch you can control the overall lighting level.

lighting track

Downlighters (left)
These can be recessed, semi-recessed or surface-mounted and provide more specific lighting. Butterfly clips usually hold the fitting in position and internally silvered lamps direct most of the light (and heat) downwards.

butterfly clips

spot lamps

on installing a new socket see Chapter 2, pages 27-30.

If you have a radial circuit in your kitchen this can easily be extended provided you don't exceed the limitations on area mentioned earlier. You'll have to break into the circuit at the last outlet. With the power off, you should then remove the outlet and connect the equivalent sized cable to it. Then extend the circuit's route so that it supplies as many extra sockets and fused connection units as you want to install. Otherwise you would install a new radial circuit to supplement an existing circuit. For further details see Chapter 4 pages 72-75.

A third option is to split a large ring circuit into two smaller ring circuits. That way you still use most of the existing cable and all of your existing power outlets. To do this sounds much more complicated than it actually is. After you've switched off the power at the mains, you should trace the cable run of the existing circuit. At the point at which it leaves the adjacent room to enter the kitchen you'll have to break into it. Using 30A cable connectors you should then attach enough 2.5mm^2 two-core and earth cable to the cable in the adjacent room to enable you to run it back to the consumer unit. On the way, of course, you can add extra power outlets where you need them. You'll have to do exactly the same in the kitchen extending the existing cable so that it, too, returns to the consumer unit via whatever extra power outlets you wish to install. You'll probably find that you'll have to make a couple of alterations

in the arrangements of fuses and cable in the consumer unit. Each circuit will require its own 30A fuse where the circuit both starts and ends. Unless you already have a spare 30A fuseway, you'll probably have to fit a new MCB or fuse in your consumer unit. If there isn't enough room in the unit then you'll have to fit a new switchfuse unit close to the existing consumer unit. For further details see Chapter 4 pages 72-75.

The ultimate way to provide power for your new socket outlets and fixed appliances is to run in a completely new ring circuit. This is undoubtedly the best way, for not only does it satisfy all your power requirements but it also means that, should a fuse blow in the other circuit, you'll still have some power on the same floor.

Siting the sockets

The best position for the socket outlets in your kitchen will depend largely on how it is laid out. Sockets for portable appliances such as kettles, toasters, food mixers and so on should be on the wall above the work surfaces so flexes are not stretched and connections strained; switched fused connection units for fixed appliances such as refrigerators, freezers and washing machines and other appliances like cooker hoods or extractor fans can be fixed at a similar height or just below the work surface if you want them out of sight. But remember they should be accessible so they can be turned on and off without any trouble. If you fit them just above skirting board level, you'll conceal them neatly behind the appliance but they'll be extremely awkward to get at.

If the appliance is fitted with flex, you'll need a unit with a special flex outlet and it should be sited as near as possible to the appliance and fitted with the appropriate fuse – 3A for loads of up to 720W and 13A for loads up to 3kW.

There is a considerable choice of socket types available and for further details on the range of electrical accessories available see pages 16-18.

Rewiring your lights

Having considered the power circuits, you'll probably want to turn your attention to the lighting in your kitchen. It's no good getting all sorts of marvellous electrical gadgetry and then not being able to see to use it!

As a rule, you'll find there's one lighting circuit for each floor and each one supplies eight or nine lampholders. If there's any danger of overloading the circuit by adding new lights then you should install a new circuit. And an additional circuit means that should a fuse blow, the downstairs of the house won't be left in the dark! For further details on installing a new light circuit see pages 6-10.

However, you might find that modifying your existing lighting will be sufficient for your needs. For instance, replacing an existing tungsten filament lamp with a fluorescent fitting is simple and effective. If your lighting circuit is wired on the junction box system then all you have to do is remove the existing light, fit the new tube holder and make the connections. If, however, you've got loop-in wiring you'll have to modify the wiring a little as there are no loop-in facilities on a fluorescent fitting (for further details see Chapter 3 pages 46-49). With quite a large kitchen you can be more adventurous in your choice of lighting and there is a wide variety of fittings available, including conventional pendant or ceiling-mounted lights, illuminated ceilings, spotlights, downlighters and concealed striplights.

Choosing your lights

Pendant lights are probably not a particularly good idea in small kitchens. Not only do they cause more shadow than other types, but their flexes tend to get quickly covered in grime. However, a pendant light fitted on a rise-and-fall fitting is perfectly suited for use over an eating area in a larger kitchen.

Fluorescent lights are ideal for general lighting in a kitchen because they cast virtually no shadows. Although they don't give a particularly attractive sort of light, diffusers and coloured tubes make them much more acceptable, while their efficiency and relative cheapness are factors strongly in their favour.

If you find fluorescent lighting ugly and too 'cold' you could incorporate it in an illuminated ceiling. With this method two or more fluorescent lights are fitted to the original ceiling and a second 'ceiling' of translucent plastic panels is fitted below. This is not difficult to do. A lattice or grid of metal bars has to be fitted below the level of the existing ceiling and the panels are then laid on top. These panels can be of different colours to provide a slightly softer effect. A partly illuminated ceiling can be achieved by cutting out sections of the existing ceiling between a pair of joists and replacing them with translucent panels. For further details on fluorescent lights and illuminated ceilings see Chapter 3 pages 46-49.

Spotlamps provide a concentrated light which is ideal for focussing on a particular area. They can be mounted on the ceiling, on the wall and singly or in groups on a track. Fitting track lighting is ideal for a kitchen as you can pick out a number of specific areas, as well as providing general lighting. For further details see pages 62-65.

Downlighters are ideal for a kitchen as they will give a concentrated beam of light on a worktop. They are usually the recessed type and therefore lie flush with the ceiling. To fit one you'll have to cut a circular hole in the ceiling to take the tubular fitting. Remember it's a good idea to fit a heat-resisting pad to the underside of the floorboards above and that way you will avoid any possible risk from the rising heat of the bulb. However, semi-recessed and surface-mounted types are also available, and are rather easier to fit. For further details on recessed lighting see pages 58-61.

Finally, **striplights** provide a very effective method of lighting worktops that lie under wall cupboards and are therefore often poorly lit. The striplights are fitted to the underside of the cupboard along with a batten to cut out the glare.

Remember, the rewiring of a kitchen or the adapting of existing circuitry are not such daunting tasks as they first seem, and the results can be both rewarding and satisfying.

REWIRING A HOUSE
1: inspection

Rewiring your home requires considerable preparation and planning. Before you actually decide to do the job, you'll have to give your circuitry a thorough inspection.

Electrical circuits, like most other things in the home, don't last for ever. If your circuits are run in rubber or lead-sheathed cable, then this indicates that they're probably about 30 years old and will have to be replaced. And if all your power circuits are wired as radials (see Chapter 1 pages 6-10), then its clear these will have to be replaced with ring circuits to cater for the needs of the modern home. At the same time, it's best to renew completely all the various wiring accessories that allow you to make use of the power carried round your home by these circuits. This is what's meant by rewiring.

Accessories such as switches, socket outlets, ceiling roses, lampholders and plugs can, and do, get broken. As many of these items form an integral part of your home's decor, the chances are you'll want to replace them if they're old-fashioned, and especially if they're damaged. Similarly, the older sort of circuit cables will inevitably have deteriorated with age, or may, like the accessories, have been damaged and will also need renewing. Only if your circuits are run in PVC-sheathed cable will it be possible to leave them in situ and merely replace the accessories. If your cables do get damaged, then they become immediately dangerous and this is the most important reason for rewiring your home: as with any home electrical work safety is the keyword. Although they could still operate satisfactorily, old circuits may be a high shock and fire risk without this being immediately apparent. That's not to say more recent installations are completely safe; bad wiring, poor quality accessories and extensions that have resulted in overloading, can all render an installation or even just part of it, dangerous.

The first step before deciding what to do is to make a thorough examination of your home's existing circuitry.

Know your cables
Old installations are likely to have been wired in either tough rubber-sheathed (TRS) or lead alloy sheathed cable. Both types were insulated with vulcanised rubber and as this was expected to last about 30 years,

many installations using these cables are still very much intact. However, the insulation tends to get brittle with age, and when handled can easily break away 'from the cores and so cause short circuits and current leakage. These faults are the principal causes of fires attributed to faulty electrical wiring. The insulation tends to deteriorate most at the ends of the cores where the cable is connected to whatever accessory it is supplying. This will become apparent when you remove the faceplate of a socket or light switch. Before replacing the faceplace of a socket or light switch. You should, as an interim measure, enclose any bare ends of cores where insulation has cracked or broken away

in PVC sleeving and insulation tape. That way the circuit can be safely used until you actually rewire, without the risk of short circuits or earthing faults.

Lead-sheathed cable can prove extremely dangerous. With this type of installation, the sheathing itself was used as the earth and so if it's damaged or no longer intact it's essential to replace it. With age the sheathing often cracks and if this has happened you need look no further; you'll have to rewire as soon as possible.

Cable that is run in light gauge steel conduit is not often found these days, but was frequently used in large blocks of flats (and occasionally in houses). Usually single-core,

INSPECTING YOUR FUSEBOARD

1 *Double-pole fusing is potentially dangerous. With a fuse in both the live and neutral poles it means if the neutral fuse blows, the circuit is still live.*

2 *Switch off at the mainswitch before removing any of the fuseholders. This type of mainswitch is obsolete and should be renewed.*

3 *Carefully remove the fuseholders so you can inspect them. Look for cracked and damaged porcelain that will expose the fuse wire.*

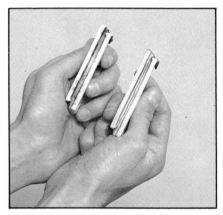

4 *Double-pole fusing should be replaced immediately with a safer system. Never use thicker fuse wire to prevent the fuses repeatedly blowing.*

Inspecting your fuseboards

If your home has a number of main switches and fuse units instead of one composite consumer unit then it's safe to assume that the installation is old and is likely to be in need of a rewire.

Old main switches and fuse units were usually an assortment of splitter units that each supplied several circuits. So, the chances are there would have been one for the light circuits, one for the power circuits and then single switchfuse units for individual circuits supplying such appliances as immersion heaters or cookers. But don't be taken in by the presence of a gleaming new consumer unit; this doesn't necessarily mean that your home has been recently rewired. It's possible that its presence is merely for cosmetic purposes and that it was installed by the previous owner prior to putting the house up for sale.

Whatever the superficial appearance of the existing units, it's best to carry out a more detailed check to see that the switches all work and, after switching off at the mains, whether any of the porcelain fuseways are broken, so exposing live wire. Watch out for two fuses per circuit which means you have what is termed double-pole fusing; this means there's a fuse in both the live and neutral poles in the unit. The big drawback of double-pole fusing is that in the event of a short circuit or overload it's possible for only the neutral fuse to blow, so leaving parts of the circuit live. With single pole fusing, which present-day regulations now require, the fuse is in the live pole of the circuit only and if it blows, the whole circuit is isolated from the live mains. If your circuits have double-pole fusing you should replace the fuse units without delay and resist the temptation merely to wire the neutral fuse with heavier fusewire to encourage the live to blow first.

Lighting circuit accessories

When inspecting the lighting circuit, it's best to start your inspection with the switches. If you have round switches with screw-on covers or ones that are secured by two screws they will have to be replaced as they are now totally obsolete. These types of switches, known as tumbler switches, are usually mounted on either hardwood blocks or plastic pattresses and either method is potentially dangerous. Standard practice during installation was to strip the cable sheathing behind the block, and that means non-sheathed ends of the insulated cores were frequently in contact with combustible material. Over the years, as the insulation grew brittle and thin, this will have turned into a potential fire risk.

Old pattern ceiling roses mounted on wooden pattress blocks and backless ceiling plates are risky for the same reason. Those

taped and braided, rubber-insulated non-sheathed cable was used, and therefore had to be completely enclosed for safety. The conduit itself should terminate in a metal box at each accessory, not only to prevent cores from being in contact with combustible material, but also to provide efficient earthing, as without the box there will be no continuity. If there isn't a box you'll have to check that the conduit has been fitted with an earth clip and an earth tail at its outlet. If your home still uses this kind of cable and if the conduit is at all rusty or loose at the joints, there is likely to be no earth continuity anyway and it should all be replaced.

Inspecting the wiring

The best place to check the general condition of your circuitry is in the loft, where access to the cables is easy. At the same time you'll also get an impression of the condition of the remainder of the cable running round your home. Only if it is neatly run and properly fixed PVC-sheathed cable is it unlikely to need rewiring. In that case, however, you should still check that at all the accessories the sheathing ends within the mounting boxes. In addition, if there's PVC cable you must make sure that it's not merely a newer extension of an older circuit.

If you want to inspect the first floor wiring, you'll have to raise a floorboard or two. It's best to pick one that looks as if it's been raised before and you'll probably find that the one running down the centre of the landing usually has most cables concealed beneath it. To check the state of the cable at the outlets it's necessary to remove the faceplates from at least one switch, one lighting fitting and one socket outlet, but you should try not to disturb the existing cable otherwise you might damage the insulation.

CHECKING SOCKET OUTLETS

1 *Socket outlets that have round holes and which make frequent use of adaptors are potentially dangerous and should be replaced.*

2 *To inspect the existing circuit cable, switch off at the mains. Then remove the cover of the switch, and check whether it is cracked or charred.*

3 *Remove the fixing screws holding the socket to the skirting. Then gently ease the socket away so that the circuit cable is exposed.*

4 *You should be able to pull a little extra cable out from the wall so that you can give each core and its sheathing a detailed inspection.*

5 *If you've damaged the insulation or sheathing during the removal of the socket, you should fit a length of PVC sleeving over any exposed core.*

6 *Finally, you must give those damaged cores extra protection by wrapping them securely in PVC insulating tape before reusing the circuits.*

Ready Reference

WHEN TO REWIRE

There are a number of tell-tale signs that will help you determine if your home needs rewiring. When you inspect your circuitry, look for
● old cable with brittle or cracked insulation
● cable with poor sheathing
● unsheathed cores that are touching combustible material
● loose, rusty or disconnected light gauge steel conduit
● poor earthing continuity
● damaged accessories
● obsolete accessories
● accessories that can't be earthed
● overloaded circuits
● frequent use of adaptors
● insufficient lighting points
● insufficient power points.

ALTERNATIVE ACTION

If you don't need to rewire, but want more sockets, you can divide an existing ring circuit to form two complete circuits.
You should
● break into the circuit at a convenient point
● extend each section so that it runs back to the consumer unit and so completes the new circuits (you need an extra fuseway).
● add new outlets on the way.

TIP: TESTING FOR EARTH CONTINUITY

It's a good idea to test your earthing continuity. For a really conclusive test you'll need an earth loop impedance tester, but these are very expensive. For a reasonable indication of the continuity you can make your own tester. You'll need a bell, a 9V battery and some cable. You'll have to
● switch off at the mains
● connect one core of the cable to the earth terminal on the consumer unit
● connect the other in turn to the main water pipe, other earthed metal and earth terminals in socket outlets.
If the bell rings it indicates earth continuity, but this is not conclusive of efficient earthing. Only professional testing can check that.

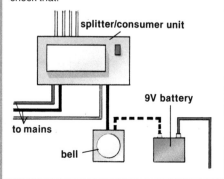

splitter/consumer unit

9V battery

to mains

bell

CHECKING PENDANT LIGHTS

1 *Before inspecting the lighting circuit, switch off at the mains. You can then remove the cover of a conveniently-located ceiling rose.*

2 *Unscrew the rose from its pattress block and ease it away so you can inspect the circuit cable. Look for any damaged or brittle sleeving.*

3 *It's also a good idea to inspect the flex at each lampholder. This can often be in poor condition and will pose a shock or fire risk.*

4 *All exposed cores must be sleeved in PVC and wrapped in insulating tape before the mainswitch is turned on and the lighting circuit used again.*

ceiling plates allowed circuit wires and flexes to be in contact with the ceiling which is especially dangerous if it's a lath and plaster one. Metal battenholders should also be replaced as, apart from the wooden pattress blocks, they weren't earthed and therefore presented a shock risk.

Socket outlets

Round pin plugs and sockets are now virtually obsolete, and as all new electrical appliances are fitted with square-pin plugs it makes sense that old sockets should be replaced in the course of rewiring. In addition, the two-pin version is dangerous as it doesn't allow the appliances to be earthed. You might well find that three-pin sockets have been fitted in place of old two-pin ones, but more often than not no extra earth core has been added. If that's the case, then you will certainly have to rewire. If the existing sockets are wired on a radial circuit there is no real advantage to be gained by inspecting the cable; you might just as well run in new cable and replace sockets when you put in a new ring circuit for the socket outlets.

But if you know that they are on a ring circuit then you should check whether the cable is in reasonable condition. If it is, you won't, of course, have to rewire it. Remember, if you do have to remove a socket you'll probably find it easier to remove one that is fixed to a wooden surface such as the skirting.

Checking the earthing

It is important that your electricity supply is connected to earth; that way if a fault develops in a circuit, current finds its way to earth and the fuse will blow to protect the circuit and its users. You can make some visual checks to get an idea of whether your circuit earthing is in order. If the electricity board's cable runs underground into your home then you should find an earth cable running from the fuseboard to a clip on the cable sheathing. It's important that all such clips and fixings are securely in place. Another method is for the earth cable to be connected to a clamp on the mains water pipe where it enters the house.

However, mains water pipes can no longer be used as the sole means of earthing. This is because of the now widespread use of plastic pipes, which interrupt earth continuity. Where the mains are run overhead, the earth cable can only be connected to a clamp on the mains water pipe or else an earth rod made of copper or wrought iron that is buried as deep as possible in the soil beneath the house. There are two important points to remember at this stage: first, even though rewiring is planned, poor connections of the main earth cable should be dealt with immediately and any corroded sections of cable replaced; and second, the presence of earthing at the mains does not mean that the earthing of individual circuits is effective.

You *can* test the earth continuity on your existing circuits using a home-made tester (see *Ready Reference*) or a proprietary plug-in tester. But such equipment will only give an indication of the efficiency of the earthing, and you should ideally call in a qualified electrician or your local Electricity Board to test the system with professional instruments. The Board must test your re-wired installation anyway, and so it is as well to rely on professional expertise at the outset rather than to have a fundamental problem discovered later.

Planning the job

Once you've inspected your home's electrics and determined that they do, in fact, need rewiring, your next step is to start planning the work. This is an extremely important part of the job, as careful and thorough preparation will mean minimum disruption to your daily routine. If you are going to rewire your home before you move in, then it makes little or no difference where you start. However, if you are already living in the house you'll probably find it best to start the job in the loft and deal with the first floor lighting.

There is bound to be an element of disruption in your home when you do the rewiring – especially as you'll have to move furniture around, lift floorcovering such as fitted carpets and lino, and raise floorboards. Inevitably you're not going to be able to do the job as quickly as a professional electrician and you should make sure that you don't try and rush the work at the expense of doing a good job.

An obvious way of cutting down on the time spent rewiring is to have a helper, and it'll also make running cable that much easier.

CHECKING LIGHT SWITCHES

1 *Round tumbler switches mounted on a block probably have worn and sparking contacts. To inspect one, isolate the circuit and remove its cover.*

2 *Loosen the terminal screws and remove the fixing screws that hold the switch in place. Then ease the switch away from the pattress.*

3 *Remove the switch, taking care not to damage any brittle insulation or sheathing. You can now examine the state of the circuit cable.*

4 *Any exposed cores present both a shock and fire risk. To lessen the danger, sleeve them temporarily in PVC and then wrap them in insulating tape.*

Ready Reference

INSPECTING CABLE

It's a good idea to inspect wiring that runs under floorboards, even though it is less likely to have been damaged since the cables are concealed. But the wiring may have been badly installed, particularly where extensions have been made to the original cable runs. You should
● look for a floorboard that has been lifted before
● lever up the end of the board with a bolster chisel
● saw through the tongue if the board still has one

● use a piece of timber as a lever to remove the board.

TIP: LABEL YOUR CABLES

After lifting the floorboards to inspect the wiring, label the cables as you identify which one feeds which circuit. That way, when you come to do the rewiring you won't have to trace all the cables again. And you won't risk removing or replacing the wrong circuits.

SHEATHING DAMAGED CORES

When you examine cables at switches, sockets and lighting points, it's very difficult not to cause further damage to already perished insulation. In that case you should
● check that the main switch is OFF
● cover each individual core in PVC sleeving
● wrap each sleeved core in PVC insulating tape
● finally, replace the accessory's face-plate.

With some assistance you'll be able to rewire the upper floor lighting and install a light in the loft in a couple of days; so you could set aside a weekend for this section of the job. For the rest of the house you should really allow about seven days.

Estimating your requirements

You'll have to cast a critical eye round your home and assess what your power and lighting needs really are before you buy any materials. The chances are that your current needs are going to be considerably greater than when the existing system was installed, and ideally you should aim to have one socket per electrical appliance. For further information on this, see the planning section on pages 135-143.

Your estimation of the cable you're going to need is likely to be less precise, and the amount you'll have to get depends on the size of your home, the number of circuits, the number of lights and the number of socket outlets you'll be installing. For the average three of four-bedroomed house that has one light and switch per room and two in the main living room and kitchen you'll probably need about ten metres of cable per light. So, as the chances are that you'll be running power to at least ten lighting points you might just as well buy a couple of 50 metres reels of cable for this part of the job. For socket outlets wired on, say, two ring circuits you'll probably need between 50 and 100 metres of 2.5mm^2 cable. It's a good idea to buy just one reel at first and then, if necessary, another – or else a specific extra length of the cable if you don't need another whole reel. But it's certainly worth taking accurate measurements of the circuit for cookers, showers and outside power because more expensive cable is used for these.

REWIRING A HOUSE: 2 starting work

Once you've decided to rewire your home and have planned what you want to do, you'll have to start thinking about buying all your materials and beginning the actual job. Here's the way to proceed.

When buying the equipment for your re-wiring, always choose good quality cable and fittings made by well-known and established firms. Obviously it's worth shopping around and it's a good idea to obtain a couple of catalogues so you can compare prices. However, beware of special bargains or similar offers of equipment from unknown sources. Make sure that the cable you buy has been produced to the relevant British Standard (see *Ready Reference*). This is likely to be stamped on the outside of the sheathing.

Itemising your requirements
Before you pay a visit to your local whole-salers, you should work out and itemise exactly what you need so that they'll be able to give you an accurate quote for all the materials. The quickest way to do this is to draw up a sketch floor plan of the house and mark on it the position of each socket outlet, light switch and light fitting, and then count up the numbers of each type of accessory you're going to need.

Work out the circuits next; an average two-storey house will probably have two lighting circuits, three ring circuits and a couple of exclusive circuits – for an immersion heater and cooker for example. That means you're likely to need a new consumer unit with at least eight fuseways, and however many circuits you need it's worth choosing a unit that will leave one fuseway spare for future use. You'll have to decide whether to use re-wirable or cartridge fuses, or else face the extra expense, but increased safety, by using MCBs and fitting an RCCB.

Decide whether you'll flush-mount or surface-mount switches and socket outlets, and note the number of each type of box you'll need. List how many ceiling roses, fused connection units, junction boxes and ceiling switches you'll need and also whether you're going to fit a shaver socket or supply unit. Finally, you should take a note of the number of switches and boxes you'll need for any special circuits you're going to run. When you've added cable, cable clips, PVC earth sleeving and other accessories to your list, you'll be ready to put it into some sort of order.

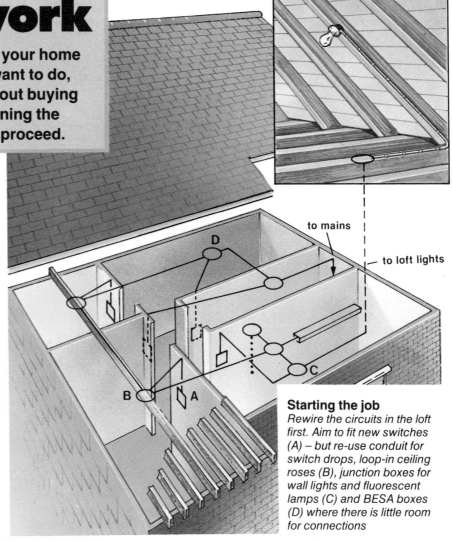

to mains

to loft lights

Starting the job
Rewire the circuits in the loft first. Aim to fit new switches (A) – but re-use conduit for switch drops, loop-in ceiling roses (B), junction boxes for wall lights and fluorescent lamps (C) and BESA boxes (D) where there is little room for connections

INSTALLING A NEW SWITCH

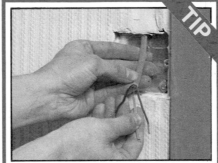

TIP

1 *Chase in the new switch cable or run it in an existing length of conduit. Strip back the sleeving on the cable and sleeve the earth core.*

2 *Mark the black core with red PVC tape to indicate that it's live. Connect the conductors to the faceplate and the earth to the box.*

FITTING A ROSE AND LAMPHOLDER

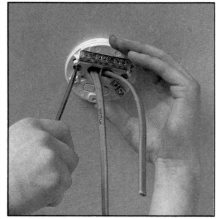

1 *Make a hole in the ceiling to let through the lighting circuit cable and the switch cable. Then fix the new rose to the ceiling.*

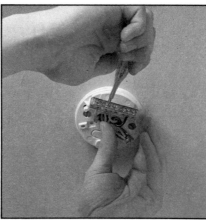

2 *With loop-in wiring, wrap the switch cable's black core in red PVC. Connect up the other cores as shown in the photograph.*

3 *With junction box wiring, the earth is connected to the earth terminal, the black conductor goes to the neutral bank and the red to the SW terminal.*

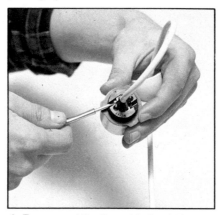

4 *To connect the flex, strip back the sheathing and insulation and connect the blue and brown conductors to the two terminals of the lampholder.*

5 *Screw on the cap and then slip the rose cover over the flex. Cut the flex to length and prepare the free end for connecting to the rose.*

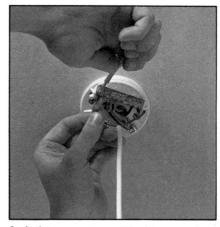

6 *At the rose, connect the blue core to the terminal on the neutral side and the red to the SW side. Remember to hook the wires over the cord grips.*

Ready Reference

BUYING THE MATERIALS

Before visiting your supplier, you should make a list of all your requirements. This should include both accessories and cable.

Accessories

For a typical three-bedroom house, with a loft and garage, your shopping list is likely to resemble the following:
25 double socket outlets plus flush/surface mounting boxes
3 single socket outlets plus boxes
14 one-gang plate-switches and boxes
3 cord-operated ceiling switches
2 two-way switches plus boxes
8 ceiling roses
8 lampholders
2 batten holders
1 close-ceiling light fitting
4 fluorescent fittings
1 shaver supply unit plus box
1 cooker switch plus box
junction boxes (optional)
1 eight-way consumer unit
8 MCBs plus an RCCB

Cable

Your cable requirements could include:
50 to 100m 1.5mm^2 two-core and earth
50 to 100m 2.5mm^2 two-core and earth
10m 1.0mm^2 three-core and earth cable
5 to 10m 1.0mm^2 flexible cord
Length of 6.0mm^2 two-core and earth cable
Length of 10mm^2 two-core and earth cable
Length of PVC-covered armoured cable
Approximately 5m 6.0mm^2 single core green/yellow PVC cable for main earthing lead
Approximately 5m 2.5mm^2 single green/yellow cable for bonding extraneous metal to earth
10m green/yellow PVC earth sleeving
Plastic cable clips

Other items you will need include wood screws, wall plugs, nails, fixing timber and PVC insulating tape.

CABLE CHECKLIST

The uses of cable varies according to its size:
1.0mm^2 and 1.5mm^2 – lighting
2.5mm^2 – power circuit, immersion heater and small water heater (up to 5kW)
4mm^2 – small cooker, 30A radial circuit, water heater (up to 7kW)
6mm^2 – cookers up to 12kW
10mm^2 – large cookers

STANDARDS

You must be sure that equipment you use corresponds to a British Standard of quality. Check that a BS number is stamped on all cable and accessories.

INSTALLING A JUNCTION BOX

1 To install a four-terminal junction box you'll have to fix a timber batten between two joists and screw the box in place onto this.

2 Connect the live cores to one terminal, the neutrals to a second and the earths to a third. The black of the switch cable (with red PVC) goes to a fourth.

3 Lay a length of 1.5mm² two-core and earth cable from the lighting point to the junction box and prepare the ends. Remember to sleeve the earth core.

4 Connect the sleeved earth core to the earth terminal, the black core to the neutral terminal and the red core to the switch terminal (top left).

Once you've made a list, take it to at least a couple of suppliers so you'll be able to get the cheapest quote – and don't forget to ask for a discount for buying in bulk.

Working in the loft

As you'll be starting work in the loft, check which existing lights are on which circuits and label them accordingly. Inspect each circuit separately, with only its fuse in position in the fuseboard at the time. Then list which lights are on it. Before starting work you must turn off the mainswitch of the fuseboard that contains the fuses controlling those lighting circuits that run in the loft. Make a note of their positions so you know which is which, but in fact, it's probably better to keep all fuses out and mainswitches off when working on the old wiring itself. You should then remove all light fittings on the floor below, that

are supplied by the wiring in the loft. That includes all switches as well, but not the two-way switch in the hall that controls the landing lighting as this is likely to get its power from a different circuit. You should then get up in the loft, taking with you a couple of battery-powered lights. This is extremely important. It's not worth working merely in torch light as you risk making errors in the wiring that could prove costly. It is possible to have electric lighting from an extension lead, but only if there is a socket outlet below that is supplied from a circuit controlled by a mainswitch independent of the lighting mainswitch. If you have a cooker control unit with a socket outlet that is supplied via a separate switch-fuse unit, then this would be perfectly suitable to use for makeshift extension lighting.

Once you're up in the loft you can pull out all the old wiring and any old conduit it's run

in. Only if conduits are sunk into plaster and run down to switch positions should they be left in place and then reused for the new cable runs. Once you've removed the cables from fittings and switches you should find only one left. This will be the circuit feed cable that runs from the mains. It's likely to be in conduit and if you want to reuse this conduit then you can use the old feed cable to fish up the new through the wall. If, on the other hand, the new feed cable is to take a different route then you can just cut off the old feed cable where it emerges from the conduit in the loft and remove it when you tackle the rewiring on the floor below. But, of course, before you do anything else you must disconnect the feed cable at its fuse unit and pull it out so there is no danger of accidentally reconnecting it.

Lighting points

Before you start making the connections, you must decide whether to use a loop-in system, a junction box system or a mixture of the two. With the loop-in system, the lighting circuit cable leaves the consumer unit and is connected to the first in a series of special loop-in ceiling roses. From this first rose, one cable will then go on to the next in the series, while another takes the power down to the switch controlling the light and back up to the light itself. The junction box system is based on much the same idea but, rather than running from rose to rose, the lighting circuit feed cable passes through a series of four-terminal junction boxes that are fixed to battens between the joists. From each box, one cable runs to the ceiling rose or light, while another serves as a switch drop and goes to the switch that controls the new light. Using a junction box system can prove particularly convenient when fitting wall lights, for example. This is because not only is there little space at the back of the fitting for looping-in, but you'll also save on cable as you won't have to run two lengths down the wall. A mixture of the two systems is the likeliest compromise, using whichever method saves the most cable at any point. For further information see Chapter 1 pages 6-10. Where your new light fittings are to be fixed in the same positions as the old, you must check that there are satisfactory fixing points above the ceiling. If not, fix a piece of 100 x 25mm (4 x 1in) timber between the joists and drill a 20mm (¾in) hole through that to co-incide with the hole in the ceiling. Do the same if you are going to fit new lights, although it is possible, if slightly fiddly, to screw a ceiling rose to the underside of a joist and still leave enough room for the cables to enter. It's also advisable to fix a batten between a couple of joists at the position of any cord-operated switch in the bathroom and for any similar switch to be fitted in a bedroom at the bedhead.

FITTING A BESA BOX

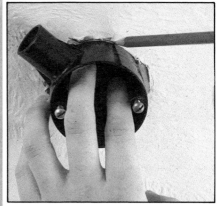

1 *Mark the position of the terminal block on the ceiling surface. Use either a pad saw or a keyhole saw to cut out the circular section.*

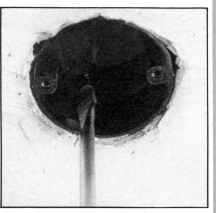

2 *Push the BESA box into the recess and screw it to the joist. Alternatively, fix a batten between the joists and screw the box in place to this.*

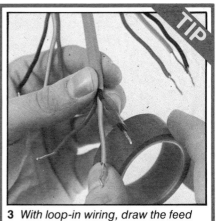

3 *With loop-in wiring, draw the feed and switch cables into the BESA box. Wrap red PVC insulating tape round the black core of the switch cable.*

4 *Connect the lives, neutral and earths up to separate connectors and the taped switch core to another. Push all four up into the box to await the light fitting.*

Running in the cable

The next thing is to install the circuit feed cable. This should be 1.5mm² two-core and earth PVC cable and should originate at a 5A fuseway. If you're going to run it in an existing conduit you must make sure that each end of the conduit is fitted with a PVC bush to prevent the cable from getting damaged on any sharp edges. You'll probably find that you have to lift at least one other floorboard to gain access to the cable and run it to the mains. You should then start running the feed cable to the lighting points in the ceiling. Push the cable through the holes and make the connections to the roses but don't, at this stage, fix the fittings to the ceiling. It's a good idea to mark the feed cables 'feed' at each point where they emerge through the ceiling so there is no possibility of subsequent confusion. You then have to run the switch

cables either from the rose itself (for loop-in wiring) or from the junction box where the feed to the light is taken (junction-box wiring) to the switch position. If there is no existing conduit just pierce a hole in the ceiling above the switch position and push the cable through. You can chase it into the plaster at a later date.

Once you've completed the wiring for the lights on the floor below, you can start wiring up a light in the loft itself. It's likely that the last light on the circuit will be close to both the first light and the trapdoor. From this last light you must extend the feed cable to a loop-in battenholder that is then screwed to one of the rafters. You then have to run a switch cable to a position on the landing below where the switch should be clearly labelled 'loft'. Alternatively, you might find it easier to break into the circuit with another four-

terminal junction box and run one cable up to the battenholder on the rafters and take another down to the landing and to a conveniently located switch.

Whichever system you decide upon, it's worth making the extra effort to install this light as it will undoubtedly prove very useful in the future.

Fixing the cable

Before leaving the loft you must check that all the cables have been run neatly between the joists. It's probably best to run the cables parallel with the joists as far as possible as that way they can be neatly clipped to them with cable clips. It's generally frowned upon to drill holes in the joists in the loft as you risk weakening them, so run cables parallel to the joists as far as the binder – the large timber cross member linking the joists. You can then clip the cable to the binder to go across the joists before running it to the position of the next light or switch. For further information on running cables, see Chapter 2 pages 31-35.

Installing the switches

When using an existing conduit for your switch drop you must make sure that it is fitted with a protective PVC bush at each end. If you want to fix surface-mounted switches, then this can be done neatly over the end of the conduit, but flush boxes have to be fixed below the conduit. If the conduit is too long it can, of course, be cut back, but you must pull back the cable first so as not to risk damaging it. If you don't have an existing conduit you'll have to cut a chase into the wall and, after fixing the switch in position and making the connections, make good with plaster filler.

Fixing the light fittings

Once you've connected up all the ceiling roses and switches, and fitted two-core PVC-sheathed flex and plastic lampholders to them, screw the light fittings to the ceiling with wood screws. Cord-operated switches should be fixed in much the same way, although some modern ones have detachable pattress blocks. Special pendant fittings that have backless ceiling plates have boxes called BESA boxes. These are fixed flush with the ceiling and secured to a timber batten fixed at the relevant height between two joists or actually to one of the joists. For further information on fitting new ceiling lights see pages 23-26 and 46-53.

Close-mounted ceiling fittings usually have a baseplate that allows them to be fixed directly to the ceiling. However, choose a totally enclosed fitting for the bathroom.

Finally, having installed all the lights and switches you can make the connections at the fuseboard/consumer unit end, insert the relevant fuse and test your new circuit.

REWIRING A HOUSE: 3 finishing off

With the new upstairs lighting cables in place, you'll be well into the job of rewiring. Here's how to tackle the next stage and finally complete the work by connecting all the cables to a consumer unit.

O nce you've completed the rewiring in the loft, you'll have to turn your attention to the rest of your home. Normally in a two-storey house this will mean working in the void between the ground floor ceiling and the floorboards of the floor above. Here you'll find the circuits for the upstairs power outlets and the downstairs lighting. And, if your house has a solid concrete ground floor, you may also find the circuit for the downstairs power outlets and possibly the cooker as well. However, if the ground floor is made up of floorboards with a void underneath then this is where the power circuits will most likely be run because it means that cables don't have to be chased down the wall from the ceiling to reach a power socket at skirting board level – and saving on expensive cable is obvious.

There are two ways of approaching this part of the rewiring job. One is to turn off the power and then to rip out the existing circuitry in a fit of enthusiasm. But what happens when the work takes longer than you anticipated? Much of the house could be left without light and power. So a more cautious approach is what's needed. Deal with each circuit individually. That way if you come across a problem that delays you you'll still be able to have some supply of electricity at the end of the day. Furthermore there's less chance of getting the circuits confused.

Dealing with the downstairs lighting

It's a good idea to rewire the lighting circuit first, as that way you'll be able to have light when you do the rest of the wiring. The first thing to do is to switch off the mainswitch controlling the circuit and then remove the fuse and disconnect the circuit cable. Take down all fittings and switches and mark the position of the old fittings you're replacing and the new lights you plan to install. If you've got fitted carpets you'll have to lift them before you raise any floorboards to gain access to the circuitry. You should aim to lift a board above each lighting point and also one that runs the length of each room. It's quite likely that many of the circuits will run along the landing so it's wise to raise a floor-board that runs the length of the landing so

The remaining stages of the job involve tackling the light and power circuits in the ground floor ceiling void, and then the power circuits under the ground floor itself.

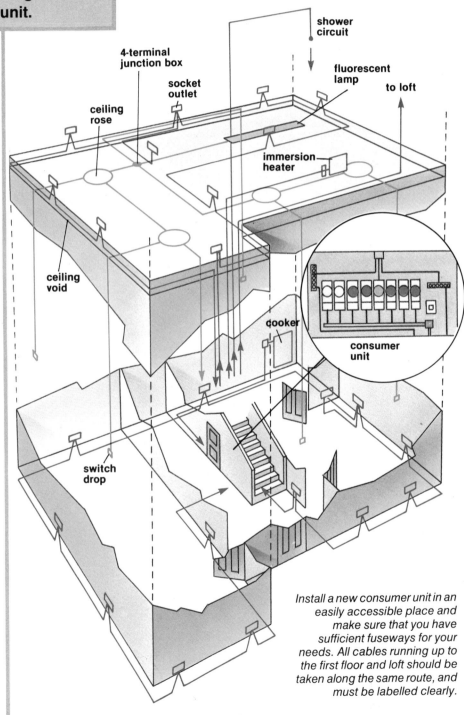

Install a new consumer unit in an easily accessible place and make sure that you have sufficient fuseways for your needs. All cables running up to the first floor and loft should be taken along the same route, and must be labelled clearly.

FITTING FLUSH SOCKETS

1 Decide where you want to position the socket, then draw a pencil line round the mounting box as a guide for where to chop out the wall.

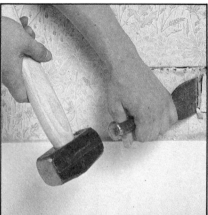

2 Drill slightly within the pencil lines to the depth of the mounting box, then work along the lines with a bolster chisel before chopping out the recess.

3 Channel a cable run down the back of the skirting using a long, thin cold chisel. Alternatively, use a long masonry bit and an electric drill.

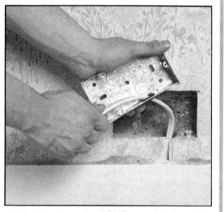

4 Push a length of PVC conduit into the hole behind the skirting, then thread the cable through the conduit and into the mounting box.

5 Push the box into position, then use a bradawl to mark where the fixing holes are to go in the recess. Remove the box and drill and plug the holes.

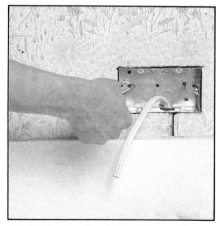

6 Set the box back into place and screw it tightly into the recess. Check that it is level, and then make good if necessary with plaster or filler.

Ready Reference

BONDING TO EARTH
The Wiring Regulations require all metal pipework, hot water radiators, metal baths, sink waste pipes and other metal work that could come in contact with electric cables to be connected to the earthing terminal.

CROSSBONDING OF SERVICES
It is also your responsibility to cross bond the gas and water mains to the earthing terminal. You should
● fix an earthing clamp to the mains water pipe on the street side of the stop-cock
● fix an earthing clamp to the mains gas pipe on the house side of the gas meter
● link the two together with 10mm^2 earthing cable sleeved in green/yellow PVC
● without cutting it, continue the cable to the board's earthing terminal near the meter.

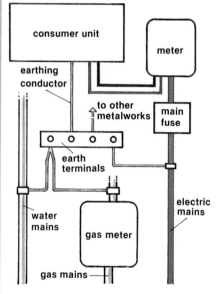

RUNNING CABLE UNDER FLOORS
Use a technique known as fishing:
● lift the floorboards at either end of the run
● thread stiff wire beneath the floor through one hole and hook it out of the other with another piece of wire
● use the longer piece of wire to pull the cable through
● if there's a gap underneath the ground floor you can 'fish' the cable diagonally across the room under the joists.
If the gap under the joists is large enough you can crawl in the space clipping the cable to the joists
● where the cable crosses the joists at right angles, run it through holes drilled 50mm (2in) below their top edges.

CONNECTING UP NEW SOCKETS

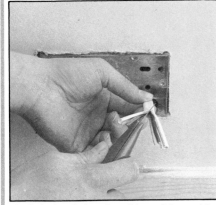

1 *Strip back the sheathing of the cable by running a sharp knife down the side, over the uninsulated earth core. Avoid damaging the other cores' insulation.*

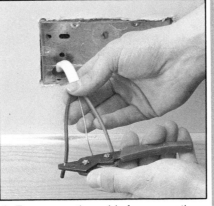

2 *To prepare the cable for connection you should set the wire strippers to the correct gauge and remove about 9mm (³/₈in) of insulation from the cores.*

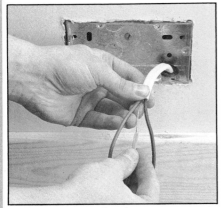

3 *Before connecting the cores you should sleeve the exposed earth core in green/yellow PVC. This is for purposes of insulation and identification.*

4 *Connect the three cores to the relevant terminals of the sockets, making sure no exposed core is showing. Then screw the socket into position.*

lighting points with 1.0mm² or 1.5mm² two-core and earth PVC-sheathed cable, and run in the switchdrops as well. At this stage, however, you needn't worry about taking cable to any wall lights. Remember, it's a good idea to label all cables so that there is no chance of any confusion at a later date.

From each wall light you should run a cable back up into the ceiling void to a four-terminal junction box fixed centrally above the lights. To obtain power you could break into the circuit with a three-terminal junction box and extend a branch cable to the four-terminal one or simply break into the mains with the four-terminal box. At this stage you should also run a cable to a porch light, a back door light or to any other light you want to fix outside the house. For further details see Chapter 3 pages 54-57. It's also a good idea to take a length of three-core and earth cable from the landing two-way switch and link it to another in the hall to give yourself two-way control of the landing and hall lights. For further details see Chapter 3 pages 66-70. Once you've made all the connections, you can fix the fittings to the ceiling and walls and temporarily connect the cable to the fuseway in your existing fuseboard so you can check that the circuit is working correctly.

Installing first-floor socket outlets

After again switching off at the mains and taking out the fuse carriers, you'll have to remove all socket outlets and lift a floorboard running to, or alongside, the skirting board or wall where each socket was fixed. Once you've done this, you can pull out all the cables and disconnect them at the fuseboard.

Start off by running two lengths of 2.5mm° two-core and earth cable down to the consumer unit position. One cable should run from the first socket outlet and the other from the last, but these two are likely to be in close proximity to each other. Link all sockets with the same sized cable, with the exception of remote sockets or fused connection units which can be supplied via spur cables wired into the nearest sockets to them. It used to be the custom to mount socket outlets on the skirting boards. However, you should position your new ones in the wall above the skirting boards and at least 150mm (6in) above the floor. Where possible it's best to install double sockets as this will cut down on the use of adaptors.

Having placed all the cables in position, and fixed all the socket outlets and fused connection units, connect the two cables to one of the existing 30A fuseways in your fuseboard. You should then replace the relevant fuse carrier and turn on the mains switch. To test the circuit, fit a 13A fused plug to a portable lamp and plug it into each socket outlet in turn.

you can pull out the cables. If your floorboards run across the landing, then raise one at each end and fish the cable through. If switch drops aren't run in conduit then you'll have to just cut the cables at ceiling level and leave them chased in the wall. Work back towards the landing and then pull out the circuit feed cable running down to the fuseboard. If you find a cable that runs under numerous floorboards, it's a good idea to attach a length of stout wire to it before pulling it out. That way you'll have a draw wire in place for the new cable and so avoid having to lift further floorboards.

You should proceed in much the same way as for rewiring the loft. If you're going to install wall lights in any of the rooms on the ground floor you'll have to make a hole in the ceiling above each light and mark the position in the room above. If the wall runs parallel to the joints on the first floor you'll find that the

cable can be 'fished' through from the raised board in the centre of the room. Otherwise you'll have to raise a floorboard directly over the lighting point. For further details on running cable see Chapter 2 pages 31-35.

Wiring the circuit

Before running in the circuit cable, you must drill holes in the joists where the cable crosses them. These should be about 19mm (³/₄in) in diameter and at least 50mm (2in) below the tops of the joists. Where you'll be running only one cable through them the holes can, of course, be slightly smaller in diameter. If you're using the loop-in system for the circuit then run a cable from the lighting point nearest the mains position down to the consumer unit and mark the end of this sheathing 'lighting circuit, ground floor'. As with the first floor lighting circuit, you must then link up the

FISHING CABLE ABOVE CEILINGS

1 Take a piece of stiff wire and check that it is just longer than is needed to reach between the cable's entry and exit holes in the ceiling.

2 Feed the wire into one hole, fish it out of the other with a second piece of wire, then tie the cable to the first wire and pull it through.

RUNNING CABLE UNDER FLOORS

1 When running cable parallel to the joists, fish it through in exactly the same way as if you were fishing through cable above a ceiling.

2 If the cable or fish wire will not pull through, check under the floor for obstructions using a small mirror and a reasonably powerful torch.

3 For cable runs at right angles to the joists, drill holes in the joists 50mm (2in) below their tops, angling these if the drill is too long to fit in.

4 Carefully thread the cable through the holes, without stretching it, so that it doesn't chafe against the side of the hole and damage the insulation.

Replacing other circuits

Working in the ground floor ceiling void will enable you to replace several other circuits at the same time. A new immersion heater circuit, for example, can be run along the same route as the old, but where the cable crosses joists, thread it through pre-drilled holes, whereas the old one was probably notched into the top.

A shower circuit is run in $6mm^2$ cable, so before running it you must again check the holes in the joists. If the holes are not large enough, drill another series which must be at least 75mm (3in) away from the old ones. For further details on installing a shower circuit see Chapter 4 pages 79-83.

If your kitchen floor is of solid concrete, you may well find that the cooker circuit is also run under the floorboards on the first floor. If you find that you do have access to under the kitchen floor then you should really re-route the circuit so that it's run on the ground floor; otherwise it'll have to follow its original route. If you decide to run the cable up through the landing void then you should take it up in conjunction with all the other circuit cables which should be taken along the same, easily identifiable, route to the ceiling void. For further details see Chapter 4 pages 88-91.

With all the cables laid on the first floor, the remaining floorboards can be relaid permanently and cable chases made good. As there are likely to be many cables on the landing, it's a good idea to fix one floorboard back with woodscrews so that it can be readily lifted at any time you want.

Ground floor wiring

The chances are that the only wiring on the ground floor will be a ring circuit for the socket outlets and, possibly, the cooker circuit. The first thing to do is to check whether the floor is suspended or solid. If it is suspended, you'll have to lift a floorboard and check the depth of the void. With a pre-1914 house, it's possible that the void will be deep enough to allow someone to go down there, in which case you'll save a lot of extra work moving furniture and floorboards. A more modern home will probably have a void depth of about 355mm (14in) and the joists will be laid and fixed to cross beams. This allows the cable to be run underneath the joists, so doing away with the necessity of drilling them. If you can't get underneath the floorboards, then much of the cable laying can be done by fishing, so reducing the number of floorboards that have to be raised.

Start pulling out the cables, but leave them in place if there is any chance of using them as drawstrings for the new cable. This will save you a lot of trouble, especially when it comes to getting cable up behind the skirting boards. Where there is more than one socket on any one wall it might be just as well to raise an extra floorboard about 500mm (20in) from the skirting board. This will save you both work and cable.

Dealing with solid floors

If your home has a solid ground floor the old wiring, most likely in conduit, will have to be left in place; then the cables at sockets outlet and at the consumer unit are chopped off flush and, together with the conduit, abandoned. New cables should be run in mini-trunking fixed to the top of the skirting board and around the architraves of doorways. An alternative is to push the cables behind the skirting boards, having first cut away the plaster. Where the cable has to cross a doorway, the architrave can be removed and the cable placed in the gap between the door frame and the wall. However, when replacing architrave or skirting take extra care not to drive nails into the cables. You could, of course, run the power circuit in the ceiling void above the ground floor. Using this method, however, would involve extensive chasing and use of a lot of extra cable.

Installing a new consumer unit

Once you've rewired all the circuits, you'll have to install your new consumer unit. You'll probably find it easiest to site it in the same place as your old fuseboard and this must be in reach of the electricity board's service fuse which will serve as the installation's main fuse. This is because the modern consumer unit has only circuit fuses, not a main fuse. If, however, you want to fix the unit away from the board's apparatus you'll have to fit a new mainswitch and main fuse unit next to the meter and then run a submains cable to the consumer unit. This is likely to be 16mm² two-core and earth cable, while the switchfuse should have a rating of 80 to 100A.

Before the new consumer unit can be connected you'll have to ask your local electricity board to disconnect the leads of the existing mainswitch units so you can remove them. You must give them a minimum of 48 hours notice for this and it's best to apply for your wiring to be reconnected to the mains at the same time. That way if you've done the lion's share of the work beforehand you can get your home reconnected to the mains the same day it's disconnected.

Before removing the old switchgear, check that each circuit is working correctly. Then, after the meter tails have been disconnected, remove the circuit cables and the old units. You'll have to fix the new unit to the wall, run in the new cable, make the connections and fit the MCBs or fuses in the correct order. For further information on connecting up a new unit see Chapter 4 pages 72-75. Finally refit the cover and await the electricity board official.

INSTALLING A COOKER CONTROL UNIT

1 *Run both the circuit cable and the cable to the cooker in conduit and chase them into the wall. Then connect the circuit cable to the mains side of the unit.*

2 *Next, make the connections on the cooker side. Remember to sleeve all the earth cores in green/yellow PVC before connecting them to the earth terminal.*

3 *When you've made all the connections, make sure that the unit is positioned square to the wall and then screw it securely onto the mounting box.*

4 *You can now fix the centre part of the faceplate. Before fixing the rest, make good and redecorate the surface of the wall.*

THE CONNECTION UNIT

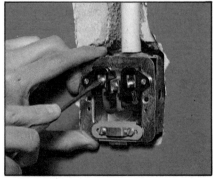

1 *Chase in the cable to the cooker and run it to the connection unit. Link the earths to the centre terminals and the other cores to the outer terminals.*

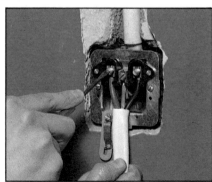

2 *Undo the clamp and hold the trailing cooker cable in place while you connect it. Remember that it should be the same size as the circuit cable.*

USING GRIDSWITCHES

There's an electrical accessory available off the shelf for most domestic requirements, but sometimes you'll wish you could have a combination of accessories to perform a specific job. That's where the gridswitch system fills the bill.

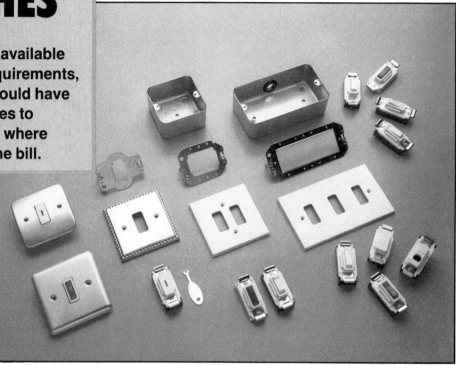

A glance through the catalogues of any major manufacturer of electrical accessories will reveal a bewildering array of switches, socket outlets and other items that enable you to control the way you take power from your home's electrical system. But because the manufacturers are catering for high demand, they can't offer an accessory for every conceivable job; the costs of tooling up a production line for a rarely-needed product would be prohibitive.

The solution that several manufacturers have adopted is to design a modular system of accessories that can be assembled in a grid system, allowing individual modules to be combined as required to produce a tailor-made unit. It's a system with many applications in the commercial and industrial field, but which can also be extremely useful for certain domestic switching and control jobs.

The system and its components

Most electrical accessories consist of two parts – a decorative faceplate, and 'the works' – switchgear, terminals for cables etc – mounted behind it. The whole unit is then fitted into a flush or surface-mounted box. With the gridswitch system, the various accessory modules are clipped side by side on a metal bar or 'grid', which is then secured within the mounting box. Finally, a faceplate with as many holes in it as there are accessories on the grid is fixed to the box to complete the gridswitch unit.

The modular gridswitch components offer a wide range of switching permutations, and a number of other functions as well. Switches rated at 5A are available in one-way and two-way versions, while 20A switches come in one-way, two-way and intermediate single-pole configurations, a one-way double-pole version and also an ingenious two-way-and-off model with a mid-position that switches the item being controlled off where the two-way section is used as a changeover switch. These are all conventional rocker switches, but in addition there are 5A and 20A switches with a push action in white, red or marked with a bell symbol.

In addition to these general switches, there is an ingenious secret key switch in one-way

and two-way versions. This can only be operated by a special key, and so is useful on circuits where unauthorised switching or tampering is to be avoided.

Other components include indicator lights in red, amber and green, flex outlet units, fused connection units which can be used with the flex outlet unit alongside to control individual appliances, blanking-off plates for assemblies with one or more unused modules, and even a television aerial outlet (although wiring regulations do not allow this to be fitted in the same enclosure as other accessories running off 240V mains). There is also a two-module dimmer switch unit.

These modules all clip onto metal grids, which are available in various sizes. For up to four modules, a single grid is used, but for larger assemblies two or even three grids are mounted one above the other in the mounting box. Faceplates can cater for 1, 2, 3, 4, 6, 8, 9, 12, 18 and 24 modules, and are available in a range of finishes – white plastic, matt chrome, satin or 'period' brass and utility 'metalclad' versions are the commonest.

One-gang and two-gang assemblies are similar in size to ordinary one-gang accessories, while three-gang and four-gang units take up about as much room as a double socket outlet. Larger assemblies have bigger mounting boxes, and in all cases special boxes must be used; ordinary accessory mounting boxes aren't deep enough to take the grid assembly. They can, of course, be flush or surface-mounted, but only metal boxes are generally available and these don't look very attractive when they're on view.

The assembly sequence

Putting together a gridswitch assembly is extremely simple – see step-by-step photographs opposite. Once the components have been clipped onto the grid in the desired order, each component is wired up in the usual way before the grid is screwed in place and the faceplate added. The grid mounting is adjustable to allow you to align the components precisely with the holes in the faceplate. The boxes are fitted with an earth terminal, but this is used only in installations involving metal conduit, where the conduit acts as the earth conductor of the circuit concerned. Otherwise all the earth cores are connected to the earth terminal on the grid itself. On complex assemblies, you may have to connect several earth cores to this terminal. It will make the connections far easier if you link all the cores to a small terminal connector block, and link this to the terminal on the grid with a single sleeved earth loop.

Gridswitch projects

As gridswitch components are comparatively expensive, there's obviously no point in using them to make up accessories that are available off-the-shelf. But the flexibility of the system allows you to create an almost limitless range of controls in combinations that are not readily available, particularly where you want to combine relatively complex two-way switching requirements with neon indicators to tell you what is on and off. Your gridswitch supplier will help you to choose the right components for any arrangement.

ASSEMBLING THE COMPONENTS

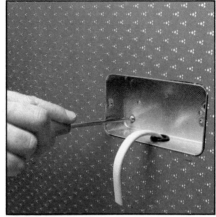

1 You need a special deep mounting box to take the gridswitch components. Run the necessary cables to the fixing point and flush- or surface-mount the box.

2 Next, position the components you want on the metal grid. Each component has two movable lugs which you squeeze together to hold it in place.

3 Use short lengths of cable core of the appropriate colour code to link the components together, and check that all the terminal screws are tight.

4 Connect the mains cable cores, and link all the earths to the terminal on the grid. Use a connector block to link the earths if the cores are too short.

5 Fit the assembled grid into the mounting box and tighten the fixing screws. One lug is adjustable to enable you to align the grid accurately.

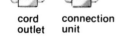

6 Finally, attach the faceplate. If you are using a flex connector, remember to thread the flex through the opening in the faceplate first.

Ready Reference

GRIDSWITCH COMPONENTS

Any gridswitch assembly consists of the same ingredients – a mounting box, a metal grid, one or more components and a faceplate. One- and two-gang assemblies have square boxes and faceplates; three- and four-gang units have rectangular ones.

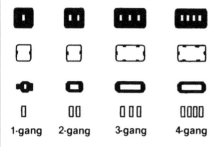

1-gang   2-gang   3-gang   4-gang

The components include one- and two-way single- and double-pole switches, indicators, flex outlet and connection units and a dimmer switch.

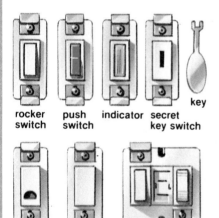

rocker switch   push switch   indicator   secret key switch   key

cord outlet   connection unit   dimmer switch (2-module)

TIP: LINK THE EARTHS

With several earth cores on complex assemblies, you can link them to the grid terminal via a small insulated connector block.

TIP: UNCLIPPING LUGS

If you wish to move a gridswitch component, simply pull the lugs out again to release it from the grid. If they won't move easily, slide the tip of a small screwdriver inside the lug and lever it out.

CHAPTER 7

MISCELLANEOUS PROJECTS

Apart from ensuring that your home has adequate lighting and power supplies, there are a number of smaller but no less important projects you can carry out with your newly-found skills.

FITTING DOOR BELLS

If you have difficulty hearing visitors when they knock on your front door, the solution is to install a new bell, buzzer or set of chimes. Should one prove inadequate, you can always connect up an extension bell as well, so your system is even more efficient.

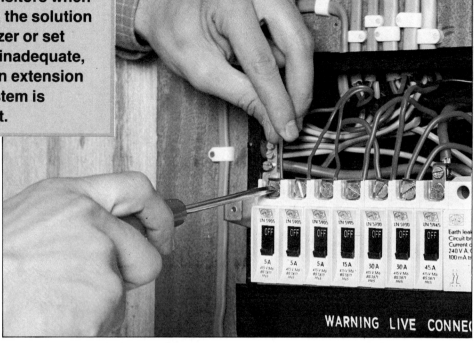

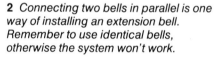
WARNING LIVE CONNE(

Imagine if someone was to knock on your front door while you were busy at the back of the house; the chances are you'd never hear them. Similarly, if you were in the garden and visitors called round, then the likelihood of them attracting your attention before they'd given up knocking on your door and gone home, is minimal. The obvious answer is to install a new bell, buzzer or set of chimes.

This needn't be a daunting job and in fact you'll find that even the most elaborate of the systems on the market is perfectly straight-forward to install. Indeed, your most difficult task is likely to be deciding what sort of sound you want to announce the arrival of your visitors. The best thing to do is to visit an electrical shop where they're likely to have a display of what is available. Then all you have to do is listen to the various tones and decide which you like; but remember, whatever you install is likely to last for a long time, so you're going to have to pick a bell, buzzer or set of chimes which won't irritate you.

Making your choice

There are two principal types of electric bell, either of which you can install in your home. The most common is the trembler bell, which operates on what is called a make-and-break system. When an electric current is passed through the bell, the cores of an electro-magnet are activated and they attract an arm, to which a striker and knob are attached; this then strikes a gong. At the same instant, the make-and-break contacts open, breaking the circuit and cutting off the current and causing the arm to return to its original position. When this happens, the circuit is reformed so the whole process is repeated – causing the arm to oscillate or 'tremble' to produce the familiar ringing of the bell – provided, of course, the bell push in the circuit is being depressed. The frequency of the trembling, and therefore the tone of the ring, can be altered simply by adjusting the contact screw. As soon as the finger is lifted off the bell push, the circuit is broken completely and the bell stops ringing. The big advantage of the trembler is that it will operate on both ordinary direct current (DC) from a battery or else on alternating current (AC)

CONNECTING BELLS TO BATTERIES

1 *If your bell has a separate battery you'll need two lengths of bell wire. The two floating cores should be joined and protected by insulating tape.*

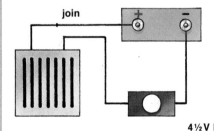
join

2 *Connecting two bells in parallel is one way of installing an extension bell. Remember to use identical bells, otherwise the system won't work.*

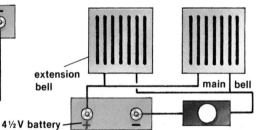
extension bell
main bell
4½V battery

3 *Connecting two bells in series is better as there is no danger of one bell starving the other of power. But don't use two trembler bells together.*

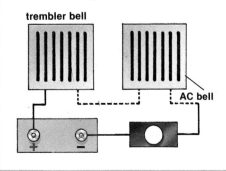
trembler bell
AC bell

4 *You can use an ordinary two-way switch as a changeover switch. That way you'll be able to select which bell you want working at a particular time.*

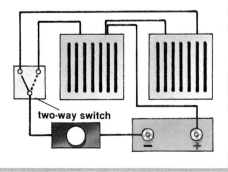
two-way switch

INSTALLING A BELL PUSH

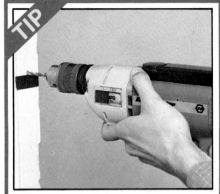

1 To make a hole in your door post, you'll probably have to drill through from both sides. Stick some tape right round the post to act as a guide.

2 Feed through the twin bell wire and check you have enough to make the connections. You can pull back the surplus after the push is fitted.

3 Connect the two cores to the two terminals on the bell push and then use a drill or bradawl to make pilot holes to fix the push to the post.

4 Finally use wood screws to fix the push securely in place. Bed the push on non-setting mastic if it will be exposed to rain.

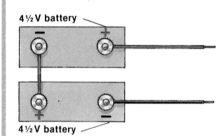
from the mains, provided it comes via a low-voltage transformer.

An AC bell is similar in principle to the trembler bell, but has no make-and-break contact device. As a result it will only operate on AC current from the mains and must therefore be connected to a suitable transformer. It is the alternating pattern of the current itself that provides the required movement in the arm to make the bell ring.

A buzzer is basically an electric bell minus the striker and bell dome. That means that it's the arm hitting the electro-magnets that produces the buzzing noise. It, too, is made in DC versions for operation from a battery and in AC versions for use from the mains.

Chimes are more elaborate than simple bells and buzzers, and are, inevitably, more expensive. When the bell push is pressed, the current activates an electro-magnet, and a double-ended plunger is drawn across to

strike one of the chime bars. When the bell push is released, it is sent back by the pressure of a spring to strike the second bar.

There is a wide range of models on the market and the most simple produces a two-note 'ding-dong' ring. Other models have special chimes playing more notes and some contain cassettes which produce familiar bars from popular tunes. Chimes can look rather ugly. This is because some models have long chime tubes that hang down underneath the casing. If you don't like the look of them, buy bar chimes which have all their apparatus concealed within the unit.

When choosing which type of bell, buzzer or chimes you want, it's well worth considering how it obtains its power, as well as what it sounds like. Where the power source is likely to be a mains transformer, either type of bell or buzzer may be used, but you'll probably find an AC bell or buzzer best. This is because

CONNECTING TO THE MAINS

1 *If you're going to connect your transformer to a spare fuseway, you'll have to fix it to the wall or back-board close to your consumer unit.*

2 *Run in the twin bell wire, fixing it to the wall with tacks or clips. Connect it to the secondary terminals that will provide the correct voltage.*

3 *Connect a length of 1.0mm² two-core and earth cable to the primary terminals. Ignore the earth core as most transformers don't need earthing.*

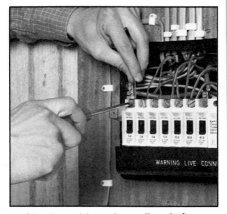

4 *Clip the cable to the wall and after switching off at the mains connect it to a spare 5A fuseway in the unit. Remember to label the fuseway.*

not only are they cheaper to buy, but with no make-and-break device there is the minimum of things that can go wrong: no contacts to corrode or burn and no adjusting screws to work loose and fall out.

Installing a bell

The simple circuit required for installing a bell is also suitable for the installation of a buzzer or a set of door chimes. You'll obviously require the new bell unit itself, a bell push, a length of twin bell wire, some tacks or insulated staples and a power source which will be either a 4½V battery or a special bell transformer. Bells, and all the necessary accessories and materials, are often available in kit form. You'll find that some bells have a special compartment in the unit for their battery; with others, the battery is housed separately. Remember, though, that circuit requirements are likely to vary between the

different models of bells, buzzers and chimes that are on the market. Before starting any installation, do make sure that you read all of the manufacturer's instructions very carefully.

The first thing to do is to fix the bell to the wall with woodscrews. It's best to fit it high up in the hall, where it'll be audible throughout the home, yet out of harm's way. If you're fixing into masonry, remember that you should drill and plug the holes before screwing the unit to the wall. You should then drill a hole about 6mm (¼in) in diameter in the front door post at the height of the bell push, so that the bell wire will be able to run straight through and into its back. Do make sure that this is at an easily accessible height for visitors, and that its position will be clearly visible. Unless you have a long drill bit, you might find that you'll have to drill in from both faces of the post. To help the two holes meet up with each other in

the middle, it's a good idea to mark the line of the intended hole on the post with a pencil or a length of tape. Provided your bell contains its battery, a single twin wire is all that's needed to link the bell and its push. This should run along as unobtrusive a route as possible and if you've got a picture rail in the hall you'll probably find it ideal to fix the wire on top. In fact the wire is so small that it's rarely noticed and can be kept in place with bell wire tacks. All you do is press the point between the two insulated cores of the bell wire and then knock it into the timber. If you don't want to go to that trouble, however, you could use self-adhesive bell wire.

You can then pass the wire through the hole drilled in the door post and, after removing the cover from the bell push, connect it to the two terminals. The wire is then drawn back through the hole so no excess wire remains on the outside of the door post, and the push can then be fixed to the door post. This is simply done by drilling a couple of pilot holes and then fixing it with wood screws; once it's fixed you can then replace the cover. The other end of the wire should then be connected to the bell terminals and, with the battery fitted, it'll be ready for use.

If, however, your battery has to be mounted separately, or else you're using a transformer, the circuitry is altered slightly. Only one of the cores from the push is connected to the bell itself and you have to run another length of bell wire from the spare bell terminal to the battery. Both cores of this second wire are then connected to the battery, while at the bell end the core which remains unconnected is joined, by means of a small connector, to the floating core running from the bell push.

Installing a transformer

The function of a transformer is to reduce the mains voltage so that it's safe to use with bells, buzzers and chimes. It's important to make sure that it is a bell transformer and is therefore designed specifically for this purpose.

The transformer will have two sets of terminals. One set is for the cable linking it to the 240V mains supply, while the others are low voltage and commonly have outputs of 3, 5 and 8 volts. You can also get transformers which have outputs of 4, 8 and 12 volts. Bells and buzzers usually require only 3 or 5 volts, while chimes are normally connected to the 8V terminals, although some models require 12V.

You can connect the transformer to the mains simply by plugging it into a spare socket, in which case the plug should have its 13A fuse replaced with a 3A one. You could also run a fused spur from the mains to the transformer – in which case you'd use a fused connection unit, also fitted with a 3A fuse.

Another way of obtaining mains power for your bell, buzzer or set of chimes is to connect

FITTING A CHIME UNIT

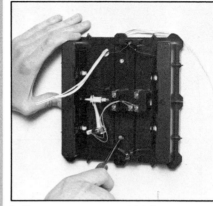

1 *Fix the bar chime unit high up on your hall wall. If you're fixing into masonry, you'll have to drill and plug the holes first.*

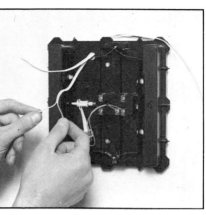

2 *Run in the twin bell wire and prepare the ends. Remember to read the maker's instructions carefully before making the connections.*

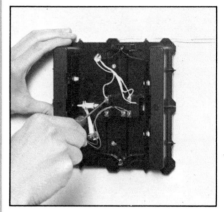

3 *Tack the wire to the wall, or if you're using self-adhesive wire make sure that it's pressed firmly in place. Then make the connections.*

4 *Finally, refit the cover of the chimes and, after switching on at the mains, check that your new system works efficiently.*

must be identical otherwise they won't work satisfactorily. In addition, the extension bell wire should not be too long, as this will result in erratic ringing.

It's probably better to connect the bells up in series. This is because the extra bell then becomes part of the whole circuit and the current must therefore pass through both bells. That means that there is no danger, as with parallel connection, of one bell 'starving' the other of current. However, if you're going to power the bells with a battery then you'll find that you can't successfully use two trembler bells in series. This is because the first bell would disrupt the current flow, and its subsequent irregular pattern would not allow the second one to work properly. The answer is to use an AC bell in conjunction with a trembler – that way there are no make-and-break contacts in the second bell – or else to modify a trembler bell by bridging the contacts with a piece of wire. In this case, the first bell will pass on identical current interruptions and so cause an identical trembling in the second bell.

An extension bell can also be connected to the terminals of door chimes, but it will ring only for the short time that the bell push is pressed by the caller. One way of avoiding this problem is to fit what is called a change-over switch. That way the caller is unlikely to hear the extension chimes and so depress the button longer.

Fitting a change-over switch

If you don't want both bells or chimes working at the same time, the answer is to fit a change-over switch. You can then have the main bell ringing when you are in the house, and the extension bell ringing when you're in the garden. The snag is, of course, that you must remember to switch the main bell back into the circuit when you come in from the garden; otherwise you'll be defeating the whole purpose of the switching arrangement. The correct switch to use is an ordinary two-way lighting switch. The twin wire from the bell push should be split, with one core going to the battery and the other going to the common terminal of the switch. From the L1 and L2 terminals of the switch, bell wire then runs to the main bell and the extension bell. For extra convenience, you could install a second bell push at the back door. If you already have a set of two-note chimes, then the front door push will give one note while the back door push will give the other; that way you'll know at which door the caller is. If, on the other hand, you already have a bell for the front door, then it's best to use a buzzer at the back so you can differentiate between them. Making the connections is not difficult, and as both pushes are unlikely to be used at the same moment both circuits can be connected to the same battery or transformer.

the transformer directly to the lighting circuit. This method should really only be used if you don't have a spare fuseway in your consumer unit or a free socket outlet, as it involves a bit of extra work. You'll have to break into the lighting circuit, and that means you'll have to lift the floorboards in the room above in order to gain access. Once you've done this and switched off at the mains, break into the circuit and fix a three-terminal junction box to a batten between two joists. Connect the cores of the lighting circuit cable to the junction box and then extend a branch cable from the box to the transformer. This cable should be $1.0mm^2$ two-core and earth cable and will run to the primary terminals on the transformer. You can then connect the twin bell wire to the secondary terminals.

But probably the best way to obtain your mains power is to connect the transformer directly to a spare 5A fuseway in the con-

sumer unit. You should place the transformer close to the unit and run a short length of $1.0mm^2$ two-core and earth cable to the spare 5A fuseway. On no account should you use bell wire for this section, as the cable will be carrying mains electricity which would overload it. (For further details on making connections to a spare fuseway see Chapter 4 pages 72-75). Once the bell wire has been connected to the two correct terminals on the other side of the transformer, the main switch can be turned on.

Installing an extension bell

There are times when your bell or buzzer can't be heard in the kitchen or garden. In that case the answer is to fit an extension bell. This is merely an extra bell or buzzer that is connected in parallel or in series to the main one (see diagram). If you are going to connect up the bells in parallel, then they

FITTING AN ENTRYPHONE

Door answering systems are usually associated with blocks of flats, but the convenience and added security they provide make them suitable for every home. And they are particularly useful for the elderly and the handicapped.

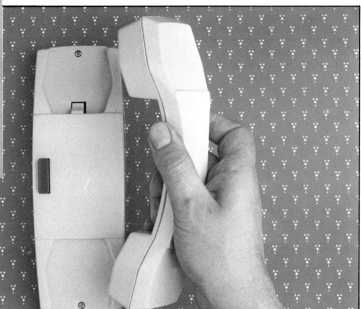

Given the high crime rate, making your home safe against intruders is essential. And fitting strong locks to doors and security devices to windows, or perhaps installing a burglar alarm to protect the whole property (see pages 167-170), will give you a fair degree of protection. So, if you've already got a door viewer and door chain fitted to your front door, why go to the added expense of an entry phone? Simply, they do offer more security – you don't have to open the door, even a little, to talk to someone. They also mean you don't have to go to the door to find out who's there – especially in flats. Furthermore, once you've established the person's identity you can let him in by remote control if an automatic door opener is fitted. And the beauty of this device is that you don't have to replace the existing door lock.

The ultimate system is a video phone which allows you to see and speak to the person at the front door.

The entry phone kit

Entry-phone systems are available in kit form, and it's far more sensible to use one of these than to buy all the components individually. The kit consists of a push-button panel which contains a microphone, a receiving amplifier and a speaker, which usually has a volume control. When the person at the door presses the button on the panel a buzzer sounds on the intercom handset. This can be installed wherever is most convenient – in the hallway, kitchen or study, for example. Lifting the receiver opens the channel to the speaker and receiver in the panel. And, by pressing a button on the handset holder, the solenoid-operated automatic door opener frees the latch, so allowing the door to be pushed open. If the buzzer is difficult to hear from other parts of the home, you can also wire the system to the existing door bell to give a general audible warning. Similarly, you can install a second handset.

The various fittings are connected using special multi-core flex. The system is powered by a low-voltage transformer which can be plugged into a 3-pin socket. It can also be run on a spur from the ring circuit or a branch from the lighting circuit.

LINKING THE COMPONENTS

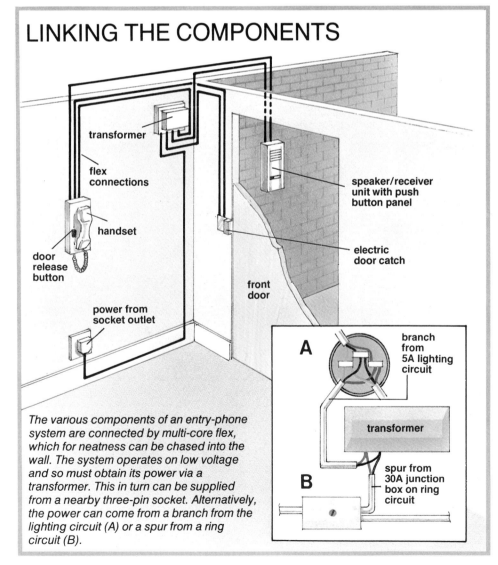

The various components of an entry-phone system are connected by multi-core flex, which for neatness can be chased into the wall. The system operates on low voltage and so must obtain its power via a transformer. This in turn can be supplied from a nearby three-pin socket. Alternatively, the power can come from a branch from the lighting circuit (A) or a spur from a ring circuit (B).

165

FITTING THE COMPONENTS

1 Make up the speaker/receiver unit and fix it in a protected place near the front door. Ideally it should be recessed, but plastic surrounds are available.

2 Wire up the flexes to the unit, and screw the push-button panel over the top. Note that flexes run on the surface should be encased in PVC conduit.

3 Screw the backplate of the handset to the wall, about 1.5m (5ft) above the floor. Make the necessary wiring connections and then replace the cover.

4 Depending on whether your door has a rim or mortise lock, the electric latch either has to be set into the door frame (illustrated) or mounted on the architrave.

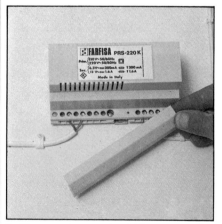

5 The transformer should be mounted where it can't be knocked accidentally. After wiring in all the flex cores, don't forget to replace the terminal cover.

THE ELECTRICAL CONNECTIONS

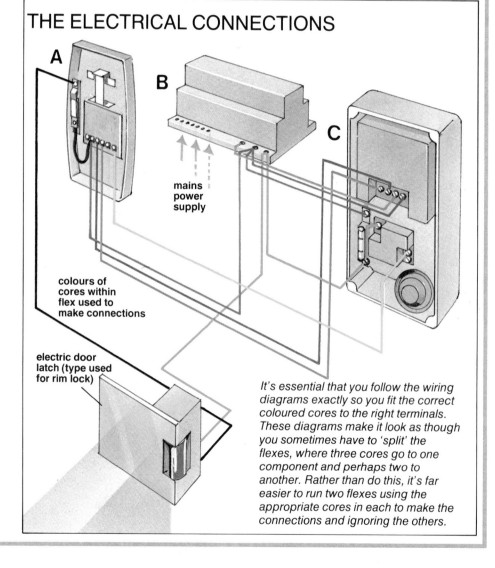

mains power supply

colours of cores within flex used to make connections

electric door latch (type used for rim lock)

It's essential that you follow the wiring diagrams exactly so you fit the correct coloured cores to the right terminals. These diagrams make it look as though you sometimes have to 'split' the flexes, where three cores go to one component and perhaps two to another. Rather than do this, it's far easier to run two flexes using the appropriate cores in each to make the connections and ignoring the others.

INSTALLING A BURGLAR ALARM

More and more people are choosing to protect their homes against intruders by fitting a burglar alarm. Here's how to install a typical kit system.

A typical domestic burglar alarm system serves two main purposes; to deter a burglar (either by warning him off when he sees the bell, or by scaring him off when it rings as he breaks in), and to alert you or your neighbours that a break-in is happening.

When you're thinking about fitting one to your home, there are several points to ponder. Firstly, even DIY kits are comparatively expensive, and you may feel that the money is better spent on locks and bolts for doors and windows all round the home – there's a very wide range to choose from. Secondly, false alarms can be a problem (and a nuisance), and the way you live may make having an alarm a distinct hindrance – for example, if you have children in and out all evening. Thirdly, if you live in a comparatively remote area, it's unlikely that anyone but the burglar will hear the bell anyway. However, if you feel that your home will be better protected (and your peace of mind guaranteed) with an alarm system fitted, the actual installation of a kit system is extremely straightforward.

What's in the kit

Most kits consist of the same ingredients. At the heart of the system is a control unit to which all the system components are linked by slim two-core cable. Most contain a battery, but with some models rechargeable batteries can be used. The main circuit cable runs out from and back to the control unit via magnetic contacts fitted to all windows and doors you want to protect (except for your main entry door, which is usually wired on a separate circuit to allow you a short time to leave the house when the system is on without activating the alarm). In addition, pressure-sensitive pads linked to the circuit can be laid under carpets to detect an intruder moving about the house, having bypassed the first line of defence. Another circuit runs from the control unit to the alarm bell, and on some systems there is also provision for a 'panic switch' which can be placed in the bedroom or by the front door; if it's pressed in an emergency, it sounds the alarm bell even if the rest of the system is switched off.

THE CIRCUITS

A typical burglar alarm system consists of circuits that link door and window sensors of various types to a central control unit. In this system there are five circuits in all.

1 *main loop to doors/windows*
2 *circuit to alarm bell*
3 *circuit to front door*
4 *circuit to warning buzzer*
5 *circuit to panic switch.*

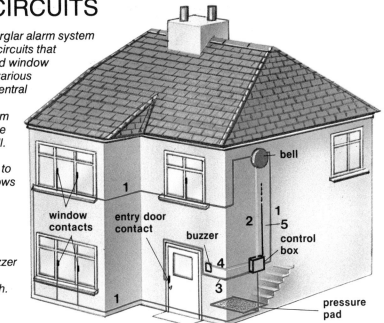

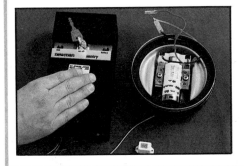

Testing the components

Before starting to install the various components of your kit, it's a good idea to carry out a bench test to familiarise yourself with the connections and to test that everything is working properly. In this case short lengths of wire are used to complete the various circuits. Have a cushion handy to smother the noise of the bell; it makes a very loud noise indoors.

INSTALLING WINDOW/DOOR CONTACTS

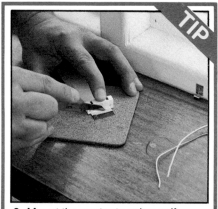

1 *Run the continuous circuit loop to each window or door to be protected, using cable clips to hold it in place. Then cut one core of the cable.*

2 *Mount the contacts using self-adhesive pads or small screws, or recess them neatly (see Ready Reference). Trim the pads to size first.*

3 *Mount the magnetic part of the contact on the moving casement or door, making sure you fit it so that the magnets face the correct way.*

Testing the system

Your first step on unpacking the contents of the kit is to read the instructions carefully and to familiarise yourself with all the components. The manufacturers usually recommend setting up a bench test of the equipment (see box, page 167), which helps you to see how everything interconnects and to check that it is functioning correctly. Have a cushion handy to smother the sound of the bell when you're testing it indoors.

The next stage is to plan how the property will be protected and where the various components of the system will be sited. It is a good idea to draw a floor plan of the areas to be protected, and from this to work out the possible points of entry and the routes within the building that an intruder is likely to take. You also need to decide on your own main entry and exit route. This is probably the front door, and it is not a good idea to have pressure pads between this door and the control unit, which may be fitted with a timer that allows about 30 seconds only for opening and closing the final exit door once the control unit is switched on. This is not quite so important with a system that has a separate main exit/entry door switch which allows the keyholder free exit and entry whilst the system is in the 'alert' condition. In the latter case, a good position for the control unit is in a concealed position in an area to be protected by the alarm system, such as in an upstairs cupboard where the wire to the alarm bell can be kept as short as possible. When the control unit has a time delay, it should be sited in a convenient position for the front door, such as in a hall cupboard or cloakroom. The warning buzzer (which sounds on entry to remind you to switch off the system) should also be placed fairly near the front door.

FITTING PRESSURE PADS

1 *Position pressure pads in areas that an intruder cannot avoid, such as at the foot of the stairs. Fit them below carpet underlay, and secure with screws or tape.*

2 *Prepare the cores of the cable connected to the mat as described in the maker's instructions; this usually involves cutting away screening wires.*

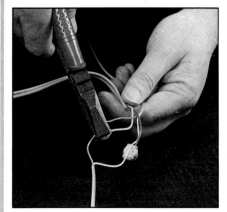

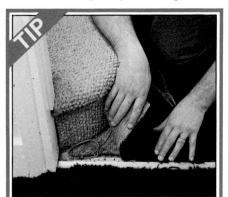

3 *Link the cores of the mat cable to the circuit cable (one core of which is cut as for fitting window contacts) using the special connectors provided.*

4 *Conceal the cable and connectors near the edge of the carpet. Avoid having the circuit cable visible – it could betray the mat's whereabouts.*

4 Then mount the switch part of the contact on the window or door frame, checking that it is parallel to and in line with the magnetic contact.

5 Connect the leads from the contact switch to the cut ends of the circuit loop by inserting both into the connectors and squeezing them with pliers.

6 Fix the two connectors and the uncut part of the circuit loop to the frame with self-adhesive pads. Use conduit to conceal the cable if you prefer.

INSTALLING THE CONTROL UNIT

1 Screw the control unit to the wall in its chosen position, and then connect up the circuit cores and the links to the bell, the main entry door and so on.

2 Check all the connections carefully against the manufacturer's instructions, and then fit the battery. The red test light will light if the battery is sound.

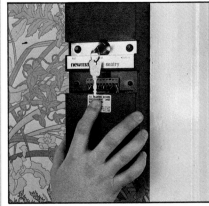

3 Replace the battery compartment cover, checking that it is pushed fully home. The red test light should go out when the cover is completely closed.

4 Fit the entry/exit warning buzzer near to the front door so that you hear it clearly whenever you enter or leave the house and the system is switched on.

Completing the installation

The alarm bell or siren should be fitted in a prominent position on the outside of the building, well out of reach of tampering. It should be as close as possible to the control unit and the cable connecting them should run through the wall immediately behind the alarm box so it is completely concealed.

Next, the control box is connected to the various sensors around the house with two-core cable which should be routed as unobtrusively as possible. Small cable clips are supplied, but where carpets are fitted the main loop cable can often be laid between carpet and skirting board. Exposed cable can, if you wish, be hidden in slim PVC electrical conduit – see *Ready Reference*.

The door and window contacts are magnetically-operated switches that are activated whenever a protected door or window is opened. Each sensor is in two parts. The switch section is fitted to the fixed frame, either on the surface or else neatly recessed into the frame – see *Ready Reference*. The magnetic section is fitted to the moving door or window, and you must ensure that both sections line up when the door or window is closed. The gap between them should not be greater than about 6mm (¼in).

Pressure pads are flat mats which in fact are electrical switches sensitive to the weight of a person through a carpet or rug. They can be used at any carpeted position where an intruder is likely to tread, such as at door thresholds between rooms, on stair treads, or beneath windows.

Once the wiring has been completed according to the installation instructions, it remains only to test the system before showing all members of the household how to use it.

Ready Reference

FITTING A PANIC SWITCH
If a panic switch is included in the kit, fit it by your bedside or near the front door, where it will be easy to reach in an emergency (A).

Run the cable from the control unit to the switch position, and connect the cores as per the manufacturer's instructions (B).

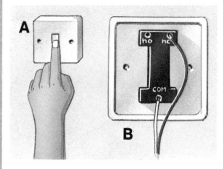

TIP: RECESS THE CONTACTS
You can make the window and door contacts far less obtrusive by recessing them into the woodwork. Mark up the positions of the recesses accurately.

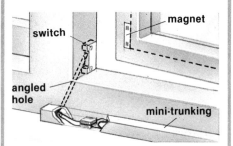

You can also conceal the circuit cable and the connectors if you wish by fitting lengths of slim PVC conduit along the rear edge of the window sill, and drilling an angled hole for the leads through the window frame.

TIP: SEAL THE BELL
The bell unit is usually fitted under the eaves, so it will get some protection from the weather. You can also seal the back of the bell housing with mastic to stop water running into the unit.

WARN YOUR NEIGHBOURS
When you install a burglar alarm
● tell your neighbours, so they'll know what's going on if the bell rings and can take appropriate action
● inform the local police, and leave a key with a neighbour so that the unit can be switched off in the event of a false alarm.
● make sure everyone in the house knows how to operate the system.

FITTING THE ALARM BELL

1 Fit the bell in a prominent position well out of reach of tampering. Put some non-setting mastic between backplate and wall to keep rain out.

3 Feed in the circuit loop cable, cut one core (as for windows) and use the connectors provided to link it to the leads from the anti-tamper switch.

5 Hook the gong into position over the lugs on the backplate, tucking all the cables neatly away behind it, and secure it to the backplate by tightening the fixing screw.

2 Feed the cable from the control unit through a hole drilled in the wall behind the bell, and connect the cores to the two bell terminals.

4 Connect the flying leads from the gong to the bell terminals, by pushing the plug pins into the terminal sockets. Check that they are pushed fully home.

6 Check that the magnet inside the bell cover lines up with the anti-tamper switch on the backplate, and then fix the cover in place. Now you can test the completed installation.

INSTALLING CONVENIENCE CONTROLS

You can make your life more comfortable and your home that much more secure by installing a variety of special controls for your lighting and electrical appliances.

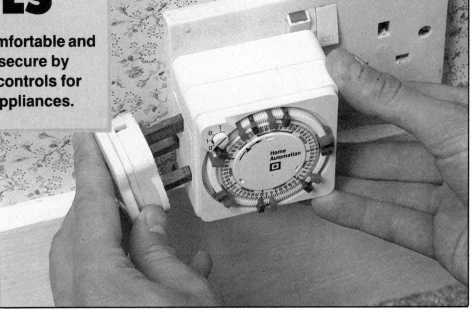

Special controls for electric appliances can be a real boon to the householder. They can make life much more comfortable by automatically switching appliances on and off, and more economic by preventing appliances from being left on to consume costly electricity. They can also help to make the home more secure by controlling lights, radios and curtains to give would-be burglars the impression that there's someone in.

But before you dash off to your local electrical supplies shop, pause for a moment's reflection. Are you being tempted by the sheer novelty of automatic controls? Remember, all automation is expensive, so it pays to take a slightly more hard-headed attitude towards making the decision. First of all, make sure that the equipment will actually do the job you have in mind. Read all the technical specifications carefully. You don't want to discover that your new dimmer light switch won't allow two-way switching or won't work on fluorescent lights. Secondly, do make sure that you know exactly what you're getting for your money. You may find out that the price quoted in the sales leaflet is just a basic 'starter kit' and that you'll have to spend more money to achieve the full performance suggested by the advertisement. Thirdly, consider whether it's actually worth automating a particular appliance; after all, many of the currently available devices perform only fairly menial tasks. Finally, remember that the development of home technology is advancing rapidly; buy now and you may well find that next year you can buy something that does more and does it cheaper.

Dimmer switches
Although dimmer switches offer no automatic form of control, they are considerably more versatile than the conventional rocker switch – allowing you greater flexibility in controlling the level of artificial lighting in the room where they are installed. They're usually used to control tungsten filament lights and spotlights. However, you can dim even a fluorescent lamp provided you have a special choke for the fitting. Various types of dimmer switches are available, ranging from those

with a simple rotary knob to those with a separate on/off switch. Touch dimmers are the most recent development.

Connecting a dimmer switch into your existing circuit is perfectly straightforward. Switch off at the mains and remove the fuse for the particular circuit you're working on; then you can switch the mains back on and have some light to work by. Unscrew the faceplate of your existing switch and pull it carefully away from the mounting box. This will give you enough room in which to disconnect the cable cores. Then simply connect up the cores to the dimmer switch according to the manufacturer's instructions and screw the faceplate to the box. If you want to put a dimmer into a two-way system then remember you can only replace one of the switches with a dimmer. Most one-gang dimmers will fit a standard plaster-depth or surface-mounted box, but some need a deeper box. Two-gang and multi-gang dimmers may need a double box.

Automatic light controls
The most basic automatic light switch is the time delay switch designed primarily for use on communal landings and stairwells. When you want light, all you do is switch on and leave the device to turn the light off again after a pre-set interval – usually anything from five to twenty minutes, depending on the model. Most versions allow you to adjust the timing to suit your needs. The most simple type works by means of a large spring-loaded button, while more sophisticated models use electronic timers and touch plate controls.

Time delay faders are a sort of cross between a dimmer and a time delay switch. They fade out the light gradually over a preset delay time and so are extremely handy for a child's bedroom, say. These are normally fitted with dual touch plate controls; the upper plate allows the switch to work like a conventional touch dimmer, the lower one triggers the dimming sequence. Time delay faders can be simply installed in the place of ordinary rocker switches, but, as a rule, they are not suitable for use with fluorescent lights.

Security switches
These switches are useful from a security point of view because lights are thereby turned on and off automatically to convince would-be burglars that you're at home. The basic switch incorporates a light-sensing device that will turn on the light at dusk and then off after a certain period of time (usually between two and ten hours). The faceplate carries a dial for selecting the time the light is on, and two switches, one to allow the switch to function as an ordinary on/off switch and the other to activate the light sensing device. It's not a good idea to fit this type of switch in unusually light or dark situations where the light-sensing device could get confused; avoid fixing it in a corner where there is little natural light or close to a window by a street light.

Photoelectric security switches don't, as a rule, incorporate on/off switches, so, if necessary, manual override will have to be provided separately. However, these switches are usually designed to be installed outside to control lights in exposed conditions. They

INSTALLING A DIMMER SWITCH

1 *Switch off at the mains and remove the lighting circuit fuse; then switch the power back on and unscrew the existing faceplate from its mounting box.*

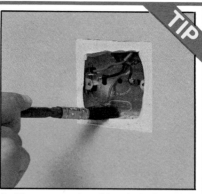

2 *Disconnect the old switch. Before fitting the dimmer switch brush away any plaster or debris that's fallen into the mounting box.*

3 *Make the connections to the new switch following the manufacturer's instructions. You may have to remove covers to get access to the terminals.*

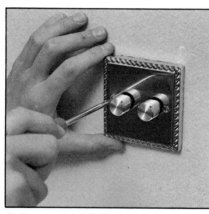

4 *If you're installing a metal switch, make sure the faceplate is earthed by linking it with the box earth terminal. Then screw the faceplate in place.*

USING A PLUG-IN DIMMER

1 *Plug-in dimmers can be easily moved, allowing you to dim any table lamps. They are not suitable for lamps below 40W or above 400W.*

2 *Simply plug the lamp into the dimmer socket. You'll then be able to control the brightness by moving the dial on the dimmer face.*

Ready Reference

INSTALLING DIMMER SWITCHES
Dimmer switches can easily replace one-way rocker switches and most two-way switches. However, in a two-way system only one switch need be replaced.

CONTROLLING THE LIGHT
There are three ways of switching lights controlled by a dimmer, depending on which model you fit;
● rotating an on/off knob
● flicking a separate rocker switch incorporated on the face plate
● tapping the touch plate.

MOUNTING BOXES
Most one-gang dimmer switches will fit into existing square plaster-depth (16mm/⅝in deep) mounting boxes (A), and have standard screw fixings.
  Some dimmer switches will require deeper boxes – either 25mm (1in) or 35mm (1⅜in). If you're installing three – or four-gang switches, then you'll probably have to install rectangular mounting boxes (B). These are also available in various depths.

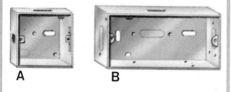

A   B

WATTAGE LIMITS
Dimmer switches operate between minimum and maximum wattage limits. Before buying one, check the light wattage of each lamp it will control. The minimum wattage is likely to be about 60W, so if you have a 40W lamp you won't be able to dim it successfully. On some switches the minimum can be as high as 120W, so a single 100W lamp would be too low.
  The maximum wattage can be as low as 400W, which means that some switches would be unable to control a section of track lighting with, say, five 100W lamps.

DEALING WITH THE CORES
When replacing switches with dimmers, always follow the manufacturer's instructions. In particular
● take note of existing core connections
● apply the equivalent coloured insulation tape round cores with faded insulation so they'll be readily identifiable in the future
● don't separate cores that are joined together. Just fit them into the same terminal on the new dimmer.

INSTALLING A TIME-DELAY SWITCH

1 *Switch off at the mains and remove the existing switch. Take off the front cover of the switch to gain access to the terminal screws.*

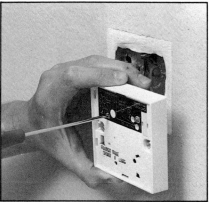

2 *Connect the cores to the terminals as indicated on the switch. You can then fix the switch to the mounting box with the screws provided.*

3 *You can set the switch so the light will be switched off up to twenty minutes after being turned on. Use the special screwdriver to adjust the delay.*

4 *Finally, fit the touch plate back in position. Switch on at the mains and test the time setting. If necessary, adjust the setting again.*

FITTING A SECURITY SWITCH

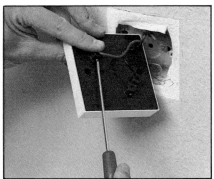

1 *Switch off at the mains and remove your old switch. Make the connections to the security switch and screw it to the mounting box.*

2 *You can programme the light switch to turn interior and exterior lights on or off automatically. Programmes can be easily cleared and overidden.*

can usually be mounted within plastic conduit systems and will switch outside lights on at dusk and off at dawn, so giving your home extra security when no one's in. And, of course, you'll have the lights on for you when you return from an evening out. Most exterior switches incorporate a designed time delay of 1 to 2 minutes so that car headlights won't cause the light to go off.

Automatic power control
Plug-in timers are merely a sort of sophisticated plug-in adaptor for ordinary power sockets. Once you have one in place, all you do is plug in whatever device you want the timer to control. This can be just about anything that can be powered from your home's ring circuit – standard lamps, radiators, blankets and radios. You programme the timer by using small pegs fixed in special holes on the dials or by moving small spring-loaded lugs; the timer will automatically turn the power on and off at these pre-set times.

The minimum period the power can be on for is thirty minutes, although you can control the timer to the nearest fifteen minutes. The on/off pegs are usually protected by a clear dust cover and spare pegs are normally provided with each timer so that more than one operation can be made in each cycle. Most basic versions will operate on a twenty-four hour cycle, although timers programmable for up to seven days are available. With these the setting intervals tend to be quite long – up to two hours in some cases. However, the timer with a longer cycle will obviously be more useful from a security point of view, since you can set it to turn lights on and off at different times each day.

Other control gear
Other devices on the market perform more specific tasks. An electric curtain controller, for example, will both open and close corded curtains provided the weight of pull on the cord required to do so is no greater than 8kg (17½lbs). The motor is controlled by a two-position switch and is simply plugged into the mains. As a safety precaution it will only operate for a period of five minutes before cutting out; that way any accidents in the event of a cord failure will be prevented.

Fan controllers are suitable for use with most electric extractor fans. They are basically specialised dimmer switches that allow you to vary the speed of the fan. They're normally fitted with a separate on/off switch and in some cases a switch for opening and closing the shutters found on very large fans. Other models also have reversing switches. Finally, immersion heater timers work in much the same way as plug-in timers, allowing a number of switching operations per day or per seven days.

FITTING A CURTAIN CONTROLLER

1 Gain access to your electric curtain controller by removing the two screws on top of the casing and then sliding it away from the housing.

2 You can only use the curtain controller with curtains that have endless cord. Feed the cord through the front slot and position it round the drive pulley.

3 Position the curtain controller where you want to fix it to the wall. The cord must not chafe on the housing. Drill and plug the wall and screw the box in place.

4 Slide the cover back onto the housing and fit the screws. Make sure the cords are in line with the top opening and there's no obstruction.

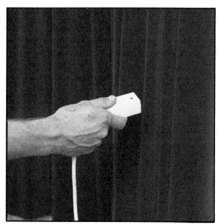

5 Plug in the power lead. You'll then be able to open and close your curtain by using the rocker switch that is already fitted to the switch cable.

6 If you find that the curtains don't close fully then you'll have to make adjustments to the pulley wheel using the small hexagon wrench provided.

PLUG-IN TIMERS

1 Programme the plug-in timer by first setting it to the correct day and time. Then slot in the nibs that will turn the appliance on and off.

2 Plug the timer in the nearest socket. You'll then be able to plug in the appliance. Finally, switch on both the appliance and the socket.

3 You can override the timer by turning the control knob anti-clockwise one position. Spare nibs for further programming are supplied with the timer.

MAINTENANCE & REPAIRS

However well equipped and installed everything electrical may be in your home, there will still be occasional problems – faults, breakdowns, everyday wear and tear – that need to be solved properly and quickly if the system is to carry on functioning.

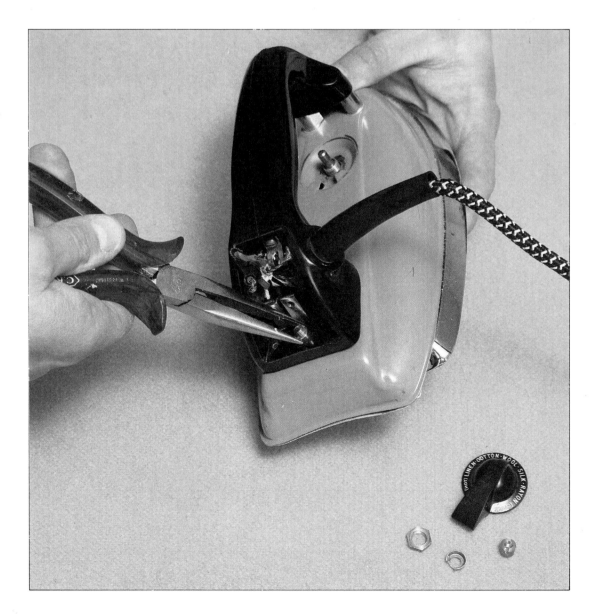

TRACING ELECTRICAL FAULTS

When the lights go out or an electrical appliance won't work, the reason is often obvious. But when it isn't, it helps to know how to locate the fault and put it right.

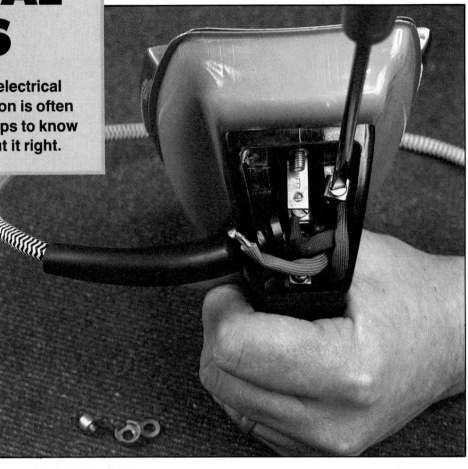

Most people's immediate reaction to something going wrong with their electricity supply is to head for the meter cupboard, muttering darkly about another blown fuse. Fuses do blow occasionally for no immediately obvious reason, but usually there is a problem that needs to be pin-pointed and put right before the power can be restored. It's no use mending a blown fuse, only to find that when the power is restored the fuse blows again because the fault is still present.

Tracing everyday electrical faults is not particularly difficult. You simply have to be methodical in checking the various possible causes, and eliminating options until you find the culprit. More serious faults on the house's fixed wiring system can be more difficult to track down, but again some careful investigation can often locate the source of the trouble, even if professional help has to be called in to put it right.

Safety first

Before you start investigating any electrical faults, remember the cardinal rule and switch off the power at the main switch. When fuses blow, it is all too easy to forget that other parts of the system may still be live and therefore dangerous, and even if you know precisely how your house has been wired up it is foolish to take risks. If the fault appears to be on an electrical appliance, the same rules apply: always switch off the appliance *and* pull out the plug before attempting to investigate. Don't rely on the switch to isolate it; the fault may be in the switch itself.

It's also important to be prepared for things to go wrong with your electrics; even new systems can develop faults, and in fact a modern installation using circuit breakers will detect faults more readily than one with rewireable or cartridge fuses, so giving more regular cause for investigation. Make sure that you keep a small emergency electrical tool kit in an accessible place where it won't get raided for other jobs; it should include one or two screwdrivers, a pair of pliers, a handyman's knife, spare fuses and fuse wire, and above all a *working* torch. For more details about tools for electrical work see pages 19-21.

Check the obvious

When something electrical fails to operate, always check the obvious first – replace the bulb when a light doesn't work, or glance outside to see if everyone in the street has been blacked out by a power cut before panicking that all your fuses have blown. Having satisfied yourself that you may have a genuine fault, start a methodical check of all the possibilities.

A fault can occur in a number of places. It may be on an appliance, within the flex or plug linking it to the mains, on the main circuitry itself or at the fuseboard. Let's start at the appliance end of things. If something went bang as you switched the appliance on, unplug it immediately; the fault is probably on the appliance itself. If it simply stopped working, try plugging it in at another socket; if it goes, there's a fault on the circuit feeding the original socket. If it doesn't go, either the second socket is on the same faulty circuit as the first one (which we'll come to later) or there may be a fault in the link between the appliance and the socket – loose connections where the cores are connected to either the plug or the appliance itself, damaged flex (both these problems are caused by abuse of the flex in use), or a blown fuse in the plug if one is fitted.

Plug and flex connections

The next step is to check the flex connections within the plug and the appliance. The connections at plug terminals are particularly prone to damage if the plug's cord grip or flex anchorage is not doing its job; a tug on the flex can then break the cores, cutting the power and possibly causing a short circuit. If the connections are weak or damaged, disconnect them, cut back the sheathing and insulation and remake the connections. Make sure that the flex is correctly anchored within the body of the plug before replacing the cover.

If the plug contains a fuse, test that it has not blown by using a continuity tester, or by holding it across the open end of a switched-on metal-cased torch – see *Ready Reference*. Replace a blown fuse with a new one of the correct current rating; 3A for appliances rated at 720W or below, 13A for higher-rated appliances (and all colour televisions).

Next, check the flex connections within the appliance itself. Always unplug an appliance before opening it up to gain access to the terminal block, and then remake any doubtful-looking connections by cutting off the end of the flex and stripping back the outer and inner insulation carefully to expose fresh conductor strands. If the flex itself is worn or

REWIRING A PLUG

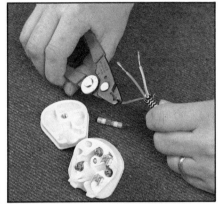

1 *Strip the outer sheathing carefully, cut each core 12mm (1/2in) longer than is necessary to reach its correct terminal and then remove 12mm of core sheathing.*

2 *Twist the strands of each core neatly and form a loop that will fit round the terminal screw. Connect the cores as shown here and screw down the studs.*

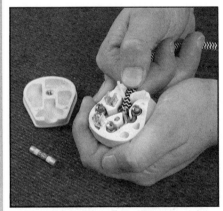

3 *Check that the core insulation reaches right to each terminal, and that there are no loose strands visible. Then fit the flex securely in the cord grip.*

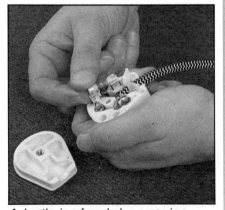

4 *Lastly, in a fused plug press in a cartridge fuse of the correct rating for the appliance concerned, and screw the plug top firmly on.*

damaged, take this opportunity to fit new flex of the correct type and current rating – see *Ready Reference*, step-by-step photographs and pages 14-15 for more details. Make sure you re-use any grommets, heat-resistant sleeving, special captive washers and the like that were fitted to the appliance.

Lastly, check the flex continuity; it is possible that damage to the flex itself has broken one of the cores within the outer sheathing. Again use a continuity tester for this, holding the two probes against opposite ends of each core in turn, or use your metal-cased torch again, touching one core to the case and the other to the battery. Replace the flex if *any* core fails the test; the appliance may still work if the earth core is damaged, but the earthing will be lost and the appliance could become live and dangerous to anyone using it in the event of another fault developing in the future.

Lighting problems

Similar problems to these can also occur on lighting circuits, where the pendant flex linking ceiling roses to lampholders can become disconnected or faulty through accidental damage or old age. If replacing the bulb doesn't work, switch off the power at the mains and examine the condition of the flex. Look especially for bad or broken connections at the ceiling rose and within the lampholder. Replace the flex if the core insulation has become brittle, and fit a new lampholder if the plastic is discoloured (both these problems are caused by heat from the light bulb). See step-by-step photographs on page 150 for details.

Mending blown fuses

A circuit fuse will blow for two main reasons, overloading and short circuits – see *Ready Reference*. Too many appliances connected

to a circuit will demand too much current, and this will melt the fuse. Similarly, a short circuit – where, for example, bare live and neutral flex cores touch – causes a current surge that blows the fuse.

If overloading caused the fuse to blow, the remedy is simple: disconnect all the equipment on the circuit, mend the fuse and avoid using too many high-wattage appliances at the same time in future. If a short circuit was to blame, you will have to hunt for the cause and rectify it before mending the fuse – see photographs on the next page.

When a circuit fuse blows, turn off the main switch and remove fuseholders until you find the one that has blown. Then clean out the remains of the old fuse wire, and fit a new piece of the correct rating for the circuit – 5A for lighting circuits, 15A for circuits to immersion heaters and the like, and 30A for ring circuits. Cut the wire over-long, thread it loosely across or through the ceramic holder and connect it carefully to the terminals. Trim the ends off neatly, replace the fuseholder in the consumer unit and turn on the power again. If the fuse blows again, and you have already checked for possible causes on appliances, flexes and lighting pendants, suspect a circuit fault – see below.

If you have cartridge fuses, all you have to do is find which cartridge has blown by removing the fuseholder and testing the cartridge with a continuity tester or metal-cased torch. A blown cartridge fuse should be replaced by a new one of the same current rating. Again, if the new fuse blows immediately, suspect a circuit fault.

If you have miniature circuit breakers (MCBs) you will not be able to switch the MCB on again if the fault that tripped it off is still present. Otherwise, simply reset it by switching it to ON or pressing in the centre button.

Residual current circuit breakers (RCCBs)

If your installation has an RCCB, it will trip off if an earthing fault occurs – for example, if a live wire or connection comes into contact with earthed metal. Like an MCB, it cannot be switched on again until the fault is rectified – a useful safety point. However, it will not trip off in the event of a short circuit between live and neutral, or when overloading occurs.

A modern high-sensitivity RCCB will, in addition to detecting earth faults, also protect against the danger of electric shocks by tripping off if it detects current flowing to earth through the human body. It can do this quickly enough to prevent the shock from causing death.

Tracing circuit faults

If you have checked appliances, flexes, plug connections and pendant lights, and a fault is still present, it is likely to be in the fixed

REPLACING FLEX

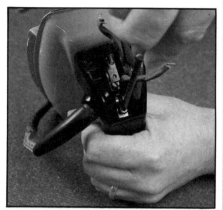

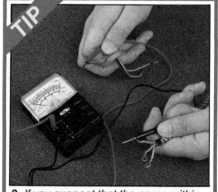

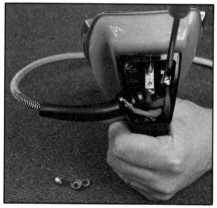

1 To replace damaged flex, remove the appropriate cover plate or panel from the appliance. Make a note of which core goes where before undoing it.

2 Loosen the cord grip within the appliance and withdraw the old flex. Here heat-resisting sleeving has been fitted; save this for re-use.

3 If you suspect that the cores within apparently undamaged flex are broken, test each core in turn with a continuity tester.

4 Connect in the new flex by reversing the disconnection sequence, re-using grommets, sleeving and washers. Make sure each connection is secure.

wiring. Here, it is possible to track down one or two faults, but you may in the end have to call in a professional electrician.

The likeliest causes of circuit faults are damage to cables (perhaps caused by drilling holes in walls or by nailing down floorboards where cables run), ageing of cables (leading to insulation breakdown, and overheating) and faults at wiring accessories (light switches, socket outlets and so on). Let's look at the last one first, simply because such items are at least easily accessible.

If the cable cores are not properly stripped and connected within the accessory, short circuits or earth faults can develop. To check a suspect accessory such as a socket outlet, isolate the circuit, unscrew the faceplate and examine the terminal connections and the insulation. Ensure that each core is firmly held in its correct terminal, and that each core has insulation right up to the terminal,

so that it cannot touch another core or any bare metal. There is usually enough slack on the mains cable to allow you to trim over-long cores back slightly. Check that the earth core is sleeved in green/yellow PVC, and try not to double over the cable as you ease the faceplate back into position; over-full boxes can lead to short circuits and damage to cable and core insulation ... and more trouble. You can carry out similar checks at light switches and ceiling roses. Any damaged accessories you find should be replaced immediately with new ones.

Damage to cables is relatively easy to cure provided that you can find where the damage is. If you drilled or nailed through a cable, you will of course be able to pin-point it immediately. Cable beneath floorboards can be repaired simply by isolating the circuit, cutting the cable completely at the point of damage and using a three-terminal junction

REPAIRING A CIRCUIT FUSE

1 *Switch off the mains and locate the blown fuse. Then remove the remains of the old fuse wire and clean off any charring that has occurred.*

2 *Feed in a length of fuse wire of the correct rating and wind each end round the terminal before tightening up the screw. Don't pull the wire taut.*

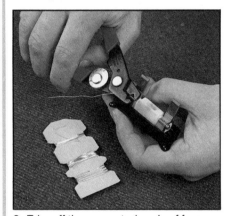

3 *Trim off the unwanted ends of fuse wire neatly with wire strippers, then replace the fuse carrier in the fuse box and restore the power.*

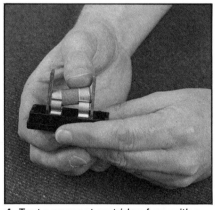

4 *Test a suspect cartridge fuse with a continuity tester or torch (see* Ready Reference*) and replace it by pressing in a new fuse of the correct rating.*

Ready Reference

CHECKLIST FOR ACTION

When something goes wrong with your electrics, use this checklist to identify or eliminate the commonest potential causes of trouble.

Fault 1
Pendant light doesn't work
Action
● replace bulb
● check lighting circuit fuse/MCB
● check flex connections at lampholder and ceiling rose
● check flex continuity.

Fault 2
Electrical appliance doesn't work
Action
● try appliance at another socket
● check plug fuse (if fitted)
● check plug connections
● check connections at appliance's own terminal block
● check flex continuity
● check power circuit fuse/MCB
● isolate appliance if fuses blow again.

Fault 3
Whole circuit is dead
Action
● switch off all lights/disconnect all appliances on circuit
● replace circuit fuse or reset MCB
● switch on lights/plug in appliances one by one and note which blows fuse again
● isolate offending light/appliance, and see Faults 1 and 2 (above)
● check wiring accessories on circuit for causes of short circuits
● replace damaged cable if pierced by nail or drill
● call qualified electrician for help.

Fault 4
Whole system is dead
Action
● check for local power cut
● reset RCCB fitted to system (and see Faults 1, 2 and 3 if RCCB cannot be reset)
● call electricity board (main service fuse may have blown)

Fault 5
Electric shock received
Action
● try to turn off the power
● grab victim's clothing and pull away from power source, but DO NOT TOUCH WITH BARE HANDS
● if victim is conscious, keep warm and call a doctor; don't give brandy or food
● if breathing or heartbeat has stopped, CALL AN AMBULANCE and give artificial respiration or cardiac massage.

box to link the cut ends. Cable buried in plaster must be cut out and a new length of cable inserted between adjacent accessories to replace the damaged length. Where this would involve a long length of cable (on a run to a remote socket, for example) it is acceptable to use junction boxes in nearby floor or ceiling voids to connect in the new length of cable. You will then have to make good the cutting-out.

Tracking down a break in the cable elsewhere in the installation is a difficult job best left to a qualified electrician. If, however, you find that your house is wired in rubbersheathed cable and faults are beginning to occur, don't waste time and effort trying to track them down; you need a rewire. For more information see Chapter 6 pages 144-157.

If you are unable to trace an electrical fault after checking all the points already de-

scribed, call in a professional electrician who will be able to use specialist test equipment to locate the fault. Do *not* attempt to bypass a fault with a makeshift wiring arrangement, and NEVER use any conducting foreign body such as a nail to restore power to a circuit whose fuse keeps blowing. Such tricks can kill.

Regular maintenance
You will find that a little common-sense maintenance work will help to prevent a lot of minor electrical faults from occurring at all. For example, it's well worth spending a couple of hours every so often checking the condition of the flex on portable appliances (especially those heavily used, such as kettles, irons, hair driers and the like) and the connections within plugs. Also, make a point of replacing immediately any electrical accessory that is in any way damaged.

EXTENDING FLEX SAFELY

Ideally, electrical appliances should be linked to the mains via an unbroken length of flex. However, there are times when you may need a longer flex – which means extending the one that's fitted, or else using a separate extension lead with its own plug and socket.

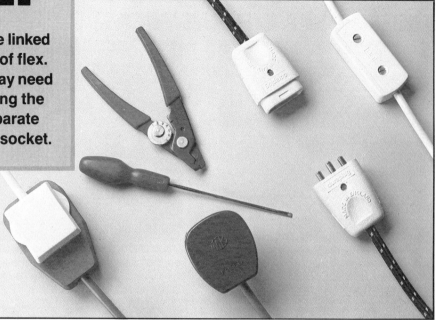

If you've got enough socket outlets in your home, you should be able to plug in most of your appliances to a nearby socket without any problem. But there are often situations where the length of flex that's fitted just isn't long enough. For example, few vacuum cleaners have enough flex to allow uninterrupted cleaning without you having to keep unplugging the appliance and moving to another socket outlet to plug it in. And most power tools come with annoyingly short leads – fine if you always use them at your workbench, but not much use elsewhere.

There are two ways round the problem. The first is to fit a longer flex – the right answer for cases like the vacuum cleaner. The second is to use a separate extension lead into which appliances with short flexes can be plugged whenever the need arises.

Extension leads
An extension lead is just a length of flex with a plug on one end (to plug into the mains) and a socket on the other (into which you plug the tool or appliance you're using). You can buy one ready-made, complete with connectors and packed loose in a bag (in which case it will have what is called a trailing socket at the 'appliance' end of the lead), or complete with a drum onto which the flex is wound when the lead is not in use (here the socket is actually mounted on the drum). Alternatively, you can buy the various components and connect them up yourself.

Earthing and current rating
Any extension lead must serve the same purpose as the flex on the appliance whose reach it is extending, and this means that above all it must provide earth continuity. Many power tools (especially those intended for use out of doors, such as lawnmowers) are double-insulated, which means that they do not need an earth connection and are fitted with two-core flex. So, in theory, you could use an extension lead with just two cores as well.

However, the extension lead you intend to use with your lawnmower may end up being used with another appliance instead – one that *does* need earthing. So any extension

lead you use should, for safety's sake, always have three-core flex. It will still work with any double-insulated appliance too, of course.

The other important thing about extension leads is the current rating of the flex used. You may have intended your lead to be used only for a power drill using, say, 400 watts – well within the capacity of a 3A 0.5mm² flex. But suppose someone unknowingly uses that same flex to power a fan heater rated at 3kW. The flex will then be heavily overloaded and unless a 3A fuse has been fitted in the lead's plug the flex will overheat and could start a fire. So play safe: always use 1.25mm² flex for an extension lead, whatever you intend to use it for.

If you're going to use the extension lead out of doors, it's best to choose an orange or white sheathed flex rather than a black one. Always use it in conjunction with an RCCB – see pages 76-78.

Safety with extension leads
There are two points to remember about using extension leads safely. The first is always to uncoil the lead from the drum before you use it, especially if it's powering a high-rated appliance. If you don't it may overheat and eventually melt. The second point is never to use a lead out of doors when it is raining, or after rain when foliage is wet and moisture could get into the socket.

Making up your own lead
The flex should, as already described, be 1.25mm² two-core and earth PVC-sheathed flex. The plug can be any conventional plug that suits your house sockets. However, a toughened plastic or moulded rubber one will stand up to knocks better.

The socket should also be toughened plastic or rubber. There's the same choice of pin type and colour as with moulded plugs, and you can have one, two or four outlets on the one socket.

It's best to keep your lead on a drum of some sort so it doesn't get kinked when coiled up. An empty cable reel is ideal, or you can make a simple drum from plywood and softwood offcuts – see *Ready Reference*.

Extending flex
On appliances like vacuum cleaners and lawnmowers, you may prefer to extend the appliance flex permanently instead of using an extension lead. The best way of doing this is to replace the existing flex completely, wiring the new flex into the appliance itself. But provided you use the right method, you can also extend the existing flex by adding on an extra length with a flex connector.

For most household appliances a one-piece connector is ideal – see the step-by-step photographs opposite. This simply links the old and new flex within a one-piece moulding. Make sure you use the right size – a 5A one for appliances rated at less than 1200 watts, a 13A one otherwise.

If you'll want to disconnect the flex extension for any reason, use a two-part connector instead. Fit a two-pin one to double-insulated appliances, a three-pin one otherwise. Remember always to connect the plug part to the appliance flex and the socket part to the extension flex. If you do it the other way round the plug pins will be live when the flex is plugged into the mains. For leads of this type being used out of doors, go for a weatherproof type with a shroud that locks the two parts together.

ASSEMBLING THE COMPONENTS

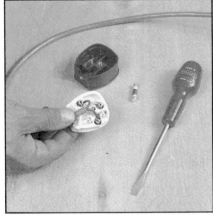

1 *If you're making up an extension lead, use orange or white 1.25mm² three-core flex and a toughened plug. Make sure the cord grip holds the flex securely.*

3 *With a two-part flex connector, prepare the cores. Thread the flex through the shrouds, connect up the cores and tighten the cord grips.*

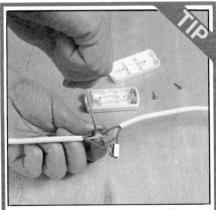

5 *With a one-piece connector it's easier to link the cores if you remove the terminals first. You may have to cut each core to a different length.*

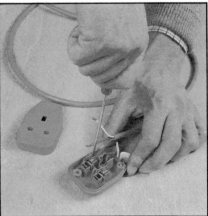

2 *Connect the other end of the flex to the correct terminals within the trailing socket. Again, make sure the cord grip is secure before fitting the cover.*

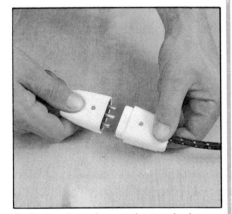

4 *Fit the shrouds over the terminal blocks. Check that you have connected the plug part to the appliance flex, the socket part to the mains flex.*

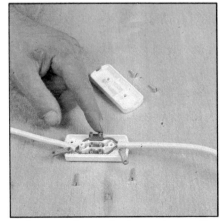

6 *Open up the cord grips and press the terminal blocks into place, laying the cores in their channels. Do up the two cord grips and fit the connector cover.*

Ready Reference

READY-MADE LEADS

You can buy extension leads ready-made and wound on plastic drums, complete with a carrying handle. Before you buy one
● check that the flex is rated at 13A rather than 5A
● check the flex length; it may be anything from 9 to 20m (30 to 66ft).
Look too for extra features like switched sockets with neons, hanging hooks and somewhere to stow the plug.

PICK THE RIGHT FLEX

For extension leads, always choose 1.25mm² two-core and earth PVC-sheathed cable – preferably orange or white rather than black. Fit a 13A fuse in the plug.

   If you're extending an appliance flex via a flex connector, use the same type of flex and make sure you choose the right current rating, according to the wattage of the appliance.

Core size	current rating	max. wattage
0.5mm²	3A	720W
0.75mm²	6A	1440W
1.0mm²	10A	2000W
1.25mm²	13A	3000W

EXTENDING OLD FLEX

The flex you're extending may have the old colour codes on its core insulation. To make sure you connect the cores correctly, remember that
● live cores were colour-coded red, but are now coded brown
● neutral cores were black, are now blue
● earth cores were green, are now green/yellow striped.

TIP: UNCOIL DRUM FLEXES

If you're using a ready-made extension reel, it's safest to uncoil the flex fully before using it. Otherwise there is a risk of the flex overheating and melting, especially if a highly-rated appliance is being used.

MAKING A REEL

If you've made up your own extension lead, it's a good idea to store it on a makeshift or home-made drum so it doesn't become kinked or knotted. You can either use an empty cable reel (A), or make up a simple drum from plywood and softwood offcuts (B).

A   B

SERVICING ELECTRICAL APPLIANCES:1

When electrical appliances go wrong getting them repaired can be a costly and time-consuming business. Here are the first steps that will enable you to undertake some simple repairs yourself.

From time to time electrical appliances will need servicing. You wouldn't dream of not looking after your car, so why your fridge or toaster? However, in spite of any servicing you might undertake, appliances do now and then go wrong, perhaps leaving you with an expensive repair bill. If an appliance packs up your first inclination may be to take it down to a local electrical repair shop, or, if it isn't portable, to call in a servicing engineer. But if you take the trouble to examine the appliance, its plug and flex, you may be able to locate the fault and make the necessary repairs so saving quite a lot of money. You could also save yourself the embarrassment of calling out an engineer only for him to discover that a fuse had blown in the plug.

However, before rushing for your screwdriver and taking your appliance to pieces, there are a number of checks you should make which may save you a lot of work.

Preliminary checks

Before examining any part of the appliance do make sure that it is unplugged. Then check that the socket, switched fused connection unit or double pole switch through which the appliance obtains its power was actually switched *on*. After all, if for some reason you're in a rush it's very easy to forget to do this. If your appliance has a thermal cut out device, or some other kind of cut out, check that this is closed otherwise it won't work. If it isn't, press the relevant button and switch on the appliance. If it trips within a minute or so you'll know that the appliance itself is faulty.

Then check that the fault isn't something as simple as a blown fuse in the plug. Remove the fuse and either test it (see Ready Reference, page 177) or merely replace it with a new fuse that you know works.

If your appliance has a loading of more than 720W, and when you remove the plug fuse you discover that it has a current rating of 3 or 5A, then you can be almost certain that it has blown. Simply replace the fuse with a 13A one and your problem should be solved. Examine the flexible cord for damage or general wear and if there is evidence of any then there could be a short circuit. If possible

you should check the flex connections at the appliance terminals as well as at the plug or fused connection unit terminals. Replace damaged or worn flex, and reconnect it if the cores at the terminals are loose or broken but it is otherwise in good condition. You should also check the flex continuity. A broken core within the outer sheathing will not be immediately apparent, for example. Use a continuity tester and if a core is damaged replace the flex immediately. For further information on how to do this see pages 176-179 again.

You should also make sure that you have power at the socket by plugging in another appliance that you know works. If there proves to be no power, you'll probably find that the circuit fuse has blown; check this and make the necessary repairs or adjustments and you'll find that your appliance works perfectly again.

If, however, after checking all these points you find that your appliance still doesn't work then it will certainly be in need of some attention.

Guarantees and service contracts

Don't immediately proceed with taking your faulty appliance to pieces in the hope that

you'll spot the fault. Electrical appliances are delicate pieces of machinery and need careful treatment. And in any case you might still be able to avoid having to do the work yourself. Before dismantling anything check whether the maker's guarantee has expired. If not then don't attempt any work on the appliance; simply follow the terms of the guarantee and you'll probably be able to get it all done by qualified electricians completely free of charge. If the guarantee has run out then check that the appliance isn't covered by some other scheme for which an annual premium is paid. You'll often find that for large and complicated appliances such as automatic washing machines it'll prove cheaper, and in the long run more satisfactory, to take out a maintenance contract. To service such appliances special tools and equipment are often required and it's a good idea to have a servicing manual as well. However, these are not as easily obtainable as those for cars, and they're only available either to authorised dealers and servicing firms or at quite a high price. And, of course, you'll have to make sure that you can get any spares you might need. After all, it would be a complete waste of time to take something to pieces only to discover that spare parts

TYPES OF ELECTRIC MOTOR

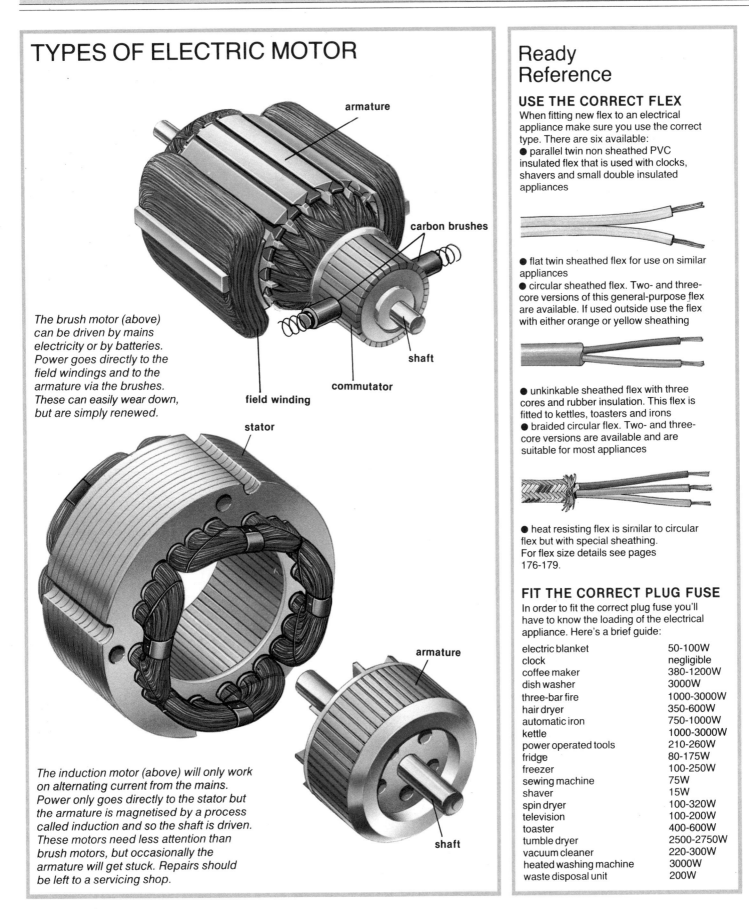

armature

carbon brushes

shaft

commutator

field winding

The brush motor (above) can be driven by mains electricity or by batteries. Power goes directly to the field windings and to the armature via the brushes. These can easily wear down, but are simply renewed.

stator

armature

shaft

The induction motor (above) will only work on alternating current from the mains. Power only goes directly to the stator but the armature is magnetised by a process called induction and so the shaft is driven. These motors need less attention than brush motors, but occasionally the armature will get stuck. Repairs should be left to a servicing shop.

Ready Reference

USE THE CORRECT FLEX

When fitting new flex to an electrical appliance make sure you use the correct type. There are six available:
● parallel twin non sheathed PVC insulated flex that is used with clocks, shavers and small double insulated appliances

● flat twin sheathed flex for use on similar appliances
● circular sheathed flex. Two- and three-core versions of this general-purpose flex are available. If used outside use the flex with either orange or yellow sheathing

● unkinkable sheathed flex with three cores and rubber insulation. This flex is fitted to kettles, toasters and irons
● braided circular flex. Two- and three-core versions are available and are suitable for most appliances

● heat resisting flex is similar to circular flex but with special sheathing.
For flex size details see pages 176-179.

FIT THE CORRECT PLUG FUSE

In order to fit the correct plug fuse you'll have to know the loading of the electrical appliance. Here's a brief guide:

electric blanket	50-100W
clock	negligible
coffee maker	380-1200W
dish washer	3000W
three-bar fire	1000-3000W
hair dryer	350-600W
automatic iron	750-1000W
kettle	1000-3000W
power operated tools	210-260W
fridge	80-175W
freezer	100-250W
sewing machine	75W
shaver	15W
spin dryer	100-320W
television	100-200W
toaster	400-600W
tumble dryer	2500-2750W
vacuum cleaner	220-300W
heated washing machine	3000W
waste disposal unit	200W

weren't available. Always check that replacement parts can be obtained and that you'll be able to buy them before you start work. In some cases parts might be made available only to trade repairers or simply not at all. Before trying to get any make sure you know the make and model of your appliance. If you're in any doubt, provided it's portable, take the appliance down to your local retailer for exact identification; that way you'll avoid making any mistakes.

How appliances work

Before undertaking any repairs to an electrical appliance it's important to understand just how it works. As a rule there are three basic types of electrical appliance. These are:
● those with heaters and which are not power driven such as cookers, toasters and kettles.
● those that have motors and which are power driven such as extractor fans, vacuum cleaners and lawn mowers.
● those that have both heaters and motors such as tumble dryers, hair dryers and washing machines.

The types of motor

While heaters in electrical appliances tend to vary a great deal, you'll probably find that your appliance is powered by one of two types of electric motor – a brush motor or an induction motor.

Both types of motor consist of two electromagnets. One is fixed and cannot move and is called the stator; the other is set so that it can revolve rapidly and is called the armature. The motor shaft is fixed to the armature, and when this spins it drives the equipment attached to it, a drill chuck, for example.

With a brush motor, power is directed straight to the stator, and also to the armature by a couple of carbon brushes which make a rubbing contact with the commutator. Both stator and armature are magnetised and so the latter is set spinning.

Brush motors can run on power from the mains or else on direct current from a battery, and are fitted to power tools, vacuum cleaners, polishers, food mixers, washing machines and lawn mowers.

Induction motors can only work on alternating current taken direct from the mains. Power goes only to the stator but by a process called induction the armature is magnetised as well. While its magnetism stays constant, the stator's magnetic field is reversed rapidly by the alternating current and so the armature and shaft are spun. This type of motor, or variations of it, are fitted to washing machines, refrigerators, fans, whisks and freezers.

Servicing brush motors

The most likely source of trouble will be the carbon brushes. These could be worn, sticking in their holders or simply in poor

SERVICING ELECTRIC DRILLS

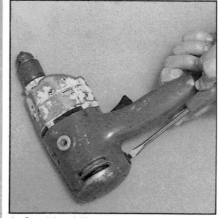

1 *On older drills, access to carbon brushes is often through insulated retaining caps on the motor casing. Don't damage the slot as you unscrew them.*

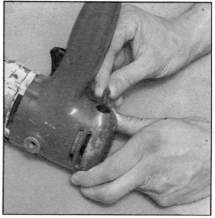

2 *Remove the caps carefully and you should be able to pull out the brushes; if not, hold the drill upside down and turn the chuck to loosen the brushes.*

5 *Finally, replace the retaining caps. If the motor sparks heavily when tested, ensure there is good contact between the brushes and commutator.*

6 *With some drills, access to the brushes is from inside the casing. Take off the back section of the drill, first removing the fixing screws.*

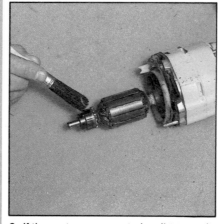

9 *If the motor appears to be dirty now is the time to clean it. Use a brush or cloth previously dipped in petrol to clean the commutator.*

10 *It's quite easy for dust and other potentially damaging debris to find its way into the armature and field windings. Clear it away with a soft brush.*

3 *If the brushes show signs of severe wear they should be replaced. Make sure you have identical brushes; otherwise they won't fit in the brush tubes.*

4 *New brushes can quite easily stick in the brush tubes. One solution is to rub down the brushes with fine glasspaper first.*

7 *If you want to service the motor at the same time, release the screws securing the chuck assembly and gear box to the main body of the drill.*

8 *Carefully pull away the front of the drill and end plate and ease the armature and commutator from the field windings. Inspect the motor's condition.*

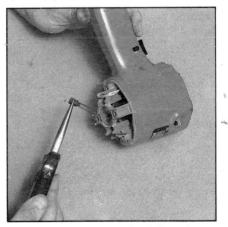

11 *As you reassemble the drill, replace the old worn brushes. When you come to refit the commutator, hold the brushes apart with a piece of card to admit it.*

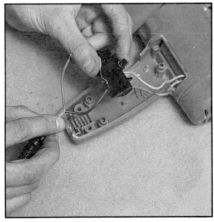

12 *Finally, if the flex is damaged fit a new one. Remove the handle piece and insert a paper clip to open the terminal clamps on the trigger switch.*

contact with the commutator. Occasionally the armature or field windings burn out but this is really only likely in power tools that are subject to considerable overloading.

Access to the brushes is usually via insulated retaining caps which are on the outside of the motor casing. However, with some motors, such as those in a horizontal vacuum cleaner, the power unit is inside the casing which means partly dismantling the machine. Remove the brushes by loosening the retaining caps or slips. Take care not to lose the springs that hold the brushes against the commutator: these are likely to pop out. You should also take note of the position of any guiding marks that will eventually help you to reset the brushes. Examine the condition of each brush and if either is worn down to as little as 5mm (⅕in) then it must be renewed. The replacement brushes must of course be identical to the old ones otherwise they won't fit into the brush tubes. If they do stick slightly then wipe them with fine glass paper before replacing the securing caps.

At the same time that you're replacing the brushes it's a good idea to examine the commutator; if it's blackened then wipe it carefully with a cloth previously dipped in petrol. You should then test the motor. If there's heavy sparking then you'll have to adjust the brushes to ensure good contact with the commutator surface. If you find that the sparking continues along with erratic running then the chances are that one of the armature coils will have burnt out. In this case you should stop the motor to avoid any further damage. Remove the motor end plate that's usually at the opposite end to the commutator and take out the armature for examination. It'll be obvious if one of the coils or a commutator segment has burnt out. You'll have to take the armature to an electrical servicing shop that offers a rewind service, although very often it's easier simply to buy a completely rewound armature. However, with some machines, such as lawn mowers, you'll probably find that in these cases you'll have to get a completely new power unit.

Servicing induction motors

Because there are no carbon brushes, a commutator and wound armature, an induction motor requires little attention during the life of the appliance. As with all motors, it should, of course, be kept clean and it's a good idea to check now and then that the armature can turn freely inside the stator. A voltage drop for some reason will mean that the induction motor won't be able to reach its correct running speed and this could result in a burnt out stator if it's not swiftly switched off. However, this and other damage that might occur is best left to a servicing shop to put right.

SERVICING ELECTRICAL APPLIANCES: 2

Kettles, irons, electric fires, cookers and vacuum cleaners are the sorts of electrical appliances that can sometimes go wrong. Here's a run through some of the repairs you can safely do yourself.

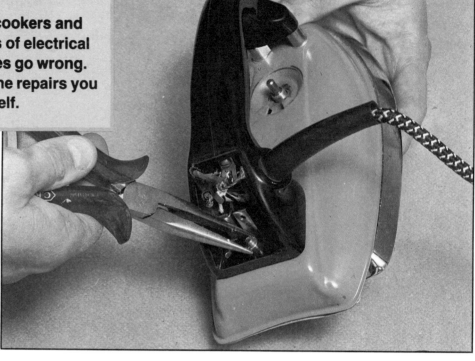

Once you've established that it's your electrical appliance that's gone wrong, and not just a blown plug fuse or damaged flex, you'll have to decide whether it's actually worth repairing. Always bear in mind the age of your appliance; after all, you might not be able to get spare parts. And, of course, you might just decide to buy a new model that is more efficient – and remember, electrical appliances are somewhat cheaper than they used to be.

Most electrical appliances differ between manufacturers so it's not possible to tell you exactly what to do if particular faults arise. However, there is a set procedure and a number of general steps you should follow for any electrical appliance repair.

Before doing anything, though, it's a good idea to contact the manufacturers or their agents and get hold of any relevant repair manuals they produce. These won't always be available to members of the public and there's bound to be a small charge. However, it is essential to know exactly what you're doing. Finally, you should make sure that all the correct spare parts are available and that you'll have all the tools required for the job. Only then should you start attempting any repairs.

Electric kettles

There are two main types of electric kettles, the non-automatic one which has to be turned off manually when the water boils, and the automatic type which switches itself off. Other than faults within the flex and plug, the most common problems are likely to be,
● a faulty element
● a burnt-out switch wiring or faulty cut-out
● leaks at the shroud.
To remove the faulty element and fit a new one (normally they are widely available) you should:
● remove the switch cover plate
● undo the screws securing the handle clamping and lift up the handle
● undo the screw fixing the switch assembly to the body of the kettle, then use long-nosed pliers or a specially shaped screwdriver to remove the earth connection screw and remove the switch assembly

● unscrew the nuts and washers securing the element, take out the old element and scrape off any rubber washer remains from the flange hole
● fit the new element by reversing the process, making sure you fit new sealing washers
● finally, check the kettle for earth continuity before using it.

Replacement switch assemblies are readily available for most makes and can be easily fitted. If you can't identify the fault on your kettle, most electrical servicing shops will test the element for you. Alternatively, test the element using an ohm meter to check the resistance level.

Electric irons

There are two types of iron – the steam iron and the dry iron. Both are thermostatically controlled and when the thermostat develops a fault – often indicated by the neon light being on but the soleplate, the shiny metal bottom of the iron, not heating up – you should take the iron to a servicing shop for repairs. Soleplates should always be regularly cleaned with a special non-abrasive solution that is readily available. On steam irons, outlets and valves should be regularly cleared with descaling liquid. You should then fill the tank only with distilled water – unless it is designed to take tap water – otherwise tap water will simply cause the iron to fur up.

An iron element will occasionally fail and will therefore have to be renewed. With some

models the element is embedded in the soleplate, in which case a new soleplate is the only answer. To replace an ordinary element you'll have to:
● remove the iron cover and cast iron pressure plate that's normally bolted to the soleplate
● disconnect the element contact strips and remove the screw from the thermostat
● lift off the asbestos heat resisting pad and remove the element
● clean the soleplate and fit the new element by reversing the order of dismantling.

Vacuum cleaners

You're likely to have either an upright or cylinder vacuum cleaner. Both types can develop faults, most of which you'll probably be able to rectify. Keep your vacuum cleaner serviced to cut down on problems: never let dust bags get too full and inspect all hoses and tools regularly – an accumulation of dust and fluff will cause blockages.

Signs of a fault developing in your vacuum cleaner are likely to be:
● a motor not running, resulting from a faulty fuse, plug or flex connections, a damaged switch, or a burnt-out motor winding (see pages 182-185).
● erratic running resulting from worn or sticking carbon brushes (which may need replacing) or loose connections (which should be re-made)
● failure to pick up dust, resulting from a full bag or blockage in the inlet. Check also that

RENEWING A DRIVE BELT

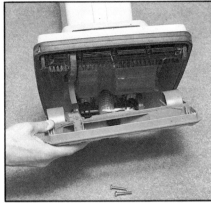

1 *Remove the casing fixing screws set in the bottom plate to gain access to the broken belt. On some vacuum cleaners you'll have to remove a front panel.*

2 *Lift out the roller brush and dispose of the broken drive belt. Also check the condition of the brushes at the same time and replace the roller if necessary.*

3 *Hook the correct-sized replacement drive belt over the drive shaft. At the same time you should also lubricate the wheels with a light machine oil.*

4 *Finally, fit the exposed section of the drive belt over the roller brushes and clip them back, making sure they are correctly located.*

Ready Reference

SAFETY FIRST
When attempting repairs to faulty electrical appliances you should:
● unplug all portable appliances at the socket outlet to which they're connected
● switch off all faulty fixed appliances at the circuit switch
● allow all heating elements and boiling rings to cool down before touching them
● make sure you have a service manual or detailed information about the faulty appliance
● make sure you have adequate tools for the job
● make sure you have the correct spare parts, if needed
● take note of all colour codes, disassembly order and screw position marks so that you'll be able to reassemble the appliance correctly.

For safety's sake some appliances should not be serviced or repaired by the do-it-yourselfer. These include microwave ovens and electric blankets.

KETTLE SWITCHES
A common fault on automatic kettles is a faulty switch. This means the kettle is slow or reluctant to switch itself off. There are several ways of dealing with this,
● simply adjust the thermostat screw found on the switch assembly of some models
● change the lid position so the steam outlet is close to the switch
● replace the switch assembly.

the drive belt hasn't slipped or broken; a sure sign of this is a fast-running motor on no load. On a cylinder model, check for badly-fitting joints
● excessive and unpleasant noise indicates that a metal object has been picked up and is making contact with the cooling fan, so check that the fan hasn't been damaged
● smell of burning caused by something hindering the belt operation; check that it is running properly
● smoke resulting from a burnt-out armature or field windings; this will probably mean a professional repair is needed.

Electric heaters
There are various types of electric heater, but the two main ones are radiant heaters, where elements operate at 'red' heat and heat up the air next to them, and convectors operating at 'black' heat and expelling warm air. Other types include fan heaters, panel heaters and radiators, and night storage heaters.

The most common fault with radiant heaters will be a faulty element or switch. To replace an element you should lift off the wire guard of the fire and undo the fixing nut at each end of the element. Connections vary between the different makes of fires, as do the lengths and types of element, so make sure the replacement element is identical to the old one.

Firebar elements comprising flat ceramic or fireclay bars with the element wires fixed in parabolic grooves can be removed from the back of the heater after first undoing the fixing screws and loosening the connecting wires. Reverse the process for fitting the new elements.

If the fan of a fan heater doesn't work then the heater must not be used; otherwise it will burn out, as no air can pass over the elements.

Remember to keep all air grilles clear of dust and any blockages. The inbuilt thermostats of panel heaters and radiators rarely go wrong. If they do, or if anything goes wrong with your storage heaters, then you'll have to call in an electrician as the repairs are likely to prove too complicated for the average do-it-yourselfer.

Power tools
Faults with drills do develop and often you can repair some of these yourself. The most likely symptoms are:
● motor does not start, resulting from worn carbon brushes or burnt-out motor windings (see pages 182-185).
● motor runs erratically due to worn or sticking brushes, or loose connections in the switch gear
● overheating resulting from overloading or a burnt-out armature or field coil.

Cookers

The most likely repair you'll have to make to your electric cooker is to replace one of the boiling rings. Remember replacements must be identical to the originals. Grill and oven elements rarely fail, but if necessary they, too, can be replaced. The signs of a fault on your cooker will be,

● no power at the control switch, caused by a blown circuit fuse

● a ring or grill that fails to heat, resulting from a burnt-out element or faulty switch

● a double-heat boiling ring or grill element that produces only half heat, which indicates that half the element has failed

● a variable-heat element that doesn't respond to control, is a sign of a faulty control

● an oven that fails to heat up properly, again the result of faulty control

● automatic controls not working, suggesting they need adjusting or replacing.

You'll probably find that repairing the control panel or thermostat will be beyond you, in which case call in an electrician.

To replace a boiling ring, lift the hob on its hinges and support it. Most rings have individual fixed conections; some are connected in pairs to a terminal block, while with other models all four rings are connected to a central terminal block. Remove the cover screws and the terminal block and release the element-connecting nuts and washers. Take out the old element and fit and connect the new ring, making sure that the terminal screws are tight.

Grill elements are replaced in much the same way, although the terminal blocks are usually either reached from the back of the cooker or from under the hob.

If you need to replace the oven element then you'll have to take off the back panel.

Washing machines

There is a limit to the repairs and servicing which you can satisfactorily undertake. Washing machines usually incorporate elements for heating the water, a motor to agitate the water and clothes, as well as a pump. Failure of the agitator or impeller to operate while the motor is indicative of a broken or slipping belt. In some cases the belt might even have come off the pulley. Failure of the water to heat means either a burnt-out element or faulty heater switch. Water leakage can usually be traced to a split hose or a loose or broken hose clip. If water isn't pumped out when the pump is switched on, then the most likely cause will either be a blocked filter, a failed inlet valve or something fouling up the pump vane. Filters can be removed for cleaning, while inlet valves are usually quite straightforward to replace. In the case of a blocked pump, disconnect the pipe to the pump and remove the blockage.

1 On a cooker lift the hob to get at the faulty ring. Most models are hinged and incorporate a special hob support; otherwise just prop it up.

2 The connections of most cooker rings are protected by a box-like cover. Undo the fixing screws and lower this cover to get at the terminals.

6 On an iron you'll have to take off the cover by undoing the nut beneath the control dial and loosening the slotted nut under the earth terminal.

7 After disconnecting the flex completely you'll be able to lift off the cover to get inside the iron. If necessary, remove the terminal screws.

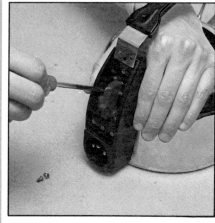

11 On a kettle remove the switch cover plate and undo the handle screws. Then undo the screws securing the switch assembly to the body.

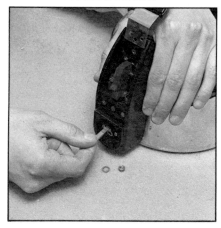

12 Undo the slotted nuts securing the earth pin and remove the earth connection screw. Use long-nosed pliers or buy a special screwdriver.

REPLACING ELEMENTS ON COOKERS, IRONS AND KETTLES

3 *In order to loosen the ring itself, you'll first have to remove the screw on the element fixing plate that secures it to the cooker frame.*

4 *You can then disconnect the faulty ring. The terminals will either be the screw or tab type. Ease the strain on the latter when disconnecting.*

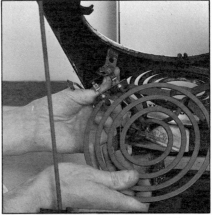

5 *Finally, replace the old ring with an identical new one, connecting the terminals in the same way. Then simply reassemble the cooker in the reverse order.*

8 *Before removing the pressure plate, you must disconnect the contact strips of the faulty element. Use an ordinary screwdriver for this task.*

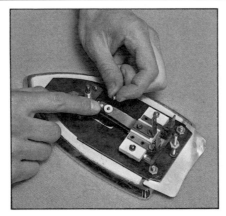

9 *You'll also have to remove the screw top of the temperature control rod, and undo the nuts at the back of the iron that fix the pressure plate in place.*

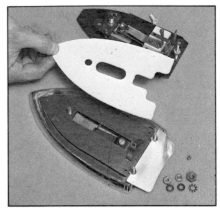

10 *Lift off the pressure plate and remove the old heat-resistant cover and element. Then fit the new element and reassemble the iron in reverse order.*

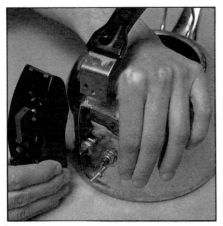

13 *In order to gain access to the element connections themselves, carefully pull away the complete switch assembly from the kettle.*

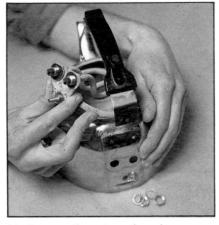

14 *Remove the nuts and washers securing the old element and lift it out. Scrape off any scale and the remains of old washers from the kettle surface.*

15 *Finally, fit the new element using the new nuts and washers supplied with it. Then reverse the dismantling process to reassemble the kettle.*

INDEX

Accessories, 16-18, 150, 158-9
Aerial sockets, 17, 136
Air bricks, use of, 103
Airing cupboard heaters, 108
Alarm bells, 170
Appliances,
    guarantees, 182
    loading guide, 183
    servicing, 182-9
Architrave mounting boxes, 56
Architrave switches, 18
Armoured cables, 113
Automatic control devices, 171-4
    lighting, 171
    power, 173

Bathroom electrics, 89, 108
    heaters, 108, 110
    rewiring, 138, 147
    safety precautions, 7, 23, 109,
        138
Batten holders, 10, 18
Bayonet caps (BC), 42
Bedrooms,
    rewiring, 137, 138, 147
Bedside switches, 45
Bell pushes, 162
Bell transformers, 163-4
BESA boxes, 50-51, 53, 65,
    152
Bi-pin end caps, 42
Blank plates, 18
Boiler electrics, 136
Bollard lights, 122, 123, 127, 128
Bonding to earth, 154
Bracket lights, 121
Brick walls, fixing into, 28
Brushes (electric drills),
    renewing, 185
Bulbs see lamps
Bulkhead lights, 122, 123
Burglar alarms, 167-70
Buzzers, 162

Cable outlets, 17
Cable runs, preparation of, 24
Cables, 6
    checking, 144-5, 148
    checklist, 150
    laying, 25, 28, 30
    lead alloy sheathed, 15, 144
    overhead, 116-8
    PVC armoured, 112
    PVC-sheathed, 14-15
    running, 31-5, 154, 156
    stripping, 24
    types of, 14-15, 75, 112
    underground, 112-5
Cartridge fuses, 12, 73
Ceiling fans, 104-7
Ceiling lights, 23-5
Ceiling roses, 10, 18, 25, 26,
    150
Ceiling switches, 17, 18, 23
Chasing out, 33
Chest freezers, 140
Chimes, door, 162, 164
Circuit fuses, replacing 13, 179
Circuit fuseways, 73, 75
Circuitry inspection,
    accessories, 145
    cables, 144-5
    fuseboards, 145
    light switches, 148
    pendant lights, 147
    socket outlets, 146
Circuits,
    checking, 27, 144-5
    current rating, 84, 86
    fault tracing, 178-9
    lighting, 10, 23
    radial, 8-9, 27, 72-5
    ring, 7-8
    special, 9
Close-ceiling light fittings, 38
Close-mounted light fittings, 50,
    52

Colour codes, cable, 13, 15
Concealed wiring, 32-5
Connection units, 17, 86, 157
Consumer units, 12, 76-7, 138,
    153, 157
Continuity testers, 21, 178
Conversion boxes, 113-5
Cookers, 141
    control units, 17, 85, 86-7, 157
    hoods, 87
    installing, 84-7
    repairing, 85, 188-9
Corner lights (external), 122,
    123
Cross-bonding of services, 15,
    154
Crown-silvered (CS) lamps, 38,
    41, 143
Current ratings, 16-17, 84, 86,
    180
Curtain controllers, 173, 174

Dimmer switches, 25, 44, 171,
    172
Di-pole (DP) switches, 17
Dishwashers, 141
Door bells, 136, 161-4
Downlighters, 38, 58, 59, 60-61,
    142, 143
Drive/path lighting, 122
Dual switches, 17

Earth continuity conductors
    (ECC), 7
Earth continuity testing, 146
Earthing, 7, 15, 23, 147, 180
Edison screw (ES) caps, 42
Electric drills, servicing, 184-5
Electric heaters, servicing, 187
Electric irons, servicing, 178,
    186, 188-9
Electric kettles, servicing, 186,
    187, 188-9

Electric motors, servicing, 183,
    184-5
Electrical terms, 7
Electricity Boards, 7, 75, 147
Electricity supply equipment, 7
Emergency supplies, 12, 21
Entryphones, 165-6
Extension bells, 162, 164
Extension leads, 180-1
Extractor fans, 100-107, 137,
    141
Eyeball light fittings, 38, 58

Fans, see ceiling fans; extractor
    fans
Fault tracing, 176-9
    checklist, 179
Filament lamps, 37, 40-41
'Fishing' (cable), 33, 34, 35, 154
    156
Flex connectors, 180-81
Flex outlet plates, 82
Flex storage reels, 181
Flexes,
    choosing, 177, 181
    extending, 180-81
    replacing, 178
    types of, 14-15, 183
Flexible cords see flexes
Floor boards, lifting, 21, 148
Fluorescent lighting, 46-9, 142,
    143
Fluorescent tubes, 37, 40, 42,
    46-9, 54, 58
    colour range, 48
    faults, 49
    starters, 47
Flush sockets, 28-9, 154
Freezers, chest, 140
Fuses, 6, 12-13
    cartridge, 12, 73, 75
    checking, 145
    testing, 177-8

Gangs, 17
Garage accessories, 119
Garage circuits, 117
Garage power supply, 116-20
Garden lighting, 126-9
Gateway lighting, 122
General Lighting Service (GLS)
    lamps, 38, 41, 143
Glare, avoiding (lighting), 39
Grid switches, 121
    system, 158-9
Guarantee on appliances, 182

Halls and passageways,
    rewiring, 138
Heated towel rails, 108, 110, 137

Illuminated ceilings, 59, 143
Immersion heaters, 137
    cable checking, 95
    replacing, 92-5
    use of, 93
Instantaneous water heaters,
    140
Intermediate switching, 69-70
Internally silvered lamps (ISL)
    38, 41, 143

Junction boxes, 10, 48
    installing, 51, 151

Kitchen improvements,139-43
    lighting, 139-40, 142-43
    power, 140-41

Lampholders, 18, 26, 150
Lamps
    garage, 120
    light output, 37
    types of, 37-8, 40-42, 143
Lead alloy sheathed cables, 15,
    144
Light bulbs see lamps
Light fittings, 37-70
    decorative, 50-51
    fluorescent, 46-9
    types of 38, 40, 142
Light/heater units (bathrooms),
    109
Lighting accessories, 18
Lighting bricks, 121
Lighting circuits, 10, 23-5, 145,
    153, 155
Lighting design, 37-45
Lighting levels, 37-8
Lighting points, 151
Living areas, rewiring, 136
Loft lights, 137
Loop-in wiring, 10, 24, 48

Low-voltage lighting, 125
Low-voltage power supply, 132
Lumens, 37

Materials listing, 150
Mineral insulated copper-
    covered cable (MICC), 112,
    113, 124
Miniature circuit breakers (MCB),
    12
Mounting boxes, 18, 30, 119, 172

Neon indicators, 109
Neon testers, 21

Outdoor lighting, 113, 121-9,
    131-2
Outside power supply, 130, 132
    cabling, 138
    safety precautions, 130
    socket outlets, 113, 136
Overhead cables, 116-8

Panic switches, 170
Parabolic aluminized reflector
    (PAR) lamps, 38, 41, 143
Path lighting, 122
Patio lighting, 122
Pendant light fittings, 23, 38, 50-
    53, 143, 147
Plaster-board walls,
    fitting to, 29
Plug fuses, 13
    ratings, 183
Plugs,
    types of, 13
    wiring of, 13, 15, 176, 177
Plumbing (for showers), 80, 83
Pond lighting, 131-2
Pond pumps, 130-31, 133
Pool heaters, 130
Porch lights, 122, 123, 136
Post-top lights, 122, 123
Power circuit accessories, 16-17
Power factor correction
    capacitors (PFCC), 47
Power points, adding, 27-30
Power tools, servicing, 187
Pressure pads, 169
Pumps (ponds), installing,
    130-31, 133
PVC armoured cables, 112
PVC-sheathed cables, 14-15

Quick-start fittings, 47

Radial circuits, 8-9, 27, 72-5
Radiant heaters, servicing, 187
Radiators, oil-filled, 108

Recessed lighting, 58-61
Reflector lamps, 38, 40
Refrigerators, 141
Residual current circuit breakers
    (RCCB), 7, 12, 76-8, 113,
        116, 136, 138, 149,
        178, 180
Rewiring, 135-57
    bedrooms and bathrooms,
        137, 138, 147
    halls and passageways, 138
    kitchens, 139-43
    living areas,136
    outside, 138
    planning, 135-8, 144-8
Ring circuits, 7-8
    checking, 28
Rise-and-fall light fittings,
    50, 53
Rose and lampholder fittings,
    150

Safety plates, 30
Safety plugs, 14
Safety tips, 15, 187
Security switches, 171, 173
Service contracts, 182
Shadows, hard - avoiding
    (lighting), 39
Shavers,
    adaptors, 17, 88, 91
    plugs, 89
    sockets, 7, 17, 88-91
    striplights, 88, 91
    supply units, 17, 88, 90
Sheathing cables, 148
Shock, treatment for, 7, 75, 179
Short circuit, 6
Showers, 79-83, 137
Silvered lamps, 38, 41, 143
Single-centre contacts, 42
Single-pole (SP) switches, 17
SL lamps, 42
Socket mountings, 30
Socket outlets, 17, 140, 147
    checking, 146
    connecting, 155
    enlarging, 143
    installing, 27-30, 155
Solid walls, chasing out, 33
Special circuits, 9
Spotlights, 142, 143
    outside, 127
    stem, 51, 52
    track-mounted, 62-5
    wall-mounted, 54
Spurs, 8, 27, 28, 56
Starters (for fluorescent tubes),
    47, 49

Striplights, 142, 143
Stud walls, cabling in, 34
Surface-mounted cables, 32-3
Surface-mounted light fittings, 52
Switches,
    changeover, 164
    checking, 148
    installing, 25, 55, 68, 80, 83,
        120, 149, 152
    security, 171, 173
    time-delay, 171, 173
    types of, 10, 17, 18
Switchfuse units, 74, 75, 118
Switching systems,
    gridswitch, 158-9
    intermediate, 69-70
    two-way, 66-70, 137

Terminal conduit boxes see
    BESA boxes
Testers, 21, 178
Time-delay switches, 171, 173
Timers, plug-in, 174
Tools, 19-21, 24
Tough rubber-sheathed (TRS)
    cable, 15, 144
Towel rails, heated, 108, 110,
    137
Track lighting, 50, 62-5, 142
Trunking, 32
Tube lamps, 40, 42, 46-9, 54, 58
Tungsten Halogen lamps, 42
Two-way switching, 66-70, 137

Underfloor cable inspection, 148
Underground cables, 112-5
Understair lighting, 138
Uplighters, 38

Vacuum cleaners, servicing, 186-7

Wall heaters, 108, 110, 137
Wall lights, 38, 54-7, 136
    external, 124
Wall panel heaters, 108
Wall washer light fittings, 38, 43,
    58
Washing machines, 140
    servicing, 188
Waste-disposal units, 141
    fault-finding, 97
    installing, 96-9
    operating, 97
Waterfalls, 130, 132
Wattage, 7, 37, 40, 172
Wire cutters and strippers, 20, 24
Wiring, checking, 145
Wiring, fixed, 14-15
Wiring Regulations, 8, 27, 154